C0-AST-727

INTRODUCTORY
COBOL

VILLANOVA UNIVERSITY

Villanova, Pennsylvania

FALVEY MEMORIAL LIBRARY

INTRODUCTORY
COBOL

Dennie Van Tassel

University of California • Santa Cruz, California

HOLDEN-DAY, INC.

San Francisco · London · Düsseldorf · Singapore · Sydney · Tokyo · New Delhi · Mexico City

Permissions

Glorobots on the first page of each chapter are printed
with the permission of Gloria A. Maxson.

Cartoon on page 12 is reprinted by permission of SIAM REVIEW (April 1973)
copyright 1973 by Society for Industrial and Applied Mathematics.

Cartoons on pages 64, 106, 273 are printed
by permission of Charles Selberg.

Poems on page 165, 276 are printed
by permission of D. M. Nessett.

Poem *Raven* by Laverne Ruby is reprinted
by permission of System Development Corporation.

Poem *Ye Olde Computer Class* is reprinted
by permission of Modern Data magazine.

Computer forms are courtesy of IBM Corporation.

Pictures of magnetic tape and disk devices
are courtesy of IBM Corporation.

Glossary is courtesy of IBM Corporation.

INTRODUCTORY COBOL

Copyright © 1980 by Dennie Van Tassel

All rights reserved.

No part of this book may be reproduced, stored in a retrieval
system or transmitted, in any form or by any means, electronic,
mechanical, photocopying, recording, or otherwise, without
permission in writing from the publisher.

Library of Congress Catalog Card Number: 78-54210
ISBN: 0-8162-9133-0

Printed in the United States of America

4567890

QA
76.73
C25V3

For my friends,
who have been good to me.

1/9/83 MIDWEST 17.06 JP

500220

PREFACE

This book is intended to introduce beginning students gradually and systematically to COBOL. No previous computer experience is necessary. Each new concept is presented by means of explanations, sample programs, and exercises.

All the programs used in this text are structured programs. Since the students learn programming by following the structured examples presented here, the students will naturally program in a structured fashion.

Since everyone is motivated by seeing the usefulness of what they are learning, the sample programs and exercises revolve around two fictitious organizations. Most of the sample programs are for a company called Ready-Cash Bank, a medium-sized bank which requires many of the same computer reports real companies need. Most of the programming assignments are to write programs for the fictitious Intellect Haven College, to produce reports similar to those used in any college.

The homework involves three types of problems: chapter review, program modifications, and new programs. The chapter review exercises are spread throughout the chapter so that they can be used soon after the material is read, while it is still fresh in the student's mind. The program modifications require the student to use the material covered in that chapter. The student is then asked to write short programs of his own, demonstrating his mastery of the material. The first modification or program in each chapter is relatively simple; later modifications and programs become more difficult and depart further from the sample programs. Thus, the beginning student can try the early exercises and more confident students can attempt the later modifications and programs. Finally, advanced students may profit from writing their own programs.

I would like to thank all my students who tested the early versions of this book in COBOL programming classes. Ardis Claire Mcleod spent many hours typing it and Jim Haynes and Evan Schaffer contributed many of the computer graffiti.

Dennie Van Tassel
Santa Cruz, 1979

CONTENTS

****

Ye Olde Computer Class

Listen, my students, for I am your tutor,
I'm going to teach you to use the computer.
You're going to learn both ASSEMBLER and COBOL,
PL/1, BASIC, and FORTRAN and SNOBOL.

You start out by writing a FORTRAN routine;
Don't use twenty cards when it works with nineteen.
You feed the compiler (it's mean as the devil),
Soon it spews out your severity level.

Your program's a failure, you're filled with dismay,
Your project has met an unplanned-for delay.
The problem, it seems, is a misspelled command
(syntactical errors computers can't stand).

You retype the program, this time it compiles:
The core dump runs ten thousand pages (two miles).
Let's give up on FORTRAN and try PL/1;
This language, it's said, is a barrel of fun.

Or you can try COBOL, if that's your decision,
Just try to remember the data division.
BASIC and SNOBOL, to name just a few,
Are languages offered, some old and some new,
In which you can program some wonderful feat,
Until the computer becomes obsolete.

The errors are many, frustrations are great,
One minute you're happy, the next you're irate.
Buy a computer, it's great fun for swingers,
Or give up, like I did, and count on your fingers.

Nathan Meyers

****

****

A Univac wept, "Although bred
To think faster than man with my head,
And put to scorn scholars,
My master still hollers
And tells me to get out the lead."

****

INTRODUCTION TO COMPUTERS

Every home may have its own household computer in the near future. Home computers already cost less than an automobile, and kits which permit you to play computer games on your television screen are cheaper than many kitchen appliances. Your telephone can be used to connect a teletypewriter or CRT console to a computer miles away.

Computers are commonplace in all large businesses and in institutions such as colleges and government agencies. You have already heard many stories about the bad and good things that computers can do. You may also have had experience with some of the bad (keeping track of your traffic offenses) or good (making your work or homework less laborious) influences of computers.

Since computers are so prevalent in modern life, it is a good idea to know how they work. The best way to learn about them is actually to use them, that is, program them. Programming is the science or art of telling the computer how to solve a problem. This must be done in a very precise manner. Once you learn how to program computers you will be better able fo judge whether the statements you hear about computers are valid. Some people have gone so far as to suggest that if you don't know how to program a computer, you are an illiterate in this society. While this is an extreme view, it does suggest modern society's involvement with computers.

PROGRAMMING A COMPUTER

There are four basic steps to follow when programming a computer:

1. Planning.
2. Coding.
3. Debugging.
4. Testing.

Planning the Program

Program planning consists of carefully outlining what you want to do. Remember, a computer is a fast but dumb helper. Your computer has no more intelligence than your lawnmower. It can do many different tasks, but it needs very explicit instructions. For example, if you wish to calculate a paycheck you cannot just say "do paycheck." Instead, you must tell the computer, in a special language such as COBOL, exactly what is to be done. This means that you must know exactly what you want done and how it can be done. The problems a computer cannot do are those for which we cannot give explicit instructions.

Coding the Program

Coding the program consists of putting the directions for solving the problem into a form and language the computer can understand. The complete set of directions, or **instructions**, is called a **program**.

If you speak English to Russians, they probably won't understand you. Even if you do speak Russian, but badly, they may still not understand you. Computers also understand only their own languages. Present-day computers cannot understand English for two reasons: (1) the computer is not as sophisticated a mechanism as a human being, and (2) English is a very imprecise language. Many English words have several meanings, and slang usage often changes the meaning of the word.

A very precise language is needed to communicate with a computer. One of the oldest and most common computer languages is FORTRAN. The name FORTRAN comes from *FOR*mula *TRAN*slation; it is a language for translating mathematical equations into the computer's internal language. Another widely used programming language is COBOL (*CO*mmon *B*usiness *O*riented *L*anguage), which is mainly used for business applications. Other business-programming languages are RPG (*R*eport *P*rogram *G*enerator), which is most commonly used on small business computers, and PL/I (*P*rogramming *L*anguage *I*), a newer, multipurpose language that hasn't yet been widely accepted because so many people are already using FORTRAN and COBOL.

The languages above—COBOL, FORTRAN, and PL/I—are called **high-level languages**. High-level languages are relatively **machine-independent**, which means they will execute on a wide variety of computers with relatively few changes. A lower-level language (sometimes called an intermediate-level language) is **assembly language**. Assembly languages are dependent on the brand of computers. The lowest level of computer language is **machine language**. A machine language can be directly executed by the computer; all the other computer languages must be converted into machine language before the program can be executed. Usually, an assembly language statement translates into a single machine-language instruction, whereas one high-level language statement will result in several machine-language-level instructions.

Modern computers are very discriminating. Every time you give an instruction to a computer, it first checks to see if the instruction is syntactically correct. This checking is called **syntax checking**.

Statements in computer programs must conform to the syntax for that language and statement. If one of the instructions in a program is not syntactically correct (e.g., if there is a spelling error), the computer rejects the complete program. Then you must correct the program and run it again.

Syntax checking is done by a program called a compiler. The computer is only a machine; it is not a sage. That is, it only requires your program to be syntactically correct; it doesn't care at all if the whole program is nonsense. You are responsible for making sure the program does what you want it to. This is called debugging and testing the program.

Debugging the Program

Debugging a program is looking for errors (called **bugs**) in the program. You will soon learn that bugs often infest programs that you write. These bugs can be instructions out of sequence. For example, if you tell a child to put on his shoes and socks and he follows your instructions exactly as a computer would, the child will be in trouble. You said put on *shoes* and socks, so the child will put on his shoes first, and then put on the socks over the shoes. Computers attempt to follow your instructions exactly as you give them, no matter how illogical the order may be.

****

Computer Graffiti

A computer is a fast, accurate moron.
A human being is a slow, error-prone genius.

****

Other mistakes can be caused by giving instructions that are syntactically correct, but do not have the meaning you intended. For example, if you wanted to say:

DIVIDE I BY X GIVING Z.

but you put the numeral 1 instead of the letter I, your instructions would be accepted by the computer as syntactically correct, but the results would not be what you desired. Mistakes such as this are called **logic errors**. It is a little like following the recipe for a cake and putting in salt instead of sugar. The possibility of getting something good exists, but the probability is low. The aim in programming is to get the exact results you want, and you will not be apt to get them if you have logic errors.

Therefore, you debug a program when it gives obviously incorrect answers. When the program *seems* to be giving correct answers, you move on to the testing stage.

Testing the Program

The final step is **testing the program**. Once you think the program is correct, you use it with some numbers for which you can predict the answers. If the computer gives you the known answers, *maybe* the program will be correct for other numbers; "maybe," because it is very difficult on a large program to decide how much testing is necessary.

Everyone has heard stories of how the computer did something obviously stupid or incorrect.

When this happens, it means that the programmers did not test their programs carefully. Many amateur programmers, and even many experienced ones, are so relieved to get their program *apparently* working that they skip the step of testing it carefully. You will soon learn just how important it is to test your program carefully.

One concluding hint: one hour of planning is usually worth five hours of programming, debugging, and testing. Programs which have not been planned are usually very time-consuming to finish. *Think* before you start writing your program.

FLOWCHARTS

Before attempting to code a program, you should plan the program. In the haste to start coding, all planning is often left by the wayside by both novice and experienced programmers. As your programs get larger and more complicated, the need for planning becomes much more important. Thus, it is important to develop the habit of planning early in your programming career.

One method of program planning is to draw a **flowchart** of the program. A flowchart is a pictorial representation of a program. What is usually desired is a high-level flowchart. That is, we do not want to map each line of code; we want to flowchart the general structure of the program. A flowchart for a simple program might look like **Figure 1.1**. This flowchart illustrates the general program flow.

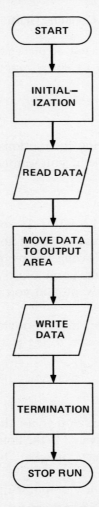

FIGURE 1.1   **A Simple Program Flowchart**

The shape of the figures in a flowchart have standardized meanings. They are drawn by using a flowcharting template (see **Figure 1.2**). The most commonly used symbols and their meanings are given in **Table 1.1**.

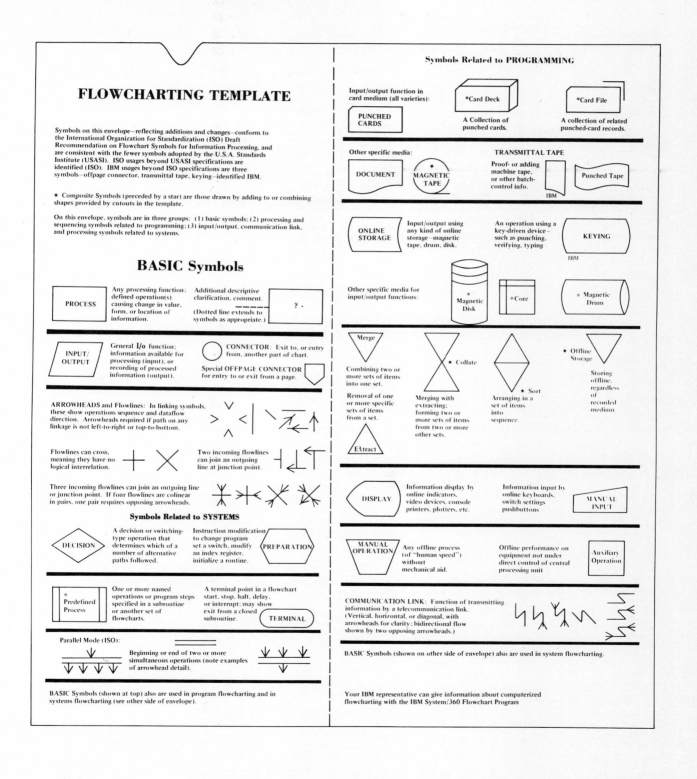

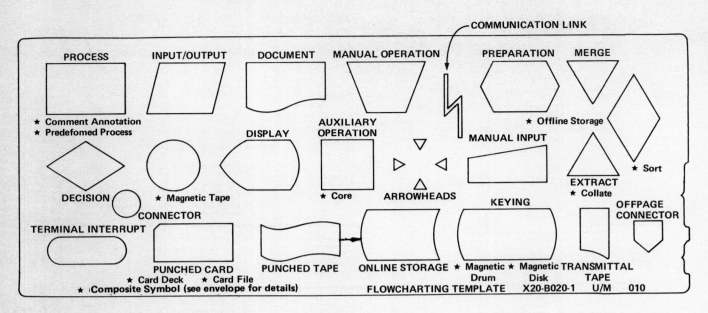

FIGURE 1.2   Flowchart Template Symbols and a Template

TABLE 1.1   FLOWCHART SYMBOLS AND THEIR USES

Symbol	Symbol Name	Symbol Use
	Input-output	Represents input operations such as the reading of a punched card* or output operations such as the printing of a line.
	Process	Represents data movement and arithmetic operations.
	Decision	Represents a question, decision, or comparison.
	Terminal	Represents the start or end of a program.
	Punched card	Represents punched card, either input or output.

Symbol	Symbol Name	Symbol Use
	Document	Represents printed results.

*Punched cards are used to record data.

Figure 1.3 is an example of a more complex flowchart.

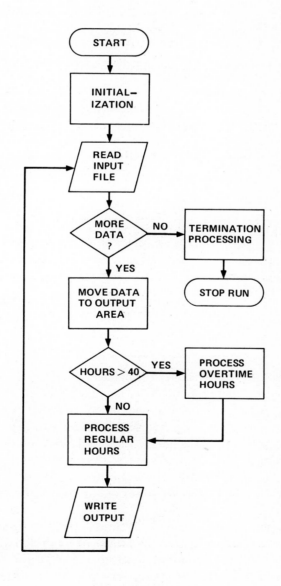

FIGURE 1.3   **A More Complex Flowchart**

```
*********************************************************************
```

A Diversion: The Computer in Fiction

Computers, so important in everyday life, have also become characters in contemporary literature. In many short stories a computer plays an important part. One of the oldest is Ambrose Bierce's "Moxon's Master" (1889), which stars a chess-playing computer. A more current example is HAL, the computer from the movie and book *2001: A Space Odyssey*.

Many novels and stories also have computers in them. Five of the best are:

Colossus, by D. F. Jones (New York: G. P. Putnam's Sons).

The Moon Is a Harsh Mistress, by Robert A. Heinlein (New York: G. P. Putnam's Sons).

Computers, Computers, Computers: In Fiction and Verse, by D. Van Tassel (New York: Thomas Nelson).

This Perfect Day, by Ira Levin (New York: Random House).

The Terminal Man, by Michael Crichton (New York: Alfred A. Knopf).

These books personify the computer as both hero and villain. Reading computer fiction can be helpful while learning how to use computers, because it offers another source of information about computers.

```
*********************************************************************
```

COBOL

If you scan the job-opportunity ads in any large metropolitan newspaper, you will see that a majority of the programmer ads are looking for COBOL programmers. COBOL is the dominant programming language of the business community, and the business community is probably the biggest user of computers.

History of COBOL

COBOL stands for *CO*mmon *B*usiness *O*riented *L*anguage. In 1959, a group of large-computer users formed a committee to develop a common business language. The committee was named *CO*nference on *DA*ta *SY*stems *L*anguage (CODASYL). The members consisted of the Department of Defense, Burroughs, IBM, RCA, Honeywell, and Sperry Rand. It was one of the first times a group of competitors worked together to develop a language that could be used by all computer manufacturers.

Before that time, most business programs were written in machine language, which is dependent on the brand of computer. If a computer user wished to use a different type of computer, all previous programs had to be rewritten. The cost of reprogramming when buying a new computer was staggering.

In 1960, a report was published by the Government Printing Office describing COBOL. From 1961 to 1965 COBOL was expanded; by 1965 it had most of its present-day features.

In 1968, the American National Standard Institute (ANSI) approved a standard COBOL language, ANSI COBOL. In 1974, COBOL was again revised: some of the rules regarding blank spaces were relaxed, and numerous other small changes were made. In addition, a few statements were added to take advantage of new hardware and new programming techniques. This 1974 version of COBOL is the most commonly used today.

An Assessment of COBOL

Some advantages of COBOL are:

1. Standard language. There is a standard COBOL to which all COBOL compilers are supposed to conform. (A **compiler** is a program which translates a high-level language, such as COBOL, into the computer's machine language.)
2. English-type language. A COBOL program is written in a standard way so that all COBOL programmers can read the program without having to be familiar with the particular computer being used.
3. Widely used and available. COBOL is available on almost all general-purpose computers.
4. Self-documenting. Because COBOL is a standard language, and the program is readable, the program can be used as part of the documentation.
5. Good file-handling techniques. COBOL easily processes the large amounts of data that are commonly needed in business applications.
6. Easy to learn and program. COBOL is much faster to learn and to program than assembly language.

Some disadvantages of COBOL are:

1. Programs may be wordy. Compared to languages such as FORTRAN or BASIC, COBOL programs tend to be rather large.
2. It is easy to write inefficient (slow) programs. In order to write efficient programs the programmer must know something about the particular computer being used.
3. Some modern programming techniques are not available. Since COBOL is such an old language, it does not have some features that were invented after COBOL was designed.

You will soon be able to decide if you agree with this list of advantages—especially the last one—and disadvantages.

Why learn COBOL? You have probably heard of other programming languages. Perhaps someone has told you that COBOL is obsolete and we all should use this new XYZ language. However, there are several *thousand* programming languages. Programming languages are invented and discarded almost daily. You can read about many of the longer-lasting programming languages in a book called *Programming Languages*, by Jean Sammet (Englewood Cliffs, N.J.: Prentice-Hall, 1969).

Why learn COBOL, then? COBOL is the predominant business-programming language. As many as 60 percent or more of all business programs are written in COBOL. There are always new programming languages, many of which undoubtedly have valuable features. However, the business community has millions of dollars tied up in COBOL programs and thousands of programmers trained to use COBOL. For these simple economic reasons, the business community will probably stay with COBOL for quite some time.

Preference for a particular programming language is similar to preference for a particular automobile. Each group of computer programmers have reasons for their preference, and it is unlikely that any group will convince any other group to change. Reason (or your interpretation of facts) does not necessarily prevail. People generally tend to prefer the programming language they learned first.

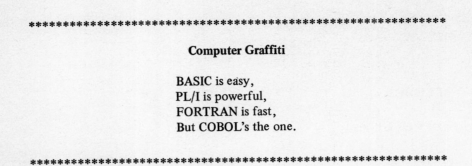

Computer Graffiti

BASIC is easy,
PL/I is powerful,
FORTRAN is fast,
But COBOL's the one.

THE COMPUTER

One of the best ways to become familiar with computers is to take a supervised tour of a computer center. (Computer centers often provide tours.) A computer is a machine designed to receive data, perform programming operations on the data, and supply results. **Figure 1.4** is a very general picture of the parts of a computer.

While some computers are bigger or more powerful than others, they all have basically the same parts. Together, all the devices or machinery of the computer are called **hardware**. This name includes the input/output devices, control unit, memory, and processing unit.

The **input device** is used to bring data into the computer. It is usually either a card reader, a teletypewriter, or a CRT (*C*athode *R*ay *T*ube) terminal. The **output device**, ordinarily some type of printer or terminal, permits the user to read the results of the program. These devices are often referred to as *input/output* and are usually abbreviated to I/O. **Figure 1.5** gives I/O devices.

The **control unit** carries out the sequence of operations, interprets instructions, and initiates commands. In other words, it tells the rest of the computer what to do.

The **memory** holds information inside the computer. This is sometimes called storage, but the word *storage* can also indicate storage outside the computer, for example, on a magnetic disk or magnetic tape.

The last major part of the computer is the processing unit, or **processor**, which is where the arithmetic and logic operations are performed.

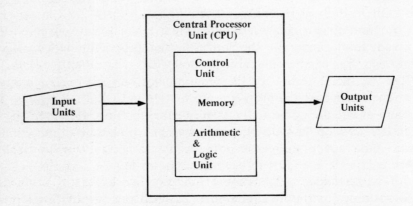

FIGURE 1.4   **Components of a Computer**

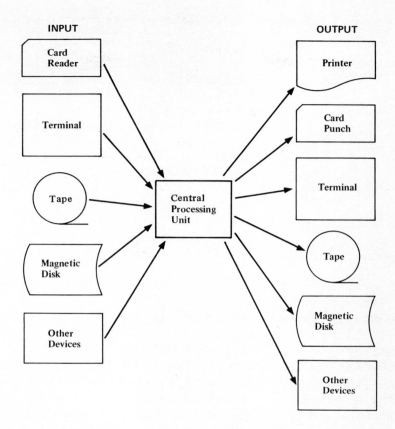

FIGURE 1.5   **Input and Output Devices**

PROCESSING

Let us examine exactly what happens when a program is submitted to the computer. **Figure 1.6** is an illustration of the process involved.

The **source program** is the set of instructions written by the programmer. It is either written directly into the computer on a terminal (a CRT or teletypewriter), or on punched cards. Punched cards are made on a **keypunch machine**, which records the data by making coded holes in blank cards.

The source program is read by the input device. The Operating System (**OS**) is a large program which allocates the resources of the computer and determines what language your program uses (for example, COBOL, FORTRAN, RPG, PL/I). Then the correct compiler is called by the operating system to process the program. The compiler checks for errors in syntax in the program. If the complier cannot understand the program, the output device just prints the program with messages describing the kinds of errors it found. Beginning programmers (and experienced programmers, too) may have to run their programs several times before they get all the errors out. As soon as the program is free from syntax errors, it is converted into machine code (the program is then called the **object program**) by the compiler, and the central processor unit then executes the program; that is, it reads and carries out the program instructions, one by one. Then the output device prints the program and the calculated results. Once the execution of the program has been completed, control is returned to the operating system.

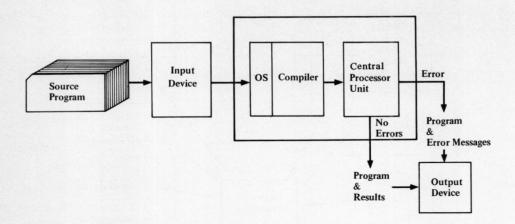

FIGURE 1.6   **Processing a Program**

The operating system and compiler are very large programs that control the computer until your program goes into execution. These large programs and other programs are called **software**. They provide a link between your program and the hardware.

A number of words and phrases have been defined in the last few pages. These words have been printed in darker type, so they are easy to find. They are all listed below. If you can't remember the definition of one of them, go back and reread that section in this chapter. These words will be used in this book and are regularly used by computer professionals. Learn them and soon you will be talking like a computer expert.

****

Efbé (Holland)

****

Reprinted with permission from Siam Review (April 1973) copyright 1973 by Society for Industrial and Applied Mathematics

CHAPTER REVIEW

Vocabulary Review

Program planning	Debugging a program	I/O
Coding a program	Logic error	Control unit
Instructions	Testing a program	Memory
Program	Flowchart	Processor
High-level language	Compiler	Source program
Machine-independent language	Hardware	Keypunch machine
Assembly language	Input device	OS
Machine language	Output device	Object program
Syntax checking		

Review Questions

1. What does COBOL stand for? When was it first developed? Name three other programming languages and try to find out on your own how they differ. Find out what other programming languages are available at your computer installation. Who uses these other languages (i.e., administrators, scientists, students)? Why doesn't everyone use the same programming language? You will get many conflicting opinions on this question.

2. Take a tour of your computer center. Find out what type of equipment is available in the computer center. Who runs the computer center? That is, is it run by a committee, a professor, or an administrator? How is it financed? Find out as much as possible about the organization, financing, and operation of the computer center.

3. Find out how to keypunch. Then keypunch your name, the alphabet, numbers, and some punctuation. Keypunch the alphabet in order and figure out the coding system. What letter is made from a 0 and 2 punch? Be sure to learn how to duplicate cards. There are often part-time keypunching jobs available at computer centers, so if you become skilled in this work you can earn extra money. Read the keypunch manual.

4. Find a computer terminal. Find out how to obtain a user account. Next, try doing some simple things on the computer terminal, such as playing games or doing arithmetic.

5. Survey the help-wanted ads under the heading *Computer* or *Programmers* to see what kinds of computer jobs are available. Can you find out what training, experience, and pay are associated with these jobs? Pick out two computer-related jobs and map plans of attack for you to obtain these jobs.

6. What are the steps in writing a program?

7.   Indicate what the following flowchart symbols represent:

8.   Draw a flowchart for walking across the street when there is a traffic light.

9.   What are some of the advantages of COBOL? What are some of the disadvantages?

10. How are source program, object program, compiler, and operating system related? That is, how do they interrelate when a typical COBOL program is run?

11. How are syntax errors found? Logic errors?

12. Read a computer-related book—fiction or nonfiction—and write a book report on it. Evaluate how well the writer understood the limits and possibilities of computers.

****

**A robot who worked like a drone
Into deep melancholia was thrown,
And confessed in analysis
A sense of paralysis
Because his will wasn't his own.**

****

COBOL PRELIMINARIES

We will now look at the characteristics of a COBOL program. COBOL coding sheets are usually used as an aid in writing neat programs.

CODING FORM

Figure 2.1 is a COBOL coding form. Each line represents a data-processing card or a line at a terminal. The columns are numbered 1 through 80—corresponding to the 80 columns of a data-processing card—so that similar items can be aligned vertically.

Columns 1-6

Columns 1-6 are used for **sequence numbers**. Sequence-numbering is optional, but it is normally used by professional programmers. The coding form's page number is generally put in columns 1-3. Line numbers are put in columns 4-6. The lines are usually numbered by 10s; this allows you to insert other sequentially numbered lines at a later stage. Pages are often numbered by 10s, too, and one page number is used for each sheet of the coding form. If you sequence-number your program, most compilers will check the sequence and warn you if lines are out of sequence.

Columns 73–80

Columns 73–80 are used for **program identification**. If, for example, you are using the name of the program as the identification, you put the same name on each line of the program in columns 73–80. This use is optional, too, but is normally used by professional programmers.

Column 7

Column 7 is used as a **continuation column**. A hyphen indicates a continuation line in an item within quotes. The hyphen goes in the second and all following continuation lines. (There will be more on this in Chapter 5.)

If an asterisk is typed in column 7, it indicates that the line is to be used for a **comment**. This means that anything put in columns 8–72 is printed but is ignored by the compiler. While this is a handy feature, it is not available with some older versions of COBOL and it may not work on non-IBM computers. Try it.

Columns 8–72

Columns 8–72 are used for the COBOL language. Only division headings, section names, paragraph names, and level indicators start in columns 8–11. (These terms are discussed later in this chapter and in the next chapter.) Columns 8–11 are called **Area A** (also called margin A). The rest of the COBOL

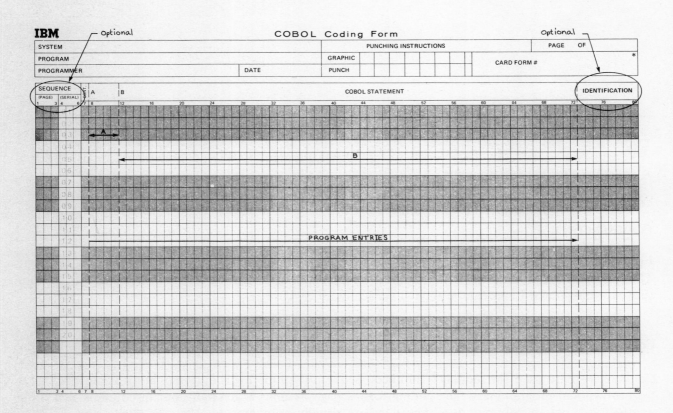

FIGURE 2.1   **A COBOL** Coding Form

program is put in columns 12–72. Columns 12–72 are called **Area B** (also called margin B). Area B items can start anywhere in any column in Area B; the same is true for Area A. **Figure 2.2** is a filled-out COBOL coding form.

IBM COBOL Coding Form

SYSTEM: PRINT PROGRAM
PROGRAM: PROGRM 2A
PROGRAMMER: D. VAN TASSEL DATE 2/1/1981
PUNCHING INSTRUCTIONS — GRAPHIC: Ø O 1 I 2 Z — PUNCH: N A N A N A
PAGE 1 OF 2

```
010010 IDENTIFICATION DIVISION.                                PROGRM2A
010020 PROGRAM-ID.                                             PROGRM2A
010030    PROGRM2A.                                            PROGRM2A
010040 ************************************************************ PROGRM2A
010050 *   SAMPLE PRINT PROGRAM.                               *PROGRM2A
010060 ************************************************************ PROGRM2A
010070 ENVIRONMENT DIVISION.                                   PROGRM2A
010080 INPUT-OUTPUT SECTION.                                   PROGRM2A
010090 FILE-CONTROL.                                           PROGRM2A
010100    SELECT RECORDS-IN                                    PROGRM2A
010110       ASSIGN TO UR-254ØR-S-SYSIN.                       PROGRM2A
010120    SELECT PRINT-OUT,                                    PROGRM2A
010130       ASSIGN TO UR-14Ø3-S-SYSPRINT.                     PROGRM2A
010140                                                         PROGRM2A
010150 DATA DIVISION.                                          PROGRM2A
010160 FILE SECTION.                                           PROGRM2A
010170 FD RECORDS-IN                                           PROGRM2A
010180    LABEL RECORDS ARE OMITTED.                           PROGRM2A
010190 Ø1 IN-RECORD              PICTURE X(8Ø).                PROGRM2A
010200 FD PRINT-OUT                                            PROGRM2A
010210    LABEL RECORDS ARE OMITTED.                           PROGRM2A
010220 Ø1 PRINT-LINE             PICTURE X(133).               PROGRM2A
010230                                                         PROGRM2A
```

IBM COBOL Coding Form

SYSTEM: PRINT PROGRAM
PROGRAM: PROGRM 2A
PROGRAMMER: D. VAN TASSEL DATE 2/1/1981
PUNCHING INSTRUCTIONS — GRAPHIC: Ø O 1 I 2 Z — PUNCH: N A N A N A
PAGE 2 OF 2

```
020010 WORKING-STORAGE SECTION.                                PROGRM2A
020020 Ø1 ADDRESS-RECORD         PICTURE X(8Ø).                PROGRM2A
020030 Ø1 OUT-LINE.                                            PROGRM2A
020040    Ø5 FILLER              PICTURE X(Ø1).                PROGRM2A
020050    Ø5 ADDRESS-LINE        PICTURE X(132).               PROGRM2A
020060                                                         PROGRM2A
020070 PROCEDURE DIVISION.                                     PROGRM2A
020080    OPEN INPUT RECORDS-IN, OUTPUT PRINT-OUT.             PROGRM2A
020090 START-PROCESSING.                                       PROGRM2A
020100    READ RECORDS-IN INTO ADDRESS-RECORD                  PROGRM2A
020110       AT END PERFORM WRAP-IT-UP.                        PROGRM2A
020120    MOVE ADDRESS-RECORD TO ADDRESS-LINE.                 PROGRM2A
020130    WRITE PRINT-LINE FROM OUT-LINE AFTER ADVANCING 1 LINES. PROGRM2A
020140 WRAP-IT-UP.                                             PROGRM2A
020150    CLOSE RECORDS-IN, PRINT-OUT.                         PROGRM2A
020160    STOP RUN.                                            PROGRM2A
```

FIGURE 2.2   **A Filled-Out Coding Form**

GENERAL STRUCTURE

A COBOL program is divided into 4 divisions. All divisions must appear, and must appear in order. **Table 2.1** shows the 4 divisions and the purpose of each one.

TABLE 2.1   THE COBOL PROGRAM DIVISIONS

Divisions	*Purpose*
Identification	Identifies the program.
Environment	Describes the computer and peripheral devices.
Data	Describes files, record layouts, and storage.
Procedure	Program logic.

The four divisions in a program are all in **Figure 2.2**.

CHARACTER SET

There are 51 COBOL characters. They are shown in **Figure 2.3**. Their uses are shown in **Figure 2.4**.

```
Digits 0 through 9
Letters A through Z
Special characters:
    Blank or space
    + Plus sign
    – Minus sign or hyphen
    * Check-protection symbol, asterisk
    / Slash
    = Equal Sign
    > Inequality sign (greater than)
    < Inequality sign (less than)
    $ Currency sign
    , Comma
    . Period or decimal point
    ' Quotation mark (or ")
    ( Left parenthesis
    ) Right parenthesis
    ; Semicolon
```

FIGURE 2.3   **COBOL Character Set**

The following characters are used for words:
  0 through 9
  A through Z
  – (hyphen)
The following characters are used for punctuation:
  ' Quotation mark (or ")
  (Left parenthesis
) Right parenthesis
  , Comma
  . Period
  ; Semicolon
The following characters are used in arithmetic expressions:
  + Addition
  – Subtraction
  * Multiplication
  / Division
  ** Exponentiation (two asterisks)
The following characters are used in relation tests:
  > Greater than
  < Less than
  = Equal to

FIGURE 2.4   Uses of COBOL Characters

IDENTIFIERS

In algebra letters are used for variables or symbolic names. In programming, such symbolic names are called **identifiers** or data names. They can be 1 to 30 characters in length, must contain an alphabetic character, and can be composed of the following:

A–Z   Alphabetic characters

0–9   Numbers

-         hyphen

No blanks or other characters are allowed. Blank spaces are used as word separators in COBOL just as they are in English. Identifiers usually start with an alphabetic character; they cannot begin or end with a hyphen. Examples:

HOURS
COST
TIME-OF-DAY
MASTER-FILE
TIME-34

RESERVED WORDS

You cannot use a **reserved word** as an identifier. There are approximately 300 reserved words. Read the list of reserved words inside the front cover and start to become familiar with them. Reserved words have special meanings in COBOL and can be used only as required by the COBOL language. A reserved word can be part of another word, however, and then it is no longer a reserved word. For example, MOVE is a reserved word but MOVE-IT is not a reserved word. **Figure 2.5** is a COBOL program with all the reserved words underlined. **Table 2.2** gives examples of illegal identifiers.

TABLE 2.2 EXAMPLES OF ILLEGAL IDENTIFIERS

Unacceptable	Reason
PRINT — FILE	No blanks allowed.
24-567	Must have at least one alphabetic character.
A.B.C.	No special characters allowed.
MOVE	A reserved word.

```
IDENTIFICATION DIVISION.
PROGRAM-ID.
     PROGRM2A.
* * * * * * * * * * * * * * * * * * * * * * * * * * * * **
*          SAMPLE COBOL PROGRAM.                          *
* * * * * * * * * * * * * * * * * * * * * * * * * * * * **
ENVIRONMENT DIVISION.
INPUT-OUTPUT SECTION.
FILE-CONTROL.
     SELECT RECORDS-IN
          ASSIGN TO UR-2540R-S-SYSIN.
     SELECT PRINT-OUT,
          ASSIGN TO UR-1403-S-SYSPRINT.

DATA DIVISION.
FILE SECTION.
FD   RECORDS-IN
LABEL RECORDS ARE OMITTED.
01   IN-RECORD                    PICTURE X(80).
FD   PRINT-OUT
LABEL RECORDS ARE OMITTED
01   PRINT-LINE                   PICTURE X(133).

WORKING-STORAGE SECTION.
01   ADDRESS-RECORD               PICTURE X(80).
01   OUT-LINE.
     05   FILLER                  PICTURE X(01).
     05   ADDRESS-LINE            PICTURE X(132).

PROCEDURE DIVISION.
     OPEN INPUT RECORDS-IN, OUTPUT PRINT-OUT.

START-PROCESSING.
     READ RECORDS-IN INTO ADDRESS-RECORD
          AT END PERFORM WRAP-IT-UP.
     MOVE ADDRESS-RECORD TO ADDRESS-LINE.
     WRITE PRINT-LINE FROM OUT-LINE AFTER ADVANCING 1 LINES.

WRAP-IT-UP.
     CLOSE RECORDS-IN, PRINT-OUT.
     STOP RUN.
```

FIGURE 2.5   Reserved Words in a COBOL Program

COBOL VERBS

A **COBOL verb** is a reserved word that expresses an action to be taken by the program. COBOL verbs can be used in the PROCEDURE DIVISION to process data. Some of the most common verbs are:

1. Input/output verbs: OPEN, CLOSE, READ, WRITE.
2. Arithmetic verbs: ADD, SUBTRACT, MULTIPLY, DIVIDE, COMPUTE.
3. Data-movement verb: MOVE.
4. Procedure-branching verbs: PERFORM, STOP, GO TO.
5. Conditional verb: IF.

SENTENCES

Sentences are used in the PROCEDURE DIVISION to tell the computer what to do with the data. **COBOL sentences** start with a verb and end with a period. COBOL sentences must be in columns 12–72 and can be placed anywhere within these columns. This allows you to paragraph and indent statements for visual clarity. If a sentence will not fit on one line, break after a blank space and continue on the next line. You should not break a word over two lines. Examples of COBOL sentences are:

```
OPEN INPUT RECORDS-IN.
MOVE SPACES TO PRINT-LINE.
CLOSE RECORDS-IN.
IF (AGE < 21 AND SEX = 'M')
    MOVE ZEROS TO TOTAL-OUT.
```

Notice that the last COBOL sentence is on two lines and the second line is indented 4 spaces. When sentences are longer than one line, the second and following lines are usually indented 4 spaces to help the human reader note that the second line is part of the previous line. There is no particular reason to indent 4 spaces rather than 3 or 5, but 4 spaces is the convention in COBOL programs.

A **COBOL statement** is a valid combination of words and symbols written in the PROCEDURE DIVISION. A sentence is a sequence of one or more statements, the last of which ends with a period. Notice that within the IF sentence above there is another complete sentence (i.e., MOVE. . .).

PUNCTUATION

You must leave blank spaces between words so that the compiler can distinguish one word from another. Extra blank spaces are acceptable. The end of the line is *not* considered a blank space, that is, if a word ends in column 72, there must be a blank space in column 12 of the following line. Arithmetic operators (+, −, *, /, **) and relational operators (>, <, =) must be preceded and followed by a blank space. Some of these punctuation rules regarding spaces before and after operators have been relaxed in newer COBOL compilers.

In COBOL each entry (e.g., sentences, labels) ends with a period. Since the period signals the end of the sentence, a sentence may continue for several lines. A blank space must follow the period. **Labels** are division names, paragraph names, and section names. These all start in columns 8–11 of the program and all end with a period. In most cases, commas have little meaning and can be used anywhere to separate items, but when a comma is used it must be followed by a blank space. Periods and commas must not be preceded by a space. Some COBOL compilers completely ignore commas, but other compilers will generate an error message if you put a comma in a particularly inappropriate place.

DATA VALUES

Three types of **data value** can be used in a COBOL program. They are:

Type	Example
Numeric literal	74.1
	256
Nonnumeric literal	'HI FOLKS'
	'GEORGE'
Figurative constant	SPACE
	ZERO

Literals

A **literal** is a constant used in a COBOL program. There are two types of literals: numeric and nonnumeric.

Numeric

Numeric literals may contain 1 to 18 digits, a sign, and a decimal point. The sign is always on the left side, but if the number is positive, the plus sign is not needed and is usually not used. If there is a decimal point, it must *not* be on the right end of the number because the decimal point is also used to terminate COBOL sentences. If a numeric literal ended with a decimal point, it would terminate the COBOL sentence. Therefore, to indicate place in a whole number, use a 0 after the decimal point. Examples of correct numeric literals are:

12.3	+.0123	−16.5
15	4.0	178.56

Notice that in COBOL, as in English, we use the symbol of a dot for two purposes, as decimal point and as period. A period must always be followed by a blank space: that is how the COBOL compiler distinguishes between a period and a decimal point. The following are *not* numeric literals:

Invalid	Reason
1,200	No comma permitted.
151.	Decimal point must not be rightmost character.
$100.00	The dollar sign is an illegal character.
14.2−	Sign must be on the left side.

The following are examples of COBOL statements in which numeric constants (underlined) are used:

```
ADD 1 TO SUM.
WRITE PRINT-LINE FROM PRINT-OUT AFTER ADVANCING 2 LINES.
PERFORM START-PROCESSING 10 TIMES.
```

Nonnumeric

Nonnumeric literals (also called **character strings**) are always enclosed within single quotes (or double quotes, depending on the compiler) and can contain any legal character except the quotation mark. Nonnumeric character-strings may be 1 to 120 characters in length. Blank spaces enclosed inside the quotation marks are treated as characters. If numbers are enclosed within quotes, they are treated as alphanumeric characters, and cannot be used in arithmetic statements. Examples of correct nonnumeric literals are:

```
'HI FOLKS'          '14.6'
'JULY 12, 1979'     '   '
'DENNIE'            '125'
```

Reserved words can be part of a literal; they cause no problems because they are enclosed within quotes and treated as character strings. For example:

```
MOVE 'MOVE TO THE END' TO MESSAGE-OUT.
```

In the nonnumeric literal above there are three reserved words, but since they are enclosed within quotes they are processed as a character string.

The following are COBOL statements in which nonnumeric literals are used (the nonnumeric literals are within quotes):

```
MOVE 'ERROR ** CHECK-IT' TO ERROR-MESSAGE.
05 FILLER        PICTURE X(04) VALUE 'SUM='.
IF (PAST-DUE = 'D') PERFORM OVER-DUE-ROUTINE.
MOVE '+' TO INDICATOR.
```

Figurative Constants

A **figurative constant** is a constant to which a specific data-name has been assigned. Examples are:

ZERO	Represents the value 0,
ZEROS	or one or more occurrences of
ZEROES	the character 0, depending
	on the context.
SPACE	Represents one or more blank
SPACES	spaces.

The singular and plural forms of a figurative constant are equivalent. Figurative constants are reserved words. Examples of their use are:

```
MOVE ZERO TO PAY.
MOVE SPACES TO PRINT-OUT.
COMPUTE A = ZERO.
05 FILLER   PICTURE XXX   VALUE SPACES.
```

REVIEW

1. What are the following columns used for in a COBOL program? Which columns are of optional use?

   Columns   1-6
   Column   7
   Columns   8-11
   Columns   12-72
   Columns   73-80

2. On your COBOL compiler, if you put an ∗ in column 7, can you use the line as a comment line?

3. List the rules for forming identifiers. Which of the following are invalid identifiers? Indicate why the invalid identifiers are invalid.

   TIME-CARD   DON'T
   1ST   GET OUT
   COBOL   APRIL
   DATE-WRITTEN   I.B.M.
   SPACE   NOTES
   89-78   END-OF-IT-

4. List the rules for use of spaces, periods, and commas in a COBOL program.

WHAT A PROGRAM LOOKS LIKE

In order for a program to be executed it must have control records and data. Together this is called a **job**. A job is usually composed of the parts shown in **Figure 2.6**.

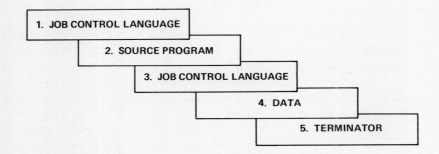

FIGURE 2.6   **A Complete Computer Job**

1. Job Control Language

The first set of job-control language (**JCL**) cards usually tells the computer who is running a program and, therefore, whom to charge for the computer usage. In addition, JCL indicates what programming language is being used. You will have to check with your instructor or at the computer center to find out the exact form of the JCL statements needed at your installation. JCL is used by the operating system.

2. Source Program

The program is used to specify in the correct language (e.g., COBOL) the task which is to be accomplished.

3. Job Control Language

This second set of JCL is used to separate the source program and the data. JCL cards are a special language and are not related to COBOL in form or syntax. JCL statements are very sensitive to errors; even the smallest error will usually prevent your job from being run.

4. Data

The **data** is the information which is to be processed. All columns of a data record can be used. If the program is processing a payroll, for example, the data will be payroll information containing employee number, name, hours, rate, deductions, etc.

5. Terminator

The terminator is used to indicate the end of the complete program. The terminator is also JCL.

****

A Diversion: A Large Program

One of the largest programs written was the IBM/360 Operating System (fondly called OS/360). OS/360 was announced with much fanfare a year or two before it was scheduled to be completed. Then anxious users waited and waited. It finally appeared late and incorrect, part by part, starting around 1966.

At its release, it consisted of over a million lines of code, and it grew to over five million lines of code. It cost 50 million dollars a year during its preparation. Between 1963 and 1966, over 5,000 person-years went into its design, construction, and documentation. At its peak, over 1,000 people were working on it—programmers, writers, machine operators, clerks, secretaries, and supervisors.

From 1966 to 1976, OS/360 went through 21 major releases and numerous minor releases. (In a release, errors are fixed and changes are made in a software package.) OS/360 had over 1,000 errors in it at all times. Because of OS/360's size and complexity, any change or correction was likely to add a new error. In fact, some observers felt it was a deteriorating system, since any change (even a correction) was likely to add an error. OS/360 was a mammoth software project and it was done in the eye of the public. It was a great project and taught us all some valuable lessons about software. Because of it, today we know a little better how to (or how not to) do large programs.

****

FORMAL NOTATION FOR COBOL STATEMENTS

There is a standard **formal notation** used in describing COBOL. This formal notation is used in COBOL textbooks and COBOL reference manuals, so it is important to become familiar with it. Here are the rules:

1. Reserved words are printed in capital letters.

2. Reserved words which are underlined are required unless the portion containing them is optional. Reserved words which are not underlined are included to improve readability but may be omitted.

3. Special symbols that are required are included in the formal notation (for example, periods and equals signs).

4. Words printed in lower-case letters are supplied by the programmer. These words must conform to the rules for programmer-defined words.

5. Square brackets [ ] enclosing items indicate that the enclosed items may be either used or omitted, depending on the requirements of the particular program.

6. Braces { } enclosing items indicate that one of the enclosed items must be used.

7. An ellipsis . . . indicates that repeated occurrences of the preceding item are permissible.

This notation will be used in this text, so you will soon gain familiarity with it. Since COBOL is rather like English, many beginning programmers assume that they can write instructions to the computer in any way they please, but COBOL really has very few of the possible English words and structures, and you can write only COBOL statements that conform to these rules of formal notation. For example:

    MULTIPLY A BY C.

is correct, but

    MULTIPLY A TIMES C.

is incorrect. When using COBOL we must use the exact syntax; no variations are allowed.

Here is a formal notation of the MOVE statement:

$$\underline{\text{MOVE}} \left\{ \begin{array}{l} \text{identifier-1} \\ \text{literal} \end{array} \right\} \underline{\text{TO}} \text{ identifier-2 [identifier-3 . . .]} .$$

In the notation above, MOVE and TO are required reserved words. The two words in braces indicate two options, one of which must be chosen. We must have an identifier-2 and we may also have additional identifiers. Here are some examples of the MOVE statement:

    MOVE X TO Y.
    MOVE 4.5 TO C.
    MOVE A TO B, C, D.

The commas in the last example are optional. Here is a more complicated example:

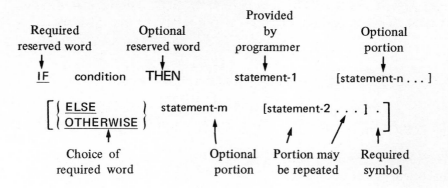

In the example above, IF is a required reserved word and THEN is an optional reserved word (some compilers do not accept THEN in the IF statement). The programmer must supply the condition and statement-1. The ELSE clause is optional, but, if used, you must use either the reserved word ELSE or OTHERWISE and supply statement-m. Here are some examples of the IF statement:

```
IF (A < B) THEN MOVE ZERO TO A.
IF (EARNINGS < 100.00) THEN MOVE ZERO TO TAX
                    MOVE EARNINGS TO PAY.
IF (PAY < ZERO) COMPUTE PAY = ZERO.
IF (HOURS > 40) THEN PERFORM OVERTIME
            ELSE PERFORM REG-TIME.
```

COBOL does not require us to put the condition inside parentheses, but the statement is easier to read if we do use the parentheses. Appendix B contains the formal notation for the COBOL statements used in this book. You will find this appendix useful for checking the syntax in your program.

REVIEW

1. Name the four COBOL divisions in order and describe the purpose of each.

2. How is a numeric literal different from a nonnumeric literal? Give the rules for composing numeric literals. Give the rules for composing nonnumeric literals. Which of the following are numeric literals? Which are nonnumeric literals? Which are neither, and why?

    a) 123.4

    b) HI

    c) 481.

    d) 'JOE'S BOOK'

    e) $278.5

    f) '14%'

    g) '12/18/79'

    h) 12345678901234567890

    i) +16

    j) ' '

k)   'MOVE'

l)   'THE "BOOK" IS'

m)   1,456

n)   MOVE

o)   1/2

p)   ZERO

3.   When reading COBOL formal notation, what does each of the following indicate?

    a)   Underlined capitalized words

    b)   Capitalized words not underlined

    c)   Lower-case words

    d)   Brackets [ ]

    e)   Braces { }

    f)   Ellipsis . . .

4.   Given the formal notation

$$\underline{\text{SUBTRACT}} \left\{ \begin{array}{l} \text{literal-1} \\ \text{identifier-1} \end{array} \right\} \left[\begin{array}{l} \text{literal-2} \\ \text{identifier-2} \end{array} \right] \ldots$$

$$\underline{\text{FROM}} \left\{ \begin{array}{l} \text{literal-m} \\ \text{identifier-m} \end{array} \right\}$$

$$\underline{\text{GIVING}} \text{ identifier-n } [\underline{\text{ROUNDED}}].$$

indicate which of the following are incorrect, and if incorrect, why:

    a) SUBTRACT 5 FROM C GIVING T.

    b) SUBTRACT 5*A FROM C GIVING Z ROUNDED.

    c) SUBTRACT A GIVING Z.

    d) SUBTRACT A B C FROM X GIVING T.

    e) SUBTRACT A AND B FROM Z.

A SAMPLE PROGRAM

Figure 2.7 and **Figure 2.10** are the sample COBOL programs. **Figure 2.8** shows the punching instructions for this job. Keypunch or type this program and run it. This will help you to become familiar with the procedure for submitting and running a COBOL program at your installation. You will need to inquire at your computer installation to learn the exact form of the JCL cards needed to execute your program. Also, the two ASSIGN clauses may require modification for your computer.

Typing Instructions

Notice the top of the coding form. The program name and programmer's name are put on the top of the form. In addition, punching instructions are given. In a professional installation someone else usually types up the program (a programmer makes three times as much as a typist, so it would be bad economics to have programmers typing their own programs). The keypunch operator who types the program will not know COBOL, so the programmer must distinguish any characters that may be confused. On the top row the programmer puts the character, and on the bottom row indicates whether the character is N (numeric) or A (alphabetic). A slash is put through the number zero to distinguish the zero from the letter "O"; also notice how the number 1 is distinguished from the letter I and the letter Z is distinguished from the number 2.

IBM COBOL Coding Form

SYSTEM PRINT PROGRAM	PUNCHING INSTRUCTIONS							PAGE 1 OF 2
PROGRAM PROGRM 2A	GRAPHIC	Ø	O	1	I	2	Z	CARD FORM #
PROGRAMMER D. VAN TASSEL DATE 2/1/1981	PUNCH	N	A	N	A	N	A	

```
SEQUENCE    A   B                                                           IDENTIFICATION
(PAGE)(SERIAL) CONT.  COBOL STATEMENT
Ø1ØØ1Ø IDENTIFICATION DIVISION.                                         PROGRM2A
Ø1ØØ2Ø PROGRAM-ID.                                                      PROGRM2A
Ø1ØØ3Ø     PROGRM2A.                                                    PROGRM2A
Ø1ØØ4Ø*****************************************************************PROGRM2A
Ø1ØØ5Ø*    SAMPLE PRINT PROGRAM.                                       *PROGRM2A
Ø1ØØ6Ø*****************************************************************PROGRM2A
Ø1ØØ7Ø ENVIRONMENT DIVISION.                                            PROGRM2A
Ø1ØØ8Ø INPUT-OUTPUT SECTION.                                            PROGRM2A
Ø1ØØ9Ø FILE-CONTROL.                                                    PROGRM2A
Ø1Ø1ØØ     SELECT RECORDS-IN                                            PROGRM2A
Ø1Ø11Ø         ASSIGN TO UR-254ØR-S-SYSIN.                              PROGRM2A
Ø1Ø12Ø     SELECT PRINT-OUT,                                            PROGRM2A
Ø1Ø13Ø         ASSIGN TO UR-14Ø3-S-SYSPRINT.                            PROGRM2A
Ø1Ø14Ø                                                                  PROGRM2A
Ø1Ø15Ø DATA DIVISION.                                                   PROGRM2A
Ø1Ø16Ø FILE SECTION.                                                    PROGRM2A
Ø1Ø17Ø FD  RECORDS-IN                                                   PROGRM2A
Ø1Ø18Ø     LABEL RECORDS ARE OMITTED.                                   PROGRM2A
Ø1Ø19Ø Ø1  IN-RECORD                   PICTURE X(8Ø).                   PROGRM2A
Ø1Ø2ØØ FD  PRINT-OUT                                                    PROGRM2A
Ø1Ø21Ø     LABEL RECORDS ARE OMITTED.                                   PROGRM2A
Ø1Ø22Ø Ø1  PRINT-LINE                  PICTURE X(133).                  PROGRM2A
Ø1Ø23Ø                                                                  PROGRM2A
```

FIGURE 2.7 **Coding Sheet for Sample Program 2A**

PUNCHING INSTRUCTIONS								
GRAPHIC	Ø	O	1	I	2	Z		
PUNCH	N	A	N	A	N	A		

FIGURE 2.8 **Punching Instructions**

Problem Description

A program is needed by Ready-Cash Bank to read a data record and print the data record on the printer. This is the simplest possible kind of program. Sample Program 2A in **Figure 2.7** and **Figure 2.10** will read and print only one record.

For the time being we will ignore everything before the WORKING-STORAGE SECTION. (The information above that section will be explained in Chapter 4.) We will now concentrate on the most interesting part of the program. COBOL is a rather difficult language to discuss, because no matter where we begin it seems as though some other part should have already been discussed. We are attempting to start you programming as soon as possible. Here is the WORKING-STORAGE SEC-TION:

```
WORKING-STORAGE SECTION.
01 ADDRESS-RECORD              PICTURE X(80).
01 OUT-LINE.
   05 FILLER                   PICTURE X(01).
   05 ADDRESS-LINE             PICTURE X(132).
```

WORKING-STORAGE

WORKING-STORAGE is used to store information needed by the program. You can think of it as a blackboard or a large piece of paper. In our program the input record is read and put into the 80-character location called ADDRESS-RECORD. This is then transferred by a MOVE command to ADDRESS-LINE so it can be printed. Then OUT-LINE (which contains ADDRESS-LINE) is printed by using a WRITE statement. **Figure 2.9** is a picture of what happens to the data record in WORKING-STORAGE. Note that you, as the programmer, must write instructions to move the data from the record area to the print area. The computer will not do that automatically, since you do not always wish to print everything; you may sometimes wish to print data in a special format; or you may wish to manipulate the data before you print it.

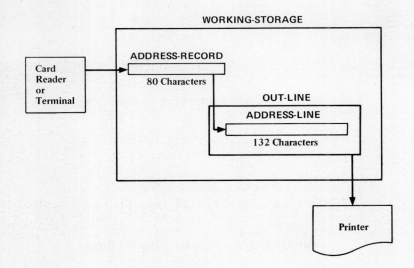

FIGURE 2.9   **A Picture of WORKING-STORAGE**

PROCEDURE DIVISION

In the DATA DIVISION we specified all the files and data to be used in the program. The PROCEDURE DIVISION specifies how to solve the problem, that is, it provides the logic of the program: the arithmetic, logical decisions, input/output, etc. First, we will discuss some of the more elementary statements in the **PROCEDURE DIVISION**. In the next chapter we will examine a more detailed description of options in **WORKING-STORAGE**. The **PROCEDURE DIVISION** begins with the two words **PROCEDURE DIVISION** starting in Area A, that is, in columns 8-11. They must be on a line by themselves and must end with a period.

Paragraphs

A **COBOL paragraph** is a set of one or more COBOL sentences, preceded by a paragraph name. Paragraph names are simply identifier names chosen by you. The paragraph name must start in Area A. In Sample Program 2A, **START-PROCESSING** and the following three lines constitute a paragraph. **WRAP-IT-UP** is the start of another paragraph. The paragraph headings begin in columns 8-11; everything else in the paragraph begins in columns 12-72. The basic structure for most small programs is very similar to this. There are usually three paragraphs. They do the following:

1. Initialization: Open files and do any other needed initialization work.
2. Processing: Read files and process data and transfer results to output.
3. Termination: Close files and do any other termination bookkeeping.

Now we can look at **Figure 2.10** and examine the commands used in this program. The first paragraph should contain all initialization; that is, all things that must be done before the main processing can start. In this sample program all we must do is open the files.

```
IBM                                    COBOL Coding Form
SYSTEM   PRINT PROGRAM                              PUNCHING INSTRUCTIONS          PAGE 2 OF 2
PROGRAM  PROGRM 2A                      GRAPHIC  0 0 1 1 2 Z
PROGRAMMER  D. VAN TASSEL    DATE 2/1/1981  PUNCH  N A N A N A    CARD FORM #

020010  WORKING-STORAGE SECTION.                                          PROGRM2A
020020  01  ADDRESS-RECORD              PICTURE X(80).                     PROGRM2A
020030  01  OUT-LINE.                                                      PROGRM2A
020040      05  FILLER                  PICTURE X(01).                     PROGRM2A
020050      05  ADDRESS-LINE            PICTURE X(132).                    PROGRM2A
020060                                                                     PROGRM2A
020070  PROCEDURE DIVISION.                                               PROGRM2A
020080      OPEN INPUT RECORDS-IN, OUTPUT PRINT-OUT.                       PROGRM2A
020090  START-PROCESSING.                                                 PROGRM2A
020100      READ RECORDS-IN INTO ADDRESS-RECORD                           PROGRM2A
020110          AT END PERFORM WRAP-IT-UP.                                PROGRM2A
020120      MOVE ADDRESS-RECORD TO ADDRESS-LINE.                          PROGRM2A
020130      WRITE PRINT-LINE FROM OUT-LINE AFTER ADVANCING 1 LINES.       PROGRM2A
020140  WRAP-IT-UP.                                                       PROGRM2A
020150      CLOSE RECORDS-IN, PRINT-OUT.                                  PROGRM2A
020160      STOP RUN.                                                     PROGRM2A
```

FIGURE 2.10 **WORKING-STORAGE and PROCEDURE DIVISIONS**

OPEN

All files must be opened before they are used. You specify the files, using file names from the **FD** part of **DATA DIVISION**. The general format of an **OPEN** statement is:

> OPEN $\left\{\begin{matrix} \text{INPUT} \\ \text{OUTPUT} \end{matrix}\right\}$ file-name-1 [,file-name-2, . . .].

Several files can be open at the same time. You may use the same statement for input and output, as in the example, or use one statement for input files and one statement for output files, as follows:

    OPEN INPUT RECORDS-IN.
    OPEN OUTPUT PRINT-OUT.

In **Figure 2.10** we open one input file, the record file, and one output file, the print file. It is done as follows:

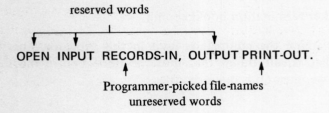

We will use **RECORDS-IN** for the input file-name and **PRINT-OUT** for the output file-name in the next few chapters. The comma is optional.

CLOSE

All files that are open must be closed before the program stops. This is to ensure that the computer processes all final records correctly before stopping. At the end of **Figure 2.10** you will see a **CLOSE** statement. The general format is:

> CLOSE file-name-1 [,file-name-2, . . .].

Figure 2.10 has a correct **CLOSE** statement. It reads as follows:

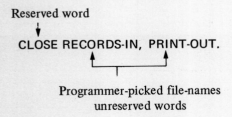

Notice that when you are closing the files, you do not indicate which are input and which are output files.

STOP RUN

The STOP RUN statement terminates the execution of the program. Every program must have a STOP RUN as the last statement of the program executed, in order to terminate the execution of the program. Notice that STOP RUN is two separate words. Both words in STOP RUN are reserved words.

   This completes the initialization and termination paragraphs for this program; as our programs get larger, the initial and final paragraphs will get larger.

READ

The READ statement transfers the data from the input medium (e.g., cards), so that the program can manipulate the data. The general format is:

```
READ file-name [INTO record-name] AT END imperative statement.
```

The file-name must be the same file-name that was used in the OPEN INPUT statement. Each time a READ statement is executed, a data record is read. The INTO record-name clause causes the input to be read and moved into the WORKING-STORAGE area defined by the record name. The data remains the same in storage until the next READ INTO this area (unless it is changed by the program). An imperative statement is a statement that specifies an action to be taken unconditionally. (This will be explained in Chapter 8.) Here is the READ sentence:

```
READ RECORDS-IN INTO ADDRESS-RECORD
    AT END PERFORM WRAP-IT-UP.
```

   The AT END option is used to indicate what is to be done when the program runs out of data, that is, what the program is to do when all the data records have been read. The AT END clause is executed only if the program tries to read a data record when there is no data-record available. The example above is all one sentence, even though it is put on two lines. Whenever a sentence is too long to fit on one line, you break at a space and then continue the rest of the sentence on the next line. The continued line should be indented 4 spaces so that someone reading the program will know that the line is a continuation of the previous line.

MOVE

The MOVE command is used to move data from one field to a new field. In our sample program we must move data from the input area to the output area so that the information can be printed. Here is the MOVE sentence:

```
MOVE ADDRESS-RECORD TO ADDRESS-LINE.
```

The general format of the MOVE sentence is:

```
MOVE data-name-1 TO data-name-2.

    or

MOVE data-name-1 TO data-name-2 [,data-name-3, . . . ].
```

As you see, you can move an item from one field to another field or you can move it to several fields at the same time.

WRITE

After the output record has been set up, the WRITE statement is used to write the record on the output device. The general format is:

```
WRITE record-name-1 [FROM record-name-2] [AFTER ADVANCING integer LINES].
```

Here is the WRITE statement:

```
WRITE PRINT-LINE FROM OUT-LINE AFTER ADVANCING 1 LINES.
```

In the next few sample programs we will use PRINT-LINE as record-name-1. The record-name-2 must be the output record-name as defined in WORKING-STORAGE. The AFTER ADVANCING option is used for vertical spacing when printing output or for skipping cards when punching output. If the AFTER ADVANCING option is used, the first position of the output record must be blank. This is achieved in the sample program by using FILLER with PICTURE X as the first column. The integer used can be 0, 1, 2, or 3. A zero would cause no spacing, which would result in overprinting, and is not often used. A 1 causes single-spacing; a 2 causes double-spacing; a 3 causes triple-spacing. Note that LINES is plural. Using the singular will generate an error on most compilers, although a few new compilers allow the singular word LINE.

****

Computer Graffiti

If computers are so fast, why do we spend so much time waiting around the computer center?

****

EXECUTION SEQUENCE

Notice that the statements in the PROCEDURE DIVISION are executed in sequence. The OPEN sentence is executed first. In this program the label START-PROCESSING only groups the following sentences, so that the next statement executed is the READ sentence. Next, the MOVE sentence is executed; it is followed by the WRITE sentence. This program will read only one record and write only one record. Finally, the CLOSE and STOP sentences are executed. The sentences must be in this order for the program to execute correctly: we must OPEN the file before we attempt to READ the file; we must READ the file before we attempt to MOVE the data; and we must MOVE the data into the WRITE area before we print the data. After the data has been processed we wish to CLOSE the files we opened and STOP the program. **Figure 2.11** is a flowchart of Sample Program 2A. **Figure 2.12** is the computer printout of Program 2A.

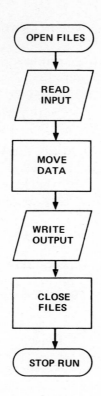

FIGURE 2.11   Flowchart for Program 2A

```
010010 IDENTIFICATION DIVISION.                                          PROGRM2A
010020 PROGRAM-ID.                                                       PROGRM2A
010030     PROGRM2A.                                                     PROGRM2A
010040* * * * * * * * * * * * * * * * * * * * * * * * * * * * **PROGRM2A
010050*     SAMPLE COBOL PROGRAM.                                        *PROGRM2A
010060* * * * * * * * * * * * * * * * * * * * * * * * * * * * **PROGRM2A
010070 ENVIRONMENT DIVISION.                                             PROGRM2A
010080 INPUT-OUTPUT SECTION.                                             PROGRM2A
010090 FILE-CONTROL.                                                     PROGRM2A
010100     SELECT RECORDS-IN                                             PROGRM2A
010110        ASSIGN TO UR-2540R-S-SYSIN.                                PROGRM2A
010120     SELECT PRINT-OUT,                                             PROGRM2A
010130        ASSIGN TO UR-1403-S-SYSPRINT.                              PROGRM2A
010140                                                                   PROGRM2A
010150 DATA DIVISION.                                                    PROGRM2A
010160 FILE SECTION.                                                     PROGRM2A
010170 FD  RECORDS-IN                                                    PROGRM2A
010180     LABEL RECORDS ARE OMITTED.                                    PROGRM2A
010190 01  IN-RECORD                   PICTURE X(80).                    PROGRM2A
010200 FD  PRINT-OUT                                                     PROGRM2A
010210     LABEL RECORDS ARE OMITTED.                                    PROGRM2A
010220 01  PRINT-LINE                  PICTURE X(133).                   PROGRM2A
010230                                                                   PROGRM2A
020010 WORKING-STORAGE SECTION.                                          PROGRM2A
020020 01  ADDRESS-RECORD              PICTURE X(80).                    PROGRM2A
020030 01  OUT-LINE.                                                     PROGRM2A
020040     05  FILLER                  PICTURE X(01).                    PROGRM2A
020050     05  ADDRESS-LINE            PICTURE X(132).                   PROGRM2A
020060                                                                   PROGRM2A
020070 PROCEDURE DIVISION.                                               PROGRM2A
020080     OPEN INPUT RECORDS-IN, OUTPUT PRINT-OUT.                      PROGRM2A
020090 START-PROCESSING.                                                 PROGRM2A
020100     READ RECORDS-IN INTO ADDRESS-RECORD                          PROGRM2A
020110        AT END PERFORM WRAP-IT-UP.                                 PROGRM2A
020120     MOVE ADDRESS-RECORD TO ADDRESS-LINE.                          PROGRM2A
020130     WRITE PRINT-LINE FROM OUT-LINE AFTER ADVANCING 1 LINES.      PROGRM2A
020140 WRAP-IT-UP.                                                       PROGRM2A
020150     CLOSE RECORDS-IN, PRINT-OUT.                                  PROGRM2A
020160     STOP RUN.                                                     PROGRM2A
```

FIGURE 2.12   Sample Program 2A

COMMON ERRORS

1. Punching your program in the wrong columns. Labels must start in columns 8–11. COBOL sentences must be contained in columns 12–72. For the time being, it is best to use the exact columns used in the sample program when typing the program.

2. Forgetting to end statements and labels with periods. If you forgot periods, you will generate many errors.

3. Making spelling errors: (1) Reserved words must be spelled exactly as they are in the text. (2) Names that you make up must be spelled the same way each time they appear in a program. (3) The number 0 (zero) and the letter O (oh) are two different characters on a terminal or a keypunch. (4) You must leave space between each word.

```
*****************************************************************
```

Desk Checking

After you type your program, carefully check each line for errors before you try to execute the program. This simple process can save you a great deal of time. *Get it right the first time.*

```
*****************************************************************
```

```
*****************************************************************
```

Automation Lament

Nature never spawned my race,
Nor do we continue it.
'Tis man who breeds
And then enslaves us
Till we're obsolete.

They curse our theft of menial jobs,
Yet only must they
Stop the lines
And we would cease to be.

They call us cold unfeeling beasts
Whose eyes just flash and blink
To the base-two rhythm
Of our hearts.

Yet, what fault of ours
That sum of parts
In silicon psychology
Cannot exceed the whole
And what emotions
Could be stirred
Within a software soul?

```
*****************************************************************
```

CHAPTER REVIEW

Vocabulary Review

Coding sheet	Reserved word	Character string
Sequence numbers	COBOL verb	Figurative constant
Program identification	COBOL sentence	Job
Continuation column	COBOL statement	JCL
Comment	Label	Formal notation
Area A	Data value	Data
Area B	Numeric literal	COBOL paragraph
Identifier	Nonnumeric literal	Desk checking

Review Questions

1. Which columns of a record are used for the COBOL program? Which columns are used for COBOL data records? How does the computer distinguish between records which are COBOL statements and records which are data?

2. Explain and trace how the output is derived from the input in the COBOL program. What is the role of the job-control records in a COBOL program?

3. Indicate which of the following begins in Area A and which in Area B:

    a) PROCEDURE DIVISION.
    b) MOVE ADDRESS-RECORD TO ADDRESS-LINE.
    c) Paragraph name.
    d) CLOSE RECORDS-IN, PRINT-OUT.

4. In an OPEN sentence what is meant when a file is designated as INPUT? As OUTPUT?

5. In your own words, explain what the function is of each of the sentences in the PROCEDURE DIVISION of Sample Program 2A. What would happen if there were no data-records?

6. Those of you who would like to read about OS/360 should look at *The Mythical Man Month* by Frederick P. Brooks, Jr. (Reading, Mass.: Addison-Wesley, 1975). Brooks was the project leader for the IBM/360 and has written a very readable and informative book on it.

Program Modifications

1. Find out exactly what JCL statements are needed to run COBOL programs at your computer center. Next, find out exactly what must go in the ASSIGN clauses for the input file and the output files. These items are different at each installation. You should be able to get this information from your instructor or computer center.

2. Next, keypunch or type Sample Program 2A and run it. This will help you to learn the procedure for submitting and running COBOL programs. If you have errors in your program, you will have to fix the errors and rerun the program. The object is to get an error-free run which prints your output data. Be sure to include an input data-record for the program to process. Notice that you can use all 80 columns for the data record.

3. Modify Program 2A so that it prints the same data-record twice. This requires you to change only the **PROCEDURE DIVISION**. Use double-spacing.

4. Using only what you know so far about COBOL, modify Program 2A so that it will read and print two *different* data-records. This requires you to change only the **PROCEDURE DIVISION**.

5. Make the following modifications in Program 2A:

   a) Change the paragraph heading **WRAP-IT-UP** to **END-IT-ALL**.
   b) Change the line **01 ADDRESS-RECORD** to **01 LOCATION-RECORD**.

   Both of these names are chosen by the programmer, so any legal name can be used, but each of the above changes will necessitate other changes in the program, too. Make the necessary changes and check them by rerunning the program. Hint: if you are having trouble, do one change at a time.

6. If all of this seems easy, combine the modifications in questions 3 to 5 into one program and run it.

7. *Errors*. One way to learn how to understand the compiler error-messages is intentionally to introduce some errors into the program. Try the following modifications, one at a time:

   a) Omit the **OPEN** sentence.
   b) Omit the whole **ADDRESS-LINE** line.
   c) Omit the **CLOSE** sentence.
   d) Omit **STOP RUN**.
   e) Omit the paragraph heading **WRAP-IT-UP**.
   f) If you omit the paragraph heading **START-PROCESSING**, will an error message be generated? Why?

8. Use the Glossary in Appendix A to determine the difference between a numeric literal and a nonnumeric literal.

****

A garrulous robot I know,
With a tongue constantly on the go,
Incessantly brags
That nobody gags
His free informational flow.

****

THE INS AND OUTS OF DATA

In Chapter 2 we read and printed a single data-processing record. In this chapter we will learn how to manipulate and print parts of a record. First, we must examine a little more closely how records can be described in WORKING-STORAGE.

Every company payroll department needs to keep information on its employees. To process a payroll for each employee the following are needed: employee number, name, pay hours, pay rate, and address. There are many ways to organize this data. Here is one way to set up a time-card record:

Field	Columns
Employee number	1–9
Last name	10–30
First name	31–39
Middle initial	40
Date	41–46
Hours	47–50

Pay rate	51–54
Department	55–68
Section	69–80
Street	81–100
City	101–120

Since a data-processing card is only 80 columns long, this data would require two cards for each record.

The method above is a useful way of organizing data: each field is indicated in order and the corresponding columns are indicated. It does not, however, indicate the relationships between items of data. Higher levels of connection can be indicated: for example, the name consists of first name, middle initial, and last name; home address consists of street and city. It is often useful to look at these relationships. **Figure** 3.1 is a tree-type illustration of the relationship of the items in the time card. Notice that this is similar to a tree structure (upside down). Items at the bottom branches of this tree are called **elementary items**, that is, all items which are not further subdivided are elementary items. Employee number, last name, month, and day, for example, are elementary items.

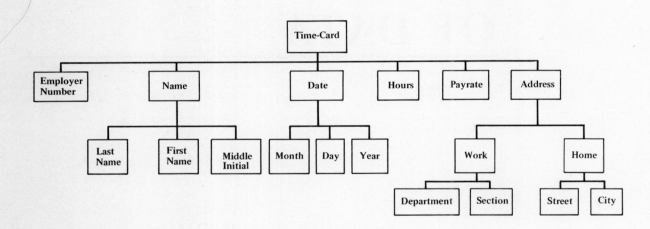

FIGURE 3.1   **A Time-Card Tree**

An item containing elementary items is called a **group item**. Examples of group items are name, date, and address. The highest or most inclusive group item is the time card. An elementary item belongs to only one group item; a group item may be part of another group item.

The dividing and grouping of elementary items may change for different purposes. Items are organized according to how they are going to be used. Thus, you subdivide items only as far as is useful. For some purposes, you may break date into month, day, and year, but for other purposes subdividing the date may not be necessary. The purpose of such subdivisions is to facilitate movement of data within the program. In COBOL, records are organized in a manner similar to that of the tree structure. The sub-tree levels are indicated by number.

Before we talk about level numbers, we need some definitions. A **file** is a collection of related records. A **record** is a collection of related fields. A **field** is an item of information in a record. **Figure 3.2** shows some simple payroll records which have employee number, name, and pay-rate fields. The relationships among files, records, fields, and characters are illustrated in this figure: the complete collection of payroll records is the file; a single card is a record; each piece of information (such as employee number) is a field.

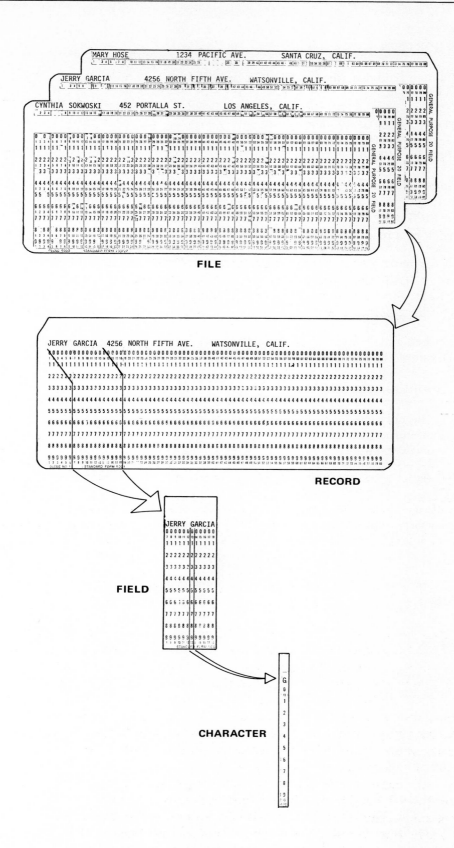

FIGURE 3.2   Relationships of Data

RECORD DESCRIPTION

An example of a date field described in COBOL notation is:

```
05 DATES.
    10 MONTHS       PICTURE X(02).
    10 DAYS         PICTURE X(02).
    10 YEARS        PICTURE X(02).
```

Each field must be described as a separate entry, and the items in each field must be described in the order in which they appear in the data record. Each elementary field described uses a level number, data name, and PICTURE clause. (These will be described in the next two sections of this chapter.) The general format of a record description entry is:

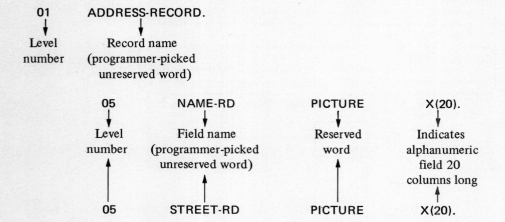

(FILLER is described a little later in the chapter.)
Here is an example of part of a record:

```
01        ADDRESS-RECORD.
```
Level   Record name
number   (programmer-picked
                unreserved word)

```
   05          NAME-RD           PICTURE        X(20).
```
          Level   Field name   Reserved   Indicates
        number   (programmer-picked   word   alphanumeric
                        unreserved word)   field 20
                                                                      columns long

```
   05          STREET-RD         PICTURE        X(20).
```

LEVEL NUMBERS

Level numbers are used to show how data items are related, that is, the hierarchy of the data. In the following example, the level numbers are **05** and **10**:

```
05 DATES.
    10 MONTHS  ...
    10 DAYS    ...
    10 YEARS   ...
```

The level numbers must always be followed by at least one blank space, and are usually followed by two blank spaces. The MONTHS, DAYS, and YEARS are subparts of the DATES field. The field DATES has the smaller level number and subfields of the DATES use a higher level number. You use the same level number for all items on the same level, that is, you wouldn't use 10 for MONTHS and 15 for DAYS, since both items are on the same level. The level numbers specify subdivisions of data for the purpose of data reference. In the example above, it is possible to reference the whole DATES field, or just one part of it, such as the DAYS field. In the fields above, MONTHS, DAYS, and YEARS are elementary items, and DATES is a group item. DATE is a reserved word on some computers, so we used DATES, which is not a reserved word.

The most inclusive level number is the 01 level. The 01 level number always goes in Area A, that is, in columns 8–11. It is reserved for records and must be used at this level. Less inclusive items use levels 02 to 49; here they are put in Area B, in columns 12–72. The actual level numbers you use are arbitrary, but it is best to leave gaps so that new levels can be inserted. Many programmers use levels 05, 10, 15, . . . in order always to have gaps available.

Here is an example in which we do not leave any gaps in the level numbers:

```
01 ADDRESS-CARD.
      02 SECTIONS        . . .
      02 DEPARTMENT  . . .
      02 STREET          . . .
      02 CITY            . . .
```

But SECTIONS and DEPARTMENT refer to a work address, and STREET and CITY refer to a home address. Later we may wish to be able to refer to home address or work address as a single unit. If gaps had been left in the level numbers, we could simply insert a new level, but in the case above the whole record description will have to be retyped. Here is a corrected version with new level numbers inserted:

```
01 ADDRESS-CARD.
   05 WORK-ADDRESS.
      10 SECTIONS        . . .
      10 DEPARTMENT  . . .
   05 HOME-ADDRESS.
      10 STREET          . . .
      10 CITY            . . .
```

Here is a picture of the relationship of data showing the levels:

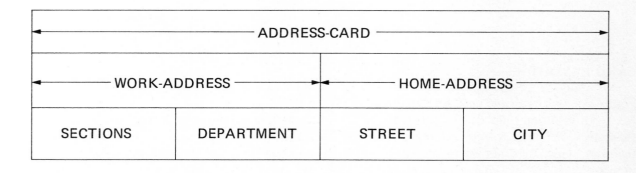

FIGURE 3.3   **Levels of Data**

Now we can use the group items of WORK-ADDRESS or HOME-ADDRESS. If gaps had been left in the level numbers in the first example, we could simply have inserted two new lines in our program.

PICTURE CLAUSE

The **PICTURE IS** clause is used to indicate the type and size of the data field. The **IS** part is optional and is often dropped. The **PICTURE** is used to give a "picture" of each elementary item. (Most compilers allow you to abbreviate the word **PICTURE** to **PIC**.) Here are three type of **PICTURE** entries:

Field Indicator

X	Alphanumeric field
9	Numeric field
A	Alphabetic or blank field

Alphanumeric field: Any computer character can be included in an alphanumeric field. Use this field until the other field indicators are discussed in more detail in a later chapter.

Numeric field: This indicates numeric fields. Only digits and sign can appear in the data field.

Alphabetic field: Only letters of the alphabet or blanks can occur in the data field. This is not much used.

The part in parentheses after the field indicator indicates the size of the field:

9(05)	5-column numeric field
X(23)	23-column alphanumeric field

Each elementary item must have a **PICTURE** clause to indicate the type of field and size. Only elementary items have **PICTURE** clauses. Since **PICTURE** clauses are necessary for elementary items, it would be a duplication to have **PICTURE** clauses on group items.

Special forms are available on which to lay out the input records and the output records. These forms are often filled out by the person who wants the program or by someone who plans the program. They are sometimes filled out by the programmer.

CARD LAYOUT

Figure 3.4 is a **multiple-card layout form**. Even though it is called a card layout form, it can be used for records other than card records. Both input and output records can be put on these forms (but there is a different form used for printed output, and there are special forms available for longer records). This form allows us to represent graphically the field size and sequence of data items in a record.

There are six bands on the form; each can be used to lay out a record. At the bottom of each band is a row of 9s, and the columns are numbered 1 to 80.

One data field is separated from the next by a vertical line. The first band is the card layout for a name-and-address record. The name field is in columns 1–20, the street field is in columns 21–45, and the city field is in columns 46–72. The last 8 columns of an 80-column card are not used in this record. **Figure 3.5** is a card which matches this card layout form.

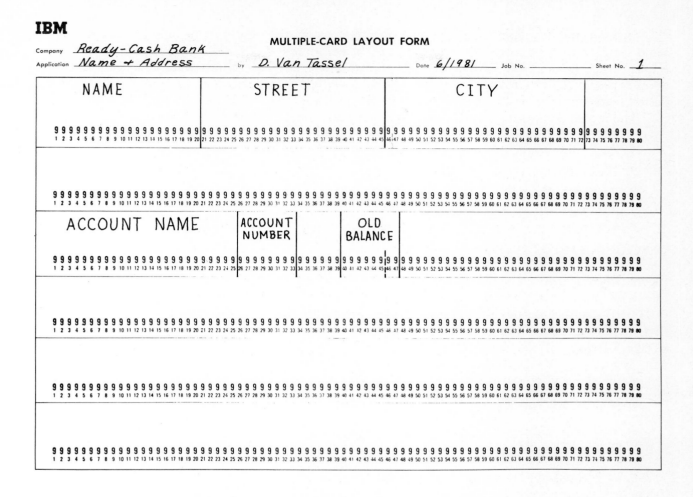

FIGURE 3.4   **A Multiple-Card Layout Form**

FIGURE 3.5   **A Name-and-Address Record**

If a job requires more than one type of input record, the other records are also laid out on the same form. Another record has been laid out in **Figure 3.4** that has numeric data with dollars and cents. Notice in the OLD BALANCE field how the decimal point is indicated. The decimal point is never typed in the input data; instead, its place is marked. The decimal point in the OLD BALANCE field is between columns 45 and 46, indicated by the dashed vertical line.

The record layouts have several purposes. They are used:

1. As a guide to the data-entry operator in preparing the data.
2. As a reference for the programmer.
3. As part of the documentation for the program.

DESCRIBING INPUT DATA

Figure 3.6 is a name-and-address record and the corresponding COBOL record description. Note that the fields must be described in the order in which they appear on the input data record. Also, the PICTURE clause indicates the type and length for each field; thus, the NAME-RD field is described first. It is 20 columns long—PICTURE X(20)—and it defines columns 1–20 of the data record. Next, STREET-RD is defined as 25 columns long—PICTURE X(25)—and it defines columns 21–45 on the data record. CITY-RD is similarly defined. These variable names are arbitrarily picked by the programmer, but your variable names should add meaning to the program.

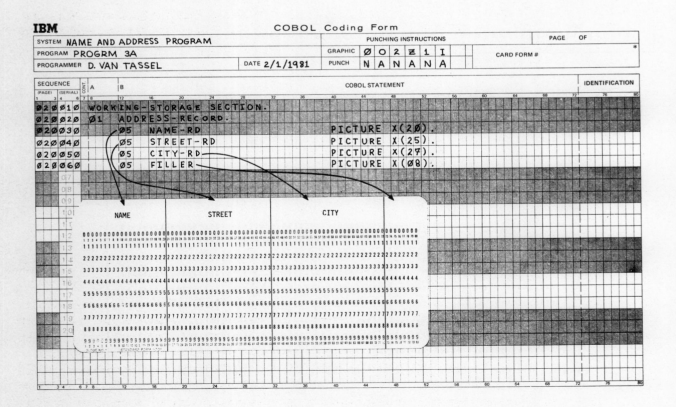

FIGURE 3.6   **A Record and Its COBOL Description**

In COBOL we must describe the whole record. Since we are using cards, or card images, which are 80 columns long, we need to describe the last 8 columns of the card. Any time you wish to specify an area in a record which you will never wish to reference, you use the reserved word FILLER and use an X specification that indicates its length, as we have done in the record description above. FILLERs can be used only at the elementary level.

Notice that each data field ends with the suffix RD. Programmers often put the same prefix or suffix on every field of a record so that items of the record can be easily spotted by the programmer. Thus, when reference is made to STREET-RD anywhere in the program, the programmer will know this field is in the input data record. This description of a record using level numbers is called a **data structure**.

Indenting

The lining up of like elements in the same column is called **indenting** or **paragraphing**. The word PICTURE is almost always started in the same column to make the program easier to read. Column 40 is usually used for PICTURE, but other columns may be used.

The field size is also usually lined up. The field sizes in the example are:

```
X(20).
X(25).
X(27).
X(08).
```

The field sizes must always add up to the total record size. In this case, that is 80 columns. Note that if the field sizes are lined up this way, the addition is easy to check. We use X(08) instead of X(8) to line up the digits. The two forms are treated by the compiler as identical, but use of the second form would make addition more difficult. For example, add these:

```
X(20).
X(25).
X(27).
X(8).
```

This is more difficult to add, because the last 8 is in the wrong column for addition.

There are several ways you can write the specifications:

```
PICTURE XX.      (or PIC XX.)
```

is the same as

```
PICTURE X(02).    (or PIC X(02).)
```

You may either write out *n* symbols (e.g., XX) or list the symbol and indicate how many (e.g., X(02)). The last method is the most commonly used by professional programmers. It makes addition easier; and the use of the number in parentheses eliminates the common error of listing one too few or one too many symbols. Finally, someone reading the program will not be forced to count the symbols.

It is usual to indent 4 spaces, as in the examples above. This indenting is not required by the COBOL compiler, but it allows the physical structure of the record to match the logical structure, that is, subfields are indented so that they appear visibly as subdivisions. A sign of an amateur COBOL programmer is the absence of indentations in the program.

The Data

The data, the information you process with your program, are the cards at the end of your program if you use cards, or a data file if you use a terminal system for your input. The data are read by the READ statement and transferred to the correct place in WORKING-STORAGE by use of the INTO record clauses. **Figure 3.5** is a data-processing card for a name-and-address record. Notice that the data fields are described by order and place. In this program the person's name must be in columns 1–20 in the data record. Alphabetic data fields are always **left-justified**, that is, they are aligned on the lefthand side. Thus, the name must start in column 1. Starting the name in some other column would be a data error.

The street is the second field. It is to be punched in columns 21–45. (Note that name required the first 20 columns, and street the next 25 columns.) The city is to be punched in the next 27 columns, columns 46–72. If, for example, the city were punched in columns 48–74 instead of in columns 46–72, only part of the city data would be read and printed. It is as important to put the data in the correct columns of the data record as it is to get the program correct. Also, notice that in data-record cards you may use all the columns, 1–80.

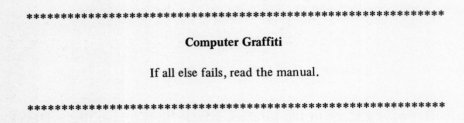

****

Computer Graffiti

If all else fails, read the manual.

****

PRINT CHART

Figure 3.7 is a **print chart**. This is used to lay out a printed report, to plan and document it graphically. This form is also a useful part of the program documentation. The form is normally numbered along the top from 1 to 150. There are 50 lines down the side of the page. Programmers lay out the report on this print chart exactly as they want it to appear in the final printed report. Thus, the programmer sees just how the report will look. Most reports have heading lines, detail lines, and total lines. These three lines are usually laid out in the printer-spacing chart. The type of line is indicated on the left margin, as follows:

H   Heading line
D   Detail line
T   Total line

Figure 3.7 illustrates the print columns used for the fields of the name-and-address records. The NAME field will be printed in columns 1–20 of the printed report. The Xs indicate the size of the field. The STREET field will be printed in columns 26–50. The CITY field will be printed in columns 56–82. The names in parentheses are the field names used in the program. Once the fields have been laid out on the print chart, this information can be used to code the print-line.

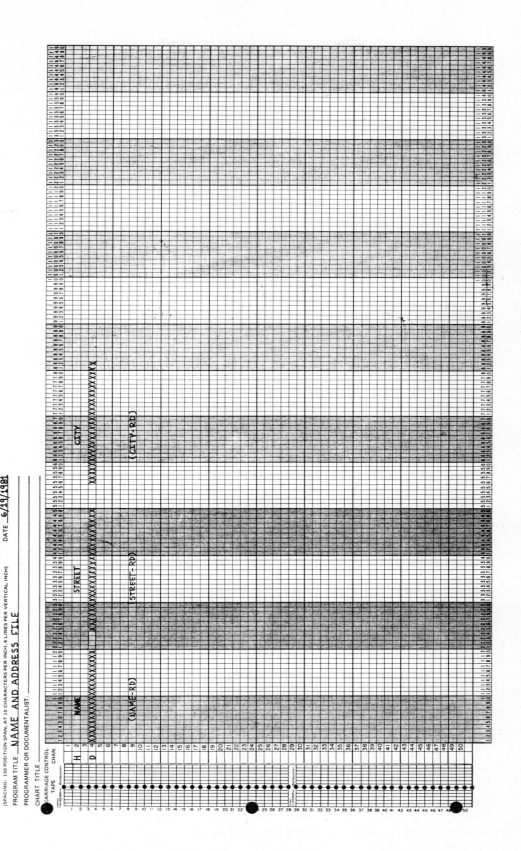

FIGURE 3.7   A Print Chart for a Name-and-Address Record

DESCRIBING OUTPUT DATA

Next, we will describe the output line in the way we did for the input record. **Figure 3.8** is a record description and the corresponding output line. First, we must give the output line a name. Here, it has been given the name ADDRESS-LINE, but any other legal COBOL name could have been used. We usually pick a name that describes the record. The first position of a print-line must not contain data to be printed. This position is reserved for carriage control (explained in detail a little later).

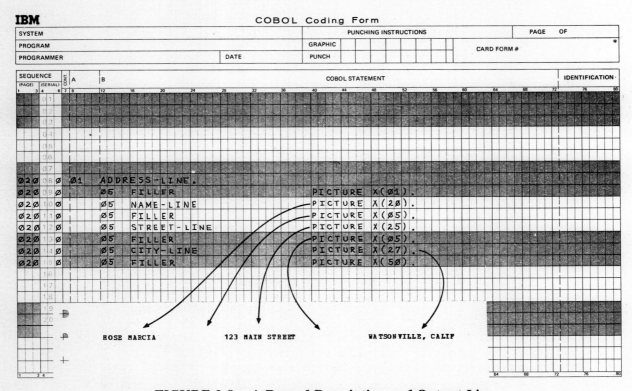

FIGURE 3.8   **A Record Description and Output Line**

Next, we start defining the fields just as we did in the input data record. Since the NAME-RD was 20 columns long on the input data record, the name field should be 20 columns on the output record. When the information is printed, there should be some blank spaces separating each field, so we put a FILLER 5 spaces long between the fields.

Note that we again used a suffix on each field name in the output record. This time LINE was used for the suffix. This will help us to identify fields from the output line later on in the program.

Finally, the whole output record must total 133 columns; so we end the record with a FILLER of size 50. Some printers use a line of 121 columns: if your printer does, you will have to adjust your line to this length by changing the last FILLER. Each time you describe a record you must describe the whole record, even if you are using only part of it.

REVIEW

1. Write the complete record description for the TIME CARD example from the beginning of this chapter. Remember, you must select the level numbers and use PICTURE clauses. Assume it will all fit on one record (which it would if we were using magnetic tape or disk).

2. Explain how and why level numbers are used in COBOL. How are level numbers like an outline structure?

3. Assuming a 80-column input record, code the input description of the following inventory record:

Field	*Name*
Part Number	1–6
Description	7–30
Location	36–46
Purchase Date	47–52 (47–48, month; 49–50, day; 51–52, year)

Which fields are group items? Which fields are elementary items? Draw a tree of this record.

4. Lay out a reasonable output-record description for the input record in question 3.

5. What columns are used for program sentences? What columns can be used for data records?

6. Why are PICTURE clauses not used with group items?

7. What is the purpose of FILLERs?

****

A Diversion: Job Description

Programmer: Programmers are people who pass themselves off as exacting experts on the basis of being able to turn out, after innumerable debugging sessions, an infinite series of incomprehensible answers calculated with micrometric precision from vague assumptions based on debatable figures taken from inconclusive documents of problematical accuracy by persons of dubious reliability and questionable mentality for the purpose of annoying and confounding a hopelessly defenseless department that was unfortunate enough to have asked for the information.

****

PROGRAM EXAMPLE

Ready-Cash Bank needs a program that will print a customer's name and address. **Figure 3.9** is the complete program for this example. Everything before WORKING-STORAGE is the same as in the previous program. In WORKING-STORAGE you will see the input record and the output record, which were discussed earlier. They complete the WORKING-STORAGE.

The PROCEDURE DIVISION is very similar to that in the last program. First, we must OPEN the input and output files. This is done with the following sentence:

OPEN INPUT RECORDS-IN, OUTPUT PRINT-OUT.

(We will continue to use RECORDS-IN and PRINT-OUT for our file names.) Next, we must move spaces to our output line. This is done by the sentence:

MOVE SPACES TO ADDRESS-LINE.

This sentence puts blanks in the whole ADDRESS-LINE. Otherwise, our ADDRESS-LINE might have anything in the FILLER fields when the line is printed. Notice that you can MOVE from or to both elementary and group items. In this statement we move spaces into the group item, blanking out the whole line with one sentence.

The START-PROCESSING paragraph is where all the processing of the record is done. (Remember, a paragraph consists of one or more sentences preceded by a paragraph name.) Paragraph names always start in Area A (columns 8–11) and end with a period. The paragraph name is chosen by the programmer; it can be any name you desire, as long as it doesn't use reserved words. The paragraph

```
010010 IDENTIFICATION DIVISION.                                   PROGRM3A
010020 PROGRAM-ID.                                                PROGRM3A
010030     PROGRM3A.                                              PROGRM3A
010040*********************************************************PROGRM3A
010050*    SAMPLE NAME AND ADDRESS PROGRAM.                      *PROGRM3A
010060*********************************************************PROGRM3A
010070 ENVIRONMENT DIVISION.                                      PROGRM3A
010080 INPUT-OUTPUT SECTION.                                      PROGRM3A
010090 FILE-CONTROL.                                              PROGRM3A
010100     SELECT RECORDS-IN                                      PROGRM3A
010110         ASSIGN TO UR-2540R-S-SYSIN.                        PROGRM3A
010120     SELECT PRINT-OUT,                                      PROGRM3A
010130         ASSIGN TO UR-1403-S-SYSPRINT.                      PROGRM3A
010140                                                            PROGRM3A
010150 DATA DIVISION.                                             PROGRM3A
010160 FILE SECTION.                                              PROGRM3A
010170 FD  RECORDS-IN                                             PROGRM3A
010180     LABEL RECORDS ARE OMITTED.                             PROGRM3A
010190 01  IN-RECORD                  PICTURE X(80).              PROGRM3A
010200 FD  PRINT-OUT                                              PROGRM3A
010210     LABEL RECORDS ARE OMITTED.                             PROGRM3A
010220 01  PRINT-LINE                 PICTURE X(133).             PROGRM3A
010230                                                            PROGRM3A
020010 WORKING-STORAGE SECTION.                                   PROGRM3A
020020 01  ADDRESS-RECORD.                                        PROGRM3A
020030     05  NAME-RD                PICTURE X(20).              PROGRM3A
020040     05  STREET-RD              PICTURE X(25).              PROGRM3A
020050     05  CITY-RD                PICTURE X(27).              PROGRM3A
020060     05  FILLER                 PICTURE X(08).              PROGRM3A
020070                                                            PROGRM3A
020080 01  ADDRESS-LINE.                                          PROGRM3A
020090     05  FILLER                 PICTURE X(01).              PROGRM3A
020100     05  NAME-LINE              PICTURE X(20).              PROGRM3A
020110     05  FILLER                 PICTURE X(05).              PROGRM3A
020120     05  STREET-LINE            PICTURE X(25).              PROGRM3A
020130     05  FILLER                 PICTURE X(05).              PROGRM3A
020140     05  CITY-LINE              PICTURE X(27).              PROGRM3A
020150     05  FILLER                 PICTURE X(50).              PROGRM3A
020160                                                            PROGRM3A
030010 PROCEDURE DIVISION.                                        PROGRM3A
030020     OPEN INPUT RECORDS-IN, OUTPUT PRINT-OUT.               PROGRM3A
030030     MOVE SPACES TO ADDRESS-LINE.                           PROGRM3A
030040                                                            PROGRM3A
030050 START-PROCESSING.                                          PROGRM3A
030060     READ RECORDS-IN INTO ADDRESS-RECORD                    PROGRM3A
030070         AT END PERFORM WRAP-IT-UP.                         PROGRM3A
030080     MOVE NAME-RD TO NAME-LINE.                             PROGRM3A
030090     MOVE STREET-RD TO STREET-LINE.                         PROGRM3A
030100     MOVE CITY-RD TO CITY-LINE.                             PROGRM3A
030110     WRITE PRINT-LINE FROM ADDRESS-LINE AFTER ADVANCING 1 LINES.  PROGRM3A
030120                                                            PROGRM3A
030130 WRAP-IT-UP.                                                PROGRM3A
030140     CLOSE RECORDS-IN, PRINT-OUT.                           PROGRM3A
030150     STOP RUN.                                              PROGRM3A
```

FIGURE 3.9   Sample Program 3A

name **START-PROCESSING** is used to group the main body of the program. It has no effect on the program in this example. (In later chapters you will see paragraph groupings that are used for a particular purpose.) Since the initialization paragraph contains only one sentence (i.e., the **OPEN** statement), it does not have a paragraph name before it, although it could have a paragraph name. In this program, paragraph names are used to group together statements that have a common purpose, that is, we grouped the initialization statements in the first paragraph, the processing statements in the second paragraph, and the termination statements in the last paragraph.

The next statement is:

    READ RECORDS-IN INTO ADDRESS-RECORD AT END PERFORM WRAP-IT-UP.

The file name **RECORDS-IN** must be the same file name that was used in the **OPEN** statement. **ADDRESS-RECORD** is the record that we declared in the **WORKING-STORAGE SECTION**. The **AT END** clause is executed when a **READ** is attempted and there is no data record to be read. (This will be explained in more detail later.)

    OPEN INPUT RECORDS-IN, . . .
    READ RECORDS-IN . . .

cause the input record to be read. The **INTO ADDRESS-RECORD** clause causes the input record to be moved into the **ADDRESS-RECORD** area in **WORKING-STORAGE**.

Next, we must **MOVE** each field which we want to print from the input-record area to the output-record area. This is done by the next three **MOVE** commands:

    MOVE NAME-RD TO NAME-LINE.
    MOVE STREET-RD TO STREET-LINE.
    MOVE CITY-RD TO CITY-LINE.

It may seem as though the computer should automatically move the input fields to the output area, but often we will not want to print the input fields exactly as read without first manipulating the fields, so the programmer must write statements to do the moving. (We will later look at the **MOVE** command in more detail.)

After all the fields have been moved into the print area, we use the **WRITE** statement to print the output line. The last line in the **START-PROCESSING** paragraph writes the **PRINT-LINE**:

    WRITE PRINT-LINE FROM ADDRESS-LINE AFTER ADVANCING 1 LINES.

The **FROM ADDRESS-LINE** clause causes the data we moved into **ADDRESS-LINE** to be moved into the print-record area, **PRINT-LINE**, so that it can be printed. The **AFTER ADVANCING 1 LINES** clause causes the printer to space 1 column vertically after printing the line in the output report.

CARRIAGE CONTROL

Carriage control determines vertical spacing on the printed page. This refers to the spacing in the printed output report, not the spacing in the listing of the program. We tell the printer whether we want single-spacing or double-spacing by using the **AFTER ADVANCING** clause of the **WRITE** statement. The normal output print-line is defined as 133 characters long (some printers use 121 characters). You must define all 133 positions, but only 132 are printable. The first character is never printed. It is always used to tell the printer what type of spacing is to take place. Thus, when you say:

    . . . AFTER ADVANCING 1 LINES.

the compiler creates code to send a line to the line-printer with a **1** in the first position. The printer inspects the first position and finds the **1**; it therefore single-spaces, and it does not print the first position.

You ask for double spacing as follows:

   . . . AFTER ADVANCING 2 LINES.

Now the computer will send the print-line to the printer with a **2** in the first position and we will get double-spacing. A **0** (zero) would indicate no spacing. **Figure 3.10** illustrates what happens when a line is printed.

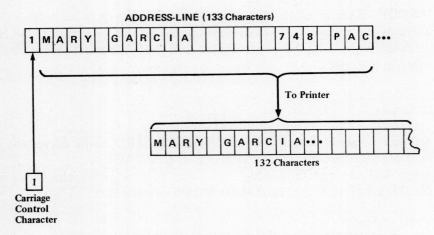

FIGURE 3.10   **Carriage Control in an Address-Line**

WRAP-IT-UP

The **WRAP-IT-UP** paragraph is the paragraph which is done last. Any other paragraph name could have been chosen. This program processes only one data record, so the next statement executed is the **CLOSE** sentence. In this paragraph we **CLOSE** the files and stop the execution of the program.

MOVE

The **MOVE** command is used to move data from one field, the **sending field**, to a new field, the **receiving field**. In our sample program we must move data from the input area to the output area so that the information can be printed.

The general format is:

```
MOVE   {data-name-1}   TO data-name-2 [data-name-3 . . . ] .
       {literal      }
```

Examples of the **MOVE** statement are:

   MOVE A TO B.
   MOVE SPACES TO Z, T.
   MOVE PRICE TO PRICE-OLD, PRICE-NEW.

Notice that, as in the last example, you can move one field to several fields. The comma is optional in these **MOVE** sentences. There are several examples of moves in Sample Program 3A. One example is:

MOVE NAME-RD TO NAME-LINE.

After this statement has been executed, the field **NAME-LINE** will have whatever was in the field **NAME-RD**. **NAME-RD** is the sending field and **NAME-LINE** is the receiving field.

Before execution:

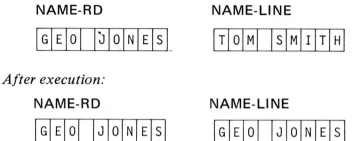

After execution:

NAME-RD

| G | E | O | | J | O | N | E | S |

NAME-LINE

| G | E | O | | J | O | N | E | S |

Notice in the example above that after the **MOVE** the original information is still in the sending field. A **MOVE** operation does not disturb the information from the sending field.

Truncation

On **MOVE**s with alphabetic or alphanumeric fields, **truncation** will occur on the right if the receiving field is too short:

MOVE OLD-ADDRESS TO NEW-ADDRESS.

Notice that the receiving field **NEW-ADDRESS** is shorter than the sending field **OLD-ADDRESS**.

Before execution:

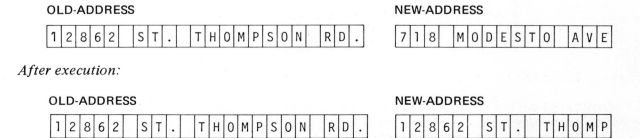

After execution:

OLD-ADDRESS

| 1 | 2 | 8 | 6 | 2 | | S | T | . | | T | H | O | M | P | S | O | N | | R | D | . |

NEW-ADDRESS

| 1 | 2 | 8 | 6 | 2 | | S | T | . | | T | H | O | M | P |

Notice that the last few letters in **NEW-ADDRESS** have been lost because the receiving field was too small. No error is generated when this occurs during execution of the program, but most compilers will provide a warning message at compile time to tell you that this may occur.

Adding Blanks

On **MOVE**s with alphabetic or alphanumeric fields, if the receiving field is larger than the sending field, the rightmost portion of the receiving field will be converted to blanks:

    05 DATES   PICTURE X(8).
     .
     .
     .

    05 PRINT-DATE   PICTURE X(13).
     .
     .
     .

       MOVE DATES TO PRINT DATES

Before execution:

    DATES

    | 0 | 6 | / | 1 | 7 | / | 7 | 4 |

    PRINT-DATE

    | J | U | N | E | | 1 | 2 | , | | 1 | 9 | 7 | 3 |

After execution:

    DATES

    | 0 | 6 | / | 1 | 7 | / | 7 | 4 |

    PRINT-DATE

    | 0 | 6 | / | 1 | 7 | / | 7 | 4 | | | | | |

You can move data from one area to several areas in one **MOVE** statement. For example:

    MOVE FIRSTS TO FIRSTS-OUT.

Before:

    FIRSTS   FIRSTS-OUT

    | B | U | Z | Z | | T | A | S | S |

After:

    FIRSTS   FIRSTS-OUT

    | B | U | Z | Z | | B | U | Z | Z |

MOVE FIRSTS TO FIRSTS-OUT, FIRSTS-RD.

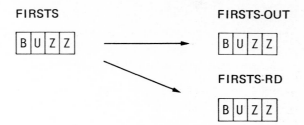

FIRSTS   FIRSTS-OUT

B U Z Z   ———————▶   B U Z Z

                                          FIRSTS-RD

                                          B U Z Z

The last **MOVE** example moves the contents of **FIRSTS** to both **FIRSTS-OUT** and **FIRSTS-RD**. Here are some examples of what happens when you move alphabetic or alphanumeric data:

MOVE A TO B.

A		B	
Sending Field		*Receiving Field*	
PICTURE	*Contents*	PICTURE	*Contents*
X(4)	A B C D	X(4)	A B C D
X(4)	A B C D	X(5)	A B C D ☐
X(4)	A B C D	X(3)	A B C
A(4)	A B C D	A(4)	A B C D
A(4)	A B C D	A(5)	A B C D ☐
A(4)	A B C D	A(3)	A B C

Data can be moved at both the group and the elementary level. For example:

```
01 A.
   05 B            PICTURE X(10).
   05 C.
      10 Z         PICTURE X(05).
      10 T         PICTURE X(07).
   05 N            PICTURE X(15).
```

Using the description of a record above, the sentence

MOVE B TO OUT-B.

moves 10 characters, an elementary item. We can also move group items. The sentence

MOVE C TO OUT-C.

moves 12 characters of data, that is, it moves both data fields **Z** and **T**. We can also move entire records. For example:

MOVE A TO OUT-A.

moves the entire record of 37 characters.

COMMON ERRORS

1. Omitting a hyphen in a data name or label. If the variable PRINT-LINE is typed PRINT LINE, the compiler will not find its reference and the program will have syntax errors.

2. Misspelling data names or reserved words. Reserved words must be spelled exactly as indicated. Data names chosen by the programmer must be spelled consistently.

3. Going past column 72. COBOL sentences and entries must be contained within columns 12–72. Sometimes this error is difficult to notice, since the compiler usually lists all columns even though it uses only the columns up to column 72.

****

Computer programming is a skill which is learned by doing. In this way it is similar to learning how to play the piano or ride a bicycle. A lecture on bicycle-riding may be of some help, but the real test of bicycle-riding (and programming) is in doing it.

****

CHAPTER REVIEW

Vocabulary Review

Elementary item	Alphanumeric field	Left-justify
Group item	Numeric field	Print chart
File	Alphabetic field	Carriage control
Record	Multiple-card layout form	Sending field
Field	Data structure	Receiving field
Level number	Indenting (Paragraphing)	Truncation

Review Questions

1. True or false:

   a) After executing a MOVE sentence, the sending field is always unchanged.

   b) After executing a MOVE sentence, the contents of the sending field and of the receiving field are always identical.

2. Most computer centers charge for computer usage. You probably do not have to pay the bill yourself, but someone does. Find out exactly how the charges are calculated and determine the cost of some of your computer runs.

3. Explain what the following COBOL verbs do:

   a) OPEN
   b) READ
   c) MOVE
   d) WRITE
   e) CLOSE

4. Answer the following questions, using this record layout:

```
01 STUDENT-RECORD.
   05 STUDENT-NAME.
      10 FIRST-NAME          PICTURE X(20).
      10 LAST-NAME           PICTURE X(20).
      10 MID-INITIAL         PICTURE X(01).
   05 STUDENT-NUMBER         PICTURE X(09).
   05 COLLEGE-BOARDS.
      10 MATH.
         15 GENERAL-MATH      PICTURE X(04).
         15 ADVANCED-MATH     PICTURE X(04).
      10 ENGLISH.
         15 GENERAL-ENG       PICTURE X(04).
         15 ADVANCED-ENG      PICTURE X(04).
      10 SPECIALTY.
         15 TOPIC             PICTURE X(10).
         15 TOPIC-SCORE       PICTURE X(04).
```

   a) How many characters long is the record?
   b) List all elementary items.
   c) List all group items.
   d) Give the column numbers for the following fields:

      1) MID-INITIAL
      2) GENERAL-ENG

   e) If **05 COLLEGE-BOARDS** is changed to **03 COLLEGE-BOARDS**, will anything else have to be changed?

5. Since the print-line is defined as 133 positions, why can we use only 132 positions for printing?

6. What is the reserved word **FILLER** used for? Could we do the following?

   MOVE FILLER TO ZAP.

7. A very interesting and readable book about programming is *The Psychology of Computer Programming*, by Gerald Weinberg (New York: Van Nostrand-Reinhold, 1972). It analyzes the craft of programming from the point of view of a psychologist. It will be worth your while to locate and read it.

Program Modifications

1. Type Sample Program 3A and run the program. Then modify the data record as follows:

Field	Columns
Name	1–18
Street	19–48
City	52–75

    Rerun the program, using this data, and look at the results. If the data were going to be typed this way, what would you have to change in the program? Make the changes and rerun the program.

2. Remove the MOVES SPACES . . . line from the program and see what happens. (The program will usually print junk in the FILLER fields, but because it uses whatever was left by the last program you may get blank spaces.)

3. There are several places you could put the MOVE SPACES . . . line. Some of these will cause the program to work correctly and some will not. Determine which of the following would still allow the program to work correctly:

    a) After the READ statement.

    b) Before the READ statement.

    c) Before the WRITE statement.

    d) After the WRITE statement.

    If you cannot decide what would happen if you placed the MOVE SPACES . . . sentence in the places listed above, try each out in your program and observe the results.

4. The order of the statements in the program will usually affect whether the program can be executed correctly, but some lines could be moved and the program would still execute correctly. Find three lines that could be moved in the PROCEDURE DIVISION which wouldn't affect results of Sample Program 3A. Can anything else be moved in the PROCEDURE DIVISION? What could be moved in the WORKING-STORAGE SECTION? If you are unsure, try out your suggested changes. How will the output be changed if you change the order of the two lines 05 NAME LINE . . . , and 05 STREET-LINE . . . in the program? Make this change and run the program to see if your guess was right. What changed?

5. You have probably already experienced a few errors in your programs. One way to develop an understanding of error messages is to put deliberate errors in a program and then look at the error messages. Add a few errors (not more than two per run) and look at the error messages they caused.

6. Modify Sample Program 3A so that instead of using LINE as a suffix on NAME-LINE it uses LN. Change the street and city fields in a similar manner. (Remember, this will cause you to have to make other changes in the PROCEDURE DIVISION.)

7. Using what you have learned so far, modify Sample Program 3A so that it reads and processes two different data records. Cause a blank line to be printed by printing a blank line between each line. Do not use double spacing.

8. *Overprinting*: Modify Sample Program 3A so that it overprints, that is, the same output line is printed twice, one line on top of the other.

9. If your postal department uses a postal code after the city, add a field for the postal code and print it as a separate field.

10. Modify Sample Program 3A so that the data is printed vertically instead of horizontally, that is, the output should look like this:

    JERRY JONES
    123 MISSION STREET
    ANYTOWN, CA

    Do not change the input records.

11. Modify Sample Program 3A so that the data is printed vertically *twice* as in question 8, but print in two columns, as follows:

JERRY JONES	JERRY JONES
123 MISSION STREET	123 MISSION STREET
ANYTOWN, CA	ANYTOWN, CA

    Do not change the input records.

Programs

1. Write a program for the storeroom of Intellect Haven College to do the following:

INPUT RECORD

	Input	Output	
Field	Columns	Format	Columns
Part number	1–5	X(05)	1–5
Description	7–40	X(34)	41–74
Location	41–60	X(20)	16–35

The program up to the **WORKING-STORAGE SECTION** is the same in this program as in Sample Program 3A; copy that part from a previous program. Then lay out your input record first, and your output record next in the **WORKING-STORAGE SECTION**. Then write the **PROCEDURE DIVISION**.

2.   Write a program to print these records for Intellect Haven College:

Field	Input Columns	Output Columns
Student number	1–9	1–9
Student name	10–30	15–35
Major	31–40	41–50
Level	42	56

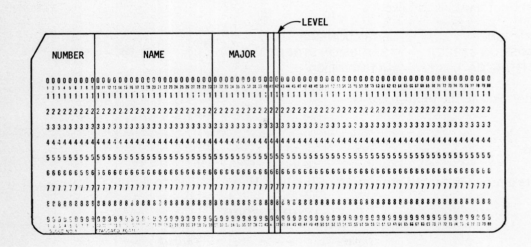

The program up to the **WORKING-STORAGE SECTION** is the same in this program as in Sample Program 3A; copy that part from a previous program. Then lay out your input record first, and your output record next in the **WORKING-STORAGE SECTION**. Then write the **PROCEDURE DIVISION**.

3.   Write a program to print these inventory records for the storeroom of Intellect Haven College:

Field	Input Columns	Output Columns
Part number	1–6	1–6
Part number	1–6	21–26
Description	7–30	31–54
Quantity on hand	31–36	61–66
Quantity on order	37–42	71–76

The program up to the **WORKING-STORAGE SECTION** is the same in this program as in Sample Program 3A; copy that part from a previous program. Then lay out your input record first, and your output record next in the **WORKING-STORAGE SECTION**. Then write the **PROCEDURE DIVISION**.

4. Write a program to process the following data for Intellect Haven College:

INPUT RECORD

Field	Columns	Format
Name	1–30	X(30)
Major	31–50	X(20)

OUTPUT RECORD

Field	Columns
Name	1–30
Major	36–55
Name	61–90
Major	96–115

The program up to the WORKING-STORAGE SECTION is the same in this program as in Sample Program 3A; copy that part from a previous program. Then lay out your input record first, and your output record next in the WORKING-STORAGE SECTION. Then write the PROCEDURE DIVISION.

****

****

```
**************************************************
      A robot sat scowling and scorning,
      And said to mechanics at Corning,
       "You know that I am
        Just not worth a damn
        Until I have my juice in the morning!"

**************************************************
```

A COMPLETE PROGRAM

IDENTIFICATION DIVISION

The IDENTIFICATION DIVISION, the first division of a program, must contain a user-supplied program name. The information you put in the IDENTIFICATION DIVISION is needed to identify the program, because even a small computer installation can have hundreds of programs. This division contains such optional information as author, date written, a description of the program, etc. **Figure 4.1** shows the general format for the IDENTIFICATION DIVISION.

The division headings and all paragraph headings must start in columns 8–11 and must end with a period. IDENTIFICATION DIVISION must be on a line by itself and must end with a period. The entries that follow the paragraph headings may be placed on the same line as the paragraph heading or on the following line, but they must be contained within columns 12–72. After each paragraph name the programmer provides an **entry**; these items are called entries because they are not sentences. (The rules for forming COBOL sentences apply only to the PROCEDURE DIVISION; the other three COBOL divisions use entries in columns 12–72.) The paragraphs listed are the only paragraphs allowed in the IDENTIFICATION DIVISION. **Figure 4.2** is a sample IDENTIFICATION DIVISION.

Structure of the Identification Division

```
IDENTIFICATION DIVISION.
PROGRAM ID. program-name.
[AUTHOR. [comment-entry] . . . ]
[INSTALLATION. [comment-entry] . . . ]
[DATE-WRITTEN. [comment-entry] . . . ]
[DATE-COMPILED. [comment-entry] . . . ]
[SECURITY. [comment-entry] . . . ]
```

FIGURE 4.1   **IDENTIFICATION DIVISION Format**

IBM   COBOL Coding Form

SYSTEM	NAME AND ADDRESS PROGRAM		PUNCHING INSTRUCTIONS			PAGE 1 OF 4
PROGRAM	PROGRM4A		GRAPHIC	Ø 0 1 I 2 Z		CARD FORM #
PROGRAMMER	D. VAN TASSEL	DATE JUNE 1981	PUNCH	N A N A N A		

| SEQUENCE | | CONT. | A | B | COBOL STATEMENT | IDENTIFICATION |
| (PAGE) | (SERIAL) | | | | | |

```
010010  IDENTIFICATION DIVISION.                                    PROGRM4A
010020  PROGRAM-ID.                                                 PROGRM4A
010030      PROGRM4A.                                               PROGRM4A
010040  AUTHOR.                                                     PROGRM4A
010050      DENNIE VAN TASSEL.                                      PROGRM4A
010060  INSTALLATION.                                               PROGRM4A
010070      READY-CASH BANK.                                        PROGRM4A
010080  DATE-WRITTEN.                                               PROGRM4A
010090      JUNE 12, 1981.                                          PROGRM4A
010100  DATE-COMPILED.                                              PROGRM4A
010110      JUNE 15, 1981.                                          PROGRM4A
010120  SECURITY.                                                   PROGRM4A
010130      NONE.                                                   PROGRM4A
010140  ****************************************************************PROGRM4A
010150* SAMPLE PROGRAM WITH ENTIRE IDENTIFICATION AND              *PROGRM4A
010160*     ENVIRONMENT DIVISION.                                  *PROGRM4A
010170  ****************************************************************PROGRM4A
010180                                                              PROGRM4A
```

FIGURE 4.2   **Sample IDENTIFICATION DIVISION**

PROGRAM-ID

The programmer provides a program name in the **PROGRAM-ID** paragraph. The name must conform to the following rules:

1. It must start with a letter.
2. It must be composed of letters and numbers only (no hyphen).
3. It must be 1 to 8 characters in length.

If the full program name is longer than 8 characters, only the first 8 characters are used in the PROGRAM-ID paragraph. This **program name**, chosen to indicate the purpose of the program, is usually placed in columns 73–80 of each line of the program. The rest of the IDENTIFICATION DIVISION is optional, but it is normally included. If the rest of the paragraphs are included, they must be in the sequence listed in the example. Entries in these paragraphs are treated as comments and have no effect on the program. Thus, the entries can be of any length and composition. Each entry is terminated with a period.

AUTHOR

Put your name after this paragraph heading.

INSTALLATION

Put the name of the computer installation here.

DATE-WRITTEN

Put the date the program was written in this paragraph. The date can be in any form desired.

DATE-COMPILED

Put the date the program is compiled in this paragraph. The date can be in any form desired. Some compilers will insert today's date in this paragraph for you.

A brief summary of what the program does is usually included here. This can be several English sentences in length. Each line should have an asterisk in column 7. Enough information should be included that someone reading these comments can understand what the program does.

ENVIRONMENT DIVISION

The ENVIRONMENT DIVISION is used to describe the characteristics of the computer and must indicate the location of each file used by the program. The ENVIRONMENT DIVISION is composed of two sections: the CONFIGURATION SECTION and the INPUT-OUTPUT SECTION. **Figure 4.3** is the general format for the ENVIRONMENT DIVISION. **Figure 4.4** is a sample ENVIRONMENT DIVISION. **Figure 4.5** shows the purpose of each of the four COBOL divisions. The ENVIRONMENT DIVISION is the most machine-dependent division in COBOL; it is the most likely to require change if a program is to be compiled and executed on a different computer.

Structure of the Environment Division

```
ENVIRONMENT DIVISION.
[CONFIGURATION SECTION.
SOURCE-COMPUTER. paragraph
OBJECT-COMPUTER. paragraph
[SPECIAL-NAMES. paragraph] ]
[INPUT-OUTPUT SECTION.
FILE-CONTROL. paragraph]
```

FIGURE 4.3   **ENVIRONMENT DIVISION** Format

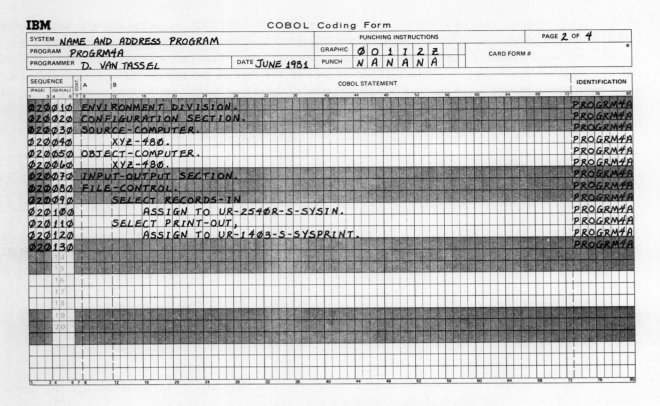

FIGURE 4.4   A Sample ENVIRONMENT DIVISION

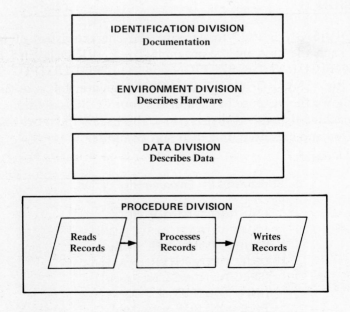

FIGURE 4.5   Purpose of the Four COBOL Divisions

CONFIGURATION SECTION

The CONFIGURATION SECTION is optional; it is often omitted. It is used to identify the computer on which the program is compiled—the **source computer**—and executed—the **object computer**. This information is used only for documentation. The example indicates that an XYZ-480 is being used as both the source and the object computer. (The SPECIAL-NAMES paragraph will be discussed in Chapter 11). A few compilers require the CONFIGURATION SECTION.

INPUT-OUTPUT SECTION

The INPUT-OUTPUT SECTION is required whenever there is input or output. It is used to identify the files to be used in our program, and to assign the file to specific I/O devices. First, we need a FILE-CONTROL paragraph. Within the FILE-CONTROL paragraph we must have a SELECT entry for each field that is being processed. On simple programs we usually have only two files: an input card or terminal file, and an output print-file. The SELECT entries assign each file to a particular input/output device such as a card reader or printer. This section is quite machine-dependent; the following description may not work for non-IBM/OS equipment.

The general format for the SELECT entry in the FILE-CONTROL paragraph is:

```
SELECT file-name ASSIGN TO class-device-organization-name.
```

where:

> file-name is a user-supplied name. Each file name must have a file description (FD) entry in the DATA DIVISION of the source program.
>
> class is a two-character abbreviation that indicates the class or type of device that is to be used for the file. The choices are:
>
> > UR   Unit-Record (card-reader, terminal, card-punch, line-printer)
> > DA   Direct Access (magnetic disk)
> > UT   Utility (magnetic tape, magnetic disk)
>
> device is the model number of the I/O device. The permissible model numbers vary, depending on the type of hardware.
>
> organization is a one-character abbreviation indicating the organization of the file.
>
> > S Sequential   (card-reader, line-printer, card-punch, magnetic tape)
> > D Direct organization (disk)
>
> name is a 1-to-8-character field specifying the user-picked **external name** appearing in the Job Control Language for the file.
>
> > SYSIN is commonly used for input.
> > SYSPRINT is commonly used for printer output.

Table 4.1 provides this information for some common devices.

TABLE 4.1   SOME I/O DEVICE SELECT INFORMATION

Device Name	Class	Device Number	Organization
Card-reader	UR	2540R	S
Line-printer	UR	1403	S
Tape drive	UT	2400	S
Magnetic disk	UT or DA	2314, 3330	S or D

Input SELECT

First, we write the SELECT sentence for the input records. Here is the input SELECT sentence:

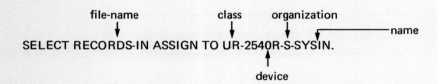

The file name is RECORDS-IN. This is a user-picked name, but once the name has been chosen it must be used in several places. The class used for sequential files is UR. Most of the programs in this book will use class UR.

The device used for the card-reader on IBM computers is 2540R. This specifies a particular device within a device class. If you are not using an IBM computer or not using card input, you will need a different device number here. The table above is only a partial list of the most common devices, so you may have to use different device names.

The organization for all programs in this book will be S, which stands for sequential. This means the file is a **sequential file**, that is, the records are in a particular sequence. All **unit-record (UR) devices** use sequential files. Unit-record devices process each record as a separate unit.

The name SYSIN is used to specify the external name. On IBM computers the card-reader is usually called SYSIN. On a different system a different name would be used.

Output SELECT

Next, we must do the same thing for the output SELECT sentence:

SELECT PRINT-OUT ASSIGN TO UR-1403-S-SYSPRINT.

The file name chosen is PRINT-OUT, which is a user-picked name. We use the class UR for the printer.

The device for an IBM printer is 1403. The printer is a sequential device, so S is used for organization. Finally, SYSPRINT is commonly used for the external name.

Warning

The ASSIGN clause is very user-installation-dependent, so check at your installation and find out what must be used. Once you get it right, you can use the same SELECT entries in almost all of your programs.

****

REVIEW

1. What is the purpose of the IDENTIFICATION DIVISION? What is required in the IDENTIFICA-TION DIVISION of the program? What is optional? What are the rules for forming the program name? What happens if you supply the DATE-COMPILED paragraph?

2. What is the purpose of the ENVIRONMENT DIVISION? What is required in the ENVIRON-MENT DIVISION? What is optional?

3. Find out exactly how your type and size of computer is indicated in the CONFIGURATION SECTION. Try it in one of your programs.

4. Find out exactly what must go in the ASSIGN clause for input files and output files at your installation. Why does this entry vary at different installations?

DATA DIVISION

The DATA DIVISION contains the description of all data to be processed by the program. This includes input data, such as data records, and output data, such as the printed results. In small programs the DATA DIVISION is often the largest of the four divisions.

The two sections of the DATA DIVISION which we will consider here are:

1. The FILE SECTION.
2. The WORKING-STORAGE SECTION.

The FILE SECTION is used to describe all input/output (I/O) files. Each column of input and output records must be specified.

The WORKING-STORAGE SECTION is used to store all information created by the program, such as intermediate results in calculations or constants like tax rates. You have already learned how to use the WORKING-STORAGE SECTION; it will be discussed further in later chapters.

FILE SECTION

Figure 4.6 is a sample FILE SECTION. The first heading is FILE SECTION, which starts in Field A, and the heading terminates with a period. Then each input/output file has an FD entry. The FD is the *F*ile *D*escription. This indicates the file name and the type of records. The abbreviated general format is:

```
┌─────────────────────────────────────────────────────┐
│                                                       │
│    FD      File-name                                  │
│            LABEL RECORDS ARE  ⎰OMITTED ⎱              │
│                               ⎱STANDARD⎰ .            │
│                                                       │
└─────────────────────────────────────────────────────┘
```

Some compilers may require additional entries.

IBM   COBOL Coding Form

SYSTEM	NAME AND ADDRESS PROGRAM	PUNCHING INSTRUCTIONS		PAGE 3 OF 4
PROGRAM	PROGRM4A	GRAPHIC	0 0 1 1 2 Z	
PROGRAMMER	D. VAN TASSEL DATE JUNE 1981	PUNCH	N A N A N A	CARD FORM #

SEQUENCE (PAGE) (SERIAL)	CONT	A	B	COBOL STATEMENT	IDENTIFICATION
030010		DATA DIVISION.			PROGRM4A
030020		FILE SECTION.			PROGRM4A
030030		FD RECORDS-IN			PROGRM4A
030040			LABEL RECORDS ARE OMITTED.		PROGRM4A
030050		01 IN-RECORD		PICTURE X(80).	PROGRM4A
030060		FD PRINT-OUT			PROGRM4A
030070			LABEL RECORDS ARE OMITTED.		PROGRM4A
030080		01 PRINT-LINE		PICTURE X(133).	PROGRM4A
030090					PROGRM4A

FIGURE 4.6   A Sample FILE SECTION

Notice that the FD must start in the A margin, that is, in columns 8–11. Everything else goes in the B margin, that is, in columns 12–72. Also notice that the FD is a single statement, with a period at the end. A common error is to put a period at the end of each line or after FD. There is only one period, and it is placed at the end of the FD entry. (A longer version of the FD will be explained in Chapter 16.)

The file name is required. It must be the same file name used in the SELECT statement of the INPUT-OUTPUT SECTION of the ENVIRONMENT DIVISION, so that the compiler can match the correct SELECT entry with the right FD entry by comparing the file names. This is how the program knows which device is used for the data.

LABEL RECORDS

This clause is required in each FD if labels are omitted or nonstandard. Card files and print files are unit-record files, and label records are omitted on all unit-record files. Tape and disk files normally use labelled files. On magnetic tape and disk, special records called **label records**, assigned to the files by the operating system, identify each file. These label records are written at the beginning and end of files on magnetic disk or tape. For tape or disk you usually put STANDARD instead of OMITTED.

File Names

Beginning programmers often fail to notice how the same file name is used in several places in the program. As was said above, the file name is an arbitrary name chosen by the programmer, but once the name is chosen it must be used in several places. **Figure 4.7** is the sample program with the input file name RECORDS-IN circled to show where it is used.

RECORDS-IN is not a reserved word. We could put any legal identifier there instead of RECORDS-IN, but then we would use this new name in all five places in the program. RECORDS-IN was picked as a suitably descriptive file name.

```
020010 ENVIRONMENT DIVISION.                                            PROGRM4A
020020 CONFIGURATION SECTION.                                           PROGRM4A
020030 SOURCE-COMPUTER.                                                 PROGRM4A
020040     XYZ-480.                                                     PROGRM4A
020050 OBJECT-COMPUTER.                                                 PROGRM4A
020060     XYZ-480.                                                     PROGRM4A
020070 INPUT-OUTPUT SECTION.                                            PROGRM4A
020080 FILE-CONTROL.                                                    PROGRM4A
020090     SELECT (RECORDS-IN)                                          PROGRM4A
020100         ASSIGN TO UR-2540R-S-SYSIN.                              PROGRM4A
020110     SELECT PRINT-OUT,                                            PROGRM4A
020120         ASSIGN TO UR-1403-S-SYSPRINT.                            PROGRM4A
020130                                                                  PROGRM4A
030010 DATA DIVISION.                                                   PROGRM4A
030020 FILE SECTION.                                                    PROGRM4A
030030 FD (RECORDS-IN)                                                  PROGRM4A
030040     LABEL RECORDS ARE OMITTED.                                   PROGRM4A
030050 01  IN-RECORD                    PICTURE X(80).                  PROGRM4A
030060 FD  PRINT-OUT                                                    PROGRM4A
030070     LABEL RECORDS ARE OMITTED.                                   PROGRM4A
030080 01  PRINT-LINE                   PICTURE X(133).                 PROGRM4A
030090                                                                  PROGRM4A
030100 WORKING-STORAGE SECTION.                                         PROGRM4A
030110 01  ADDRESS-RECORD.                                              PROGRM4A
030120     05   NAME-RD                 PICTURE X(20).                  PROGRM4A
030130     05   STREET-RD               PICTURE X(25).                  PROGRM4A
030140     05   CITY-RD                 PICTURE X(27).                  PROGRM4A
030150     05   FILLER                  PICTURE X(08).                  PROGRM4A
030160                                                                  PROGRM4A
030170 01  ADDRESS-LINE.                                                PROGRM4A
030180     05   FILLER                  PICTURE X(01).                  PROGRM4A
030190     05   NAME-LINE               PICTURE X(20).                  PROGRM4A
030200     05   FILLER                  PICTURE X(05).                  PROGRM4A
030210     05   STREET-LINE             PICTURE X(25).                  PROGRM4A
030220     05   FILLER                  PICTURE X(05).                  PROGRM4A
030230     05   CITY-LINE               PICTURE X(27).                  PROGRM4A
030240     05   FILLER                  PICTURE X(50).                  PROGRM4A
030250                                                                  PROGRM4A
040010 PROCEDURE DIVISION.                                              PROGRM4A
040020     OPEN INPUT (RECORDS-IN,) OUTPUT PRINT-OUT.                   PROGRM4A
040030     MOVE SPACES TO ADDRESS-LINE.                                 PROGRM4A
040040                                                                  PROGRM4A
040050 START-PROCESSING.                                                PROGRM4A
040060     READ (RECORDS-IN) INTO ADDRESS-RECORD                        PROGRM4A
040070         AT END PERFORM WRAP-IT-UP.                               PROGRM4A
040080     MOVE NAME-RD TO NAME-LINE.                                   PROGRM4A
040090     MOVE STREET-RD TO STREET-LINE.                               PROGRM4A
040100     MOVE CITY-RD TO CITY-LINE.                                   PROGRM4A
040110     WRITE PRINT-LINE FROM ADDRESS-LINE AFTER ADVANCING 1 LINES.  PROGRM4A
040120                                                                  PROGRM4A
040130 WRAP-IT-UP.                                                      PROGRM4A
040140     CLOSE (RECORDS-IN,) PRINT-OUT.                               PROGRM4A
040150     STOP RUN.                                                    PROGRM4A
```

FIGURE 4.7   **Use of File Name**

The output file name is used in a similar manner, with one crucial difference. The WRITE statement does not use the file name. Instead, you must use the record name in the 01 record description under the FD as follows:

```
FD   PRINT-OUT
     LABEL RECORDS ARE OMITTED.
01   PRINT-LINE     PICTURE X(133).
         .
         .
         .
     WRITE PRINT-LINE FROM . . .
```

The record name is PRINT-LINE, a programmer-picked identifier. The reason COBOL requires you to put the record name here is that you can have several different types of output records described and you must indicate which one is to be used. **Figure 4.8** shows the relationships of output files.

****

A Diversion: A Historical View

You probably know that computers are relatively new, but their development and evolution from punched-card equipment is much older. Cards punched with holes were used in the 1800s to store patterns for the weaving looms in England. In the 1890s a card-sorter was used by the U.S. Census Bureau to process the census. If you would like to read about the history of computers, you may enjoy looking at the picture book *A Computer Perspective*, by Charles and Ray Eames (Cambridge, Mass.: Harvard University Press, 1973). This book gives the IBM view of the history of computers. A nice readable book is *Think*, by William Rogers (New York: Stein and Day, 1969). During the 1930s and 1940s IBM used to have large sales meetings. One of the highlights of the meetings was the singing of songs from the *IBM Songbook*. I include one of these songs for your enjoyment:

Hail to the IBM

Lift up our proud and loyal voices,
    Sing out in accents strong and true,
With hearts and hands to you devoted,
    And inspiration ever new;
Your ties of friendship cannot sever,
    Your glory time will never stem,
We will toast a name that lives forever,
    Hail to the IBM.

Our voices swell in admiration:
    Of T. J. Watson proudly sing;
He'll ever be our inspiration,
    To him our voices loudly ring;
The IBM will sing the praises,
    Of him who brought us world acclaim,
As the volume of our chorus raises,
    Hail to his honored name.

****

```
020010 ENVIRONMENT DIVISION.                                          PROGRM4A
020020 CONFIGURATION SECTION.                                         PROGRM4A
020030 SOURCE-COMPUTER.                                               PROGRM4A
020040     XYZ-480.                                                   PROGRM4A
020050 OBJECT-COMPUTER.                                               PROGRM4A
020060     XYZ-480.                                                   PROGRM4A
020070 INPUT-OUTPUT SECTION.                                          PROGRM4A
020080 FILE-CONTROL.                                                  PROGRM4A
020090     SELECT RECORDS-IN                                          PROGRM4A
020100        ASSIGN TO UR-2540R-S-SYSIN.                             PROGRM4A
020110     SELECT PRINT-OUT,                                          PROGRM4A
020120        ASSIGN TO UR-1403-S-SYSPRINT.                           PROGRM4A
020130                                                                PROGRM4A
030010 DATA DIVISION.                                                 PROGRM4A
030020 FILE SECTION.                                                  PROGRM4A
030030 FD  RECORDS-IN                                                 PROGRM4A
030040     LABEL RECORDS ARE OMITTED.                                 PROGRM4A
030050 01  IN-RECORD                     PICTURE X(80).               PROGRM4A
030060 FD  PRINT-OUT                                                  PROGRM4A
030070     LABEL RECORDS ARE OMITTED.                                 PROGRM4A
030080 01  PRINT-LINE                    PICTURE X(133).              PROGRM4A
030090                                                                PROGRM4A
030100 WORKING-STORAGE SECTION.                                       PROGRM4A
030110 01  ADDRESS-RECORD.                                            PROGRM4A
030120     05  NAME-RD                   PICTURE X(20).               PROGRM4A
030130     05  STREET-RD                 PICTURE X(25).               PROGRM4A
030140     05  CITY-RD                   PICTURE X(27).               PROGRM4A
030150     05  FILLER                    PICTURE X(08).               PROGRM4A
030160                                                                PROGRM4A
030170 01  ADDRESS-LINE.                                              PROGRM4A
030180     05  FILLER                    PICTURE X(01).               PROGRM4A
030190     05  NAME-LINE                 PICTURE X(20).               PROGRM4A
030200     05  FILLER                    PICTURE X(05).               PROGRM4A
030210     05  STREET-LINE               PICTURE X(25).               PROGRM4A
030220     05  FILLER                    PICTURE X(05).               PROGRM4A
030230     05  CITY-LINE                 PICTURE X(27).               PROGRM4A
030240     05  FILLER                    PICTURE X(50).               PROGRM4A
030250                                                                PROGRM4A
040010 PROCEDURE DIVISION.                                            PROGRM4A
040020     OPEN INPUT RECORDS-IN, OUTPUT PRINT-OUT.                   PROGRM4A
040030     MOVE SPACES TO ADDRESS-LINE.                               PROGRM4A
040040                                                                PROGRM4A
040050 START-PROCESSING.                                              PROGRM4A
040060     READ RECORDS-IN INTO ADDRESS-RECORD                        PROGRM4A
040070        AT END PERFORM WRAP-IT-UP.                              PROGRM4A
040080     MOVE NAME-RD TO NAME-LINE.                                 PROGRM4A
040090     MOVE STREET-RD TO STREET-LINE.                             PROGRM4A
040100     MOVE CITY-RD TO CITY-LINE.                                 PROGRM4A
040110     WRITE PRINT-LINE FROM ADDRESS-LINE AFTER ADVANCING 1 LINES.  PROGRM4A
040120                                                                PROGRM4A
040130 WRAP-IT-UP.                                                    PROGRM4A
040140     CLOSE RECORDS-IN, PRINT-OUT.                               PROGRM4A
040150     STOP RUN.                                                  PROGRM4A
```

FIGURE 4.8   Relationships of Output Files

ORGANIZATION WITHIN A COBOL PROGRAM

It is very important that you understand the way a COBOL program is organized, so we will review the program organization. The COBOL program has four divisions. Divisions can have sections, for example, the ENVIRONMENT DIVISION has a CONFIGURATION SECTION and an INPUT-OUTPUT SECTION. The DATA DIVISION has SECTIONs but no paragraphs. You can identify a section because sections always have the reserved word SECTION, just as divisions always have the reserved word DIVISION. The next level of organization is the paragraph. Paragraphs are indicated by programmer-picked names or reserved words. Paragraphs may be grouped into sections, but are not always so grouped: in the IDENTIFICATION DIVISION there were no sections, although there were several paragraphs. Anything in Field A—columns 8-11—of a COBOL program will probably be a division, section, or paragraph heading. Divisions and sections are indicated by the reserved word DIVISION or SECTION in the heading.

In the first three divisions, each paragraph heading is followed by an entry. These entries must conform to the required form for that particular entry. Paragraphs in the PROCEDURE DIVISION are composed of COBOL sentences. Groups of sentences form paragraphs, and paragraphs may be combined to form sections. **Figure 4.9** is a picture to illustrate this COBOL program structure.

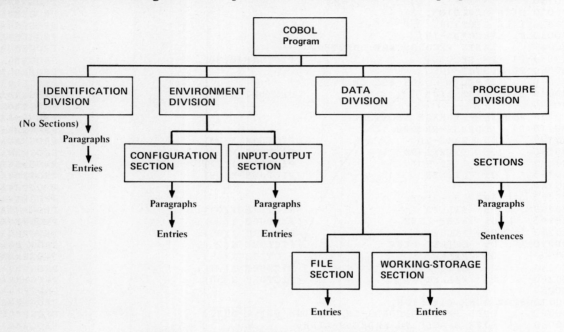

FIGURE 4.9   **Structure of a COBOL Program**

REVIEW

1. What are the two sections in the DATA DIVISION? What is each used for? How are sections, divisions, sentences, entries, and paragraphs related in a COBOL program?

2. What does FD stand for? What are the FD clauses discussed so far?

3. What is the purpose of the INPUT-OUTPUT SECTION? What is the purpose of the FILE SECTION? What is the purpose of the WORKING-STORAGE SECTION? How are these three areas linked together?

4. In the COBOL PROCEDURE DIVISION we READ___INTO___and we WRITE___FROM___. Fill in the blanks, choosing from: fields, files, records.

5. In what section are the hardware devices described in a COBOL program? In what section are the files described? In what section are the records described?

6. In what division(s) can you select your own section names? In what division(s) can't you select your own paragraph names? What division(s) has no sections? No sentences?

PROCESSING MORE DATA RECORDS

Ready-Cash Bank would like the sample program modified so that it will print the names and addresses of all the employees in the same listing. All the sample programs used so far read and process only one data record. Obviously, we want our program to process more than one data record. If we had only one or a few data records, it would be easier to process the data without a computer, because it is a great deal of work to set up a computer program. But once a program has been set up, it can process any number of data records and can be used as often as needed. This is where the savings result from using a computer—in the processing of large volumes of similar data.

Look at **Figure 4.10** and determine what we would have to repeat to process two data records. If we repeated the **START-PROCESSING** paragraph twice, we could read and process and print two data records. **Figure 4.11** is a sample program in which this is done.

```
040010  PROCEDURE DIVISION.                                               PROGRM4A
040020      OPEN INPUT RECORDS-IN, OUTPUT PRINT-OUT.                      PROGRM4A
040030      MOVE SPACES TO ADDRESS-LINE.                                  PROGRM4A
040040                                                                    PROGRM4A
040050  START-PROCESSING.                                                 PROGRM4A
040060      READ RECORDS-IN INTO ADDRESS-RECORD                           PROGRM4A
040070          AT END PERFORM WRAP-IT-UP.                                PROGRM4A
040080      MOVE NAME-RD TO NAME-LINE.                                    PROGRM4A
040090      MOVE STREET-RD TO STREET-LINE.                                PROGRM4A
040100      MOVE CITY-RD TO CITY-LINE.                                    PROGRM4A
040110      WRITE PRINT-LINE FROM ADDRESS-LINE AFTER ADVANCING 1 LINES.   PROGRM4A
040120                                                                    PROGRM4A
040130  WRAP-IT-UP.                                                       PROGRM4A
040140      CLOSE RECORDS-IN, PRINT-OUT.                                  PROGRM4A
040150      STOP RUN.                                                     PROGRM4A
```

FIGURE 4.10   **PROCEDURE DIVISION of Program 4A**

```
040010  PROCEDURE DIVISION.                                               PROGRM4A
040020      OPEN INPUT RECORDS-IN, OUTPUT PRINT-OUT.                      PROGRM4A
040030      MOVE SPACES TO ADDRESS-LINE.                                  PROGRM4A
040040                                                                    PROGRM4A
040050  START-PROCESSING.                                                 PROGRM4A
040060      READ RECORDS-IN INTO ADDRESS-RECORD                           PROGRM4A
040070          AT END PERFORM WRAP-IT-UP.                                PROGRM4A
040080      MOVE NAME-RD TO NAME-LINE.                                    PROGRM4A
040090      MOVE STREET-RD TO STREET-LINE.                                PROGRM4A
040100      MOVE CITY-RD TO CITY-LINE.                                    PROGRM4A
040110      WRITE PRINT-LINE FROM ADDRESS-LINE AFTER ADVANCING 1 LINES.   PROGRM4A
040120                                                                    PROGRM4A
040060      READ RECORDS-IN INTO ADDRESS-RECORD                           PROGRM4A
040070          AT END PERFORM WRAP-IT-UP.                                PROGRM4A
040080      MOVE NAME-RD TO NAME-LINE.                                    PROGRM4A
040090      MOVE STREET-RD TO STREET-LINE.                                PROGRM4A
040100      MOVE CITY-RD TO CITY-LINE.                                    PROGRM4A
040110      WRITE PRINT-LINE FROM ADDRESS-LINE AFTER ADVANCING 1 LINES.   PROGRM4A

040130  WRAP-IT-UP.                                                       PROGRM4A
040140      CLOSE RECORDS-IN, PRINT-OUT.                                  PROGRM4A
040150      STOP RUN.                                                     PROGRM4A
```

FIGURE 4.11   **Processing Two Data Records**

Although this works for two records, the approach is a little clumsy if we want to process 10 or 100 or 1,000 records. We need some way to perform a paragraph as many times as needed. We have already seen how the **PERFORM** verb can be used to execute a paragraph of code.

PERFORM

There is another form of PERFORM which allows us to execute a paragraph repeatedly. Here is the general format:

```
PERFORM paragraph  { variable }  TIMES.
                   { integer  }
```

Examples are:

> PERFORM START-PROCESSING 10 TIMES.

or

> PERFORM START-PROCESSING K TIMES.

But K has to be declared and to have a value. **Figure 4.12** is a modification of a previous program so that it will process 10 data cards. Let us review what happens. First, we OPEN the file and MOVE spaces into the print area as before. Next, we PERFORM the START-PROCESSING paragraph 10 times. Each time the START-PROCESSING paragraph is performed, a data record is read, processed, and written. Thus, 10 data records will be processed. As soon as the PERFORM clause is done it simply moves on to the next statement, which is to CLOSE the files and STOP the run. **Figure 4.13** is a flowchart for Sample Program 4B.

```
0 10010 IDENTIFICATION DIVISION.                                               PROGRM4B
010020 PROGRAM-ID.                                                             PROGRM4B
0 10030     PROGRM4B.                                                          PROGRM4B
010040* * * * * * * * * * * * * * * * * * * * * * * * * * * * * * * * **PROGRM4B
0 10050*    SAMPLE PROGRAM THAT READS 10 DATA RECORDS.                      *PROGRM4B
0 10060* * * * * * * * * * * * * * * * * * * * * * * * * * * * * * * * **PROGRM4B
010070 AUTHOR.                                                                 PROGRM4B
0 10080     DENNIE VAN TASSEL.                                                 PROGRM4B
010090 INSTALLATION.                                                           PROGRM4B
0 10100     READY-CASH BANK.                                                   PROGRM4B
010110 DATE-WRITTEN.                                                           PROGRM4B
010120     JUNE 12, 1981.                                                      PROGRM4B
010130 DATE-COMPILED.                                                          PROGRM4B
0 10140     JULY 14, 1981.                                                     PROGRM4B
010150 SECURITY.                                                               PROGRM4B
0 10160     NONE.                                                              PROGRM4B
010170                                                                         PROGRM4B
020010 ENVIRONMENT DIVISION.                                                   PROGRM4B
020020 CONFIGURATION SECTION.                                                  PROGRM4B
0 20030 SOURCE-COMPUTER.                                                       PROGRM4B
020040     XYZ-480.                                                            PROGRM4B
020050 OBJECT-COMPUTER.                                                        PROGRM4B
020060     XYZ-480.                                                            PROGRM4B
020070 INPUT-OUTPUT SECTION.                                                   PROGRM4B
020080 FILE-CONTROL.                                                           PROGRM4B
0 20090     SELECT RECORDS-IN                                                  PROGRM4B
020100         ASSIGN TO UR-2540R-S-SYSIN.                                     PROGRM4B
020110     SELECT PRINT-OUT,                                                   PROGRM4B
020120         ASSIGN TO UR-1403-S-SYSPRINT.                                   PROGRM4B
0 20130                                                                        PROGRM4B
030010 DATA DIVISION.                                                          PROGRM4B
030020 FILE SECTION.                                                           PROGRM4B
030030 FD  RECORDS-IN                                                          PROGRM4B
030040     LABEL RECORDS ARE OMITTED.                                          PROGRM4B
030050 01  IN-RECORD                       PICTURE X(80).                       PROGRM4B
0 30060 FD  PRINT-OUT                                                          PROGRM4B
```

```
030070        LABEL RECORDS ARE OMITTED.                            PROGRM4B
030080 01   PRINT-LINE                  PICTURE X(133).             PROGRM4B
030090                                                              PROGRM4B
030100 WORKING-STORAGE SECTION.                                     PROGRM4B
030110 01   ADDRESS-RECORD.                                         PROGRM4B
030120      05   NAME-RD                PICTURE X(20).              PROGRM4B
030130      05   STREET-RD              PICTURE X(25).              PROGRM4B
030140      05   CITY-RD                PICTURE X(27).              PROGRM4B
030150      05   FILLER                 PICTURE X(08).              PROGRM4B
030160                                                              PROGRM4B
030170 01   ADDRESS-LINE.                                           PROGRM4B
030180      05   FILLER                 PICTURE X(01).              PROGRM4B
030190      05   NAME-LINE              PICTURE X(20).              PROGRM4B
030200      05   FILLER                 PICTURE X(05).              PROGRM4B
030210      05   STREET-LINE            PICTURE X(25).              PROGRM4B
030220      05   FILLER                 PICTURE X(05).              PROGRM4B
030230      05   CITY-LINE              PICTURE X(27).              PROGRM4B
030240      05   FILLER                 PICTURE X(50).              PROGRM4B
030250                                                              PROGRM4B
040010 PROCEDURE DIVISION.                                          PROGRM4B
040020      OPEN INPUT RECORDS-IN, OUTPUT PRINT-OUT.                PROGRM4B
040030      MOVE SPACES TO ADDRESS-LINE.                            PROGRM4B
040040      PERFORM START-PROCESSING 10 TIMES.                      PROGRM4B
040050                                                              PROGRM4B
040060 WRAP-IT-UP.                                                  PROGRM4B

040070      CLOSE RECORDS-IN, PRINT-OUT.                            PROGRM4B
040080      STOP RUN.                                               PROGRM4B
040090                                                              PROGRM4B
040100 START-PROCESSING.                                            PROGRM4B
040110      READ RECORDS-IN INTO ADDRESS-RECORD                     PROGRM4B
040120          AT END PERFORM WRAP-IT-UP.                          PROGRM4B
040130      MOVE NAME-RD TO NAME-LINE.                              PROGRM4B
040140      MOVE STREET-RD TO STREET-LINE.                          PROGRM4B
040150      MOVE CITY-RD TO CITY-LINE.                              PROGRM4B
040160      WRITE PRINT-LINE FROM ADDRESS-LINE AFTER ADVANCING 1 LINES.  PROGRM4B
```

FIGURE 4.12   **Sample Program 4B**

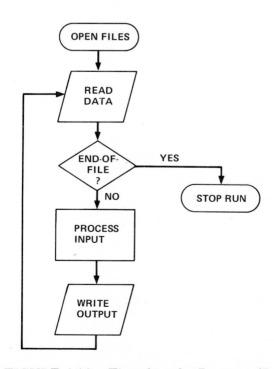

FIGURE 4.13   **Flowchart for Program 4B**

Note:

1. If the integer or variable is negative or zero when the PERFORM statement is first executed, control immediately passes to the next statement following the PERFORM.

2. Otherwise, the indicated paragraph is executed the desired number of times. **Figure 4.14** is a flowchart of the PERFORM-statement logic.

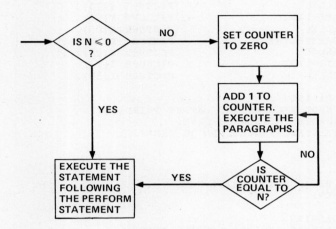

FIGURE 4.14   **Flowchart of PERFORM Statement**

****

Computer Graffiti

To err is human;
to really mess things up you need a computer.

****

DIAGNOSTICS

By now you have probably all seen some diagnostics produced by the compiler. **Diagnostics** are the messages produced when the compiler finds a syntax error in your program. A syntax error means that the compiler could not understand some part of the program. Each type of compiler uses a slightly different format for its diagnostics but they all look somewhat similar to the following:

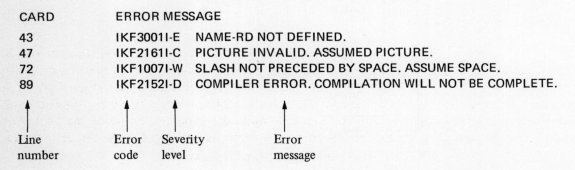

CARD	ERROR MESSAGE			
43	IKF3001I-E	NAME-RD NOT DEFINED.		
47	IKF2161I-C	PICTURE INVALID. ASSUMED PICTURE.		
72	IKF1007I-W	SLASH NOT PRECEDED BY SPACE. ASSUME SPACE.		
89	IKF2152I-D	COMPILER ERROR. COMPILATION WILL NOT BE COMPLETE.		

Line
number

Error
code

Severity
level

Error
message

The first two-column number is the line number where the error occurred in your program. When your program is listed, the COBOL compiler generates a unique line number for each line in your source program. You may have sequence-numbered your source program yourself, but the sequence numbers used for associating the error messages with a particular line in the program are the sequence numbers the compiler generated and listed.

The next seven-column code is the error code assigned to that type of error. These are listed in the back of the manufacturer's reference manual for COBOL and a little additional (although usually not much) information can be found by looking up that error code.

The one-column code, the **severity level**, indicates the severity of the diagnostic. There are usually four levels of severity code, as follows:

Code	Meaning
W	Warning
C	Conditional
E	Error
D	Disaster

A *warning diagnostic* calls attention to a potential problem. Examples are forgetting to leave space after a period, or a truncation during a MOVE operation. The compiler will still generate executable code and the program will probably be all right.

A *conditional diagnostic* is a more serious error, one which requires the compiler to make some assumption. The compiler makes a standard assumption, but often that assumption is wrong. The compiler will still generate executable code but the results will be of questionable validity. The programmer should correct the problem before compiling the program again. An example of an error of this type is an illegal PICTURE. The compiler assumes some standard PICTURE, but it will seldom be the one you want.

An *error diagnostic* indicates a serious error. This error must be corrected before executable code can be generated by the compiler. Examples of this type of error are misspelled variable names or incorrectly formed COBOL statements.

A *disaster diagnostic* is an error so bad that the compilation can't be continued. This type of error is rather rare.

In the last part of the diagnostic are the **error messages**. The error message attempts to indicate what caused the syntax error. The diagnostic messages vary in clarity and precision depending on the compiler used and the error detected. If the programmer has seen this type of error before, the error message will usually be sufficient, but if the error message is new to the programmer, it may be difficult to interpret the error message. You can learn to read error messages by purposely causing syntax errors in your source program and then examining the error message generated. Since you caused the error deliberately you will already know what the syntax error message is trying to tell you.

Hints on Correcting Syntax Errors

First, correct the errors in the order in which they occur. Syntax errors in the first three divisions will often cause several spurious errors to be generated in later lines of code. If you have many errors try to correct each one, but do not spend a lot of time on any one error. If something serious is wrong, such as an incorrect SELECT statement or misspelled variable names, many extra error messages will be generated. Correct as many errors as you can and recompile the program. Some of the syntax errors you couldn't fathom will then disappear, because they were caused by one of the errors you did correct.

The error message does not always point to the place of the error. For example, suppose we misspelled **TO** as follows:

    MOVE NAME-RD TX NAME-LINE.

then the error is in the line above. But if we misspell **NAME-RD** in **WORKING-STORAGE** as follows:

    05 NAME-ZZ   PICTURE X(20).
        .
        .
        .
        MOVE NAME-RD TO NAME-LINE.

the error message will refer to the **MOVE** statement, although the error is really in **WORKING-STORAGE**.

Notice that one syntax error can cause several error messages. In the example above, each reference to **NAME-RD** will cause a diagnostic, but there is only one error—the misspelling of **NAME-RD** in **WORKING-STORAGE**—and none of the diagnostics will point to the place where the error actually occurred.

COMMON ERRORS

1. Leaving the dash out of **DATE-WRITTEN** and **DATE-COMPILED**.
2. Using one file-name in the **SELECT** sentence and a different name in the other places where the file name must go.
3. Using a file name instead of a record name in the **WRITE** sentence.
4. Putting periods at the end of clauses in the **FD**. Remember, this is all one entry with just one period at the end, and there is no period after **FD**.

****

****

CHAPTER REVIEW

Vocabulary Review

Entry	External name	Diagnostics
Program name	Sequential file	Severity level
Source computer	Unit-record device	Error message
Object computer	Label record	

Review Questions

1. Explain:

   a) DATE-COMPILED.

   b) CONFIGURATION SECTION.

   c) INPUT-OUTPUT SECTION.

   d) File-name.

   e) DA.

   f) UT.

   g) SELECT clause.

   h) FILE SECTION.

2. *Errors.* Modify your program so that it contains the following errors; run it and see what happens:

   a) Description of input record is too long or too short.

   b) Description of output record is too long or too short.

   c) Spell the file name wrong in the SELECT clause.

   d) Omit the DATA DIVISION line.

   e) Omit the LABEL RECORDS ARE OMITTED clause.

3. Explain how the PERFORM verb works. What happens next, after the PERFORM sentence has been executed?

4. In the following code how many times is each statement executed?

```
            OPEN INPUT RECORDS-IN, OUTPUT PRINT-OUT.
            PERFORM DO-IT 8 TIMES.
        DO-IT.
            READ RECORDS-IN INTO . . .
                .
                .
                .
        WRAP-IT-UP.
            CLOSE RECORDS-IN, PRINT-OUT.
            STOP RUN.
```

5. *Errors.* Certain errors often cause the compiler to go wild. Try some of the following to see what happens:

    a) Include only the IDENTIFICATION DIVISION, omitting all the rest of the program.

    b) Misspell some of the division headings.

    c) Misspell or omit the INPUT-OUTPUT SECTION line.

    d) Put a period after FD.

    e) Misspell SELECT as SETECT in one of the SELECT clauses.

6. What is wrong with the following record description?

```
01 BOOK-RECORD.
   05 TITLE              PICTURE X(30).
   05 AUTHOR             PICTURE X(40).
   05 DATE-WRITTEN       PICTURE X(06).
   05 FILLER             PICTURE X(04).
```

Program Modifications

1. Type Sample Program 4B and run it.

2. Modify Sample Program 4B so that it prints each data record twice. Use double-spacing.

3. Modify Sample Program 4B so that it prints only the odd data records, that is, the first, third, fifth. . . . Use double-spacing.

4. Modify Sample Program 4B so that it prints only the even data-records, that is, the second, fourth, sixth. . . . Use double-spacing.

5. Make the following changes in the sample program: Change SELECT RECORDS-IN to SELECT GEORGE . . . and change SELECT PRINT-OUT to SELECT SALLY. . . . Feel free to use your own name or another name. Remember, make all the other necessary changes before you rerun the program.

6. Modify Sample Program 4B so that it prints only the last 5 of 10 records.

7. *Syntax Errors.* Modify Sample Program 4B with the goal of getting the greatest number of *different* error messages. If you get the same error message in several places it counts as only one error message. Number the different error messages. Over 25 is difficult.

8. In Sample Program 4B, what would happen if there were 15 data records and the program said to read only 10? What would happen if there were only 7 data records? Try each of these by adjusting the number of data records; then explain what happened.

9. Modify one of the exercise programs from a previous chapter so that the program processes 6 data records.

10. Modify one of the previous programs so that it will print the same data record 25 times.

Programs

1. The last time we ran our mailing labels, it was pointed out by the Ready-Cash Bank manager that the name and street fields were too short. We have now expanded our name-and-address file so that we read two input-records for each person's name and address. Here is what the input looks like:

DATA RECORD 1

Field	Columns	Format
Name	1–40	X(40)
Street	41–80	X(40)

DATA RECORD 2

Field	Columns	Format
City	1–40	X(40)

Write a report to print 2-up labels (each label twice) so that they look like this:

```
Joan Programmer      Joan Programmer
123 Main Street      123 Main Street
Watertown, SD        Watertown, SD
```

The labels should start printing in column 2 and column 52 of the output line.

2. Write a program to read the following data records for the Ready-Cash Bank:

Field	Columns	Format
I.D. number	1–5	X(05)
Last name	6–25	X(20)
First name	26–35	X(10)
Middle initial	36	X(01)
Age	37–38	X(02)
Department	39–48	X(10)
Location	49–58	X(10)

Write a program to print the information above on two lines of output, as follows:

LINE 1

Field	Print Positions
I.D. number	1-5
Last name	11-30
First name	36-45
Middle initial	50

LINE 2

Field	Print Positions
Age	7-8
Location	13-22
Department	30-39

Single-space between the two lines, but double-space between input records.

3. The input records for married housing at Intellect Haven College are as follows:

Field	Input Columns
Name	1–30
Sex	31
Age	32–33
Marriage date	34–39

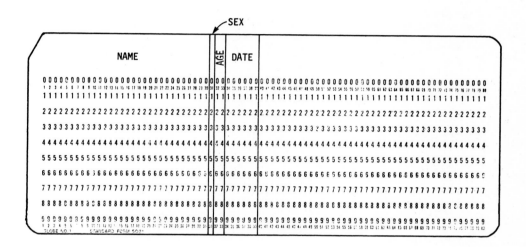

Write a program to read two data records and print the following output line:

Field	Output Columns	
Name	1–30	from 1st record
Sex	36	from 1st record
Age	42–43	from 1st record
Marriage date	49–54	from 1st record
Name	61–90	from 2nd record
Sex	96	from 2nd record
Age	102–103	from 2nd record

4. Write a program to process the following input records for Intellect Haven College:

Field	Input Columns	Output Columns
Birthdate	1–6	1–6
Student number	7–15	13–21
Student name	16–35	26–45
Major	36–45	26–35

Place the major on the second line of the output. The output should look like this:

```
071546    503990685        JOE STUDENT
                            MATHEMATICS
```

Chapter

5

```
**************************************************
            A robot took pleasure immense
            In programmings of sexual sense,
              And beholding a pail
              He thought was female,
            Cried out, "Vive la difference!"

**************************************************
```

QUALIFICATION AND HEADINGS

In all the sample programs used so far we have made sure that each data-name is unique. Sometimes it is convenient to use the same data-name in more than one place in the program: for example, you may have a STREET of sender and a STREET of receiver, and you wish to use the variable name STREET for both data-names.

We can use the same data-name in two or more places as long as the group items have different data-names. We will be using the same program used in the last chapter, but the data-names in the files will be changed so that they are identical in the input and the output files.

When we wish to specify a particular field, we must qualify it by including the group data-name. For example:

        MOVE NAME OF ADDRESS-RECORD TO . . .

or

        MOVE NAME IN ADDRESS-RECORD TO . . .

Either reserved word, OF or IN, can be used to indicate the **qualification**. The example above indicates that the NAME field from ADDRESS-RECORD is being used. As you see, a **nonunique data-name** can be made unique by qualifying it with a group data-name.

When a data-name is not unique, any reference to the data-name must always be qualified. This is a slight disadvantage, because it means names used in the PROCEDURE DIVISION are much longer. On the other hand, using the qualification with good mnemonic names aids in documentation of the program, by indicating which record the field is in.

As many levels of qualification as are needed may be used. The rule is that the data name must be uniquely specified, that is, the data name must not be pointing at two different variables. This may require several levels of qualification. Here is an example:

```
01 MASTER-FILE.
    .
    .
    .

    05 SALE-DATE.
        10    MONTHS ...
        10    DAYS    ...
        10    YEARS   ...
    05 DUE-DATE.
        10    MONTHS ...
        10    DAYS    ...
        10    YEARS   ...
        10    AMOUNT ...
01 DETAIL-FILE.
    .
    .
    .

    05 SALE-DATE.
        10    MONTHS ...
        10    DAYS    ...
        10    YEARS   ...
    05 DUE-DATE.
        10    MONTHS ...
        10    DAYS    ...
        10    YEARS   ...
        10    AMOUNT ...
```

There are four data-fields named MONTHS. To specify one of them would require two levels of qualification. The qualification MONTHS OF SALE-DATE does not provide a unique reference, because it could be in either record. Here is a correct qualification:

```
MONTHS OF SALE-DATE OF MASTER-FILE
```

The qualifier is not always the next higher group-name. In the example above, the AMOUNT field must be qualified by the record name, not by the group item DUE-DATE, because DUE-DATE is in both records: thus, you would say AMOUNT OF MASTER-FILE. There are often several ways you can qualify something correctly.

Note:

1. All references to nonunique data-names must be qualified.

2. Any reference to a data name must provide a unique reference. There may be more than one way to do this.

3. Data names may be qualified even if it is not necessary.

SAMPLE PROGRAM 5A

In Sample Program 5A (**Figure 5.1**), the input record and the output record use the same names for the fields, so qualification of names must be used in the START-PROCESSING paragraph to move the fields.

```
010010 IDENTIFICATION DIVISION.                                    PROGRM5A
010020 PROGRAM-ID.                                                 PROGRM5A
010030    PROGRM5A.                                                PROGRM5A
010040*****************************************************************PROGRM5A
010050*    SAMPLE PROGRAM USING QUALIFICATION.                      *PROGRM5A
010060*****************************************************************PROGRM5A
010070                                                             PROGRM5A
010080 ENVIRONMENT DIVISION.                                       PROGRM5A
010090 INPUT-OUTPUT SECTION.                                       PROGRM5A
010100 FILE-CONTROL.                                               PROGRM5A
010110    SELECT RECORDS-IN,                                       PROGRM5A
010120       ASSIGN TO UR-2540R-S-SYSIN.                           PROGRM5A
010130    SELECT PRINT-OUT,                                        PROGRM5A
010140       ASSIGN TO UR-1403-S-SYSPRINT.                         PROGRM5A
010150                                                             PROGRM5A
020010 DATA DIVISION.                                              PROGRM5A
020020 FILE SECTION.                                               PROGRM5A
020030 FD   RECORDS-IN                                             PROGRM5A
020040    LABEL RECORDS ARE OMITTED.                               PROGRM5A
020050 01   IN-RECORD              PICTURE X(80).                   PROGRM5A
020060 FD   PRINT-OUT                                              PROGRM5A
020070    LABEL RECORDS ARE OMITTED.                               PROGRM5A
020080 01   PRINT-LINE             PICTURE X(133).                 PROGRM5A
020090                                                             PROGRM5A
020100 WORKING-STORAGE SECTION.                                    PROGRM5A
020110 01   ADDRESS-RECORD.                                        PROGRM5A
020120    05   NAME               PICTURE X(20).                   PROGRM5A
020130    05   STREET             PICTURE X(25).                   PROGRM5A
020140    05   CITY               PICTURE X(27).                   PROGRM5A
020150    05   FILLER             PICTURE X(05).                   PROGRM5A
020160                                                             PROGRM5A
020170 01   ADDRESS-LINE.                                          PROGRM5A
020180    05   FILLER             PICTURE X(01).                   PROGRM5A
020190    05   NAME               PICTURE X(20).                   PROGRM5A
020200    05   FILLER             PICTURE X(05).                   PROGRM5A
020210    05   STREET             PICTURE X(25).                   PROGRM5A
020220    05   FILLER             PICTURE X(05).                   PROGRM5A
020230    05   CITY               PICTURE X(27).                   PROGRM5A
020240    05   FILLER             PICTURE X(50).                   PROGRM5A
020250                                                             PROGRM5A
030010 PROCEDURE DIVISION.                                         PROGRM5A
030020    OPEN INPUT RECORDS-IN, OUTPUT PRINT-OUT.                 PROGRM5A
030030    MOVE SPACES TO ADDRESS-LINE.                             PROGRM5A
030040    PERFORM START-PROCESSING 10 TIMES.                       PROGRM5A
030050                                                             PROGRM5A
030060 WRAP-IT-UP.                                                 PROGRM5A
030070    CLOSE RECORDS-IN, PRINT-OUT.                             PROGRM5A
030080    STOP RUN.                                                PROGRM5A
030090                                                             PROGRM5A
030100 START-PROCESSING.                                           PROGRM5A
030110    READ RECORDS-IN INTO ADDRESS-RECORD                      PROGRM5A
030120       AT END PERFORM WRAP-IT-UP.                            PROGRM5A
030130    MOVE NAME OF ADDRESS-RECORD TO NAME OF ADDRESS-LINE.     PROGRM5A
030140    MOVE STREET OF ADDRESS-RECORD TO STREET OF ADDRESS-LINE. PROGRM5A
030150    MOVE CITY OF ADDRESS-RECORD TO CITY OF ADDRESS-LINE.     PROGRM5A
030160    WRITE PRINT-LINE FROM ADDRESS-LINE AFTER ADVANCING 1 LINES. PROGRM5A
```

FIGURE 5.1   Sample Program 5A

MOVE CORRESPONDING

In many cases, you wish to move all or most data-fields of a record to another record. In the previous examples we had to move each field individually. Another form of the MOVE command allows you to transfer data from items of the same name simply by specifying the group items to which they belong. The group items must have unique names.

We can change the names of the ADDRESS-RECORD and ADDRESS-LINE so that the two have the same elementary names, as we did in the previous example. Then we replace the other MOVE commands with the following MOVE:

    MOVE CORRESPONDING ADDRESS-RECORD TO ADDRESS-LINE.

This statement moves each data-field which has a name common to both ADDRESS-RECORD and ADDRESS-LINE.

If an elementary item does not have a matching name, that data-field is not moved or changed. For example:

    MOVE CORRESPONDING IN-SET TO OUT-SET

with the following declaration:

```
05 IN-SET.                 05 OUT-SET.
    10    NAME    ...        10    NAME    ...
    10    STREET ...         10    AGE     ...
    10    ZIP     ...        10    STREET ...
    10    FILLER ...         10    FILLER ...
```

Since NAME and STREET are in both group-items, these fields are moved. The contents of ZIP is not moved because there is no ZIP in OUT-SET, and AGE is not changed because there is no AGE in IN-SET. Both ZIP and AGE can be used in any other way desired. By using qualifications, NAME or STREET could be used individually. The contents of a FILLER is never moved or changed.

SAMPLE PROGRAM 5B

Sample Program 5B (**Figure 5.2**) illustrates the use of MOVE CORRESPONDING. None of the old MOVE commands is needed when we use MOVE CORRESPONDING. Notice how many MOVE statements are eliminated by use of the MOVE CORRESPONDING statement.

Note:

1. When using MOVE CORRESPONDING, only items with the same name will be moved or changed. If there are sublevels, the group names must also match for the MOVE to take place.
2. Items are moved only if the data names are exactly the same and at least one of them is an elementary item.
3. FILLERs are not affected by MOVE CORRESPONDING.
4. Record names must always be unique.

```
0 10010 IDENTIFICATION DIVISION.                                    PROGRM5B
0 10020 PROGRAM-ID.                                                 PROGRM5B
0 10030    PROGRM5B.                                                PROGRM5B
0 10040******************************************************************PROGRM5B
0 10050*    SAMPLE PROGRAM USING MOVE ... CORRESPONDING.           *PROGRM5B
0 10060******************************************************************PROGRM5B
0 10070                                                             PROGRM5B
0 10080 ENVIRONMENT DIVISION.                                       PROGRM5B
0 10090 INPUT-OUTPUT SECTION.                                       PROGRM5B
0 10100 FILE-CONTROL.                                               PROGRM5B
0 10110    SELECT RECORDS-IN,                                       PROGRM5B
0 10120       ASSIGN TO UR-2540R-S-SYSIN.                           PROGRM5B
0 10130    SELECT PRINT-OUT,                                        PROGRM5B
0 10140       ASSIGN TO UR-1403-S-SYSPRINT.                         PROGRM5B
0 10150                                                             PROGRM5B
0 20010 DATA DIVISION.                                              PROGRM5B
0 20020 FILE SECTION.                                               PROGRM5B
0 20030 FD   RECORDS-IN                                             PROGRM5B
0 20040    LABEL RECORDS ARE OMITTED.                               PROGRM5B
0 20050 01   IN-RECORD                  PICTURE X(80).              PROGRM5B
0 20060 FD   PRINT-OUT                                              PROGRM5B
0 20070    LABEL RECORDS ARE OMITTED.                               PROGRM5B
0 20080 01   PRINT-LINE                 PICTURE X(133).             PROGRM5B
0 20090                                                             PROGRM5B
0 20100 WORKING-STORAGE SECTION.                                    PROGRM5B
0 20110 01   ADDRESS-RECORD.                                        PROGRM5B
0 20120    05   NAME                    PICTURE X(20).              PROGRM5B
0 20130    05   STREET                  PICTURE X(25).              PROGRM5B
0 20140    05   CITY                    PICTURE X(27).              PROGRM5B
0 20150    05   FILLER                  PICTURE X(08).              PROGRM5B
0 20160                                                             PROGRM5B
0 20170 01   ADDRESS-LINE.                                          PROGRM5B
0 20180    05   FILLER                  PICTURE X(01).              PROGRM5B
0 20190    05   NAME                    PICTURE X(20).              PROGRM5B
0 20200    05   FILLER                  PICTURE X(05).              PROGRM5B
0 20210    05   STREET                  PICTURE X(25).              PROGRM5B
0 20220    05   FILLER                  PICTURE X(05).              PROGRM5B
0 20230    05   CITY                    PICTURE X(27).              PROGRM5B
0 20240    05   FILLER                  PICTURE X(50).              PROGRM5B
0 20250                                                             PROGRM5B
0 30010 PROCEDURE DIVISION.                                         PROGRM5B
0 30020    OPEN INPUT RECORDS-IN, OUTPUT PRINT-OUT.                 PROGRM5B
0 30030    MOVE SPACES TO ADDRESS-LINE.                             PROGRM5B
0 30040    PERFORM START-PROCESSING 1000 TIMES.                     PROGRM5B
0 30050                                                             PROGRM5B
0 30060 WRAP-IT-UP.                                                 PROGRM5B
0 30070    CLOSE RECORDS-IN, PRINT-OUT.                             PROGRM5B
0 30080    STOP RUN.                                                PROGRM5B
0 30090                                                             PROGRM5B
0 30100 START-PROCESSING.                                           PROGRM5B
0 30110    READ RECORDS-IN INTO ADDRESS-RECORD                      PROGRM5B
0 30120       AT END PERFORM WRAP-IT-UP.                            PROGRM5B
0 30130    MOVE CORRESPONDING ADDRESS-RECORD TO ADDRESS-LINE.       PROGRM5B
0 30140    WRITE PRINT-LINE FROM ADDRESS-LINE AFTER ADVANCING 1 LINES. PROGRM5B
```

FIGURE 5.2   **Sample Program 5B**

****

Computer Graffiti

Never debug standing up.

****

REVIEW

1. Provide examples of when qualification is necessary and when it is not. What are the advantages and disadvantages of using qualified names?

2. When we use MOVE CORRESPONDING to move group items, which two types of items do *not* get moved in the sending group-item? Which two types of elementary items do *not* get changed in the receiving group-item?

3. Indicate which data fields will be moved or changed in the following:

        MOVE CORRESPONDING IN-RECORD TO OUT-RECORD.
        01 IN-RECORD.
            05 A   PICTURE X(04).
            05 FILLER   PICTURE X(03).
            05 B   PICTURE X(17).
            05 D   PICTURE X(05).
            05 E.
                10 X   PICTURE X(03).
                10 Y   PICTURE X(04).
        01 OUT-RECORD.
            05 A   PICTURE X(04).
            05 FILLER   PICTURE X(03).
            05 D   PICTURE X(05).
            05 C   PICTURE X(17).
            05 F.
                10 Z   PICTURE X(04).
                10 X   PICTURE X(03).

4. In the problem above how does

        MOVE CORRESPONDING IN-RECORD TO OUT-RECORD.

    differ from

        MOVE IN-RECORD TO OUT-RECORD.

    Exactly what will happen in each case?

5. If the order of the NAME and STREET fields was switched in the description of the output record in Sample Program 5B, what effect would this have on the printed output? Try it.

Program Modifications

1. Type Sample Program 5A and run it.

2. Type Sample Program 5B and run it. Then change it so that the NAME field in the ADDRESS-RECORD is called NAME-X. Change the name of the CITY field in the ADDRESS-LINE to TOWN. Then rerun the program and notice the results. Next, modify the PROCEDURE DIVISION so that the program also prints the name and city.

3. Modify one of the programs in the exercises at the end of Chapter 3 or Chapter 4 so that the input and output fields have the same data-names. Then move the fields by using qualification, and rerun the program. Next, modify the same program so that you can use MOVE CORRE-SPONDING, and rerun the program.

4. Modify Sample Program 5B so that the first six characters of the NAME field are printed but there is a blank space between each character in the name. For example, the name GARCIA would print as follows:

G A R C I A

Ignore the other fields in the record. Do not modify the data record.

5. Modify Sample Program 5B so that the first 6 characters of the NAME print vertically. For example, the name GARCIA would print as follows:

G
A
R
C
I
A

Single-space the name but double-space between names. Ignore the other fields in the record. Do not modify the data record.

PROPER TEST-DATA

You have all heard stories about computer errors. People are sent checks for $1,000,000 or bills for $0.00, or get a hundred magazines after ordering one. Many of these problems are caused by program errors, and some by data errors. Often the program has not been tested properly. Most beginning programmers (and many experienced programmers) are so relieved to get answers from the program that they do not check to see if they are getting the correct answers.

****

When a program provides output it is just providing results, not necessarily the correct results. Your job is to ensure that the program is providing the *correct* results.

****

The first thing you must ascertain is that the program is reading the correct columns in the data. Suppose you have a name field like this:

05 NAME-RD   PICTURE X(20).

If the **test data** you use is "JO LU" you have no assurance that the program is processing all 20 columns, because the following would also process the test-data correctly:

05 NAME-RD   PICTURE X(05).

One method for checking field size is to fill the data fields and see if all columns are read and processed. For the field above, test data could be 20 columns of the letter A. Then a different letter would be used for the next field to be tested. This method lets you verify easily that all columns are read and lets you see where one field stops and the next field starts. A variation of this is to run through the alphabet in each field, starting the alphabetic sequence over in each new field. Do one or the other of these when testing your program.

Another good way to assure yourself that the correct columns are read is to use some standard test-records which illustrate the columns being read. These input records are constructed as follows:

First record:
    0   columns 1–9
    1   columns 10–19
    2   columns 20–29
    3   columns 30–39
    .
    .
    .

Second record:
    1   column 1
    2   column 2
    3   column 3
    .
    .
    .
    9   column 9
    0   column 10
    1   column 11
    2   column 12
    .
    .
    .

If you have a data field in columns 18–23, when you read the previous two records your printed output should look like this:

```
112222
890123
```

Notice that when you read *down* you read the columns being read by the program, that is, the example above indicates that columns 18, 19, . . . , 23 are being read.

****

Computer Graffiti

Why do we never have time to do it right, but always have time to do it over?

****

A final useful test-record is a record with all zeros. This type of record is useful for checking out zero suppression (explained in Chapter 7). One must be careful not to use all zeros in a field that is going to be used as a divisor, however, or the program will stop executing when it attempts to divide by zero. The other types of test record may also have to have some fields changed if the program is to execute properly.

Suppose our program was to process the following:

Field	Input Columns
Location	1-7
Year	8-11
Owner	12-27

The test records could be:

```
AAAAAAABBBBCCCCCCCCCCCCCCCC
00000000011111111112222222
12345678901234567890123456 7
00000000000000000000000000
Z-24    1976DEPARTMENT Z
```

These test data would make it easy to check for proper columns being read, because the printed output would look like this:

```
AAAAAAA  BBBB  CCCCCCCCCCCCCCCC
0000000  0011  1111111122222222
1234567  8901  2345678901234567
0000000  0000  0000000000000000
Z-24     1976  DEPARTMENT Z
```

You have now seen four types of test data. Programs ought to be completely correct, if they are worth writing at all. Nearly correct programs are very dangerous, because people rely on them in making decisions. So, from now on use the standard test-records above to check your programs. (We will have more on testing in later chapters.)

```
**************************************************************
```

A Diversion: An $18,500,000 Program Error

Most computer program errors are hidden, but since this one took place on national television it became very visible. On July 27, 1962, the omission of a hyphen in a program caused the loss of the $18,500,000 Mariner I spacecraft. The spacecraft veered off course about four minutes after its launching from Cape Kennedy, Florida, and had to be destroyed in the air. I have always wondered if the programmer who left out the hyphen lost his or her job!

```
**************************************************************
```

PROBLEM DESCRIPTION

The manager of Ready-Cash Bank has requested that a heading line be printed at the top of the name-and-address report. This seems like a useful suggestion, so we will add it to our program.

HEADINGS

So far we have printed data, but have never printed any **headings** indicating what the printed data is. For the program used in this chapter it would be useful to print the following heading:

```
        NAME            ADDRESS         TOWN
   MARY STUDENT      123 MAIN ST.     ANYTOWN
        .                .              .
        .                .              .
        .                .              .
```

It is important to use headings. The people reading the reports are often not familiar with the program, and headings can help to remind the user of what each column of information represents.

Figure 5.3 is the print chart for the report and headings. It is much easier to code the heading if it is first laid out on a print-chart form. This can be done by setting up another print-line in the WORKING-STORAGE SECTION. Here is what it would look like:

```
01 HEADING-LINE.
   05 FILLER            PICTURE X(02)        VALUE SPACES.
   05 FILLER            PICTURE X(04)        VALUE 'NAME'.
   05 FILLER            PICTURE X(21)        VALUE SPACES.
   05 FILLER            PICTURE X(07)        VALUE 'ADDRESS'.
   05 FILLER            PICTURE X(24)        VALUE SPACES.
   05 FILLER            PICTURE X(04)        VALUE 'TOWN'.
   05 FILLER            PICTURE X(71)        VALUE SPACES.
```

This uses the VALUE clause. The VALUE clause can be used in the WORKING-STORAGE SECTION to initialize variables. The VALUE clause is used to **initialize** an elementary item, to set it to a specified value. Once a field is initialized it keeps that value until it is changed by a statement in the PROCEDURE DIVISION.

We have already used the reserved word SPACES. In this example the field is set to blank spaces:

```
05 FILLER   PICTURE X(21)                    VALUE SPACES.
```

This initializes a 21-column field to blank spaces. It is used to set up blank spaces between heading items. We use the reserved word FILLER for these fields because we never wish to manipulate any of the elementary fields.

Fields can also be initialized to alphanumeric values. For example:

```
05 FILLER   PICTURE X(04)                    VALUE 'NAME'.
```

This sets up a 4-column field with 'NAME' in it. Notice that 'NAME' must have single quotes, designating a character string. You must always use these quotes when initializing an alphabetic or alphanumeric field because there can be blank spaces in the character string; the quotes indicate exactly where the character string starts and stops. Headings are usually first laid out on a print chart in order to get everything properly lined up.

After the heading is coded, it must be printed. We want to print this at the beginning of the output, so we place the WRITE sentence after the OPEN file sentence. Here is the sentence which prints the heading:

```
WRITE PRINT-LINE FROM HEADING-LINE AFTER ADVANCING 1 LINES.
```

(Program 5C in **Figure 5.4** is a sample program with headings. **Figure 5.5** is some printed output for Program 5C, including a heading.)

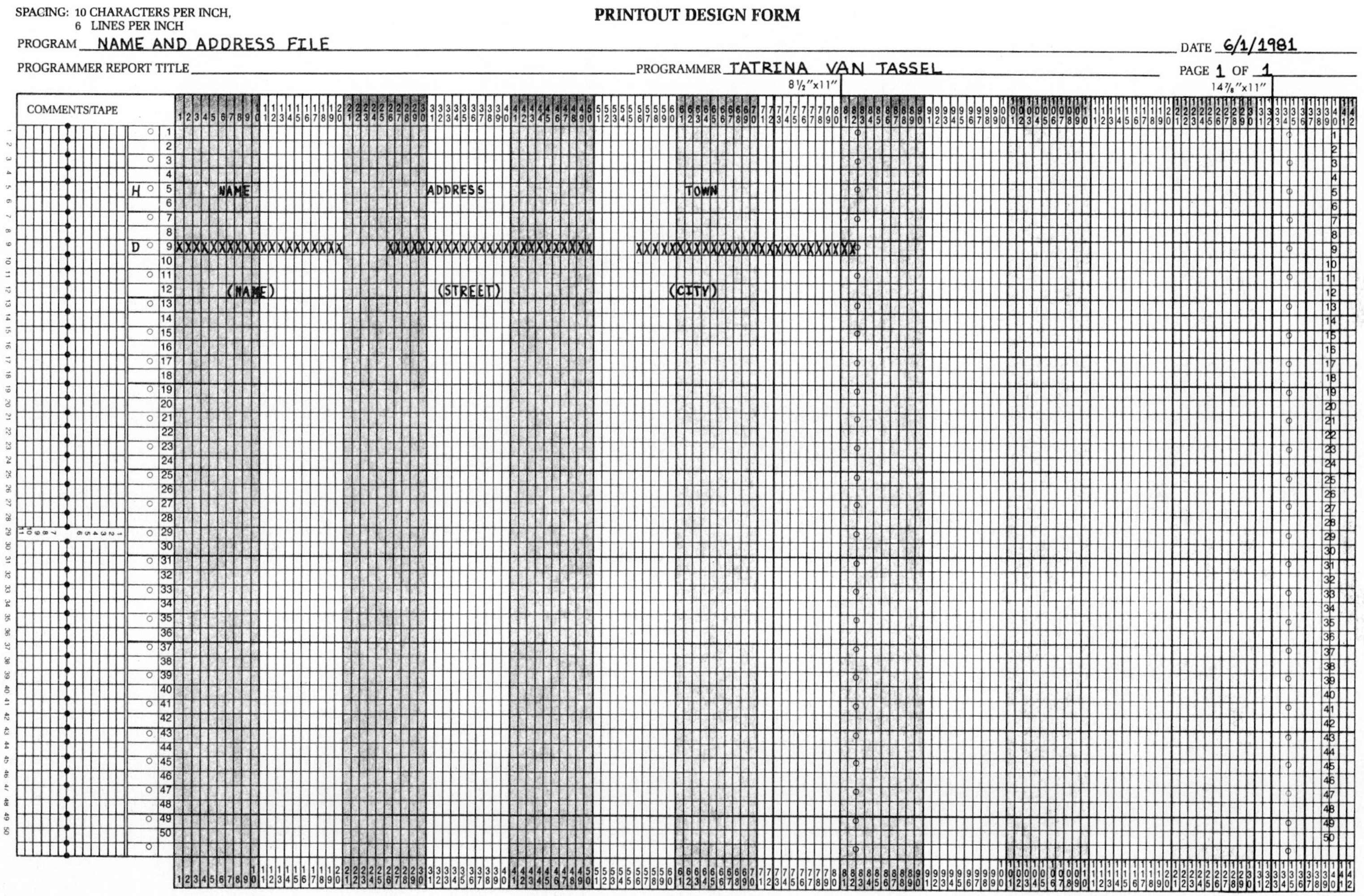
SPACING: 10 CHARACTERS PER INCH,
6 LINES PER INCH
PRINTOUT DESIGN FORM
PROGRAM NAME AND ADDRESS FILE
DATE 6/1/1981
PROGRAMMER REPORT TITLE
PROGRAMMER TATRINA VAN TASSEL
PAGE 1 OF 1
8½"x11"
14⅞"x11"
COMMENTS/TAPE
H
NAME
ADDRESS
TOWN
D
XXXXXXXXXXXXXXXXXXXX
XXXXXXXXXXXXXXXXXXXXXXXXX
XXXXXXXXXXXXXXXXXXXXXXXXXX
(NAME)
(STREET)
(CITY)

FIGURE 5.3 **Print Chart for Program 5B**

```
010010 IDENTIFICATION DIVISION.                                              PROGRM5C
010020 PROGRAM-ID.                                                           PROGRM5C
010030     PROGRM5C.                                                         PROGRM5C
010040* * * * * * * * * * * * * * * * * * * * * * * * * * * * * * * **PROGRM5C
010050*    SAMPLE PROGRAM WITH A HEADING.                                    *PROGRM5C
010060* * * * * * * * * * * * * * * * * * * * * * * * * * * * * * * **PROGRM5C
010070                                                                       PROGRM5C
010080 ENVIRONMENT DIVISION.                                                 PROGRM5C
010090 INPUT-OUTPUT SECTION.                                                 PROGRM5C
010100 FILE-CONTROL.                                                         PROGRM5C
010110     SELECT RECORDS-IN,                                                PROGRM5C
010120         ASSIGN TO UR-2540R-S-SYSIN.                                   PROGRM5C
010130     SELECT PRINT-OUT,                                                 PROGRM5C
010140         ASSIGN TO UR-1403-S-SYSPRINT.                                 PROGRM5C
020010                                                                       PROGRM5C
020020 DATA DIVISION.                                                        PROGRM5C
020030 FILE SECTION.                                                         PROGRM5C
020040 FD  RECORDS-IN                                                        PROGRM5C
020050     LABEL RECORDS ARE OMITTED.                                        PROGRM5C
020060 01  IN-RECORD                   PICTURE X(80).                        PROGRM5C
020070 FD  PRINT-OUT                                                         PROGRM5C
020080     LABEL RECORDS ARE OMITTED.                                        PROGRM5C
020090 01  PRINT-LINE                  PICTURE X(133).                       PROGRM5C
020100                                                                       PROGRM5C
020110 WORKING-STORAGE SECTION.                                              PROGRM5C
020120 01  ADDRESS-RECORD.                                                   PROGRM5C
020130     05  NAME                    PICTURE X(20).                        PROGRM5C
020140     05  STREET                  PICTURE X(25).                        PROGRM5C
020150     05  CITY                    PICTURE X(27).                        PROGRM5C
020160     05  FILLER                  PICTURE X(08).                        PROGRM5C
020170                                                                       PROGRM5C
020180 01  HEADING-LINE.                                                     PROGRM5C
020190     05  FILLER      PICTURE X(02)    VALUE SPACES.                    PROGRM5C
020200     05  FILLER      PICTURE X(04)    VALUE 'NAME'.                    PROGRM5C
020210     05  FILLER      PICTURE X(21)    VALUE SPACES.                    PROGRM5C
020220     05  FILLER      PICTURE X(07)    VALUE 'ADDRESS'.                 PROGRM5C
020230     05  FILLER      PICTURE X(24)    VALUE SPACES.                    PROGRM5C
020240     05  FILLER      PICTURE X(04)    VALUE 'TOWN'.                    PROGRM5C
020250     05  FILLER      PICTURE X(71)    VALUE SPACES.                    PROGRM5C
020260                                                                       PROGRM5C
020270 01  ADDRESS-LINE.                                                     PROGRM5C
020280     05  FILLER                  PICTURE X(01).                        PROGRM5C
020290     05  NAME                    PICTURE X(20).                        PROGRM5C
020300     05  FILLER                  PICTURE X(05).                        PROGRM5C
020310     05  STREET                  PICTURE X(25).                        PROGRM5C
020320     05  FILLER                  PICTURE X(05).                        PROGRM5C
020330     05  CITY                    PICTURE X(27).                        PROGRM5C
020340     05  FILLER                  PICTURE X(50).                        PROGRM5C
020350                                                                       PROGRM5C
030010 PROCEDURE DIVISION.                                                   PROGRM5C
030020     OPEN INPUT RECORDS-IN, OUTPUT PRINT-OUT.                          PROGRM5C
030030     MOVE SPACES TO ADDRESS-LINE.                                      PROGRM5C
030040     WRITE PRINT-LINE FROM HEADING-LINE AFTER ADVANCING 1 LINES.       PROGRM5C
030050     PERFORM START-PROCESSING 1000 TIMES.                              PROGRM5C
030060                                                                       PROGRM5C
030070 WRAP-IT-UP.                                                           PROGRM5C
030080     CLOSE RECORDS-IN, PRINT-OUT.                                      PROGRM5C
030090     STOP RUN.                                                         PROGRM5C
030100                                                                       PROGRM5C
030110 START-PROCESSING.                                                     PROGRM5C


030120     READ RECORDS-IN INTO ADDRESS-RECORD                              PROGRM5C
030130         AT END PERFORM WRAP-IT-UP.                                   PROGRM5C
030140     MOVE CORRESPONDING ADDRESS-RECORD TO ADDRESS-LINE.               PROGRM5C
030150     WRITE PRINT-LINE FROM ADDRESS-LINE AFTER ADVANCING 1 LINES.      PROGRM5C
```

FIGURE 5.4   Sample Program 5C

```
    NAME                    ADDRESS                 TOWN
    JOSE GARCIA             456 MAIN STREET         WATERTOWN, SD
    JERRY JONES             123 MISSION STREET      LOS ANGELES, CALIF.
    JOAN WOO                524 SOQUEL DRIVE        SAN JOSE, CALIF.
    MIKE MOORE              425 N. PACIFIC AVE      CASTROVILLE, CALIF.
    JOE SMITH               6542 MISSION STREET     SANTA CRUZ, CALIF
```

FIGURE 5.5   Output from Program 5C

CONTINUATION

You may remember that when we discussed coding sheets we said that column 7 was the continuation column. Sometimes you have a nonnumeric literal which is too long to fit on one line. To continue it you put a hyphen in column 7 of the **continuation line** (the second line) and continue your nonnumeric literal in field B of the continuation line. For example, if we combine the first three separate fields of the heading line it will look like this:

New way:

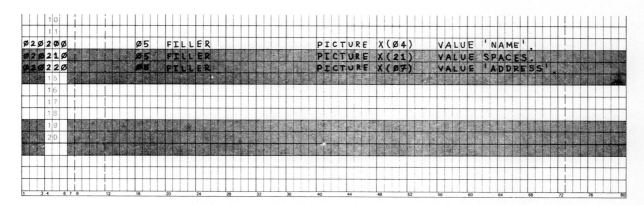

Old way:

These two statements are equivalent. Notice that all columns up to and including column 72 are part of the literal, even though there are some blank spaces. Also notice that you need a quotation mark in column 12 (or wherever the nonnumeric literal is to be started after column 12) of the continuation line. There is no quotation mark in column 72 of the first line when nonnumeric literals are continued.

COMMON ERRORS

1. Forgetting to use qualification with non-unique names.
2. Forgetting that using MOVE CORRESPONDING requires all the group names to match at all levels if the MOVE is to take place.
3. Failing to test the program completely. Testing the program is as important as writing the program.

CHAPTER REVIEW

Vocabulary Review

Qualification   Test data   Initialize
Nonunique data-name   Heading   Continuation line

Review Questions

1. Explain the uses of MOVE CORRESPONDING. What criteria must be met in using this command? When would it be useful?

2. Describe four good types of test-data records.

3. Collect some examples of program errors described in the popular media. For an interesting and humorous description of what can go wrong when a new user decides to use the computer, I suggest you read *Travels in Computerland*, by Ben R. Schneider, Jr. (Reading, Mass.: Addison-Wesley, 1974).

4. *Errors*. What do you think would happen if you made the following errors?

   a) Using a nonunique reference field.

   b) Using MOVE CORRESPONDING when there are no common names.

   c) Attempting to VALUE a field that is 4 columns long with something 6 columns long, and vice versa.

   If you are unsure of what would happen in any of these, try it in a program.

5. In Sample Program 5C, what would happen if in the initialization paragraph you added the line MOVE SPACES TO HEADING-LINE.?

Program Modifications

(From now on, all your programs should have adequate test-data.)

1. Add headings to one of the programs in the exercises at the end of Chapter 3 or Chapter 4.

2. Use two heading lines. Use Sample Heading Program 5C and print as the first heading 'COMPANY NAME AND ADDRESS FILE'. Have this heading centered on your printout. Use single-spacing for the data lines, but get two blank lines between the heading and the output data.

3. In Program 5C, what would happen if:

    a) The WRITE . . . HEADING-LINE was placed before the OPEN statement?

    b) The WRITE . . . HEADING-LINE was placed in the START PROCESSING paragraph?

    c) The WRITE . . . HEADING-LINE was placed after the CLOSE statement?

    Run the program with each of these changes.

4. Sometimes you want the same character repeated in a value clause. For example:

    ```
    05 FILLER   PICTURE X(06)        VALUE '$$$$$$'.
    ```

    There is an easier way to do this: using the figurative constant ALL. Here is an example:

    ```
    05 FILLER   PICTURE X(06)        VALUE IS ALL '$'.
    ```

    This will achieve the same result as the first example. When the figurative constant ALL is used, the literal following ALL is repeated as many times as needed. Modify Program 5C, using the ALL clause, so that a line of all dashes is printed between the heading lines and the detail lines.

5. Modify Program 5C so that instead of using several different FILLERs for the heading, there are only two FILLERs, that is, combine several of the fields into long nonnumeric literals.

6. Modify the sample name-and-address program from Chapter 4 so that it prints 2-up labels that look like this:

    ```
    JERRY JONES         JOAN SMITH
    123 MISSION STREET  567 MAIN
    ANYTOWN, CA         BIG CITY, USA
    ```

    The program should print the first record on the left and the second record on the right, and continue to alternate printing the records. Single-space within the records, but double-space between records. Do not change the input data records.

7. Modify one of the sample programs from this chapter so that it prints ALL DONE. as the last line of the output listing. This must be printed by the program, not by using input data.

Programs

1. Write a program to process the following data for the library of Intellect Haven College:

Field	Input Columns	Output Columns
Author	1–20	1–20
Title	21–40	26–45
Call number	41–52	60–71
Year	53–56	50–53

Use **MOVE CORRESPONDING**; put headings on the output report.

2. Write a program to process the following data for Intellect Haven College:

Field	Columns	Format
Student number	1–5	X(05)
Student name	11–30	X(20)
Major	31–40	X(10)

Output line:

Field	Columns
Student number	1–5
Student number	16–20
Student name	31–50
Major	61–70

The last three items in the output line should be labelled by a heading line. Use MOVE CORRESPONDING to move as much of the data as possible.

3. Intellect Haven College needs the following report for each class:

Field	Input Columns	Output Columns
Student number	1–9	1–9
Student name	10–30	15–35
Major	31–40	41–50

In addition, on each detail line, starting in column 61 print the following:

_ _ _ YES _ _ _ NO

Print headings; over this last field print the heading FULL TIME. Use MOVE CORRESPONDING for processing the data.

4.   Intellect Haven College needs the following computer printout for the students to fill out in each class:

Columns	Print
1–4	NAME
6–33	dashes
40–44	MAJOR
46–70	dashes
76–80	CLASS
82–100	dashes

There is no input. Double-space the printout; print a one-page sample.

****

****

****
A robot as glum as a mummy,
Uncommunicative as a dummy,
Got all hysterical
When the numerical
Buttons were pressed in his tummy.

****

ARITHMETIC

We have not yet done any calculations with the data processed. Obviously, if we are going to write useful business programs, we must be able to do arithmetic. There are several ways to do arithmetic in COBOL. Here is an example:

```
COMPUTE OUT-D = A + B.
```

This takes the value of A and the value of B, adds them together, and places the result in OUT-D. The values of A and B are not changed.

To perform this operation, the variable locations A and B must have values stored in them. Let us review what we have discussed so far on numerical variables. You may remember that if we want to indicate a numeric field we use 9 instead of X to indicate the field type. For example:

```
WORKING-STORAGE SECTION.
77 A PICTURE 9999    VALUE 5.
77 B PICTURE 9(04)    VALUE 2.
```

Either of the forms above can be used to indicate a numeric field 4 positions long.

LEVEL-NUMBER 77

You probably noticed that we used a new level-number. Level-number-77 items are **independent items** (not part of a record). All **level-77** items must be declared at the top of the WORKING-STORAGE SECTION, before any records are declared. Thus, the level 77s go before level numbers 01 through 49. Level 77s cannot be subdivided and are not themselves subdivisions. Thus, level-number-77 items are considered elementary items. They are commonly used to reserve space for calculations, but they can be used to store alphanumeric data. If you wish to group items together, you group them together into records.

Note:

1. Independent items are defined as level-number-77 items. They must be placed at the beginning of the WORKING-STORAGE SECTION.
2. Each level-77 item is composed of the level-number 77 (in Area A), a programmer-picked name, and a PICTURE clause.
3. A VALUE clause can be used to initialize the variable.

NUMERIC VALUE CLAUSE

As you may remember from the previous chapter, if variables need to be set to an initial value, the VALUE clause is used. In this example we are initializing numeric variables. Alphanumeric or alphabetic values are enclosed within quotes, but numeric values for numeric specifications are *not* enclosed in quotes. In the example above, the compiler places zeros on the left as needed. Thus, with a PICTURE 9999 and a VALUE 5, the number that will be stored is **0005**. For numeric specifications, only the numbers 0 through 9 can be used. A numeric field cannot be more than 18 digits. (In the next chapter we will see how to indicate sign and the placement of the decimal point.) Variables initialized with a VALUE clause keep that initial value until changed by a program statement during execution of the program.

THE COMPUTE STATEMENT

The **COMPUTE** verb is used to do arithmetic operations. Any of the normal arithmetic operations can be accomplished by using the **COMPUTE** verb. The general format is:

$$\text{COMPUTE data-name-1} = \begin{cases} \text{arithmetic expression} \\ \text{data-name-2} \\ \text{numeric literal} \end{cases}$$

The expression on the right of the replacement sign (=) must result in a numeric value. The expression on the right is calculated and the result is stored in the variable or data-name-1 on the left.

COMPUTE variable = expression.

All variables in the expression must be elementary numeric items, that is, in a COMPUTE statement you can use only level 77s or elementary items of a record. Any data-name used on the right side of the COMPUTE equation must already have a value assigned to it. Here are some examples of COMPUTE statements:

```
COMPUTE   A = 0.
COMPUTE   A = ZERO.
COMPUTE   A = B + C.
```

In all of these COMPUTE statements the value of the expression on the right is calculated and the result is stored in the variable on the left, that is, in A.

There are five arithmetic operators. They are:

**	exponentiation (raising a number to a power)
/	division
*	multiplication
−	subtraction
+	addition

Each of these operators must be preceded and followed by a blank space. The = sign also must be preceded and followed by a blank space. Can you think why this is required? What is A−B? It is a single variable "A−B". But A − B is an operation, A minus B. Thus, you must leave a blank space before and after the minus sign so that the COBOL compiler can tell that you are using a minus sign for subtraction and not simply a hyphen. Most of the symbols above probably seem appropriate to you. The symbol for multiplication is a single asterisk because it would be misleading to use a dot or an x. For exponentiation COBOL uses two asterisks. No blank spaces are permitted between the two asterisks. Here are some examples:

Addition:

```
COMPUTE A = B + C.
```

The values of B and C are added together and the result is stored in A. B and C are not changed.

Subtraction:

```
COMPUTE A = B − C.
```

The value of C is subtracted from the value of B and the result is stored in A. B and C are not changed.

Multiplication:

```
COMPUTE A = B * C.
```

The value of B is multiplied by the value of C and the result is stored in A. B and C are not changed.

Division:

```
COMPUTE A = B / C.
```

The value of C is divided into the value of B and the result is stored in A. B and C are not changed.

Exponentiation:

   A = B ** 3.

The value of **B** is taken to the exponent **3**; in other words, **B** is multiplied by itself **3** times and the result is placed in **A**. The exponent can be fractional or negative. **B** is not changed.

   It is acceptable to have the same variable on both sides of the replacement sign. The symbol = is usually called a **replacement sign** instead of an equals sign because in COBOL it really signifies replacement. For example:

   COMPUTE A = A + 1.

Obviously, the statement above is not an equality. The expression on the right is evaluated and the resulting value replaces the value in the variable on the left. Thus, 1 is added to the value of **A** and the result is stored in **A**.

Numbers

Some of the arithmetic expressions we have discussed use numbers in their calculations. Numbers can be used anywhere on the right side of the **COMPUTE** statement. Numbers in COBOL never contain commas or other special symbols. Decimal points *are* allowed with numbers. Here are some examples:

   COMPUTE TAX = PRICE * 0.06.
   COMPUTE PI = 3.1415.
   COMPUTE A = B * 4.0 + C.

Notice that when a constant is used it must never end with a decimal point—decimal points must always have a zero or other number after them, to distinguish them from periods, which must always have a space after them. The following would be incorrect:

   COMPUTE A = B * 4. + C.
                       ↗
                  incorrect

It is incorrect because **4.** indicates the end of the COBOL sentence.

Order of Evaluation

You may use as many arithmetic operators in one expression as you need. Thus, you can have an expression such as:

   COMPUTE A = B + C * D.

Notice, however, that in the expression above you get one answer if you add first, and a different answer if you multiply first. Evaluate the following expression by adding first, then by multiplying first:

   COMPUTE A = 2 + 3 * 4

As you see, there must be an **order of evaluation** for arithmetic expressions. Parentheses may be used in arithmetic expressions to specify the order in which elements are to be calculated. Expressions within parentheses are evaluated first, proceeding from the innermost pair of parentheses. COBOL requires the following spacing for parentheses: A left parenthesis must not be immediately followed by a space; a right parenthesis must not be immediately preceded by a space. For example:

```
                No spaces
                allowed.


    COMPUTE A = (B + C) * D.


                Spaces
                required.
```

Some of the newer COBOL compilers do not insist on these spacing requirements around parentheses. When parentheses are not used, the order of evaluation is:

1. − (negation)
2. **
3. * and /
4. + and −
5. Left to right.

Before we go any further you should understand the difference between negation and subtraction. For example:

Negation: − 6
Subtraction: 4 − 3

In **negation** there is no value on the left side of the − sign. In subtraction there is a value on each side of the − sign. Thus, negation is called a **unary (one) operation**, while subtraction is called a **binary (two) operation**. There is only one case in which this makes any difference; it will be explained in the last example.

Here are some examples:

COMPUTE A = B + C * D.

is the same as

COMPUTE A = B + (C * D).

because multiplication is done before addition.

COMPUTE A = B + C / D ** 2.

is the same as

COMPUTE A = B + (C / (D ** 2)).

because exponentiation is done first, then division, and finally addition. When you have operations of the same level, such as addition and subtraction, the order of evaluation is from left to right.

COMPUTE A = B + C - D.

is the same as

COMPUTE A = (B + C) - D.

and

COMPUTE A = B * C / D.

is the same as

COMPUTE A = (B * C) / D.

Now, here is a tricky one. What is the answer to the following?

COMPUTE A = - 3 ** 2.

The answer is **+9** because this is the same as

COMPUTE A = (- 3) ** 2.

Here is a case in which negation is done before exponentiation.

Using Parentheses

Parentheses are used to indicate the order of evaluation. Unnecessary parentheses are allowed, so feel free to use as many pairs as may be useful. Parentheses are cheaper than errors—many errors are caused by leaving out necessary parentheses. Say you wished to program the following:

$$Z = \frac{2X + 5}{6X + 8}$$

and you wrote it as:

COMPUTE Z = 2 * X + 5 / 6 * X + 8.

Because of the ordering rules, here is what you would actually have programmed:

$$Z = 2X + \frac{5X}{6} + 8$$

This is not even close to what you wanted. You must use two sets of parentheses to get the correct grouping. The correct code is:

COMPUTE Z = (2 * X + 5) / (6 * X + 8).

Most programmers make use of parentheses to increase readability and avoid errors. In general, the rule is: use parentheses to remove any possible doubt.

SAMPLE PROGRAM 6A

Sample Program 6A (**Figure 6.1**) does some simple arithmetic. Notice that there is no input file in this program. This is unusual; it seldom happens in the real world. This program has all the data in level-number-77 items, and the data is initialized with the **VALUE** clause.

```
010010 IDENTIFICATION DIVISION.                                         PROGRM6A
010020 PROGRAM-ID.                                                      PROGRM6A
010030    PROGRM6A.                                                     PROGRM6A
010040* * * * * * * * * * * * * * * * * * * * * * * * * * * * * **PROGRM6A
010050*    PROGRAM THAT DOES SIMPLE ARITHMETHIC.                       *PROGRM6A
010060* * * * * * * * * * * * * * * * * * * * * * * * * * * * * **PROGRM6A
010070                                                                  PROGRM6A
010080 ENVIRONMENT DIVISION.                                            PROGRM6A
010090 INPUT-OUTPUT SECTION.                                            PROGRM6A
010100 FILE-CONTROL.                                                    PROGRM6A
010110    SELECT PRINT-OUT,                                             PROGRM6A
010120       ASSIGN TO UR-1403-S-SYSPRINT.                             PROGRM6A
010130                                                                  PROGRM6A
020010 DATA DIVISION.                                                   PROGRM6A
020020 FILE SECTION.                                                    PROGRM6A
020030 FD  PRINT-OUT                                                    PROGRM6A
020040    LABEL RECORDS ARE OMITTED.                                    PROGRM6A
020050 01  PRINT-LINE              PICTURE X(133).                      PROGRM6A
020060                                                                  PROGRM6A
020070 WORKING-STORAGE SECTION.                                         PROGRM6A
020080 77  A           PICTURE 9999   VALUE 6.                          PROGRM6A
020090 77  B           PICTURE 9999   VALUE 2.                          PROGRM6A
020100 01  PRINT-ANSWER.                                                PROGRM6A
020110    05  FILLER                PICTURE X(01).                      PROGRM6A
020120    05  OUT-A                 PICTURE 9(04).                      PROGRM6A
020130    05  FILLER                PICTURE X(05).                      PROGRM6A
020140    05  OUT-B                 PICTURE 9(04).                      PROGRM6A
020150    05  FILLER                PICTURE X(06).                      PROGRM6A
020160    05  OUT-D                 PICTURE 9(06).                      PROGRM6A
020170    05  FILLER                PICTURE X(95).                      PROGRM6A
020180                                                                  PROGRM6A
030010 PROCEDURE DIVISION.                                              PROGRM6A
030020    OPEN OUTPUT PRINT-OUT.                                        PROGRM6A
030030    MOVE SPACES TO PRINT-ANSWER.                                  PROGRM6A
030040    MOVE A TO OUT-A.                                              PROGRM6A
030050    MOVE B TO OUT-B.                                              PROGRM6A
030060                                                                  PROGRM6A
030070 MAIN-PARAGRAPH.                                                  PROGRM6A
030080    COMPUTE OUT-D = A + B.                                        PROGRM6A
030090    WRITE PRINT-LINE FROM PRINT-ANSWER AFTER ADVANCING 2 LINES.   PROGRM6A
030100    COMPUTE OUT-D = A - B.                                        PROGRM6A
030110    WRITE PRINT-LINE FROM PRINT-ANSWER AFTER ADVANCING 2 LINES.   PROGRM6A
030120    COMPUTE OUT-D = A * B.                                        PROGRM6A
030130    WRITE PRINT-LINE FROM PRINT-ANSWER AFTER ADVANCING 2 LINES.   PROGRM6A
030140    COMPUTE OUT-D = A / B.                                        PROGRM6A
030150    WRITE PRINT-LINE FROM PRINT-ANSWER AFTER ADVANCING 2 LINES.   PROGRM6A
030160                                                                  PROGRM6A
030170 ALL-DONE.                                                        PROGRM6A
030180    CLOSE PRINT-OUT.                                              PROGRM6A
030190    STOP RUN.                                                     PROGRM6A
```

FIGURE 6.1   **Sample Program 6A**

UNDEFINED VARIABLES

You cannot assume that any variable has a value in it until the program places a value in the storage location reserved for that variable. Variables are not automatically initialized to zero or a blank; they are undefined until initialized by the program. Using **undefined variables** is a common source of programming errors. Here is an example:

```
77   A   PICTURE 9999   VALUE 6.
77   B   PICTURE 9999.
77   C   PICTURE 9999.
     .
     .
     .
     COMPUTE C = A + B.
```

In this code, the variable **B** has not been initialized; it is undefined. Exactly what will happen depends on what COBOL compiler you use. Some compilers will catch this error during execution and warn you. Other compilers will simply use whatever was left in those storage locations by the last program. That means that if you ran the program twice you could get two different answers, neither of which might be correct. Sometimes the data in the variable location will be so inappropriate that the program will stop executing and a system error will result. In the sample code above, the variable **C** does not have to be initialized with a **VALUE** clause because it is used on the *left* side of the replacement symbol. The result of the calculation will be stored in **C** after the statement is executed.

As you see, it is important to make sure that there are no undefined variables. While the undefined variable above is fairly obvious, they are not always this obvious. One way to avoid undefined variables is to **VALUE** as many variables as possible.

Note:

1. The variables on the right side of the replacement symbol in the **COMPUTE** statement must be elementary numeric items. These variables used in numeric calculations can be level-number-77 items or elementary items in a record.

2. All data variables used on the right side of the replacement symbol must be assigned values before they are used in a **COMPUTE** statement.

3. A data variable on the right side of the replacement symbol is not modified during execution of the **COMPUTE** statement unless the same variable is used on the left side. For example:

```
COMPUTE A = A + 1.
```

will modify **A**.

4. The receiving data-variable on the left side of the replacement symbol is used to store the result. This data-variable must be numeric or an edited numeric variable (explained in Chapter 7).

5. The size of the receiving data-variable determines the size of intermediate values; even though the final result may fit, an invalid answer may result from an intermediate calculation. See program modification 8 at the end of this chapter.

****

A Diversion: Famous Programs

These may be mythical programs, but they make good stories.

Lawrence Livermore Laboratory Program. The computer reads a one-card program, the machine computes for twenty-four hours, and prints one line.

Los Alamos Scientific Laboratory Program. The computer reads a one-card program, computes for one second, and then prints for twenty-four hours.

ZAP. In the United States there is a great network of computers called the ARPANET. This is a network of computers that can send data and programs back and forth across the United States. Thus, if you have access to the ARPANET you can send a program from the West Coast to an East Coast computer and execute the program there, and have the results sent elsewhere. Somewhere in the ARPANET sleeps a program called ZAP. At random intervals ZAP wakes up, is sent to one of the ARPANET computers. ZAP executes, takes over the computer, and prints out this message on the operator console:

        ZAP IS TAKING OVER,
        CATCH ME IF YOU CAN.

After ZAP has done its thing, it goes back to sleep somewhere else. Somewhere in ARPANET ZAP is sleeping now.

Cancer or Virus Program. This is a program that runs on a multiprogram computer, a computer which can run several programs at once. Each program requires a computer storage area for itself, in which to execute. The virus starts executing and keeps expanding and tying up all available storage as other programs release storage. Eventually the virus program has the whole computer tied up, because it controls all available storage.

A more sophisticated version of the cancer program was supposedly released through the ARPANET. This program crept through the ARPANET tying up computer after computer until it had tied up most of the computers in ARPANET.

Anonymous. The last program is unnamed and the person responsible is unnamed, for reasons that will become apparent. Supposedly this happened at Michigan, but my source was a little unreliable. A great Professor had spent most of his or her life working on a problem that required immense amounts of computer time, even on Michigan's large computer. The Professor had been cornering the machine every time there was a three-day weekend and the computer load was light. Finally, Christmas Day fell on a Thursday; so by persistence and academic political clout the Professor was able to corner the computer from Wednesday night, Christmas Eve, until Monday morning. The problem was one of those great unsolved problems that abound in mathematics, and the first person to find a solution would have his or her name in math books for the next few centuries.

The Professor started the program on Wednesday, Christmas Eve, and it ran and ran through Thursday, Friday, Saturday, and Sunday. In the early hours of Monday morning the Professor stood anxiously before the computer; it had not yet printed a solution, and defeat was near. Then, just before it was time to give up the computer to its mundane daily tasks, the computer printed "Yes, there is a solution." Elated, the Professor went home. Next day the Professor told all his or her math colleagues that there was indeed a solution. Their first question was, "What is the solution?" Alas, the Professor had forgotten to print the solution, and has never been able to get five days of computer time to do it again.

Now remember, I don't *really* think any of this is true, but it all makes a good tale.

****

REVIEW

1. When are level 77s used? Where must they be placed? Write the following level-number-77 items, using the variable name ZAP:

   a) A 60-column item initialized to blank spaces.

   b) A 60-column item initialized to 'HI FOLKS'.

   c) A 4-column numeric item.

   d) A 6-column numeric item initialized to zeros.

   e) A 3-column numeric item initialized to 4.

   f) A 3-column alphanumeric item initialized to 123.

2. If you saw VALUE '861', what would the PICTURE clause have to be? Could this field be used in a COMPUTE statement?

3. Name the six types of entries that must begin in Area A.

4. What would be the result stored in X in the following expressions?

   W = 2
   Y = 2
   Z = 4

   a) COMPUTE X = W + Y * Z.

   b) COMPUTE X = W * Y + Z.

   c) COMPUTE X = W + Z / Y.

   d) COMPUTE X = W / Y + Z.

   e) COMPUTE X = W + Z ** W.

5. If A = 4, B = 8, C = 2, what is the value of:

   a) COMPUTE X = A + B / C.

   b) COMPUTE X = B / A / C.

   c) COMPUTE X = B / A + C.

   d) COMPUTE X = -C ** 3.

   e) COMPUTE X = A + B / C ** 2.

   f) COMPUTE X = A * B / C.

6. Each of the following **COMPUTE** statements contains at least one error. List the error(s):

   a) COMPUTE A + B = C.
   b) CONPUTE C = A + B.
   c) COMPUTE – C = C.
   d) COMPUTE C = – C
   e) COMPUTE 12 = I.
   f) COMPUTE A = B = 0.
   g) COMPUTE A = B + F(D+A)).
   h) COMPUTE A = B * (1. + A) * 2.4.

7. Write the following, using the **COMPUTE** verb:

   a) $Y = \dfrac{ax + b}{c}$

   b) $Y = \dfrac{ax + b}{az + b}$

   c) $Y = \dfrac{c}{ax + b}$

8. In Sample Program 6A, why do we not have to **OPEN** an input file? What other things are not done in this program that have always been done before?

9. List the rules for order of evaluation in **COMPUTE** statements.

10. Write all the necessary COBOL statements to exchange the contents of data fields X and Y.

Program Modifications

1. Modify Sample Program 6A so that the following values are used:

   A initialized at 21
   B initialized at 7.

   Rerun the program, using this pair of values.

2. Set up a new variable Z; use Z to sequence-number the line. Print Z on the righthand side of each output line.

3. Set up a paragraph in the sample program with the following statement in it:

   COMPUTE A = A + 1.

   Initialize A to 5. Then **PERFORM** this N times, where N is a level-number-77 item set to 10. Print the answer each time.

4. Write a program which prints values of the expression:

$$3X^2 + X + 5$$

where

$$X = 0 \text{ to } 10$$

by increments of 1. Print the results for each iteration.

5. Write a program that prints out powers of 2

$$2^N$$

where

$$N = 0 \text{ to } 10$$

by increments of 1.

Print the results for each iteration.

6. Write a program that starts with X = 2, then double X (i.e., X = X + X) for fifteen iterations. Print the results for each iteration.

7. *Problems*: The following conditions will cause you problems because you do not yet know how to handle them. All of these will be discussed in the next chapter. Modify one of the programs in this chapter so that you get the following:

    a) A negative result, e.g., 4 − 6.
    b) Too large a result, e.g., 9999 * 999.
    c) A fractional result, e.g., 1/3.
    d) Division by zero.

    Try to guess what will happen before you run the program.

ALPHANUMERIC MOVES OF LITERALS

The program used in this chapter does some arithmetic operations, but the output gives no indication of what arithmetic operation was done. Since the mathematical operation changes on each line, we cannot use the VALUE clause to indicate what is being done. Instead, we can MOVE in an alphanumeric character-string each time. An example of this type of MOVE is:

    MOVE '*' TO INDICATOR.

The symbol '*' will be stored in the field INDICATOR. The quotes are used only with alphanumeric or alphabetic fields. If the sending literal is shorter than the receiving field, **padding** takes place, that is, blanks pad out the righthand side of the receiving field. (Padding may also be done with zeros.) If the receiving field is too short, the literal will be truncated on the right. Most compilers will generate a warning message if the receiving field is too short, since this is normally an error. (This type of MOVE for numeric fields will be discussed in the next chapter.)

Another example is:

MOVE 'A' TO INDICATOR.

In the statement above we are moving character string 'A'—not the value of the variable A. It is important to understand this distinction. Sample Program 6B (**Figure 6.2**) is a modification of the previous program, now indicating what is being done. **Figure 6.3** is the printed output.

```
010010 IDENTIFICATION DIVISION.                                          PROGRM6B
010020 PROGRAM-ID.                                                       PROGRM6B
010030     PROGRM6B.                                                     PROGRM6B
010040* * * * * * * * * * * * * * * * * * * * * * * * * * * **PROGRM6B
010050*   SAMPLE MOVES OF ALPHUNUMERIC STRINGS.                           *PROGRM6B
010060* * * * * * * * * * * * * * * * * * * * * * * * * * * **PROGRM6B
010070                                                                    PROGRM6B
010080 ENVIRONMENT DIVISION.                                             PROGRM6B
010090 INPUT-OUTPUT SECTION.                                             PROGRM6B
010100 FILE-CONTROL.                                                     PROGRM6B
010110     SELECT PRINT-OUT,                                             PROGRM6B
010120         ASSIGN TO UR-1403-S-SYSPRINT.                            PROGRM6B
010130                                                                    PROGRM6B
020010 DATA DIVISION.                                                    PROGRM6B
020020 FILE SECTION.                                                     PROGRM6B
020030 FD  PRINT-OUT                                                     PROGRM6B
020040     LABEL RECORDS ARE OMITTED.                                   PROGRM6B
020050 01  PRINT-LINE                      PICTURE X(133).               PROGRM6B
020060                                                                    PROGRM6B
020070 WORKING-STORAGE SECTION.                                          PROGRM6B
020080 77  A            PICTURE 9999       VALUE 6.                      PROGRM6B
020090 77  B            PICTURE 9999       VALUE 2.                      PROGRM6B
020100 01  PRINT-ANSWER.                                                 PROGRM6B
020110     05  FILLER                       PICTURE X(01).               PROGRM6B
020120     05  OUT-A                        PICTURE 9(04).               PROGRM6B
020130     05  FILLER                       PICTURE X(02).               PROGRM6B
020140     05  INDICATOR                    PICTURE X(01).               PROGRM6B
020150     05  FILLER                       PICTURE X(02).               PROGRM6B
020160     05  OUT-B                        PICTURE 9(04).               PROGRM6B
020170     05  FILLER                       PICTURE X(02).               PROGRM6B
020180     05  REPLACE                      PICTURE X(01).               PROGRM6B
020190     05  FILLER                       PICTURE X(02).               PROGRM6B
020200     05  OUT-D                        PICTURE 9(06).               PROGRM6B
020210     05  FILLER                       PICTURE X(108).              PROGRM6B
020220                                                                    PROGRM6B
030010 PROCEDURE DIVISION.                                               PROGRM6B
030020     OPEN OUTPUT PRINT-OUT.                                       PROGRM6B
030030     MOVE SPACES TO PRINT-ANSWER.                                 PROGRM6B
030040     MOVE '=' TO REPLACE.                                         PROGRM6B
030050     MOVE A TO OUT-A.                                             PROGRM6B
030060     MOVE B TO OUT-B.                                             PROGRM6B
030070                                                                    PROGRM6B
030080 MAIN-PARAGRAPH.                                                   PROGRM6B
030090     COMPUTE OUT-D = A + B.                                       PROGRM6B
030100     MOVE '+' TO INDICATOR.                                       PROGRM6B
030110     WRITE PRINT-LINE FROM PRINT-ANSWER AFTER ADVANCING 2 LINES.  PROGRM6B
030120     COMPUTE OUT-D = A - B.                                       PROGRM6B
030130     MOVE '-' TO INDICATOR.                                       PROGRM6B
030140     WRITE PRINT-LINE FROM PRINT-ANSWER AFTER ADVANCING 2 LINES.  PROGRM6B
030150     COMPUTE OUT-D = A * B.                                       PROGRM6B
030160     MOVE '*' TO INDICATOR.                                       PROGRM6B
030170     WRITE PRINT-LINE FROM PRINT-ANSWER AFTER ADVANCING 2 LINES.  PROGRM6B
030180     MOVE '/' TO INDICATOR.                                       PROGRM6B
030190     COMPUTE OUT-D = A / B.                                       PROGRM6B
030200     WRITE PRINT-LINE FROM PRINT-ANSWER AFTER ADVANCING 2 LINES.  PROGRM6B
030210                                                                    PROGRM6B
030220 ALL-DONE.                                                         PROGRM6B
030230     CLOSE PRINT-OUT.                                             PROGRM6B
030240     STOP RUN.                                                    PROGRM6B
```

FIGURE 6.2   **Sample Program 6B**

```
0006   +   0002   =   000008

0006   -   0002   =   000004

0006   *   0002   =   000012

0006   /   0002   =   000003
```

FIGURE 6.3   **Output for Program 6B**

****

Computer Graffiti

Definition of an optimist: A programmer who writes code using ink.

****

ANOTHER METHOD OF ARITHMETIC

There is another way to do arithmetic, but it can only be used when you wish to do a single arithmetic operation, and it cannot do exponentiation.

ADD

The **ADD** statement is used to accumulate values. Examples are:

    ADD 4 TO B.
    ADD A TO B.

For example:

	A	B
Before	10	5
After	10	15

The statement above adds the values of A and B, placing the result in B. The value of A is not changed. Several values can be added, and the values can be variables or numbers. For example:

    ADD A, B, 6 TO C.

This accumulates the values of A, B, 6, C and puts the result in C. The values in A and B are not changed.

ADD . . . GIVING

In the previous example the resultant field is used in the accumulation. Often you will wish to store the result in a new variable. Here is a way to do that:

ADD A, B GIVING C.

For example:

	A	B	C
Before	4	3	10
After	4	3	7

The values of A and B are added together and the result is placed in C. Neither A nor B is changed. It does not matter what was in C originally, because the old value is destroyed when the new, computed value is put in C. The initial value of C is not used in the calculation. Also, notice that the reserved word TO is not used with the GIVING clause.

SUBTRACT

The SUBTRACT verb works much like the ADD verb. Examples are:

SUBTRACT 5 FROM B.
SUBTRACT A FROM B.

	A	B
Before	3	8
After	3	5

In the statement above, the value of A is subtracted from the value of B and the result is stored in B. A is not changed. Several variables or constants can be used. For example:

SUBTRACT A, B, 6 FROM C.

A, B, and 6 are subtracted from C and the result is stored in C. A and B are not changed.

SUBTRACT . . . GIVING

In the SUBTRACT . . . GIVING statement, the resultant field is changed. Sometimes you do not wish to change the field being subtracted from; you therefore store the result in a new field. Here is an example:

SUBTRACT A, B FROM C GIVING D.

	A	B	C	D
Before	2	3	10	35
After	2	3	10	5

A and B are subtracted from C and the result is placed in D. Notice that C, A, and B are not changed. The value of D is not used in this calculation. The result is placed in D.

MULTIPLY

The MULTIPLY verb allows you to multiply one data-value by another. Examples are:

    MULTIPLY 3 BY A.
    MULTIPLY A BY B.

	A	B
Before	5	6
After	5	30

In the statement above, the value of A is multiplied by the value of B and the result is stored in B. The value of A is not changed.

MULTIPLY . . . GIVING

The GIVING option with MULTIPLY works the same as it did with previous verbs. For example:

    MULTIPLY A BY B GIVING C.

	A	B	C
Before	2	3	19
After	2	3	6

A is multiplied by B and the result is placed in C. The values of A and B are not changed. Notice that in one MULTIPLY statement only two values can be multiplied together.

DIVIDE . . . INTO

The DIVIDE verb works similarly to the MULTIPLY verb. Here are some examples:

    DIVIDE 4 INTO B.
    DIVIDE A INTO B.

	A	B
Before	3	6
After	3	2

In the statement above, the value of **A** is divided into the value of **B** and the result is stored in **B**. **A** is not changed.

DIVIDE . . . GIVING

The **GIVING** option is also available for the **DIVIDE** verb. Here is an example:

DIVIDE A INTO B GIVING C.

	A	B	C
Before	4	8	13
After	4	8	2

The remainder is occasionally needed after a division. There is a special clause available to obtain the remainder after division. Here is an example:

DIVIDE A INTO B GIVING C REMAINDER D.

	A	B	C	D
Before	3	17	29	18
After	3	17	5	2

If **3** is divided into **17**, the remainder of **2** is stored in **D**.

DIVIDE . . . BY

There is another form of the **DIVIDE** statement. Here is an example:

DIVIDE F BY E GIVING G.

	F	E	G
Before	12	4	21
After	12	4	3

Notice that E is divided into F. If we used INTO instead of BY we would have to write:

    DIVIDE E INTO F GIVING G.

The dividend and the divisor are reversed in the two versions of the DIVIDE statement.

Note:

1. In these operations, all data names and literals must be numeric, with one exception: the data variable used in the GIVING clause can be an edited numeric field (explained in Chapter 7).
2. All data variables, except the data variable used in the GIVING option, must be initialized to a numeric value.
3. Only the data variable receiving the result has its value modified by use of arithmetic statements.
4. Be careful that you never accidentally make a numeric constant the receiving variable. For example:

    ADD B TO 6.

This statement says to store the resulting value in 6. Different compilers handle this error differently. Not all compilers can catch it. Some people recommend that in order to avoid this type of error you should always use the GIVING clause.

COMPUTER ALGORITHMS

Suppose you had to exchange the values in two locations, that is, take the contents of A and store it in B and store the contents of B in A. How would you do it? Think about it for a couple of minutes and see if you can do it.

Will the following work correctly?

    MOVE A TO B.
    MOVE B TO A.

The way to check this is to hand-simulate it. We could hand-simulate the code above as follows:

Before:

        A   B
       TAP   ZIP
    MOVE A TO B.

After first MOVE:

        A   B
       TAP   TAP
    MOVE B TO A.

After second MOVE:

        A   B
       TAP   TAP

The algorithm above for exchanging values in two variables did not work: we lost the original value of B. Here is another try at the algorithm:

```
MOVE A TO TEMP.
MOVE B TO A.
MOVE TEMP TO B.
```

Hand-simulate the code above to verify that it works correctly.

This algorithm for exchanging values in two variables is quite simple and you probably won't forget it. But before you discover it, you can spend quite a bit of time trying to figure it out. Donald Knuth has collected many of the computer algorithms into a series of books called *The Art of Computer Programming* (Reading, Mass.: Addison-Wesley, 1969). These books are very mathematical, but every programmer should be familiar with them.

CHAPTER REVIEW

Vocabulary Review

Independent item	Order of evaluation	Binary operation
Level-77 item	Negation	Undefined variable
Replacement sign	Unary operation	Padding

Review Questions

1. Explain:

   a) Alphanumeric **MOVE** of literals.

   b) Exponentiation.

   c) **GIVING** clause.

2. Write **COMPUTE** statements for:

   a) Increase X by 1.

   b) Square X.

   c) Set J to zero.

   d) Decrease K by 2.

   e) Replace R by P.

   f) Divide X by 3.

   g) Raise A to the 3rd power.

   Which of the above can be done with **ADD, SUBTRACT, MULTIPLY, DIVIDE**?

3. Write COBOL sentences for the following (assume the variables are defined):

    a) Pay = hours $*$ rate.
    b) Y = A/−B.
    c) A = (X + B) (X + C)
    d) A = πr^2
    e) A = 5. $*$ P $*$ H

    Do each two ways.

4. From the following code-segment, draw a picture of the contents of the variables after the MOVE is processed:

    ```
    77 X   PICTURE XXX    VALUE 'COD'.
    77 A   PICTURE X(4).
    77 B   PICTURE XXXX  VALUE 'FISH'.
    77 C   PICTURE XX.
       MOVE X TO A, B, C.
    ```

5. What advantages, if any, does the COMPUTE verb have over the other four arithmetic verbs?

6. What is the difference between each pair of statements?

    a) ADD A, B TO C.
        ADD A, B GIVING C.
    b) MOVE SPACES TO ZZZ.
        MOVE 'SPACES' TO ZZZ.
    c) DIVIDE A INTO B GIVING C.
        DIVIDE A BY B GIVING C.

7. What is an undeclared variable? What is an undefined variable?

8. Write an equivalent COMPUTE statement for each of the following:

    a) ADD A TO B.
    b) ADD A TO B GIVING C.
    c) DIVIDE X INTO Y GIVING Z.
    d) DIVIDE N BY M GIVING P.

Program Modifications

1. Modify Sample Program 6B so that it prints headings for the variables.

2. Modify Sample Program 6A so that the complete operation is printed alongside the printed results. That is, for:

    ```
    COMPUTE OUT-D = A + B
    ```

print the character string 'A + B ='. Do this for all the arithmetic expressions in the program. Also, label each variable (e.g., 'A =') on the line on which it is printed.

3. Modify Sample Program 6B so that you do not need the MOVE '=' . . . line in the program (but the '=' must still print).

4. Do the following exponentiation:

    a) Square a number.

    b) Take the square root of 36.

    c) Try some other values for exponentiation.

5. Divide some numbers and print the remainders.

6. *Errors.* Modify one of the programs in this chapter so that the following errors occur. Then you can see how your compiler handles these errors:

    a) Use an undefined variable:

        COMPUTE C = A + B.

    where B is undefined.

    b) Try the following:

        ADD A TO 5.

    c) Use an alphanumeric variable:

        COMPUTE A = B + C.

    where A is PICTURE XXXX.

    d) In the statement in question 6c, make A numeric and B alphanumeric:

        77 B   PICTURE XXXX   VALUE '4'.

7. Modify Sample Program 6A so that it uses ADD, SUBTRACT, MULTIPLY, and DIVIDE instead of COMPUTE.

8. On some compilers, the size of the receiving field determines the maximum size of any intermediate calculations. Thus, even though the final answer would fit, high-order digits will be lost. Check this by running the following:

        77 A PICTURE 9   VALUE 8.
        77 B PICTURE 9   VALUE 5.
        77 C PICTURE 9.
           .
           .
           .
           COMPUTE C = (A * B) / 5.

    Then rerun the program using the following new declaration:

        77 C PICTURE 999.

9. The **ALL** option can also be used with a **MOVE** command. For example:

    MOVE '$$$$$' TO OUT-AREA.

    can be changed to:

    MOVE ALL '$' TO OUT-AREA.

    Modify Sample Program 5C so that a line of all dashes is printed as in modification 4 at the end of Chapter 5, but this time set up a blank heading-line in **WORKING-STORAGE**, and use **MOVE ALL** to get the dashes in the output line.

Programs

1. A gidget sells for 347. Write a COBOL program to print out a table of the prices of 1 to 25 gidgets. For example:

        01   00347
        02   00694
         .   .
         .   .
         .   .

2. Ready-Cash Bank needs a program to print a table of principal and compound interest for 10 years when $1,000 is invested at 6%. For example:

        00   1000
        01   1060
        02   1123
         .   .
         .   .
         .   .

3. Write a program to print the addition tables for two variables, A and B, where both variables range from 0 to 5. Print a self-explanatory report.

4. Write a program to print the multiplication tables for two variables, A and B, where both variables range from 0 to 5. Print a self-explanatory report.

Chapter
7

```
*****************************************************
        A privacy data lab keeps
        Unsavory secrets in heaps
           It cannot disclose,
          Suggestive of prose
    In diaries by Boswell and Pepys.

*****************************************************
```

ARITHMETIC AND OUTPUT EDITING

In the last chapter we were unable to handle **noninteger data**. Much data is noninteger—an obvious example is dollars and cents—so we need some way to process data with decimal places.

Only the numbers 0 to 9 can be used in **numeric data-fields**: no blank spaces, commas, decimal points, or alphabetic characters are allowed. Obviously, we need some way to indicate some of these characters in numeric fields. This is called **editing** the field. When we wish to print out results, we can edit-in special characters such as dollar signs, commas, and decimal points. This will be covered later when we discuss output editing. First, we will discuss input editing.

NUMERIC INPUT

As discussed above, only the numbers 0 to 9 can be used as input data for numeric fields. A blank space is considered an alphabetic character; if it is read in a numeric data-field it may cause the program to stop executing at some later point. Since a decimal point is not allowed in a field of an input record, we must indicate the *place* of the decimal point. This is done by using the letter V. For example:

> ... PICTURE 99V99.

This indicates a 4-place (*not* 5-place) numeric field with a decimal point implied between the second and third position. The V does not take up a place in the input field; it simply marks the place of the decimal point. The decimal point is never placed in the input data: thus, using the PICTURE above, the data **1234** would be read as **12.34**. Here are some examples of numbers and the values stored:

INPUT DATA

Value as Punched	PICTURE	Number Stored
1234	99V99	12ˬ34
0042	99V99	00ˬ42
00149	999V99	001ˬ49
1436	9V999	1ˬ436
125	V999	ˬ125
125	999	125ˬ

A sufficient number of zeros must be used to fill out the field in the input record completely, on both the lefthand and righthand sides. Blank spaces are not allowed for filling out unused positions of the numeric data-field. Integer numbers must be right-justified in the field.

The V is not needed when the decimal point is on the right.

> PICTURE 9999V.

is the same as

> PICTURE 9999.

Figure 7-1 is a sample input record for a payroll. Let's lay out the payroll record. The fields are in the following columns:

Name	Employee Number	Hours	Rate
1–30	31–39	40–42 (99.9)	43–46 (99.99)

```
01 PAY-RECORD.
    05 NAME      PICTURE X(30).
    05 EMP-NO    PICTURE X(09).
    05 HOURS     PICTURE 99V9.
    05 RATE      PICTURE 99V99.
    05 FILLER    PICTURE X(34).
```

Add up how many columns are specified in the payroll record. If you didn't count the **V** and if you added correctly, you should have a total of 80 columns.

EMPLOYEE NAME	EMP NO.	HOURS	RATE	

```
0 0 0 0 0 0 0 0 0 0 0 0 0 0 0 0 0 0 0 0 0 0 0 0 0 0 0 0 0 0|0 0 0 0 0 0 0 0 0|0 0 0|0 0 0 0|0 0 0 0 0 0 0 0 0 0 0 0 0 0 0 0 0 0 0 0 0 0 0 0 0 0 0 0 0 0 0 0 0 0 0 0 0 0
1 1 1 1 1 1 1 1 1 1 1 1 1 1 1 1 1 1 1 1 1 1 1 1 1 1 1 1 1 1|1 1 1 1 1 1 1 1 1|1 1 1|1 1 1|1 1 1 1 1 1 1 1 1 1 1 1 1 1 1 1 1 1 1 1 1 1 1 1 1 1 1 1 1 1 1 1 1 1 1 1 1 1
2 2 2 2 2 2 2 2 2 2 2 2 2 2 2 2 2 2 2 2 2 2 2 2 2 2 2 2 2 2|2 2 2 2 2 2 2 2 2|2 2 2|2 2 2 2|2 2 2 2 2 2 2 2 2 2 2 2 2 2 2 2 2 2 2 2 2 2 2 2 2 2 2 2 2 2 2 2 2 2 2 2 2 2
3 3 3 3 3 3 3 3 3 3 3 3 3 3 3 3 3 3 3 3 3 3 3 3 3 3 3 3 3 3|3 3 3 3 3 3 3 3 3|3 3 3|3 3 3 3|3 3 3 3 3 3 3 3 3 3 3 3 3 3 3 3 3 3 3 3 3 3 3 3 3 3 3 3 3 3 3 3 3 3 3 3 3 3
4 4 4 4 4 4 4 4 4 4 4 4 4 4 4 4 4 4 4 4 4 4 4 4 4 4 4 4 4 4|4 4 4 4 4 4 4 4 4|4 4 4|4 4 4 4|4 4 4 4 4 4 4 4 4 4 4 4 4 4 4 4 4 4 4 4 4 4 4 4 4 4 4 4 4 4 4 4 4 4 4 4 4 4
5 5 5 5 5 5 5 5 5 5 5 5 5 5 5 5 5 5 5 5 5 5 5 5 5 5 5 5 5 5|5 5 5 5 5 5 5 5 5|5 5 5|5 5 5 5|5 5 5 5 5 5 5 5 5 5 5 5 5 5 5 5 5 5 5 5 5 5 5 5 5 5 5 5 5 5 5 5 5 5 5 5 5 5
6 6 6 6 6 6 6 6 6 6 6 6 6 6 6 6 6 6 6 6 6 6 6 6 6 6 6 6 6 6|6 6 6 6 6 6 6 6 6|6 6 6|6 6 6 6|6 6 6 6 6 6 6 6 6 6 6 6 6 6 6 6 6 6 6 6 6 6 6 6 6 6 6 6 6 6 6 6 6 6 6 6 6 6
7 7 7 7 7 7 7 7 7 7 7 7 7 7 7 7 7 7 7 7 7 7 7 7 7 7 7 7 7 7|7 7 7 7 7 7 7 7 7|7 7 7|7 7 7 7|7 7 7 7 7 7 7 7 7 7 7 7 7 7 7 7 7 7 7 7 7 7 7 7 7 7 7 7 7 7 7 7 7 7 7 7 7 7
8 8 8 8 8 8 8 8 8 8 8 8 8 8 8 8 8 8 8 8 8 8 8 8 8 8 8 8 8 8|8 8 8 8 8 8 8 8 8|8 8 8|8 8 8 8|8 8 8 8 8 8 8 8 8 8 8 8 8 8 8 8 8 8 8 8 8 8 8 8 8 8 8 8 8 8 8 8 8 8 8 8 8 8
9 9 9 9 9 9 9 9 9 9 9 9 9 9 9 9 9 9 9 9 9 9 9 9 9 9 9 9 9 9|9 9 9 9 9 9 9 9 9|9 9 9|9 9 9 9|9 9 9 9 9 9 9 9 9 9 9 9 9 9 9 9 9 9 9 9 9 9 9 9 9 9 9 9 9 9 9 9 9 9 9 9 9 9
```

FIGURE 7.1   **Input Record for Program 7A**

Sign

One other symbol is commonly used in input: the **S** is used to indicate there may be a **sign**. This is required for negative numbers. An example of a field with a sign is:

PICTURE S999V99

The **S** does not count in determining the size of the elementary item, either, so this is only a 5-column field. Unless specified, COBOL assumes that all numeric fields are positive. Thus, to avoid losing the negative sign, the **S** should *always* be used with computational data. The **S** and **V** are also used in level-number 77s to indicate the sign and decimal place.

Note:

1. The complete number is punched right-justified with as many zeros on the left as are necessary to fill out the field.
2. Decimal points are not punched, but the field must be aligned according to the specified position of the decimal point.
3. For negative numbers, a minus sign is punched over the rightmost digit of the input field. Thus, given

   PICTURE S99V99.

   and the data −3.12, the data would be punched as

   031$\bar{2}$

If you are using a keypunch, you can punch the right **2** and then backspace and punch the negative character, but a − sign and a **2** is the letter **K**, so you can more easily punch **K**.

TABLE 7.1   INPUT EDITING CHARACTERS

Character	Meaning
9	Numeric data
X	Alphanumeric data
A	Alphabetic data
V	Decimal-point place indicator
S	Sign indicator

Common Errors in Input Data

1. Punching the decimal point in a numeric field. The data record *must not* have decimal points in numeric fields.
2. Leaving blank spaces in a numeric field. Numeric fields *may not* have blank spaces. Instead, the numeric fields in input records must be filled with zeros in unused columns.

ROUNDED

When two decimal numbers are multiplied together, the result has more digits to the right of the decimal point than either of the original numbers has. For example:

4.1 * 2.2 = 9.02

If too few places are declared for the resulting answer, the extra digits on the right are truncated. **Truncation** means simply dropping the extra digits without taking any account of their value. It normally occurs if, after the calculation, there are more digits after the decimal point than there is room for in the receiving data-name. For example:

```
77 PAY   PICTURE 99999V99.
   COMPUTE PAY = HOURS * RATE.
         35.70       Hours
          5.01       Rate
         ────
         3570
      1785000
      ────────
      178.8570       Pay
```

Since **PAY** has two places to the right of the decimal point, the result stored, using truncation, will be 178.85.

On some calculations it is desirable to obtain rounded results. Programmers must specify if they wish their result rounded off. To obtain rounded results we use this general format:

$$\text{COMPUTE data-name-1 [ROUNDED]} = \left\{ \begin{array}{l} \text{data-name-2} \\ \text{numeric-literal} \\ \text{arithmetic-expression} \end{array} \right\}.$$

An example of the calculation above is:

```
COMPUTE PAY ROUNDED = HOURS * RATE.
```

Now the computed results, using the figures in the previous example, will be 178.86. Here are some more examples using ROUNDED:

Computed Result	PICTURE	ROUNDED Result
123.436	999V99	123.44
123.150	999V99	123.15
12.5001	99V9	12.5
12.999	99V99	13.00

The ROUNDED option can also be used in the other forms of arithmetic operation. Here is an example of rounded addition:

```
ADD A, B TO C ROUNDED.
ADD X, Y, Z GIVING W ROUNDED.
```

Subtraction works in a similar fashion:

```
SUBTRACT A, B FROM C ROUNDED.
SUBTRACT X, Y FROM Z GIVING W ROUNDED.
```

The ROUNDED option is not much used with addition and subtraction, because we usually have the same number of places to the right of the decimal in all the participating fields; however, in division and multiplication the ROUNDED option is often needed. Here are two examples of the form for multiplication:

```
MULTIPLY A BY B ROUNDED.
MULTIPLY X BY Z GIVING W ROUNDED.
```

To get ROUNDED results in division, use the form

```
DIVIDE A INTO B ROUNDED.
```

or

```
DIVIDE X INTO Y GIVING Z ROUNDED.
```

or

```
DIVIDE Y BY X GIVING Z ROUNDED.
```

VALUE CLAUSE

The VALUE clause can be used with decimal values. Examples are:

```
77 A   PICTURE 99V99   VALUE 11.5.
77 B   PICTURE 99V99   VALUE  6.21.
```

Notice that the decimal points, typed in the data number, are used to align the value in storage. If a value is negative, the sign must be indicated in both the PICTURE clause and the VALUE clause. For example:

    77 B   PICTURE S99V9   VALUE –12.4.

The compiler will pad zeros on either the right or left side of the constants as needed, but it will not truncate constants. Most compilers will generate an error message if truncation would be necessary.

REVIEW

1. If a field is declared numeric, exactly what characters can be in the data record for that field? How is a sign indicated in the data record? In a PICTURE clause? In a VALUE clause? How is a decimal point indicated in each of the above?

2. In the following, what value will be stored by using the indicated field?

Input Data	PICTURE
012	999
012	99V9
012	999V
012	V999
012	9V9
012	S999

3. Given the number 1234 in a data record, what value would be stored if its PICTURE were:
   a) 9999
   b) 9V999
   c) V9999
   d) 999V9

4. Complete the following table:

Calculated Result	PICTURE	Value after Truncation	Value after Rounding
34.56	99V9		
34.5	99V		
34.501	99V99		
99.999	99V99		
15.500	99V9		

5. What happens if a variable is declared without the sign indicator (i.e., S) and the variable has a negative value stored in it?

Program Modifications

1. Modify Sample Program 6A so that variables A and B have the following values. Predict the results and then run the program to check your predictions.

   a) Initialize A to 7.50.

      Initialize B to 1.50.

   b) Initialize A to 7.51.

      Initialize B to 1.50.

2. Make the changes in Sample Program 6A requested in question 1, but use the ROUNDED option in the COMPUTE statements.

****

A Diversion: The Anti-Computer Movement

The anti-computer movement isn't very strong, but there are a few people pointing out that computers can't do everything. You can probably think of a few things computers can't yet do, and of a few things you wouldn't want a computer to do. Here are some of the best sources for considering computer limitations:

Computers and Common Sense: The Myth of the Thinking Machines, by Mortimer Taube (New York: Columbia University Press, 1961). This is an old book, but it still presents very concise arguments on computer limitations: mechanical language translation, learning machines, defense system uses, and a section on the fads and fallacies of science.

What Computers Can't Do: A Critique of Artificial Reason, by Hubert L. Dreyfus (New York: Harper and Row, 1972). This book examines claims of near-success in obtaining near-human artificial intelligence and shows how these projects have failed. Good food for thought.

Computer Power and Human Reason, by Joseph Weizenbaum (San Francisco: W. H. Freeman, 1976). The author argues that there are many things a computer shouldn't do even if it could (for example, being a judge in a court), because many essential aspects of human life are outside a machine's experience.

****

BASIC OUTPUT EDITING

One of COBOL's advantages is its large number of options for easy editing of printed reports. Some of the common editing symbols are the dollar sign, comma, decimal point, and debit or credit symbols. In addition, leading zeros can be replaced by blank spaces or asterisks (for checks). Well-edited and well-printed reports are very important. The ultimate user of a report is unlikely to see a listing of the program; a carefully laid-out report will indicate to the user that the programmer is a skilled craftsperson.

The editing symbol is inserted in the PICTURE clause in the desired position, but all these editing symbols can be used only in the output line. Editing is done automatically when a data field is moved to an edited field. *Once a numeric field has been edited, it can no longer be used in numeric operations.* Editing a numeric field changes it to a character string. This is obvious when you look at an edited field; for example, the edited field can have commas and dollar signs in it. Therefore, edit symbols are used only in the output print-line; once numbers are placed in these editing fields, no more arithmetic can be done on the fields.

Decimal Point

The decimal point is used when the numeric field is to be printed. It should only be used in print-lines. In fact, if you put a decimal point instead of a V in a field you are using for numeric calculations, your program will stop executing, because the decimal point is an editing character. Here are some examples of the use of the decimal point:

Stored Value	PICTURE	Printed Output
125ᴧ85	999.99	125.85
45ᴧ23	99.9	45.2

Zero Suppression

Special action must be taken if you wish **zero suppression**, that is, replacing the lefthand zeros (in the printed results) with spaces. This is usually desirable. A Z is used in a PICTURE clause to suppress left zeros. For example:

Stored Values	PICTURE	Printed Output
00946	ZZZZ9	946
12345	ZZZZ9	12345
00005	ZZZ99	05
00010	ZZZZZ	10
00000	ZZZZZ	
00000	ZZZZ9	0
000ᴧ00	ZZZ.99	.00
10000	ZZZZ9	10000

Although left zeros should usually be suppressed, notice that if you use all Z's and the result is zero, nothing will print. At least one 9 should generally be placed on the right in the edit field; two, if you are working with dollars and cents.

Commas

Commas can be inserted in the output, for example, to indicate thousands and millions. Here is a table of sample edited output:

Stored Value	PICTURE	Printed Output
123456	ZZZ,ZZ9	123,456
1467	999,999	001,467
121	999,999	000,121
1467	ZZZ,ZZ9	1,467
182ᴧ45	ZZ,ZZZ.99	182.45

Notice that when in the last example left zeros are suppressed, unneeded left commas are also suppressed.

Blanks

Blanks are occasionally desirable in printed numbers. B indicates a blank position. Here is a sample table:

Stored Value	PICTURE	Printed Output
12345	99B999	12 345
071281	99B99B99	07 12 81
503697868	999B99B9999	503 69 7868
503697868	XXXBXXBXXXX	503 69 7868

This edit symbol is one of the few which can be used with alphanumeric fields. All the rest of the edit symbols described here can be used only in numeric fields.

Signs

No sign will print unless you use a + or a − as an editing character. The sign can be printed at either side of the number. If a number has a sign it takes up a print position on the printed line. Numbers with no sign are assumed to be positive.

Negative Sign

The minus sign is used for negative values. If the value is positive, no sign prints. Here are some examples:

Stored Value	PICTURE	Printed Output
−123	−999	−123
−123	999−	123−
483	−999	483
145	999−	145
−12	−9999	−0012

****

THE PERFECT PROGRAM

NO PROGRAM'S THAT PERFECT,
THEY SAID WITH A SHRUG.
THE CLIENT IS HAPPY—
WHAT ONE LITTLE BUG.

BUT HE WAS DETERMINED
THE OTHERS WENT HOME
HE DUG OUT THE FLOW CHART
DESERTED. ALONE.

NIGHT PASSED INTO MORNING
THE ROOM WAS QUITE CLUTTERED
WITH CORE DUMPS AND PUNCH CARDS.
"I'M CLOSER." HE MUTTERED.

CHAIN SMOKING, COLD COFFEE.
LOGIC, DEDUCTION.
"I'VE GOT IT". HE CRIED. JUST
CHANGE ONE INSTRUCTION.

THEN CHANGE TWO, THEN, THREE MORE
AS YEARS FOLLOWED YEAR.
AND STRANGERS WOULD COMMENT
IS THAT GUY STILL HERE.

HE DIED AT THE CONSOLE
OF HUNGER AND THIRST
NEXT DAY HE WAS BURIED
FACE DOWN, NINE EDGE FIRST.

****

Floating Minus-Sign

The minus sign can be **floated** from the left side of the negative number so that it prints immediately next to the number. Leading zeros are suppressed at the same time. Here are some examples:

Stored Value	PICTURE	Printed Output
-0123	----9	-123
0012	----9	12
0000	----9	0
-0046	----9	-46

Notice that the sign requires a print position.

Plus Sign

Occasionally, we want the + sign to print. The positive sign can be printed on either side. When the + sign is used as an editing character, negative values receive the − sign and positive values receive the + sign. Here are some examples:

Stored Value	PICTURE	Printed Output
123	+999	+123
−123	+999	−123
123	999+	123+
−123	999+	123−
−16	+999	−016
0	+999	000

Zero is neither positive nor negative.

Floating Plus-Sign

The plus sign can also be floated from the left side of a number. When the value is negative, a − sign prints, and when the value is positive a + sign prints. Here are some examples:

Stored Value	PICTURE	Printed Output
0123	++++9	+123
0012	++++9	+12
−0123	++++9	−123
−0012	++++9	−12
0000	++++9	0

Credit and Debit Symbols

Credit and debit symbols are used in some business reports. They are placed on the righthand side of the number. When CR or DB is placed on the righthand side of the PICTURE, the CR or DB prints if the number is negative. Two blank columns are printed if the number is positive.

Stored Value	PICTURE	Printed Output
123	999CR	123
−123	999CR	123CR
123	999DB	123
−123	999DB	123DB

Fixed Dollar Sign

It is often desirable to print a **fixed dollar-sign** in a fixed column before numbers in a report. The dollar sign is placed on the left side of the PICTURE. Here are some examples:

Stored Value	PICTURE	Printed Output
1234	$ZZZZZ	$ 1234
12ᴧ34	$ZZZ.99	$ 12.34
1234ᴧ56	$Z,ZZZ.99	$1,234.56
−1234ᴧ56	$Z,ZZZ.99CR	$1,234.56CR
−1234ᴧ56	$Z,ZZZ.99−	$1,234.56−

The dollar sign requires a position in the printed output report. In the examples above, the dollar sign prints in a fixed column. In many other cases we want the dollar sign to be floated up next to the leftmost nonzero digit. If a dollar sign is on the left side of the field and a minus sign is required, the minus sign must print on the righthand side of the field.

Check Protection

When printing money amounts on checks or other documents, it is necessary to print the dollar sign directly against the amount, to prevent fraud. For example, if a check amount was printed as:

$ 1.23

anyone could take the check to a typewriter and add some numbers after the dollar sign:

$101.23

To prevent this by printing

$1.23

we use a **floating dollar-sign**, as in the following examples:

Stored Value	PICTURE	Printed Result
10ᴧ23	$$$$.99	$10.23
00ᴧ05	$$$.99	$.05
00ᴧ05	$$9.99	$0.05

The dollar sign requires a print position, so the usable field length is always one less than the total field length.

Asterisks

We may also use asterisks for check protection, by inserting them in all specified blank columns. The asterisks float up to the first nonzero digit. For example:

Computed Results	PICTURE	Printed Results
10ᴧ23	$***.99	$*10.23
00ᴧ05	$**.99	$**.05
1ᴧ41	$***.99	$**1.41
00ᴧ00	$**.99	$**.00

Notice that a single fixed dollar-sign is commonly put on the left of the PICTURE field. Both methods of check protection are commonly used; neither is considered better than the other. Which one you use is a matter of personal preference or company policy.

Space for Editing Characters

Notice that all *output* editing characters use print positions and are counted whether they are used or not. For example:

PICTURE $ZZ,ZZZ.99CR.

The output field above is twelve columns long. Input fields are counted differently: on input the V and the S do not require a position. They are simply markers or indicators. For example, in

PICTURE S9999V99.

the input field is 6 columns long. In both input and output fields, the final period does not count. Here are some more examples:

OUTPUT EDITING EXAMPLES

Stored Value	PICTURE	Printed Output
123ᴧ45	ZZZZ.99	123.45
112ᴧ45	$ZZ,ZZZ.99	$ 112.45
112ᴧ45	$$$,$$$.99	$112.45
4123ᴧ51	$ZZ,ZZZ.99	$ 4,123.51
00ᴧ00	ZZ.99	.00
1ᴧ25	$***.99	$**1.25
1ᴧ25	$$$$.99	$1.25
−127ᴧ45	$Z,ZZZ.99CR	$ 127.45CR
−127ᴧ45	$Z,ZZZ.99−	$ 127.45−
127ᴧ45	$Z,ZZZ.99CR	$ 127.45
1234ᴧ	$Z,ZZZ.99	$1,234.00

BLANK WHEN ZERO

Suppose we have the following declaration for an output line:

    05 AMOUNT   PICTURE $Z,ZZZ.99.

If AMOUNT is zero, it will be printed as follows:

    $ .00

Often we do not want anything at all to print if there is a zero value. This is achieved by using a new clause:

    05 AMOUNT   PICTURE $Z,ZZZ.99   BLANK WHEN ZERO.

Now when the AMOUNT field is zero, the output field will contain only blanks. Even the dollar sign is suppressed. The BLANK WHEN ZERO clause can be used only on numeric or numeric edited elementary items. The word WHEN may be omitted.

TABLE 7.2   OUTPUT EDITING CHARACTERS

Replacement Characters

Z	Replace leading zeros with blanks.
*	Replace leading zeros with asterisks.

Insertion Characters

B	Insert a blank space.
,	Insert a comma.
.	Insert a decimal point.
$	Insert a currency symbol.

Sign Insertion Characters

+	Plus sign.
–	Minus sign.
CR	Credit sign.
DB	Debit sign.

SAMPLE PROGRAM 7A

Figure 7.2 is the print chart for the payroll program. Notice that the necessary editing is indicated on the print chart: the hourly RATE field is shown as $ZZ.99. This indicates that a dollar sign is to precede the number, and that the left zeros are to be suppressed.

    Ready-Cash Bank needs a program to calculate gross pay for its hourly employees. Sample Program 7A **(Figure 7.3)** calculates a simple payroll. The PAY-CARD is the card we laid out earlier in the chapter. The output line PAY-LINE provides several examples of output editing. **Figure 7.4** is some sample output for this program. Notice that the decimal points are printed in the correct position in the output numbers, and that a dollar sign is printed alongside the amount.

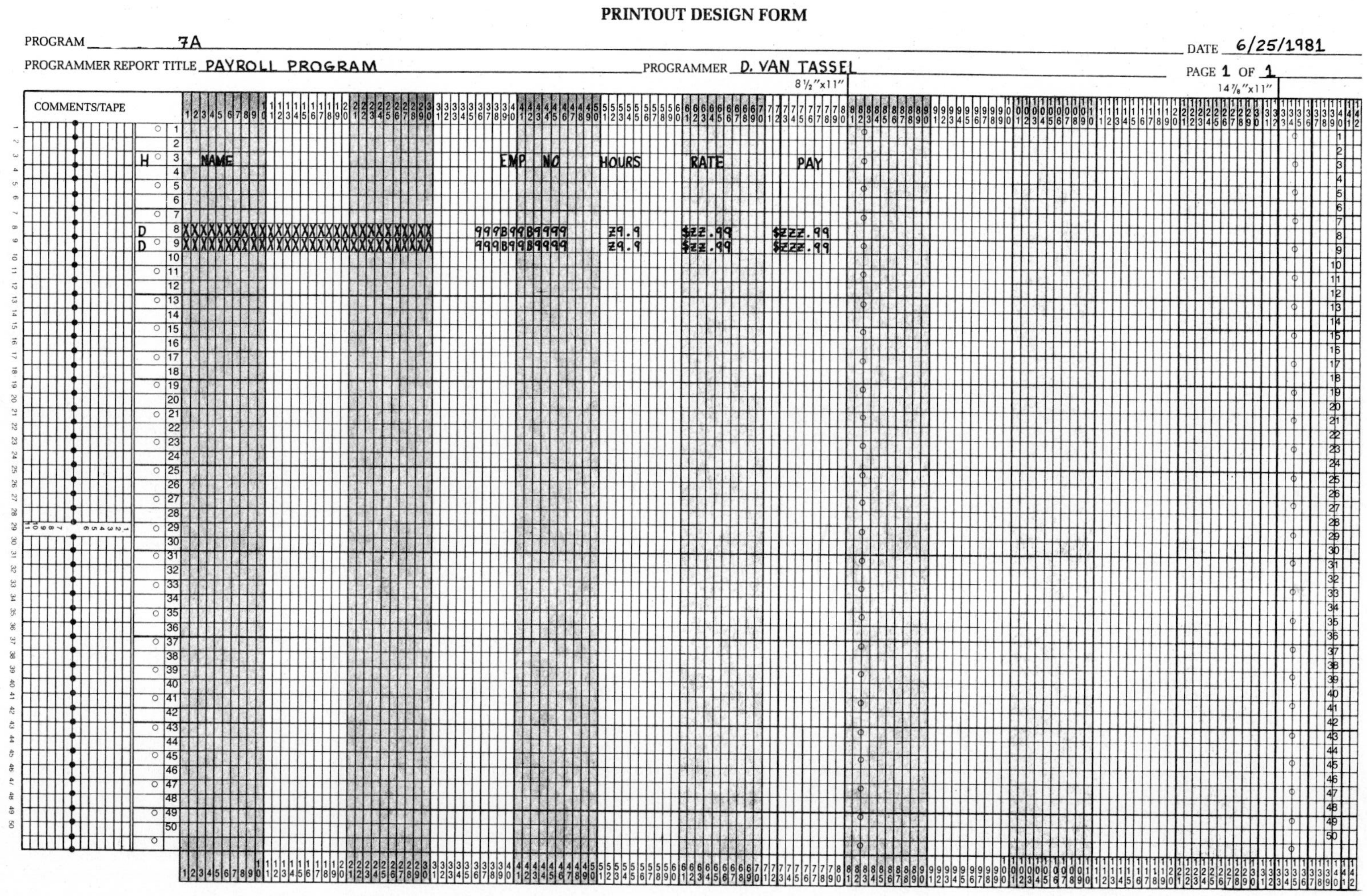

PRINTOUT DESIGN FORM

PROGRAM ____7A____

PROGRAMMER REPORT TITLE __PAYROLL PROGRAM__

PROGRAMMER __D. VAN TASSEL__

DATE __6/25/1981__

PAGE __1__ OF __1__

FIGURE 7.2 Print Chart for Program 7A

```
010010 IDENTIFICATION DIVISION.                                    PROGRM7A
010020 PROGRAM-ID.                                                 PROGRM7A
010030     PROGRM7A.                                               PROGRM7A
010040* * * * * * * * * * * * * * * * * * * * * * * * * * * **PROGRM7A
010050*    ARITHMETIC AND EDITING.                                 *PROGRM7A
010060* * * * * * * * * * * * * * * * * * * * * * * * * * * **PROGRM7A
010070                                                             PROGRM7A
010080 ENVIRONMENT DIVISION.                                       PROGRM7A
010090 INPUT-OUTPUT SECTION.                                       PROGRM7A
010100 FILE-CONTROL.                                               PROGRM7A
010110     SELECT RECORDS-IN,                                      PROGRM7A
010120         ASSIGN TO UR-2540R-S-SYSIN.                         PROGRM7A
010130     SELECT PRINT-OUT,                                       PROGRM7A
010140         ASSIGN TO UR-1403-S-SYSPRINT.                       PROGRM7A
010150                                                             PROGRM7A
020010 DATA DIVISION.                                              PROGRM7A
020020 FILE SECTION.                                               PROGRM7A
020030 FD  RECORDS-IN                                              PROGRM7A
020040     LABEL RECORDS ARE OMITTED.                              PROGRM7A
020050 01  IN-RECORD              PICTURE X(80).                   PROGRM7A
020060 FD  PRINT-OUT                                               PROGRM7A
020070     LABEL RECORDS ARE OMITTED.                              PROGRM7A
020080 01  PRINT-LINE             PICTURE X(133).                  PROGRM7A
020090                                                             PROGRM7A
020100 WORKING-STORAGE SECTION.                                    PROGRM7A
020110 01  PAY-RECORD.                                             PROGRM7A
020120     05  NAME              PICTURE X(30).                    PROGRM7A
020130     05  EMP-NO            PICTURE 9(09).                    PROGRM7A
020140     05  HOURS             PICTURE 99V9.                     PROGRM7A
020150     05  RATE              PICTURE 99V99.                    PROGRM7A
020160     05  FILLER            PICTURE X(34).                    PROGRM7A
020170                                                             PROGRM7A
020180 01  PAY-LINE.                                               PROGRM7A
020190     05  FILLER            PICTURE X(01).                    PROGRM7A
020200     05  NAME              PICTURE X(30).                    PROGRM7A
020210     05  FILLER            PICTURE X(05).                    PROGRM7A
020220     05  EMP-NO            PICTURE 999B99B9999.              PROGRM7A
020230     05  FILLER            PICTURE X(05).                    PROGRM7A
020240     05  HOURS             PICTURE Z9.9.                     PROGRM7A
020250     05  FILLER            PICTURE X(05).                    PROGRM7A
020260     05  RATE              PICTURE $ZZ.99.                   PROGRM7A
020270     05  FILLER            PICTURE X(05).                    PROGRM7A
020280     05  PAY               PICTURE $ZZZ.99.                  PROGRM7A
020290     05  FILLER            PICTURE X(54).                    PROGRM7A
020300                                                             PROGRM7A
030010 PROCEDURE DIVISION.                                         PROGRM7A
030020     OPEN INPUT RECORDS-IN, OUTPUT PRINT-OUT.                PROGRM7A
030030     MOVE SPACES TO PAY-LINE.                                PROGRM7A
030040     PERFORM CALCULATE-PAY 1000 TIMES.                       PROGRM7A
030050                                                             PROGRM7A
030060 ALL-DONE.                                                   PROGRM7A
030070     CLOSE RECORDS-IN, PRINT-OUT.                            PROGRM7A
030080     STOP RUN.                                               PROGRM7A
030090                                                             PROGRM7A
030100 CALCULATE-PAY.                                              PROGRM7A
030110     READ RECORDS-IN INTO PAY-RECORD                         PROGRM7A
030120         AT END PERFORM ALL-DONE.                            PROGRM7A
030130     MOVE CORRESPONDING PAY-RECORD TO PAY-LINE.              PROGRM7A
030140     COMPUTE PAY ROUNDED = RATE OF PAY-RECORD *              PROGRM7A
030150                             HOURS OF PAY-RECORD.            PROGRM7A
030160     WRITE PRINT-LINE FROM PAY-LINE AFTER ADVANCING 1 LINES. PROGRM7A
```

FIGURE 7.3   Sample Program 7A

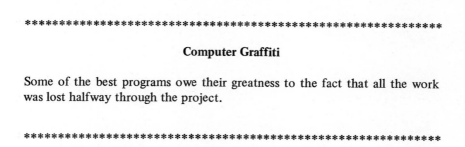

FIGURE 7.4   Output from Program 7A

****

Computer Graffiti

Some of the best programs owe their greatness to the fact that all the work
was lost halfway through the project.

****

COMMON ERRORS IN OUTPUT EDITING

1. Putting output-editing symbols in a field used for calculations. If the field is used in calculations (except as a resultant field), it can only have a V for decimal alignment and an S for sign indication.

2. Using an edited field in calculations. Once a data field has been edited, that data-item cannot be used for further calculations.

3. Attempting to use characters for editing which are not allowed. One cannot use *any* character for editing. Most of the permissible editing characters have been explained here.

REVIEW

1. Which of the following are input fields and which are output fields? What is the length of each field?

   a) 999V999

   b) S999

   c) 999.99

   d) 9999

   e) $99.99

   f) ZZZZ

   g) X(10)

   h) A(10)

   i) $99,999.99CR

   j) 9(4)V99

2. What will be printed by using the following stored values and PICTUREs?

Stored Value	PICTURE
0000	9999
0000	ZZZZ
0000	ZZZ9
00ᴧ00	ZZ99
0000	999B9
0000	ZZ.99
1234	9.999
123	$ZZZ.99
123	-999
-123	+999
-123	999
-12	-ZZZ
129ᴧ47	Z,ZZZ.99
-129ᴧ47	$Z,ZZZ.99CR

3. Given the number stored as 123ᴧ456, what would be printed if you used the following PICTUREs?

a) 9999.99
b) 999.999
c) 9999.9
d) ZZZZ.99
e) ZZZ,ZZZ.99
f) $**,***.99
g) 99.99
h) $ZZ.9999

4. What are the largest and smallest values which could print with the following edited numeric fields?

PICTURE
999
99.99
+999
++++9
-9
$$$.99
$$$.99CR
$***.99
$***.99DB

5. Given the following input value and the following PICTURE, show exactly what would have to be in the input field of the data record:

Needed Value	PICTURE
0	999
14	9999
7.3	99V99
−4.1	S99V9
15	S999V99
−15.20	S999V9

6. An edited field *can* be used as the receiving field in an arithmetic statement when the GIVING option is used or when the COMPUTE statement is used. Otherwise, all fields used in arithmetic statements must be elementary numeric fields. Why can't an edited field be used elsewhere in arithmetic statements?

Program Modifications

1. Modify Sample Program 6A so that A is initialized to −1.5. Then print A on one line, using each of the following PICTURE clauses:

   a) −999.99

   b) 999.99

   c) ZZZ.99

   d) −ZZZ.99

   e) −−−−.99

   f) .99

   Ignore the other fields in the sample program. Which PICTURE clauses print the result correctly?

2. Modify Sample Program 6A so that A is initialized to −1234.56. Then print A, using the following PICTURE clauses:

   a) $ZZ,ZZZ.99CR

   b) $ZZ,ZZZ.99

   c) $$$,$$$.99CR

   d) 99999.99CR

   e) 99B99.99

   f) 999.99

   Ignore the other fields in the sample program. Which PICTURE clauses print the result correctly?

3. Modify Sample Program 6A so that left zeros are suppressed in the output. Allow for negative values and decimal values both in calculations and in the printout. Round results when necessary. Use some different data to check the changes.

4. Modify Sample Program 6B so that several values for A and B can be read in as data. The data should be set up for both negative and positive input, with two decimal places. Make sure the output will print properly. Round results when necessary.

5.   Write a program that prints values for the expression

$$\frac{2.5x^2 + 3x + 1}{2x}$$

where X = 1 to 10 by increments of 0.5. Print the results for each iteration.

NUMERIC MOVEs

Numeric values can be moved into storage locations. For example, we can move the constant 2.5 into storage location A as follows:

        77 A   PICTURE S99V99.
           .
           .
           .
            MOVE 2.5 TO A.

Notice that the number 2.5 is *not* enclosed in quotes; if it were, it would be a character string and the A field would have to have PICTURE XXXXX. When the value is stored, the decimal point in the constant is aligned with the V in the picture, and zeros are padded on both sides. You could do the same thing with a COMPUTE statement, as follows:

        COMPUTE A = 2.5.

Which method you use is simply a matter of personal preference. Another way to initialize the variable A would be to use a VALUE clause, as follows:

        77 A PICTURE S99V99   VALUE 2.5.

When you MOVE variables instead of constants, the decimal points will be aligned and necessary zeros are padded on both sides. Thus, in this statement:

        MOVE A TO B.

A is the sending field and B is the receiving field. If the receiving field has too few places on either the righthand or the lefthand side of the decimal, the extra digits are truncated. While this does not always cause a problem on the righthand side of the decimal point, it is clearly disastrous on the lefthand side, because the high-order digits will be lost. Here are some examples of numeric MOVEs and the data that will be stored:

A *Value*	B PICTURE	B *Stored Result*
123	999	123
12	999	012
12ˬ34	99V99	12ˬ34
1ˬ23	99V99	01ˬ23
1ˬ2	99V99	01ˬ20
12ˬ345	99V99	12ˬ34
123ˬ456	99V99	23ˬ45
1234	99V99	34ˬ00

You will have less trouble if you always move fields into like fields, that is, into the same length and type of field. This is also the most efficient type of MOVE. As we saw above, you may move a short data-field to a long data-field, and vice versa, but this causes either truncation or padding.

Some MOVEs are illegal: for example, you cannot move an alphabetic field to a numeric field. The field types which have been discussed so far are:

1. Alphabetic items: PICTURE consists of A's only.
2. Alphanumeric items: PICTURE consists of X's only.
3. Numeric items: PICTURE consists of 9's, V's and S.
4. Numeric edited items: PICTURE consists of 9's, Z's, decimal points, etc.

Remember, numeric edited fields are character strings, so they are similar to alphanumeric fields. Here is a table of legal and illegal MOVEs:

PERMISSIBLE MOVEs

Sending Item	Receiving Item			
	Alphabetic	Alphanumeric	Numeric	Numeric edited
Alphabetic	OK	OK	Illegal	Illegal
Alphanumeric	OK	OK	Whole numbers only	Whole numbers only
Numeric	Illegal	Whole numbers only	OK	OK
Numeric edited	Illegal	OK	Illegal	Illegal

ON SIZE ERROR

If the number of integer places to the left of the decimal point in a field is insufficient to hold the result, a SIZE ERROR occurs. For example:

```
05 PAY          PICTURE 999.99
    COMPUTE PAY = HOURS * RATE.
        25.00   Rate
        40.0    Hours
      _____
      1000.00   Pay
```

In the example above, 1000.00 is too large to be placed in PAY. If nothing is done by the programmer, the program will fit as much as it can into the field and any high-order digits will be lost. Since this is an undesirable action, we can do the following:

```
COMPUTE PAY ROUNDED = HOURS * RATE
    ON SIZE ERROR MOVE 'ERROR ** CHECK IT' TO ERROR-MESSAGE.
```

In the example above, the variable PAY receives no value if the ON SIZE ERROR clause is executed. A SIZE ERROR will also be generated when division by zero is to take place. The general format of the COMPUTE statement with ON SIZE ERROR is:

```
COMPUTE data-name [ROUNDED]= arithmetic-expression
        [ON SIZE ERROR imperative-statement] .
```

The SIZE ERROR applies only to the results and not to intermediate values.

The ON SIZE ERROR clause can also be used with the other forms of arithmetic statement. For example:

```
MULTIPLY HOURS BY RATE GIVING PAY
    ON SIZE ERROR MOVE 'ERROR ** CHECK IT' TO ERROR-MESSAGE.
```

The ON SIZE ERROR clause can be used with any arithmetic statement.

SAMPLE PROGRAM 7B

The manager of Ready-Cash Bank said that a data-entry error in the hours field had caused an incorrect paycheck to be printed last week. Someone had typed **90.0** hours when **40.0** hours should have been typed. No weekly paycheck which is $1,000.00 or over is to be printed without the manager's approval. The payroll program is to be modified to flag any pay totals that are too large. Sample Program 7B (**Figure 7.5**) is very much like the previous sample program, but now the program checks for SIZE ERROR. If a SIZE ERROR occurs, PAY is set to zero and an error message is printed. **Figure 7.6** contains some sample output from this program.

DETERMINING THE SIZE OF THE RESULT

The ON SIZE ERROR clause is expensive both in storage space and in execution time. This is obvious when you realize that a set of extra instructions must be generated each time an arithmetic operation with the ON SIZE ERROR clause is executed. Thus, it is better to avoid using this clause except when it is really necessary. Examples of necessary use of the ON SIZE ERROR clause are:

1. When a maximum amount is to be controlled, as for payrolls.
2. When field size must be limited because of record length limitations.

It is easy to determine what the maximum size of a result field must be. If, for example, we wish to add a two-column number and a three-column number, the largest such number would be one filled with all 9s:

```
  999
+  99
-----
 1098
```

As you see, if in adding two fields the result field has one more position than the largest field, the result field will always be large enough to contain the total. (Work out the same example, but use two decimal positions in each field; devise a rule for this case.) The rules for subtraction are the same as the rules for addition, since numbers can be either positive or negative.

```
010010 IDENTIFICATION DIVISION.                                          PROGRM7B
010020 PROGRAM-ID.                                                       PROGRM7B
010030    PROGRM7B.                                                      PROGRM7B
010040* * * * * * * * * * * * * * * * * * * * * * * * * * * * **PROGRM7B
010050*    ARITHMETIC WITH ON SIZE ERROR CLAUSE.                          *PROGRM7B
010060* * * * * * * * * * * * * * * * * * * * * * * * * * * * **PROGRM7B
010070                                                                   PROGRM7B
010080 ENVIRONMENT DIVISION.                                             PROGRM7B
010090 INPUT-OUTPUT SECTION.                                             PROGRM7B
010100 FILE-CONTROL.                                                     PROGRM7B
010110    SELECT RECORDS-IN,                                             PROGRM7B
010120       ASSIGN TO UR-2540R-S-SYSIN.                                 PROGRM7B
010130    SELECT PRINT-OUT,                                              PROGRM7B
010140       ASSIGN TO UR-1403-S-SYSPRINT.                               PROGRM7B
010150                                                                   PROGRM7B
020010 DATA DIVISION.                                                    PROGRM7B
020020 FILE SECTION.                                                     PROGRM7B
020030 FD  RECORDS-IN                                                    PROGRM7B
020040    LABEL RECORDS ARE OMITTED.                                     PROGRM7B
020050 01  IN-RECORD                  PICTURE X(80).                     PROGRM7B
020060 FD  PRINT-OUT                                                     PROGRM7B
020070    LABEL RECORDS ARE OMITTED.                                     PROGRM7B
020080 01  PRINT-LINE                 PICTURE X(133).                    PROGRM7B
020090                                                                   PROGRM7B
020100 WORKING-STORAGE SECTION.                                          PROGRM7B
020110 01  PAY-RECORD.                                                   PROGRM7B
020120    05  NAME                    PICTURE X(30).                     PROGRM7B
020130    05  EMP-NO                  PICTURE 9(09).                     PROGRM7B
020140    05  HOURS                   PICTURE 99V9.                      PROGRM7B
020150    05  RATE                    PICTURE 99V99.                     PROGRM7B
020160    05  FILLER                  PICTURE X(34).                     PROGRM7B
020170                                                                   PROGRM7B
020180 01  PAY-LINE.                                                     PROGRM7B
020190    05  FILLER                  PICTURE X(01).                     PROGRM7B
020200    05  NAME                    PICTURE X(30).                     PROGRM7B
020210    05  FILLER                  PICTURE X(05).                     PROGRM7B
020220    05  EMP-NO                  PICTURE 999B99B9999.               PROGRM7B
020230    05  FILLER                  PICTURE X(05).                     PROGRM7B
020240    05  HOURS                   PICTURE Z9.9.                      PROGRM7B
020250    05  FILLER                  PICTURE X(05).                     PROGRM7B
020260    05  RATE                    PICTURE $ZZ.99.                    PROGRM7B
020270    05  FILLER                  PICTURE X(05).                     PROGRM7B
020280    05  PAY                     PICTURE $ZZZ.99.                   PROGRM7B
020290    05  FILLER                  PICTURE X(03).                     PROGRM7B
020300    05  ERROR-MESSAGE           PICTURE X(17).                     PROGRM7B
020310    05  FILLER                  PICTURE X(34).                     PROGRM7B
020320                                                                   PROGRM7B
030010 PROCEDURE DIVISION.                                               PROGRM7B
030020    OPEN INPUT RECORDS-IN, OUTPUT PRINT-OUT.                       PROGRM7B
030030    PERFORM CALCULATE-PAY 1000 TIMES.                             PROGRM7B
030040                                                                   PROGRM7B
030050 ALL-DONE.                                                         PROGRM7B
030060    CLOSE RECORDS-IN, PRINT-OUT.                                   PROGRM7B
030070    STOP RUN.                                                      PROGRM7B
030080                                                                   PROGRM7B
030090 CALCULATE-PAY.                                                    PROGRM7B
030100    MOVE SPACES TO PAY-LINE.                                       PROGRM7B
030110    READ RECORDS-IN INTO PAY-RECORD                               PROGRM7B
030120       AT END PERFORM ALL-DONE.                                    PROGRM7B
030130    MOVE CORRESPONDING PAY-RECORD TO PAY-LINE.                     PROGRM7B
030140    COMPUTE PAY ROUNDED = RATE OF PAY-RECORD *                     PROGRM7B


030150                          HOURS OF PAY-RECORD                      PROGRM7B
030160       ON SIZE ERROR MOVE ZERO TO PAY                             PROGRM7B
030170                MOVE 'ERROR ** CHECK IT' TO ERROR-MESSAGE.         PROGRM7B
030180    WRITE PRINT-LINE FROM PAY-LINE AFTER ADVANCING 1 LINES.        PROGRM7B
```

FIGURE 7.5   Sample Program 7B

```
JOAN GARCIA                                  742 53 2421      30.0    $ 9.00      $270.00
NANCY WOO                                    741 25 8963      38.0    $10.00      $380.00
BBBBBBBBBBBBBBBBBBBBBBBBBBBBBB               333 33 3333      44.4    $44.44      $  .00      ERROR ** CHECK IT
AAAAAAAAAAAAAAAAAAAAAAAAAAAAAA               123 45 6789       1.2    $34.56      $ 41.47
TERRY GONZALES                               753 65 4357      20.0    $14.50      $290.00
```

FIGURE 7.6   **Output from Program 7B**

The maximum result-field size needed with multiplication is the sum of the length of the two multiplying fields. For example:

```
     999    (3 places)
x     99    (2 places)
    ─────
    8991
  8991
  ───────
  98901     (5 places)
```

Note:

1. Division by zero always causes a **SIZE ERROR**.
2. The **SIZE ERROR** is generated by the *integer* part and not by the fractional part of the result.
3. If an **ON SIZE ERROR** clause is executed, the receiving field is not changed.
4. It is generally best to make the receiving field large enough that you don't need the **ON SIZE ERROR** clause.

SENTENCES VS. STATEMENTS

Both statements and sentences only occur in the **PROCEDURE DIVISION**; the other three divisions have entries. A COBOL **sentence** starts with a verb, is grammatically correct, and ends with a period. If all the conditions above are met except that the period is omitted, the result is a **statement**. For example:

```
MOVE A TO B.
MOVE Z TO T.
```

are two COBOL sentences. The following is one COBOL sentence:

```
MOVE A TO B
MOVE Z TO T.
```

Notice that the first line does not have a period at the end of the statement. Thus, we have two statements within one sentence. Either of these examples would provide the same results; both are grammatically correct. In this chapter and in Chapter 8 we will see several good reasons for omitting the period at the end of some statements.

Many programmers use the words *statement* and *sentence* interchangeably, but a distinction should be made.

GROUPING

We can **group** several COBOL statements together into one sentence by leaving out the period on all but the last statement. This is often desirable when you want to do several things if some condition happens. For example, suppose that we wish to calculate a value for PAY, and MOVE the error message when an ON SIZE ERROR condition happens. This may be done as follows:

```
COMPUTE PAY ROUNDED = HOURS * RATE
     ON SIZE ERROR MOVE ZERO TO PAY
              MOVE 'ERROR ** CHECK-IT' TO ERROR-MESSAGE.
```

There is only one period, at the end of the sentence. This causes two statements to be done if the ON SIZE ERROR condition happens.

Notice the importance of the periods. When a period is omitted at the end of a sentence, two sentences are treated as one and executed together. Often, a missing period does not cause an error, but occasionally it does, and this type of error can be very subtle and difficult to locate.

The example above could also be done with PERFORM, as follows:

```
COMPUTE PAY ROUNDED = HOURS * RATE
     ON SIZE ERROR PERFORM ERROR-PROCESSING.
   .
   .
   .
ERROR-PROCESSING.
   MOVE ZERO TO PAY.
   MOVE 'ERROR ** CHECK-IT' TO ERROR-MESSAGE.
```

INDENTING

Remember, indenting is used to show how a statement is related to surrounding statements. Let's go back to the example:

```
COMPUTE PAY ROUNDED = HOURS * RATE
     ON SIZE ERROR MOVE ZERO TO PAY
              MOVE 'ERROR ** CHECK-IT' TO ERROR-MESSAGE.
```

The ON SIZE ERROR clause in the example above is indented 4 columns to indicate that it is a continuation of the previous line.

Notice how the two MOVE sentences are aligned. This is done to remind us that both are to be executed if the ON SIZE ERROR happens. Indenting, in helping to make the program more readable, helps you to avoid programming errors.

CHAPTER REVIEW

Vocabulary Review

Noninteger data	Truncation	Floating dollar-sign
Numeric data-field	Zero suppression	Sentence
Editing	Floating sign	Statement
Sign	Fixed dollar-sign	Grouping

Review Questions

1. In the following, by using

    MOVE A TO B.

    what value will be stored?

A *Stored Value*	A PICTURE	B PICTURE
123∧	999	9999
123∧	999	999.99
123∧	999	99
12∧34	99V99	999.99
12∧34	99V99	9.9
AXE	XXX	XXXX
AXE	XXX	XX

2. Given the following code segments, draw a picture of the contents of the variables after the MOVE is processed (use b for blank spaces):

    ```
    77 X PICTURE 999V99     VALUE 010.01.
    77 A PICTURE 99999V99.
    77 B PICTURE ZZ,ZZZ.99.
    77 C PICTURE $ ****.99.
    77 D PICTURE 999.9.
    77 E PICTURE   9.9.
    77 F PICTURE 999.999.
        MOVE X TO A, B, C, D, E, F.
    ```

3. Given the following data description and data values, which of the following statements are allowed and which are not? (if not allowed, indicate why not):

    ```
    77 A PICTURE 99V99    VALUE 1.40.
    77 B PICTURE 99V9     VALUE 4.1.
    77 C PICTURE 99.99    VALUE 12.41.
    77 D PICTURE $ZZ.99   VALUE 11.00.
    ```

```
ADD A TO B.
ADD A B GIVING C.
ADD A B TO C.
COMPUTE C = A - B.
SUBTRACT B FROM 9.0.
COMPUTE D = A + B.
SUBTRACT A FROM D.
SUBTRACT A FROM B GIVING D.
ADD 15, A GIVING C.
ADD '40', B GIVING C.
COMPUTE C = C * D.
MOVE A + B TO C.
MOVE ZERO TO B.
MOVE ZEROS TO D.
MOVE SPACES TO B.
MOVE SPACES TO D.
```

4. In Sample Program 7B the **MOVE SPACES TO PAY-LINE** occurs inside the main processing paragraph, so it is executed each time a record is processed. Is this necessary? Why can't it be put right after the **OPEN** sentence so it is executed only once?

5. Describe what the **ROUNDED** clause does. Describe what the **ON SIZE ERROR** clause does. Should you always use either one or both of these?

6. What symbols (e.g., $, 9, V, . . .) can be used in the character string of a **PICTURE** clause for:

   a) Input field?

   b) Calculation field in **WORKING-STORAGE SECTION**?

   c) Output field?

7. If the following **VALUE** clause were used in a program, what would the **PICTURE** have to be?

   a) **VALUE 14.67.**

   b) **VALUE '14.67'.**

   c) **VALUE 'HI'.**

   d) **VALUE 16.**

8. Indicate exactly what are the contents of the receiving fields after the following **MOVE** sentences:

   a)   77 Z   PICTURE XXXX.
         .
         .
         .
         MOVE '2.5' TO Z.

   b)   77 W   PICTURE 99V99.
         .
         .
         .
         MOVE 2.5 TO W.

9. Devise a set of rules for determining the needed length of result fields for the following operations (assume all variables have two decimal places):

   a) Adding two fields.

   b) Subtraction.

   c) Multiplying two fields.

   d) Division.

10. On the following we want two decimal places in the result field. Indicate the needed field-length for the result field:

    a) 99.99 + 99.9 =

    b) 99.99 + .999 =

    c) 99.99 – .999 =

    d) 9.9 * 9.9 =

    e) 99.9 * 9.9 =

    f) 9.99 * 9.9 =

    g) 99.99 * 9.99 =

11. What is the difference between a COBOL statement and a COBOL sentence? Are they ever the same? When?

12. Given the following code:

```
COMPUTE PAY ROUNDED = HOURS * RATE
    ON SIZE ERROR MOVE ZERO TO PAY
                    MOVE ERROR TO ERR-MSG.
MOVE RATE-RD TO RATE-LINE.
```

    What would happen if the period were missing after the word ERR-MSG? What would happen if there were a period after the word PAY on the second line?

Program Modifications

1. Add headings to Sample Program 7A. Then try adding labels on the lines (that is, 'NAME='). Which method looks best?

2. Modify Sample Program 7B so that there are dashes instead of blank spaces in the printed employee-number, e.g., 503-40-0688 instead of 503 40 0688. Also, fix the dollars-and-cents output so that the dollar sign floats up to the decimal point. Use MULTIPLY instead of COMPUTE for the calculation.

3. Modify Program 7B so that there is a 6% deduction for federal tax and a standard $10.00 deduction for medical insurance. Then calculate take-home pay. Print the federal-tax rate as follows: 06%. Print all pertinent output.

4. Check to see how smart your compiler is. All of the following should cause error messages to be generated by the compiler. What is the error? What happens on your compiler?

a) 77 A PICTURE 99   VALUE 123.

b) 77 B PICTURE XX   VALUE 'JET'.

c) 77 C PICTURE 99V9 VALUE 12.34.

d) 77 D PICTURE 99.
   MOVE 123 TO D.

e) 77 E PICTURE 99V9.
   MOVE 12.34 TO E.

f) 77 F PICTURE XX.
   MOVE 'ABC' TO F.

If your compiler doesn't catch the error, print the result so that you can see what it stores.

5. Modify Sample Program 7B so that the termination paragraph is no longer necessary. (You will have to move the termination statements elsewhere in the program. Hint: Use groupings.)

Programs

1. Ready-Cash Bank sells data-processing services. Write a program to read in a data record in this format:

Salesperson no.	Name	Quota	Sales
1-5	6-30	31-36	41-46

(Both quota and sales have two decimal places.) A report is to be printed that indicates what the sales were in terms of percentage of the quota, using the following format:

Salesperson no.	Name	Quota	Sales	Percentage
1-5	10-34	41-49	51-59	61-67
		$Z,ZZZ.99	$Z,ZZZ.99	ZZZ.99 %

That is, if sales are equal to quota, then the percentage is 100.00%. If quota was $1,000 and sales were $1,200, then the percentage would be 120.00%.

2.   Write a program which processes student data-records for Intellect Haven College, as follows:

Student File		
Name	1–30	Alphanumeric
Sex	31	Alphanumeric
Age	32–33	Numeric
Test 1	34–36	Numeric
Test 2	37–39	Numeric
Test 3	40–42	Numeric
Test 4	43–45	Numeric

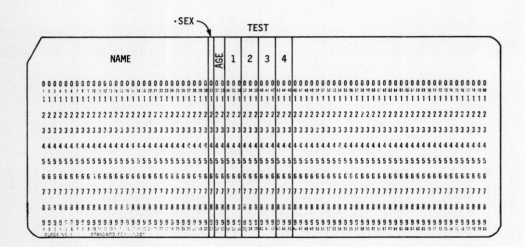

Print a report which lists all the information above, plus the average test-score. On the output line, leave 9 blank columns between the items; put a heading on the report. The average test-score should be printed as an integer value after it has been rounded. Print an asterisk next to the average score.

3.   Compound Interest. Read in the following data:

Field	Column	Format
Account number	1–5	X(05)
Principal	11–17	9(5)V99
Annual interest rate	18–20	V999
Number of years	22–23	99

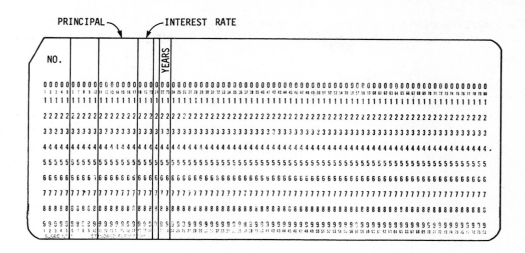

Then write a program for Ready-Cash Bank to do some or all of the following:

a) Calculate simple interest, using the formula:

$$A = P(1 + ni)$$

where P is the principal, placed at interest at a rate of i for a period of n years.

b) Calculate interest compounded annually, using the formula:

$$A = P(1 + i)^n$$

c) Calculate interest compounded q times a year, using the formula:

$$A = P(1 + i/q)^{nq}$$

Try it first for quarterly interest (that is, $q = 4$). Then try it for monthly interest (that is, $q = 12$). This program could be generalized so you could read in q as data. Label your output carefully. When you print the percentage, print the % symbol alongside the percentage (for example, 8.5%). *Warning:* Intermediate results will be truncated if the result field has only two decimal places.

4. Write a program for Ready-Cash Bank to compute the monthly payment necessary to pay off a house loan. Here is the formula:

$$P = \frac{I * A(1 + I)^M}{(1 + I)^{M-1}}$$

where

P = the payment
I = the monthly interest rate
A = the loan amount
M = the number of months

Read in the following data:

Field	Columns	Format
Amount	1-6	9(06)
Yearly interest	10-13	99V99
Number of months	14-16	999

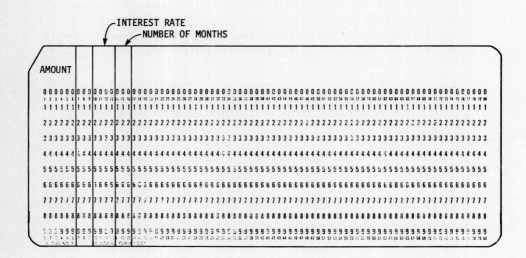

Warning: Intermediate results will be truncated if the result field has only two decimal places.

Chapter

8

```
**************************************************
```
A Soviet robot confessed
His treatment was not of the best,
    So he willfully broke,
    And the Communists spoke
Of him as "a defect to the West."
```
**************************************************
```

CONDITIONAL STATEMENTS

Often in programming, a statement should be executed only if some condition is true. There are two types of COBOL statement, imperative and conditional. An **imperative statement** specifies that an unconditional action is to be taken by the program. For example:

    MOVE A TO B.

always causes the data value of A to be moved to B. Other imperative verbs are:

    ADD
    MULTIPLY
    SUBTRACT
    DIVIDE
    COMPUTE
    PERFORM
    STOP
    OPEN
    CLOSE
    WRITE
    MOVE

A conditional statement contains a condition that is tested to determine which of the alternate paths of the program flow is to be taken. You have already seen two conditional statements:

```
READ ... AT END....
COMPUTE ... ON SIZE ERROR ....
```

In both of the above, the last part of the statement is done only if a certain condition occurs. In the READ statement we execute the AT END clause when an attempt has been made to read an input record and no data records are left. In the COMPUTE statement, the ON SIZE ERROR clause is executed whenever there is an arithmetic overflow. Both statements are dependent for their execution on some condition being met.

We often wish to execute statements of a program if some condition is present in the data. For example, employees who work over 40 hours in a week may be entitled to overtime pay; or, we may wish to send reminders to people who have not paid their bills. We do not wish to send the reminders to everyone, only to the people who have not paid. In both these situations we need some way to do something conditionally. No meaningful program can be written in COBOL without the conditional statement. After you complete this chapter, your programs will become much more interesting and closer to real-life programs.

Here is another conditional statement:

```
IF (PAST-DUE = 'D') PERFORM PROCESSING.
MOVE C TO E.
```

In the example above, only if the PAST-DUE is 'D' will the paragraph PROCESSING be executed. In either case the next sentence (i.e., MOVE) is executed afterward. **Figure 8.1** is a flowchart of this logic.

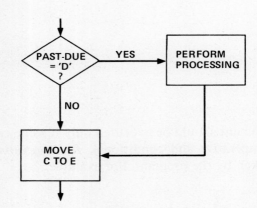

FIGURE 8.1   **Flowchart of a Conditional Statement**

Here is another example:

```
IF (AGE < 21) PERFORM UNDER-AGE-ROUTINE.
      |                        |
   condition        statement to be executed
                      if condition is true.
```

Conditional verbs are:

IF ...

ADD ...
SUBTRACT ...
MULTIPLY ... } (ON SIZE ERROR)
DIVIDE ...
COMPUTE ...

PERFORM ... UNTIL
READ ... AT END

ADD without the ON SIZE ERROR clause is an imperative statement; when the clause is included, ADD is a conditional statement. The general format of the IF statement is:

IF (condition) statement-1

The parentheses are not required around the condition, but they improve the readability of the program. The condition must result in a *true* or *false* evaluation. If the condition is true, statement-1 is executed. If the condition is false, statement-1 is not executed. Three types of test or condition that can be checked for with an IF statement are relation, sign, and class. (The class test will be discussed in Chapter 10.)

RELATION TEST

The most common condition is a **relation condition**. A relation condition is used to compare two quantities, which can be identifiers, literals, or arithmetic expressions. The general format of the relation expression is:

identifier-1		identifier-1
literal-1	relational-operator	literal-1
arithmetic expression-1		arithmetic expression-1

Examples are:

IF (HOURS < 40) ...
IF (CODE = 'B') ...
IF (PRICE − PROFITS < COST) ...
IF (C EQUAL A) ...
IF (A * B IS NOT < 0) ...
IF (X IS GREATER Y − T) ...
IF (NA = '**') ...
IF (PRICE NOT EQUAL ZERO) ...

The first operand is called the **subject of the condition**; the second operand is called the **object of the condition**. Either of these may be an identifier, a literal, or an arithmetic expression. Thus, in

```
IF (HOURS < 40) . . .
        |         |
     subject    object
```

HOURS, an identifier, is the subject of the condition, and **40**, an arithmetic expression, is the object of the condition.

The **relational operators** indicate what type of comparison is going to take place. The COBOL relational operators are listed in the following table:

Relational operator	Meaning	Math equivalent
IS <u>GREATER</u> THAN IS >	Is greater than	$>$
IS <u>NOT GREATER</u> THAN IS <u>NOT</u> >	Is not greater than Is less than or equal to	$\leqslant$
IS <u>LESS</u> THAN IS <	Is less than	$<$
IS <u>NOT LESS</u> THAN IS <u>NOT</u> <	Is not less than Is greater than or equal to	$\geqslant$
IS <u>EQUAL</u> TO IS =	Is equal to	$=$
IS <u>NOT EQUAL</u> TO IS <u>NOT</u> =	Is not equal to	$\neq$

(You may use either **EQUAL** or **EQUALS**.)

IS, **THAN**, and **TO** are not required in any of these relational operators; thus, you may simply use the word **GREATER** or the symbol > for the greater-than comparison. Some compilers require you to use the word (e.g., **GREATER**) instead of the symbol (e.g., >). When you use a symbol as a relational operator, you must precede and follow the symbol with a blank space.

For example, you could check **HOURS** to see if they are over 40 hours and, if so, calculate overtime, as follows:

```
IF (HOURS > 40) PERFORM OVER-TIME.
IF (HOURS NOT > 40) PERFORM REGULAR-TIME.
```

If the overtime calculation is only one statement, you may do the calculation in the same statement:

```
IF (HOURS > 40)
   COMPUTE PAY = (40 * RATE) + (HOURS - 40) * RATE * 1.5.
IF (HOURS NOT > 40)
   COMPUTE PAY = HOURS * RATE.
```

****

Call Magic

One day while cleaning off my desk there came
Into my hands a scrap, upon it writ
Five lines of code—a subroutine whose name
Was "Magic" which required no arguments.

My curiosity begin to itch.
I wrote a simple driver with but one
"Call Magic" statement—then submitted it
And walked outside to bask beneath the sun.

Four hours later I awoke in pain.
A sunburn had decided that it should
Take out a lease and dwell upon my skin.
So I returned inside in no sweet mood.

I claimed my job—my reason was enraged.
Queer looks were given me when I exclaimed,
"Great Caesar's Ghost," for on its final page
Was "For your sunburn try some *Solarcaine.*"

Three times I ran that job—three times amazed.
For once it solved a problem that had been
My tormentor for months and *sans* arrays
It gave a winning strategy for Gin.

The second run output a proof which showed
That every map with four colors may be
Completely marked and all adjacent nodes
Have different hues for their identity.

The third described a model of the skies
Which made the Einstein formulation seem
As trivial as one plus four is five
And yet could be explained to a Marine.

Just one more time I ran that job and while
It executed I sat deep in thought.
I concentrated all my earthly guile
On making "Magic" show the key to Luck.

The world is full of greed and avarice.
It spins on axes hewn from Mankind's lust.
Small children learn—avoid the precipice
Of grabbing for that final piece of crust.

No trace of "Magic" could be found by this
Sad author after I turned in that job
Which disappeared with all the previous
Results collected—dust to worthless dust.

Dr. D. M. Nessett

****

SAMPLE PROGRAM 8A

The Ready-Cash Bank manager pointed out that the previous payroll program did not calculate the overtime pay correctly. We are now going to modify the payroll program so that overtime pay is correctly calculated. Employees who work over 40 hours in one week are to be paid 1.5 times their normal hourly rate for all hours over 40. Sample Program 8A (**Figure 8.2**) processes data for a simple payroll. The input record consists of name, employee number, hours worked, and hourly rate. If the employee works over 40 hours, the employee receives time-and-a-half for all overtime hours. **Figure 8.3** is some sample output from Program 8A.

COMPARISON OF NUMERIC ITEMS (PICTURE 9)

Numeric items are compared by using their algebraic values. The length of the numbers does not matter, that is, fields of unequal size can be compared. The decimal point or the implied decimal point is used to align the two values: thus, **12.34** is equal to **012.340**. Here are some examples:

Field A	Field B	Result
123.4	0123.40	=
123.0	12.30	>
12.35	12.3	>
12.35	12.4	<
−99.00	1.0	<
0.0	0	=

Note:

1. The decimal points in the subject and object fields are aligned.
2. Necessary zeros are padded on the lefthand or righthand side to make the subject and object fields the same size.
3. The subject and object fields are then compared with respect to their algebraic values.

COMPARISON OF ALPHANUMERIC ITEMS (PICTURE X OR A)

Alphabetic or alphanumeric items of unequal length can be compared. The comparison proceeds from the left side, comparing character by character until a pair of unequal characters are found. Thus, if we compare 'AXES' to 'AXTB', the first field is found to be less than the second field when the pair of characters 'E' and 'T' are compared, since E comes before T in the alphabet. If the characters are all equal, the shorter field is considered less than the longer field (unless the remainder of the longer item consists solely of blank spaces, in which case the items are considered equal). For the purpose of comparison, blank spaces are padded on the right side of the shorter field.

```
010010 IDENTIFICATION DIVISION.                                    PROGRM8A
010020 PROGRAM-ID.                                                 PROGRM8A
010030     PROGRM8A.                                               PROGRM8A
010040* * * * * * * * * * * * * * * * * * * * * * * * * * * * **PROGRM8A
010050*  SAMPLE CONDITIONAL STATEMENTS  IF STATEMENT.            *PROGRM8A
010060* * * * * * * * * * * * * * * * * * * * * * * * * * * * **PROGRM8A
010070                                                             PROGRM8A
010080 ENVIRONMENT DIVISION.                                       PROGRM8A
010090 INPUT-OUTPUT SECTION.                                       PROGRM8A
010100 FILE-CONTROL.                                               PROGRM8A
010110     SELECT RECORDS-IN,                                      PROGRM8A
010120        ASSIGN TO UR-2540R-S-SYSIN.                          PROGRM8A
010130     SELECT PRINT-OUT,                                       PROGRM8A
010140        ASSIGN TO UR-1403-S-SYSPRINT.                        PROGRM8A
010150                                                             PROGRM8A
020010 DATA DIVISION.                                              PROGRM8A
020020 FILE SECTION.                                               PROGRM8A
020030 FD  RECORDS-IN                                              PROGRM8A
020040     LABEL RECORDS ARE OMITTED.                              PROGRM8A
020050 01  IN-RECORD                  PICTURE X(80).               PROGRM8A
020060 FD  PRINT-OUT                                               PROGRM8A
020070     LABEL RECORDS ARE OMITTED.                              PROGRM8A
020080 01  PRINT-LINE                 PICTURE X(133).              PROGRM8A
020090                                                             PROGRM8A
020100 WORKING-STORAGE SECTION.                                    PROGRM8A
020110 01  PAY-RECORD.                                             PROGRM8A
020120     05  NAME-RD                PICTURE X(30).               PROGRM8A
020130     05  EMP-NO-RD              PICTURE 9(09).               PROGRM8A
020140     05  HOURS-RD               PICTURE 99V9.                PROGRM8A
020150     05  RATE-RD                PICTURE 99V99.               PROGRM8A
020160     05  FILLER                 PICTURE X(34).               PROGRM8A
020170                                                             PROGRM8A
020180 01  PAY-LINE.                                               PROGRM8A
020190     05  FILLER                 PICTURE X(01).               PROGRM8A
020200     05  NAME-LN                PICTURE X(30).               PROGRM8A
020210     05  FILLER                 PICTURE X(05).               PROGRM8A
020220     05  EMP-NO-LN              PICTURE 999B99B9999.         PROGRM8A
020230     05  FILLER                 PICTURE X(05).               PROGRM8A
020240     05  HOURS-LN               PICTURE Z9.9.                PROGRM8A
020250     05  FILLER                 PICTURE X(05).               PROGRM8A
020260     05  RATE-LN                PICTURE $ZZ.99.              PROGRM8A
020270     05  FILLER                 PICTURE X(05).               PROGRM8A
020280     05  PAY-LN                 PICTURE $ZZZZ.99.            PROGRM8A
020290     05  FILLER                 PICTURE X(53).               PROGRM8A
020300                                                             PROGRM8A
030010 PROCEDURE DIVISION.                                         PROGRM8A
030020     OPEN INPUT RECORDS-IN, OUTPUT PRINT-OUT.                PROGRM8A
030030     PERFORM CALCULATE-PAY 1000 TIMES.                       PROGRM8A
030040                                                             PROGRM8A
030050 ALL-DONE.                                                   PROGRM8A
030060     CLOSE RECORDS-IN, PRINT-OUT.                            PROGRM8A
030070     STOP RUN.                                               PROGRM8A
030080                                                             PROGRM8A
030090 CALCULATE-PAY.                                              PROGRM8A
030100     MOVE SPACES TO PAY-LINE.                                PROGRM8A
030110     READ RECORDS-IN INTO PAY-RECORD AT END PERFORM ALL-DONE. PROGRM8A
030120     MOVE NAME-RD TO NAME-LN.                                PROGRM8A
030130     MOVE EMP-NO-RD TO EMP-NO-LN.                            PROGRM8A
030140     MOVE HOURS-RD TO HOURS-LN.                              PROGRM8A
030150     MOVE RATE-RD TO RATE-LN.                                PROGRM8A
030160     IF (HOURS-RD NOT > 40)                                  PROGRM8A

030170         COMPUTE PAY-LN = HOURS-RD * RATE-RD.                PROGRM8A
030180     IF (HOURS-RD > 40)                                      PROGRM8A
030190         COMPUTE PAY-LN = (40 * RATE-RD) + (HOURS-RD - 40) * PROGRM8A
030200                         RATE-RD * 1.5.                      PROGRM8A
030210     WRITE PRINT-LINE FROM PAY-LINE AFTER ADVANCING 1 LINES. PROGRM8A
```

FIGURE 8.2   Sample Program 8A

```
BBBBBBBBBBBBBBBBBBBBBBBBBBBBBBBB      333 33 3333     44.4     $44.44      $2070.90
AAAAAAAAAAAAAAAAAAAAAAAAAAAAAA       123 45 6789      1.2     $34.56      $   41.47
MARY T. WHISTLE                      425 78 6354     40.0     $12.00      $  480.00
ZERO TEST                            000 00 0000      0.0     $   .00     $     .00
JOSEPH LITTLE                        124 53 5241     20.0     $ 9.00      $  180.00
JUAN GARCIA                          742 51 4324     50.0     $11.00      $  605.00
```

FIGURE 8.3   **Output from Program 8A**

COLLATING SEQUENCE

A **collating sequence** is the arrangement of all characters in order, for example, the collating sequence of the alphabet is A, B, C, ... Here is the EBCDIC (Extended Binary Coded Decimal Interchange Code) collating sequence, listing the most common special characters:

	blank space	(lowest)
.	period	
<	less than	
(	left parenthesis	
+	plus symbol	
$	currency symbol	
*	asterisk	
)	right parenthesis	
;	semicolon	
-	hyphen or dash	
/	slash	
,	comma	
>	greater than	
'	single quote	
=	equals sign	
"	double quote	
A through Z		
0 through 9		(highest)

Some non-IBM computers use a slightly different collating sequence. If you are not using IBM equipment, consult the manufacturer's COBOL manual to determine the collating sequence for your computer.

Here are some examples of comparisons, with their results:

Field X	Field Y	Result
'ABC '	'ABC'	X = Y
'ABC'	'ABC '	X = Y
'AB'	'ABC'	X < Y
'A B'	'AB '	X < Y
' AB'	'AB '	X < Y
'AB5'	'ABC'	X > Y
'$'	'T'	X < Y
'4X'	'4C'	X > Y
'14.1'	'14.2'	X < Y
'5.30'	'05.3'	X > Y
'12 '	'120'	X < Y
'12 '	' 12'	X > Y
'1.20'	'01.4'	X > Y

Notice that alphanumeric and alphabetic comparisons are done character by character, starting on the left side.

Note:

1. If character strings are not of equal length, the shorter character-string is padded on the right with blank spaces until the two fields are of equal length.
2. Comparison starts from the left side, character by character.
3. The first unequal pair signals the ordering, that is, determines what the result of the comparison will be.
4. The COBOL collating sequence used by your computer determines the ordering.

Only fields used in arithmetic calculations should be declared with PICTURE 9 (numeric).

Use PICTURE X (alphanumeric) on all other fields. This will eliminate many errors and abnormal terminations of your program.

REVIEW

1. How are alphanumeric comparisons done? How are numeric comparisons done? What happens if the fields are of unequal length?

2. IF (A < B) MOVE C TO D.

In the statement above identify:

   a) The conditional portion.
   b) The statement portion.
   c) The object of the condition.
   d) The relational operator.
   e) The subject of the condition.

3. If you punched special symbols (e.g., #, $, &) on a data-processing card, how could you determine the collating sequence from the holes in the card? Devise a set of rules for determining sequence by using the holes punched in cards. (Hint: first punch the alphabet in collating sequence.)

4. In the following table, indicate whether A is equal to, greater than, or less than B:

A	B
1.0	01.
−16.1	18.5
'ABC'	'A C'
4	4.0
'B'	'#'
'5'	'A'
'1.0'	'1'
' '	'A'
−12.2	0.7

5. Write the code for the following:

   a) Compare A and B, then store the smaller value in T.
   b) If A is less than 10, add 1 to COUNT.

Hand-simulate the code with some test-data to verify that it works.

Program Modifications

1. We used Sample Program 3A to print mailing labels. We now wish to print mailing labels only of people whose payments are past-due. This is indicated in the data by a 2 in column 80 of the input record. Print a report with labels for all past-due customers.

2. Add headings to Sample Program 8A. Print regular hours, overtime hours, and total hours as three separate fields. Do the same for pay.

3. Add headings to Sample Program 8A. Modify 8A so that if a paycheck is over $800.00 the warning message **CHECK THIS ONE** is printed to the right of the pay amount. (Remember, you cannot do the comparison on the edited value of pay.)

4. Modify Sample Program 8A so that the following deductions are taken from the paycheck:

   a) 4% tax for checks with gross pay less than $300, 8% tax otherwise.
   b) $12.00 for medical insurance.
   c) $5.00 for union dues.

   If the resulting pay would be negative, cancel the medical and union deductions. Print all pertinent results and label your report.

****

A Diversion: Computerized Mailing Lists

Every time you join an organization, request information by mail, or buy something by mail your name ends up on a mailing list. These mailing lists are kept by computer, and these names are a saleable commodity. The worth of the name and address is governed by how much is known about you and how current the information is. For example, if you buy a magazine subscription on organic gardening for small farmers, you can easily be classified as a certain type of customer. Your name and address can be sold to mail-order organizations which wish to sell to organic farmers. By contrast, if you join a society of professional engineers, you will be asked to fill out a membership questionnaire. This information will be used to classify you further. Then a book company can request from the engineering society a list of electrical engineers under 30 working for large corporations, and attempt to sell books to the people on that list. The price your name and address is worth varies from five cents a name if little is known about you (for example, your telephone listing), to over a dollar if the list is very current and highly categorized (for example, a medical doctor between 30 and 40, living in a small town). Many organizations and businesses make a good share of their income by selling your name and address.

There is an easy way to keep track of who sells your name to whom: code your name when you fill out a form. If you join a book club and your name is Joan Smith, put your name down as Joan B. Smith. You can then remember that every time you get unsolicited mail addressed to Joan *B.* Smith, it comes from the book-club mailing list. You can easily make it more obvious than this, by using the name Book C. Smith. Then whenever Book C. Smith gets a letter, you will know your name has been passed on to another source. You will soon find this fictitious person is being told she was specially picked for her intelligence or foresight and being asked to send $20.00 for zapping lessons.

Computerized mailing-lists are so valuable that they are seeded, that is, the owner of the list adds a few phony names with the company address or the address of an employee. Then, if these fictitious people start receiving unauthorized mail, it serves as legal evidence that the mailing list has been stolen.

****

SIGN TEST

The IF statement can be used in a **sign condition**, that is, to check a numeric variable or arithmetic expression to see whether it is positive, zero, or negative. The sign-test commands are:

    ZERO
    NOT ZERO
    POSITIVE
    NOT POSITIVE
    NEGATIVE
    NOT NEGATIVE

Zero is neither positive nor negative.

The general format of the sign condition is:

$$\left\{ \begin{array}{l} \text{identifier} \\ \text{arithmetic-expression} \end{array} \right\} \text{ IS [\underline{NOT}] } \left\{ \begin{array}{l} \text{POSITIVE} \\ \text{NEGATIVE} \\ \underline{\text{ZERO}} \end{array} \right\}$$

The sign test is often used in COBOL programs. Examples are:

    IF ((A * B − 4) IS NOT NEGATIVE) PERFORM OVER-ROUTINE.
    IF (A IS POSITIVE) PERFORM ZERO-ROUTINE.

Notice that if a variable is to be used in a sign test, it must have a sign symbol in its declaration; otherwise it is always positive or zero. For the example above, A could be declared as follows:

    77 A PICTURE S9999.

To prevent errors, you should acquire the habit of always using the sign symbol when declaring variables. Variables used in the sign test must be unedited numeric variables. Notice that POSITIVE is not the same as NOT NEGATIVE; NOT NEGATIVE includes zero.

The sign test is often used to check computations for illegal operations. Suppose you want to do the following:

    COMPUTE A = B / (C − D).

You cannot do the arithmetic if (C − D) is zero, because you would be asking for division by zero. Here is how you may check for the above:

    IF (C − D IS NOT ZERO)
        COMPUTE A = B / (C − D)
    IF (C − D IS ZERO)
        PERFORM CALC-ERROR.

This checks the denominator to see if it is zero, and if so, performs an error routine.

Note:

1. The sign test determines whether a variable or arithmetic expression is negative, zero, or positive.

2. A numeric variable without a sign symbol can be only positive or zero.

LOGICAL OPERATORS

Three **logical operators** are used in COBOL. They are:

    NOT
    OR
    AND

You have seen **NOT** in the previous examples. It is used to reverse a comparison.

    OR and **AND** are used to do two or more comparisons in a single statement. In an **OR** statement, if either or both are true the condition is true. For example:

    IF (AGE < 21) OR (AGE > 30)
        PERFORM AGE-ROUTINE.

In this example, if either of the conditions is true, the **AGE-ROUTINE** paragraph will be performed. Parentheses are often used to avoid ambiguity.

    When you use **AND**, both comparisons must be true for the condition to be true. For example:

    IF (AGE < 21) AND (SEX = 'M') PERFORM YOUNG-MALE.

Only if both conditions are true will the **YOUNG-MALE** paragraph be performed. The following truth-table shows the relationship between the logical operators:

A	B	A OR B	A AND B	NOT A
T	T	T	T	F
T	F	T	F	F
F	T	T	F	T
F	F	F	F	T

Thus, you may code

    IF (A < B) . . .
    IF (A NOT < B)

NOT will negate the relational operator. **NOT** also can be used to negate the comparison. For example:

    IF NOT (A < B) . . .

This is particularly handy when you wish to negate a complicated comparison. For example:

    IF (AGE < 21) AND (SEX = 2) PERFORM FIRST-GROUP.

The negation would be:

    IF NOT ((AGE < 21) AND (SEX = 2)) PERFORM OTHER-GROUP.

The compiler uses a particular order of evaluation with logical expressions. For example:

    IF (A < B OR B > C + 4 AND D = E)

The expression could be evaluated in either of two ways (i.e., OR first or AND first) if there were no evaluation rules. The rules are:

1. Logical expressions within parentheses are evaluated first, beginning with the innermost set of parentheses.
2. Otherwise, the order is as follows:

    a) Arithmetic expressions.
    b) Relational operators.
    c) NOT.
    d) AND.
    e) OR.
    f) Left to right.

The expression

    IF (A < B OR B > C + 4 AND D = E) . . .

is evaluated as follows:

    IF ((A < B) OR ((B > C + 4) AND D = E)) . . .

You should remember that using extra parentheses is often a good way to avoid errors.

IF . . . ELSE

In the payroll program we wish to do one set of calculations if the hours are fewer than or equal to 40, and a different set of calculations if they are not:

    IF (HOURS NOT > 40) PERFORM REGULAR-TIME.
    IF (HOURS > 40) PERFORM OVER-TIME.

This kind of situation often comes up in programming, so there is a way to do this all in one statement, as follows:

    IF (HOURS > 40) PERFORM OVER-TIME
        ELSE PERFORM REGULAR-TIME.

The general format for this type of IF statement is:

```
IF (condition) statement-1
   [ ELSE statement-2 ].
```

In the example above, if the condition is true, **statement-1** is executed, but if the condition is false, **statement-2** is executed. Notice that there is no period before the ELSE clause. There should never be a period before the ELSE clause since the IF . . . ELSE is all one statement. Here is another example:

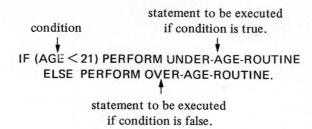

A flowchart representation of the IF statement looks like this:

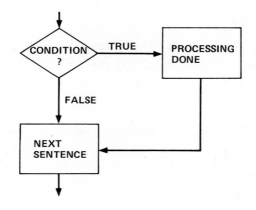

FIGURE 8.4   **Flowchart of the IF Statement**

A flowchart representation of the IF . . . ELSE statement looks like this:

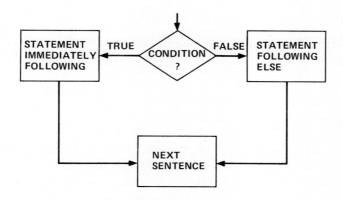

FIGURE 8.5   **Flowchart of the IF . . . ELSE Statement**

SAMPLE PROGRAM 8B

Figure 8.6 is Sample Program 8B. In this program an IF . . . ELSE statement is used to calculate regular-time pay and overtime pay. This program uses the following IF . . . ELSE statement:

```
IF (HOURS-RD NOT > 40)
      COMPUTE PAY-LN = HOURS-RD * RATE-RD
ELSE
      COMPUTE PAY-LN = (40 * RATE-RD) + (HOURS-RD – 40) * RATE-RD * 1.5.
```

Otherwise this sample program is the same as Sample Program 8A.

Program Modifications (*test carefully*)

1. Modify Sample Program 8B so that tax is deducted according to the following schedule:

    a) If total pay is less than or equal to $200, the tax rate is 3%.

    b) If total pay is over $200, but less than $350, the tax rate is 5%.

    c) If total pay is over $350, the tax rate is 8%.
    Print and label all fields.

2. Modify Sample Program 8A so that the employee's pay is calculated as follows:

    a) Regular pay for the first 40 hours.

    b) Time-and-a-half for the next 10 hours.

    c) Double-time for all hours over 50 hours.
    Print and label all fields.

3. Modify Sample Program 8B so that withholding tax is deducted according to the following schedule:

    a) 5% on the first $200.00.

    b) 8% on the next $150.00.

    c) 12% on all the rest.
    Print and label all fields.

GROUPING

We have already talked about grouping statements. We can use grouping with the IF statement so that several statements are executed, depending on the condition. For example:

```
IF (HOURS-RD NOT > 40)
      MOVE ZERO TO OVER-HOURS-LN, OVER-PAY-LN
      COMPUTE PAY-LN = HOURS-RD * RATE-RD.
```

Both the MOVE statement and the COMPUTE statement are executed if the condition is true. In general, all statements up to the period are executed if the condition is true. These statements are indented 4 spaces to show that they are part of the IF statement. Notice how important the periods are. There is no period at the end of the MOVE statement before the COMPUTE statement; therefore the two statements are executed together. There *is* a period at the end of the COMPUTE statement, which ends the sentence. If this final period should be left out, the next sentence would also be attached to the IF statement.

```
010010 IDENTIFICATION DIVISION.                                      PROGRM8B
010020 PROGRAM-ID.                                                   PROGRM8B
010030     PROGRM8B.                                                 PROGRM8B
010040* * * * * * * * * * * * * * * * * * * * * * * * * * * * * * **PROGRM8B
010050*     SAMPLE IF ... ELSE STATEMENT.                           *PROGRM8B
010060* * * * * * * * * * * * * * * * * * * * * * * * * * * * * * **PROGRM8B
010070                                                               PROGRM8B
010080 ENVIRONMENT DIVISION.                                         PROGRM8B
010090 INPUT-OUTPUT SECTION.                                         PROGRM8B
010100 FILE-CONTROL.                                                 PROGRM8B
010110     SELECT RECORDS-IN,                                        PROGRM8B
010120         ASSIGN TO UR-2540R-S-SYSIN.                           PROGRM8B
010130     SELECT PRINT-OUT,                                         PROGRM8B
010140         ASSIGN TO UR-1403-S-SYSPRINT.                         PROGRM8B
010150                                                               PROGRM8B
020010 DATA DIVISION.                                                PROGRM8B
020020 FILE SECTION.                                                 PROGRM8B
020030 FD   RECORDS-IN                                               PROGRM8B
020040     LABEL RECORDS ARE OMITTED.                                PROGRM8B
020050 01  IN-RECORD               PICTURE X(80).                    PROGRM8B
020060 FD   PRINT-OUT                                                PROGRM8B
020070     LABEL RECORDS ARE OMITTED.                                PROGRM8B
020080 01  PRINT-LINE              PICTURE X(133).                   PROGRM8B
020090                                                               PROGRM8B
020100 WORKING-STORAGE SECTION.                                      PROGRM8B
020110 01  PAY-RECORD.                                               PROGRM8B
020120     05  NAME-RD             PICTURE X(30).                    PROGRM8B
020130     05  EMP-NO-RD           PICTURE 9(09).                    PROGRM8B
020140     05  HOURS-RD            PICTURE 99V9.                     PROGRM8B
020150     05  RATE-RD             PICTURE 99V99.                    PROGRM8B
020160     05  FILLER              PICTURE X(34).                    PROGRM8B
020170                                                               PROGRM8B
020180 01  PAY-LINE.                                                 PROGRM8B
020190     05  FILLER              PICTURE X(01).                    PROGRM8B
020200     05  NAME-LN             PICTURE X(30).                    PROGRM8B
020210     05  FILLER              PICTURE X(05).                    PROGRM8B
020220     05  EMP-NO-LN           PICTURE 999B99B9999.              PROGRM8B
020230     05  FILLER              PICTURE X(05).                    PROGRM8B
020240     05  HOURS-LN            PICTURE Z9.9.                     PROGRM8B
020250     05  FILLER              PICTURE X(05).                    PROGRM8B
020260     05  RATE-LN             PICTURE $ZZ.99.                   PROGRM8B
020270     05  FILLER              PICTURE X(05).                    PROGRM8B
020280     05  PAY-LN              PICTURE $ZZZZ.99.                 PROGRM8B
020290     05  FILLER              PICTURE X(53).                    PROGRM8B
020300                                                               PROGRM8B
030010 PROCEDURE DIVISION.                                           PROGRM8B
030020     OPEN INPUT RECORDS-IN, OUTPUT PRINT-OUT.                  PROGRM8B
030030     PERFORM CALCULATE-PAY 1000 TIMES.                         PROGRM8B
030040                                                               PROGRM8B
030050 ALL-DONE.                                                     PROGRM8B
030060     CLOSE RECORDS-IN, PRINT-OUT.                              PROGRM8B
030070     STOP RUN.                                                 PROGRM8B
030080                                                               PROGRM8B
030090 CALCULATE-PAY.                                                PROGRM8B
030100     MOVE SPACES TO PAY-LINE.                                  PROGRM8B
030110     READ RECORDS-IN INTO PAY-RECORD AT END PERFORM ALL-DONE.  PROGRM8B
030120     MOVE NAME-RD TO NAME-LN.                                  PROGRM8B
030130     MOVE EMP-NO-RD TO EMP-NO-LN.                              PROGRM8B
030140     MOVE HOURS-RD TO HOURS-LN.                                PROGRM8B
030150     MOVE RATE-RD TO RATE-LN.                                  PROGRM8B
030160     IF (HOURS-RD NOT > 40)                                    PROGRM8B


030170         COMPUTE PAY-LN = HOURS-RD * RATE-RD                   PROGRM8B
030180     ELSE                                                      PROGRM8B
030190         COMPUTE PAY-LN = (40 * RATE-RD) + (HOURS-RD - 40) *   PROGRM8B
030200                         RATE-RD * 1.5.                        PROGRM8B
030210     WRITE PRINT-LINE FROM PAY-LINE AFTER ADVANCING 1 LINES.   PROGRM8B
```

FIGURE 8.6   Sample Program 8B

INDENTING

There are several ways to indent IF statements. When IF statements are short, they can easily all be placed on one line. For example:

    IF (AGE < 21) PERFORM UNDER-21.

On longer IF statements, put the IF and the conditions on the first line; put the statements to be executed on subsequent lines indented 4 spaces:

    IF (ACCOUNTS-DUE > 500.00 AND PAST-DUE > 3)
        ADD 1 TO PAST-DUE
        PERFORM LARGE-AMOUNT-ROUTINE
        PERFORM PAST-DUE-4-ROUTINE.

Notice that only the last statement ends with a period; thus, all three statements are done if the condition is true. When we have ELSE clauses and nested IF statements, the indenting becomes more important. One way to handle these is to line up the IFs and ELSEs. For example:

    IF   (condition)
              statements
    ELSE
              statements.

Complex conditional expressions are usually also lined up and parenthesized, to avoid errors and provide maximum clarity. For example:

    IF ((A LESS THAN B)
        AND (C GREATER THAN B))
        OR (T LESS THAN D)
        PERFORM PROCESSING.

By combining proper indenting and maximum use of parentheses, an otherwise confusing and unreadable set of code can become much clearer. There are no ironclad rules. Always try to write a program that is easy to read, because you and others will have to read it.

SAMPLE PROGRAM 8C

The Ready-Cash Bank manager wants overtime pay printed as a separate field. Sample Program 8C (**Figure 8.7**) calculates the overtime pay separately, and then adds the overtime pay and regular pay to get total pay. Several statements are grouped together under the IF statement. **Figure 8.8** is some sample output from Program 8C.

```
010010 IDENTIFICATION DIVISION.                                    PROGRM8C
010020 PROGRAM-ID.                                                 PROGRM8C
010030     PROGRM8C.                                               PROGRM8C
010040* * * * * * * * * * * * * * * * * * * * * * * * * * * * * **PROGRM8C
010050*       PAYROLL, CALULATES AND PRINTS OVERTIME PAY.          *PROGRM8C
010060* * * * * * * * * * * * * * * * * * * * * * * * * * * * * **PROGRM8C
010070                                                             PROGRM8C
010080 ENVIRONMENT DIVISION.                                       PROGRM8C
010090 INPUT-OUTPUT SECTION.                                       PROGRM8C
010100 FILE-CONTROL.                                               PROGRM8C
010110     SELECT RECORDS-IN,                                      PROGRM8C
010120        ASSIGN TO UR-2540R-S-SYSIN.                          PROGRM8C
010130     SELECT PRINT-OUT,                                       PROGRM8C
010140        ASSIGN TO UR-1403-S-SYSPRINT.                        PROGRM8C
010150                                                             PROGRM8C
020010 DATA DIVISION.                                              PROGRM8C
020020 FILE SECTION.                                               PROGRM8C
```

```
020030 FD   RECORDS-IN                                                     PROGRM8C
020040      LABEL RECORDS ARE OMITTED.                                     PROGRM8C
020050 01   IN-RECORD                      PICTURE X(80).                  PROGRM8C
020060 FD   PRINT-OUT                                                      PROGRM8C
020070      LABEL RECORDS ARE OMITTED.                                     PROGRM8C
020080 01   PRINT-LINE                     PICTURE X(133).                 PROGRM8C
020090                                                                     PROGRM8C
020100 WORKING-STORAGE SECTION.                                            PROGRM8C
020102 77   REG-PAY                        PICTURE 9999V99.                PROGRM8C
020104 77   OVER-PAY                       PICTURE 9999V99.                PROGRM8C
020106 77   OVER-HOURS                     PICTURE 99V9.                   PROGRM8C
020110 01   PAY-RECORD.                                                    PROGRM8C
020120      05   NAME-RD                   PICTURE X(30).                  PROGRM8C
020130      05   EMP-NO-RD                 PICTURE 9(09).                  PROGRM8C
020140      05   HOURS-RD                  PICTURE 99V9.                   PROGRM8C
020150      05   RATE-RD                   PICTURE 99V99.                  PROGRM8C
020160      05   FILLER                    PICTURE X(34).                  PROGRM8C
020170                                                                     PROGRM8C
020180 01   PAY-LINE.                                                      PROGRM8C
020190      05   FILLER                    PICTURE X(01).                  PROGRM8C
020200      05   NAME-LN                   PICTURE X(30).                  PROGRM8C
020210      05   FILLER                    PICTURE X(05).                  PROGRM8C
020220      05   EMP-NO-LN                 PICTURE 999B99B9999.            PROGRM8C
020230      05   FILLER                    PICTURE X(05).                  PROGRM8C
020240      05   HOURS-LN                  PICTURE Z9.9.                   PROGRM8C
020250      05   FILLER                    PICTURE X(05).                  PROGRM8C
020260      05   RATE-LN                   PICTURE $ZZ.99.                 PROGRM8C
020270      05   FILLER                    PICTURE X(05).                  PROGRM8C
020280      05   REG-PAY-LN                PICTURE $Z,ZZZ.99.              PROGRM8C
020290      05   FILLER                    PICTURE X(05).                  PROGRM8C
020300      05   OVER-HOURS-LN             PICTURE Z9.9.                   PROGRM8C
020310      05   FILLER                    PICTURE X(05).                  PROGRM8C
020320      05   OVER-PAY-LN               PICTURE $Z,ZZZ.99.              PROGRM8C
020330      05   FILLER                    PICTURE X(05).                  PROGRM8C
020340      05   PAY-LN                    PICTURE $Z,ZZZ.99.              PROGRM8C
020350      05   FILLER                    PICTURE X(03).                  PROGRM8C
020360                                                                     PROGRM8C
030010 PROCEDURE DIVISION.                                                 PROGRM8C
030020      OPEN INPUT RECORDS-IN, OUTPUT PRINT-OUT.                       PROGRM8C
030030      PERFORM CALCULATE-PAY 1000 TIMES.                             PROGRM8C
030040                                                                     PROGRM8C
030050 ALL-DONE.                                                           PROGRM8C
030060      CLOSE RECORDS-IN, PRINT-OUT.                                   PROGRM8C
030070      STOP RUN.                                                      PROGRM8C

030080                                                                     PROGRM8C
030090 CALCULATE-PAY.                                                      PROGRM8C
030100      MOVE SPACES TO PAY-LINE.                                       PROGRM8C
030110      READ RECORDS-IN INTO PAY-RECORD AT END PERFORM ALL-DONE.      PROGRM8C
030120      MOVE NAME-RD TO NAME-LN.                                       PROGRM8C
030130      MOVE EMP-NO-RD TO EMP-NO-LN.                                   PROGRM8C
030140      MOVE HOURS-RD TO HOURS-LN.                                     PROGRM8C
030150      MOVE RATE-RD TO RATE-LN.                                       PROGRM8C
030160      IF (HOURS-RD NOT > 40)                                         PROGRM8C
030170          MOVE ZERO TO OVER-HOURS-LN, OVER-PAY-LN                   PROGRM8C
030180          COMPUTE REG-PAY = HOURS-RD * RATE-RD                      PROGRM8C
030190          MOVE REG-PAY TO REG-PAY-LN, PAY-LN                        PROGRM8C
030200      ELSE PERFORM OVERTIME.                                         PROGRM8C
030210      WRITE PRINT-LINE FROM PAY-LINE AFTER ADVANCING 1 LINES.       PROGRM8C
030220                                                                     PROGRM8C
030230 OVERTIME.                                                           PROGRM8C
030240*    ****   DO CALCULATIONS FOR FIRST 40 HOURS.   ****              PROGRM8C
030250      MOVE 40 TO HOURS-LN.                                           PROGRM8C
030260      COMPUTE REG-PAY = 40 * RATE-RD.                               PROGRM8C
030270      MOVE REG-PAY TO REG-PAY-LN.                                    PROGRM8C
030280*    ****   NOW DO OVERTIME CALCULATIONS.   ****                    PROGRM8C
030290      SUBTRACT 40 FROM HOURS-RD GIVING OVER-HOURS.                  PROGRM8C
030300      MOVE OVER-HOURS TO OVER-HOURS-LN.                             PROGRM8C
030310      COMPUTE OVER-PAY = OVER-HOURS * RATE-RD * 1.5.                PROGRM8C
030320      MOVE OVER-PAY TO OVER-PAY-LN.                                  PROGRM8C
030330      COMPUTE PAY-LN = REG-PAY + OVER-PAY.                          PROGRM8C
```

FIGURE 8.7   Sample Program 8C

BEEEEBBBBBBBBBBBBBBBBBBB	333 33 3333	40.0	$44.44	$1,777.60	4.4	$ 293.30	$2,070.90
AAAAAAAAAAAAAAAAAAAAAA	123 45 6789	1.2	$34.56	$ 41.47	0.0	$ .00	$ 41.47
MARY T. WHISTLE	425 78 6354	40.0	$12.00	$ 480.00	0.0	$ .00	$ 480.00
ZERO TEST	000 00 0000	0.0	$ .00	$ .00	0.0	$ .00	
JOSEPH LITTLE	124 53 5241	20.0	$ 9.00	$ 180.00	0.0	$ .00	$ 180.00
JUAN GARCIA	742 51 4324	40.0	$11.00	$ 440.00	10.0	$ 165.00	$ 605.00

FIGURE 8.8   Output from Program 8C

NESTED IF STATEMENTS

A **nested IF statement** is an IF statement which contains another IF statement. There are several situations in which nested IF statements are very useful. Suppose you have a data field, ZAP, that is supposed to have a 1 or 2 in it. If ZAP is 1, you wish to PERFORM CODE-1; if ZAP is 2, you wish to PERFORM CODE-2. A poor way to code this would be:

```
IF (ZAP = 1) PERFORM CODE-1
    ELSE PERFORM CODE-2.
```

This assumes that everything not a **1** is a **2**. This overlooks an error condition, when ZAP might be neither. A better way to do it is:

```
IF (ZAP = 1) PERFORM CODE-1
ELSE IF (ZAP = 2) PERFORM CODE-2
        ELSE PERFORM CODE-ERROR.
```

This takes care of the error conditions, which can be common. The coding technique above is called **completing the decision**, that is, it takes care of all possibilities. Here is a flowchart of this sentence:

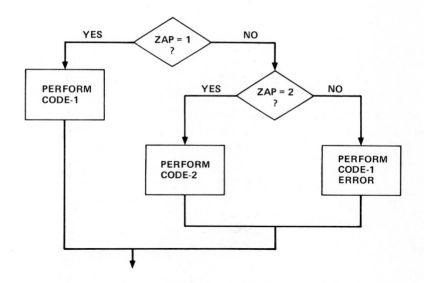

FIGURE 8.9   **Flowchart of a Nested IF Statement**

Common Errors:

1. Trying to use an edited variable in a numeric comparison.
2. Forgetting to complete your decision.
3. Comparing incompatible variables (e.g., alphabetic and numeric).

NEXT SENTENCE

The NEXT SENTENCE option is used to improve readability and to avoid certain types of error. The general format of the IF statement with the NEXT SENTENCE option is:

```
IF (condition)   { statement-1 ...              }
                 { NEXT SENTENCE                 }
    [  ELSE      { statement-2 ...          } ]
                 { NEXT SENTENCE            }
```

Sometimes NEXT SENTENCE is used to improve readability of the program. For example:

```
IF (A < B) NEXT SENTENCE
    ELSE PERFORM LESS-ROUTINE.
```

That is the same as:

```
IF (A NOT < B) PERFORM LESS-ROUTINE.
```

When the NEXT SENTENCE clause is executed by the program, the program goes on to the next sentence in the program. The NEXT SENTENCE clause can be used only with the IF statement.

In one situation the NEXT SENTENCE clause is required: when using nested IF statements, and the inner IF does not have a matching ELSE, you *must* use NEXT SENTENCE. For example:

```
IF (A < B)
    IF (B < C) PERFORM SMALL-ROUTINE
ELSE PERFORM OTHER-ROUTINE.
```

The ELSE clause is paired with the inner IF statement, which is not correct, according to the indenting. Either the indenting above is misleading, or we have made an error in coding. We cannot put a period before the ELSE to terminate the inner IF statement, because then the ELSE would be unmatched. If the ELSE is to be paired with the first IF statement, we must do the following:

```
IF (A < B)
    IF (B < C) PERFORM SMALL-ROUTINE
    ELSE NEXT SENTENCE
ELSE PERFORM LARGE-ROUTINE.
```

The ELSE clause is always paired with the previous unpaired IF statement. The relationship can be portrayed as follows:

```
IF ...   IF ...   IF ...   ELSE ...   ELSE ...   ELSE ...
```

Incorrect pairing of the IF and ELSE can make it difficult to locate logic errors in your program. One way to avoid this type of error, when using nested IF statements, is always to use both the IF and ELSE, and to use NEXT SENTENCE wherever necessary.

****

Computer Graffiti

I am working on the last bug.

****

CONDITION NAMES

It is often convenient to name values of variables for use in IF statements. For example:

    IF (SEX = 1) PERFORM PROCESS-MALES.

When writing the statement above you must remember that the 1s are the males and the 2s are the females. If you become confused about which are 1s and which are 2s, your program will be incorrect; when you have many different values, this kind of confusion is especially easy to fall into. COBOL gives you a way to assign condition names to particular values of a variable.

A **condition name** is a name assigned to values of data items in the DATA DIVISION. The general format is:

```
88 condition-name     VALUE IS literal.
```

Condition names are formed according to the rules for variable names. Each condition name must have a VALUE associated with it. Here is an example:

    05 SEX   PICTURE   9.
       88 MALE   VALUE 1.
       88 FEMALE VALUE 2.

Now we can change our IF statement to:

    IF MALE PERFORM PROCESS-MALE.

This makes the program much more readable. Level-88 entries must be preceded by the conditional variable being named. The type of value in the VALUE clause must also be consistent with the PICTURE clause of the conditional variable. In the example above, SEX is the conditional variable, and MALE and FEMALE are condition names. The level-88 entry does not assign a value to either name: instead, it *associates* a value with a name. When you say

    IF FEMALE PERFORM PROCESS-FEMALE.

it is the same as coding

    IF (SEX = 2) PERFORM PROCESS-FEMALE.

A condition name can also represent a range of values. This is done with the THRU clause. For example:

    05 AMOUNT   PICTURE 999V99.
       88 UNDER-LIMIT   VALUE   0.00 THRU 49.99.
       88 VALID-LIMIT   VALUE 50.00 THRU 99.99.
       88 OVER-LIMIT   VALUE 100.00 THRU 999.99.

Now you can use the condition names above to check conditions. For example:

    IF OVER-LIMIT PERFORM OVER-ROUTINE.

The OVER-ROUTINE will be done only if AMOUNT is equal to or greater than 100.00. Both ranges and individual values can be used in the condition names for the same variable.

Note:

1. The condition name must immediately follow the conditional variable.
2. The type of value in the **VALUE** clause must be consistent with the **PICTURE** clause of the conditional variable.
3. The level-88 items are not elementary items and can be used only as conditions. Level-88 items have no **PICTURE** clause.

CHAPTER REVIEW

Vocabulary Review

Imperative statement	Subject of the condition	Logical operator
Conditional statement	Object of the condition	Nested IF statement
Relation condition	Collating sequence	Completing the decision
Relational operator	Sign condition	Condition name

Review Questions

1. Give examples of the two conditional statements covered so far.

2. Criticize the following **IF** statements:
   a) IF (AGE < 21 AND AGE > 30) MOVE Z TO T.
   b) IF (5 < 6) MOVE A TO B.
   c) IF (P < 10 OR P NOT < 10) PERFORM ZAPPER.
   d) IF (12. < A) PERFORM ZIPPER.
   e) IF NOT (A NOT < B) MOVE M TO N.
   f) IF (A < B) MOVE Z TO ZZ ELSE NEXT SENTENCE.
   g) 77 A PICTURE 99.
       IF (A POSITIVE) MOVE XX TO BB.

3. Programmer-supplied names are used in eight places within a COBOL program. Can you name the eight places?

4. List the possible level-numbers used in a COBOL program.

5. Rewrite all the following, using relational operators (GREATER, LESS, etc.):

    a) A IS ZERO.
    b) A IS NOT ZERO.
    c) A IS POSITIVE.
    d) A IS NOT POSITIVE.
    e) A IS NEGATIVE.
    f) A IS NOT NEGATIVE.

6. Write COBOL IF statements to do the following:

    a) If ZAPPER is not zero
        execute paragraph ZIPPER.
    b) If STORE-CODE is 0
        execute paragraph STORE-ERROR.
    c) If COST plus MARGIN is greater than PRICE
        add COST and MARGIN obtaining NEW-PRICE,
        and move zero to PRICE.

7. Given the variable description.

    05 EDUCATION   PICTURE XX.

    write condition names to define the following values:

    a) Less than high school   <   12
    b) High-school graduate   =   12
    c) Some college   =   13–15
    d) College graduate   =   16
    e) Some graduate school   >   16 →

Program Modifications

1. Modify Sample Program 3A so that it prints only the mailing labels of people whose names start with the letters A or B.

2. Modify Sample Program 3A so that it prints only the labels of people whose names start with the letters A, B, or P.

3. Modify Sample Program 3A so that it prints only the labels of people whose names start with the letters B through N.

4. Add a line at the end of the report for the program in question 3 to print the number of records read and the number printed.

5. *Errors.* Try to do some of the following, to find out how your compiler handles these errors:

    a) Use a sign test on a variable that does not have a sign (that is, S) in the field.
    b) Try to do a sign test on a variable that is edited (e.g., PICTURE –999.99).
    c) Compare a numeric variable (PICTURE 9) to a alphabetic variable (PICTURE A).

Programs

1. Write a program to process the following enrollment-listings for Intellect Haven College:

Field	Columns
Department	1–6
Course number	7–10
Instructor name	11–40
Minimum enrollment	41–43
Actual enrollment	44–46

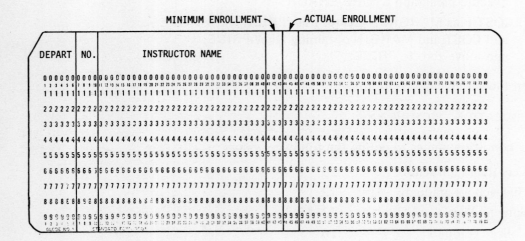

If the actual enrollment is less than the minimum enrollment, print the word UNDER to the right of that printed record. Lay the report out carefully and print all fields. Put headings on the report.

2. Ready-Cash Bank sells computer time on its computers. For each user the following data-record is created:

Field	Columns
Account number	1–4
Date	5–10 (MMDDYY)
Starting time	11–14 (HHMM)
Elapsed CPU time	15–21 (HHMMSS.S)
I/O requests	22–26

Computer time is charged as follows:

$300.00/hour	8 A.M. to 5 P.M.
$200.00/hour	5 P.M. to 8 A.M.
I/O requests	$2.25 per thousand.

(The starting time is used to determine hourly rate.) Print all information and label fields. Calculate charges for computer usage. Assume that all jobs start and stop within the time period 0000–2400.

3. Ready-Cash Bank processes bills for the local water-company. The Municipal Water Company charges the following rates for city users:

.37   per unit for the first 25 units.
.30   per unit after the first 25 units.

In addition, there is a service fee of $1.50 per month. Non-city water-users pay 1.5 times the total bill for city use.

INPUT RECORD

Field	Columns
Customer name	1–20
Customer number	21–25
Last meter reading	27–30
New meter reading	31–34
Resident code	36

    1 City resident

    2 Non-city resident

Print and label all pertinent information in your report.

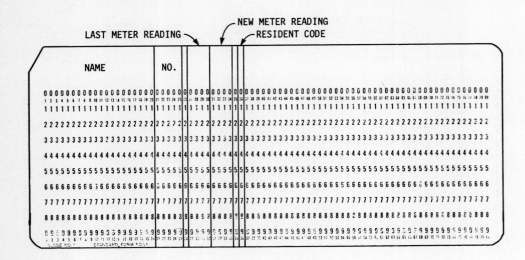

4. Salespeople who sell data-processing services for Ready-Cash Bank are paid commission at the following rates:

Sales Code	Commission Rate
A	\$100 + 1% commission of (total sales − base)
B	\$200 + 0.5% commission of (total sales − base)
C	1% commission of (total sales − base)

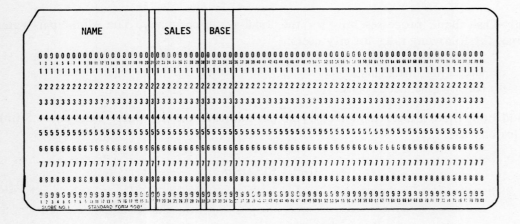

INPUT RECORD

Field	Columns
Salesperson name	1–20
Sales code	21
Total sales (dollars)	22–29
Base (dollars)	31–35

Use condition names for sales codes. Print and label all pertinent information in your report.

Chapter

9

```
****************************************************
          Refusing to work like a brute,
          A robot has claimed in a suit
            For full disability—
            He has no mobility,
          And he is blind, deaf, and mute.

****************************************************
```

HOW TO PROGRAM

We have looked at many sample programs and have tried making modifications in those programs. This is an obvious way to start to learn how to program. After all, we learn to write by reading first, so it is not surprising that we should learn to program by reading programs. Read all the programs you can. Find other programs: obvious sources are other textbooks, friends, and the computer-center recycling stack of printouts. You should be able to read most COBOL programs. We have covered much of COBOL by now; glance back through the early chapters and review what you now understand.

We have not yet approached the question of how to program. Since programming is still relatively new, no one is really sure how to teach it. Our approach to teaching programming is similar to teaching Russian: giving you some sentence structure (formal notation), and then giving you a Russian dictionary and telling you to start speaking Russian. Not surprisingly, many beginning programmers are confused.

Programming, however, is like many other skills, such as riding a bicycle or playing a piano: it is something you learn by doing. In playing the piano or riding a bicycle, and also in programming, you will probably do very badly at first, but you will improve with practice.

This book started by asking you to modify simple programs. To do this you had to read and understand the sample program before you were able to modify it. If you turn back to Chapter 2 or 3 and look over the program modifications, you will see that those modifications, which looked so difficult then, seem trivial now. You have learned quite a bit about COBOL programming!

After learning how to modify programs, the next step was to try to write simple programs. So far, the programs you have "written" were really modifications of the sample programs. You may want to begin writing complex programs now. Don't confuse complexity with size, however. All your programs should be simple, even if they are large. Complex programs are difficult to get right and difficult to keep right. A good large program is just a group of simple programs put together. It is not easy to put a large program together: therefore, it is all the more important to keep the parts simple.

How do we learn to program? Here are the first three steps:

1. Learn how to read programs.
2. Learn how to modify programs.
3. Learn how to write small programs.

As you advance through these steps you will be able to attack more complicated problems and, we hope, still end up with simple programs.

STYLE

As you read this book, you have seen suggestions on how to write good readable programs. Now some of these style guidelines should be summarized. Anyone can write these simple programs after a bit of study, but the goal is to write *good* programs, that is, simple, clear programs that work correctly. If the program is readable, it will be easier to read, to maintain, and to modify. Here are some guidelines.

Programmer-Picked Names

The section, paragraph, and variable names should be picked to indicate what is happening. For example:

    COMPUTE T = A * Z.

tells us only what arithmetic is being done. Now look at this:

    COMPUTE PAY = HOURS * RATE.

Now we have a better idea of what is happening beyond simple multiplication. The first rule of program style is to pick meaningful variable-names. This includes file names, record names, and paragraph names. Use the word *file* in file names, and use the word *record* in record names. When using variable names composed of two words, use a hyphen to connect the two words.

In describing records we learned that it was often useful to put a prefix or suffix on all fields in a record so that it would be easy to know what was being moved or manipulated in the PROCEDURE DIVISION without having to check the DATA DIVISION. An example is:

    01 IN-RECORD.
       05 NAME-RD   . . .
       05 STREET-RD . . .
       05 CITY-RD   . . .

All the fields above use the suffix **RD**, so when you see the statement

    MOVE STREET-RD TO . . .

you will know what is being moved. This technique also can be used in WORKING-STORAGE by placing the suffix WS on all variables in WORKING-STORAGE.

Indenting

The next style guideline is line indenting (also called **paragraphing**) and **alignment** of items in your program; all PICTURE and VALUE clauses should be aligned vertically. Next, indent levels in the DATA DIVISION to indicate structure. For example:

    01 MAIN-RECORD.
       05 FIELD-A.
          10 SUB-A   . . .
          10 SUB-A1 . . .
       05 FIELD-B.

The second type of indenting is that of statements which are too long for one line. The second and following lines are usually indented 4 spaces. For example:

    IF (HOURS NOT >40)
        MOVE ZEROS TO OVER-PAY
        COMPUTE PAY = HOURS * RATE.

The verb in each statement is ordinarily started in column 12. By indenting these verbs to column 16 we make it clear that the indented line is part of the previous line.

There are other rules of indenting. Programmers often align the IF and ELSE in long statements, as follows:

    IF (COST - OVERHEAD > PRICE)
        PERFORM   . . .
    ELSE
        PERFORM   . . .

These are some ways you can improve the readability of your programs. There are also ways in COBOL you can destroy readability. Some are so terrible we have hidden them until now. One is to write several statements on one line. For example:

IBM   COBOL Coding Form

SYSTEM			PUNCHING INSTRUCTIONS		PAGE	OF	
PROGRAM			GRAPHIC			CARD FORM #	*
PROGRAMMER	DATE		PUNCH				

```
SEQUENCE                                COBOL STATEMENT                              IDENTIFICATION
01  START-PROCESSING.  READ RECORD-IN INTO IN-RECORD AT END PREFORM
02     WRAP-IT-ALL.  MOVE NAME-IN TO NAME-OUT.  MOVE CITY-IN TO
03     CITY-OUT.  MOVE ZIP-IN TO ZIP-OUT.  WRITE PRINT-LINE FROM
04     ADDRESS-LINE AFTER ADVANCING 1 LINES.
05
06
07
08
09
```

This is perfectly good COBOL, but it is difficult to read. Also, if you needed to add a line, you would have to redo several sentences. You can do even worse than this. Remember, nonnumeric literals can be continued onto a second line by putting a dash in column 7 of the second line. Any other items can be continued in the same way. For example:

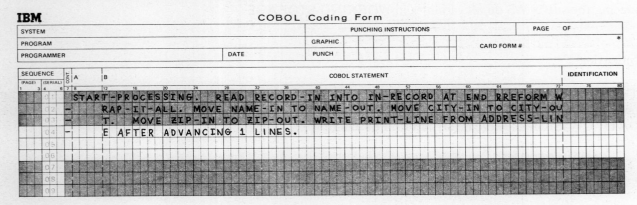

Use of this option completely destroys the readability of the program and cancels out the value of any indenting you may have done.

Blank Lines

Of course, each paragraph should accomplish a separate action. A technique to improve readability is to put blank lines or blank cards before division or paragraph names. If you choose your names carefully, this makes it easy to find the paragraphs you want.

Numbering Paragraphs

In long COBOL paragraphs, programmers often number the paragraphs in the PROCEDURE DIVISION by tens. For example, if the first three paragraphs are:

```
    START-UP.
        .
        .
        .
    CHECK-INPUT.
        .
        .
        .
    PROCESS-DATA.
```

they would be changed to:

```
    START-UP-010.
        .
        .
        .
    CHECK-INPUT-020.
        .
        .
        .
    PROCESS-DATA-030.
```

If a paragraph is referenced in the program, the number in the paragraph name helps indicate where the paragraph is. This can be quite useful when you wish to locate a paragraph in a thirty-page program.

****

A Diversion: Your Social-Security Number

Notice that the title is *your* social-security number. People so often demand that you hand over your social-security number (SSN), you may forget that it is really your number. In fact, you do not have to give it to most groups or organizations who ask for it. Federal privacy-laws have put severe restrictions on who can demand your SSN. The general rule is that you must give your SSN when receiving income, and in a few other situations connected with money. You are required to give it to your employer because the income you receive must be reported for tax purposes. If you have a savings account at a bank you must give the bank your SSN because you receive interest, which is also income. But if you have a checking account which pays no interest, the bank cannot legally demand your SSN or make it a condition for doing business with you. You do not have to give your social-security number to your school, or to the Department of Motor Vehicles or to any similar organization.

When you are asked for your SSN, you can usually simply decline to give it. Most organizations will accept that, although they will be unhappy about it. If they pressure you, you can tell them that they are violating federal privacy-laws by attempting to coerce you into handing over your SSN.

Why shouldn't you give out your SSN? Because of computers. Social-security numbers are a way to identify you uniquely. It is difficult to identify someone uniquely by a name, because there are many duplicate names and people can spell their names differently at different times. The SSN is gradually turning into a National Identification Number. Once a group has your SSN, they can take diverse files—often, especially in government-related agencies, files from other groups or agencies—and match them by using a computer, thus building up an information bank about you. Since this is done without your permission or knowledge, and for purposes over which you have no control, it is apt to be nonbeneficial to you. For example, information you give on a medical form can later be used to deny you employment or insurance. The next time some group wants your SSN, try turning them down. If computer-related privacy problems interest you, look at *Databanks in a Free Society* by Alan F. Weston and Michael A. Baker (New York: Quadrangle Books, 1972).

Sometimes you want something and you do not have the time or patience to talk the group out of taking your SSN. Once a clerk refused to sell a discount bus-pass unless he got the customer's SSN. It was obvious that the bus company wanted it merely to simplify their bookkeeping, but there was also no reason why they should have it. One customer solved the problem by saying that his SSN was 123-45-6789. The clerk couldn't believe that, but the customer pointed out that it was a valid SSN: someone had to have that number. All his life, he said sadly, every time he gave out his SSN others always thought he was kidding. By the time he left, the clerk had not only accepted the fictitious number, but he felt sorry for poor SSN 123-45-6789. The moral of this story is, most of the time people don't care what number you give them, as long as they get a number.

****

REVIEW

1. Write one sentence that indicates how to do each of the program modifications at the end of Chapter 2 and Chapter 3.

2. Write the worst program you can. Put multiple statements on the same line, split words over lines, don't indent, etc.

3. List several places where indenting can be used to improve program readability.

4. How many techniques can you list to help program readability?

5. Develop a style guideline for COBOL. Three good references for program style are:

   a) *Program Style, Design, Efficiency, Debugging, and Testing,* by D. Van Tassel (2nd edition, Englewood Cliffs, N.J.: Prentice-Hall, 1978).

   b) *The Elements of Programming Style,* by Brian Kernighan and P. J. Plauger (New York: McGraw-Hill, 1974).

   c) *COBOL with Style,* by Louis Chmura and Henry Ledgard (Rochelle Park, N.J.: Hayden, 1976).

   Compare your COBOL style guidelines with those of the rest of the class, to see if you can get a consensus. Then send me a copy of your final version.

PLANNING

We have talked a little about program planning. A basic rule is that an hour of planning is worth five hours of programming, debugging, and testing. To put it another way, one hour of planning before you start programming will save you five hours later. Some people sit down and hastily start typing the program with no advance planning, but when they run the program, if they don't have to start completely over, they usually must make major revisions.

It is much easier to revise a flowchart than to revise a coded program. You should do at least a rough flowchart of the program before you start coding. This forces you to examine the problem closely and to think about it long enough that you will have a chance of succeeding.

GETTING IT RIGHT

Remember, a program is supposed to produce *correct* results, not just any results. The first step in getting it right is to hand-simulate the flowchart. If you get correct results after following the flowchart, then you can start coding.

Where do you start coding? At the beginning. Do the COBOL divisions in order. The first two divisions should be quite simple. Then code the DATA DIVISION before the PROCEDURE DIVISION. Describe the records first. Finally, start on the PROCEDURE DIVISION, realizing you may have to go back and add items to the DATA DIVISION.

Once the program has been coded, compare it to the flowchart, looking for coding errors and things left out. You can then hand-simulate the code. Finally, desk-check the code after it is typed, reading each line looking for typing and other errors. The code is still fresh in your mind and this is the best time to desk-check. Have this as your goal:

Get the program to execute correctly the first run!

Imagine how much time you will save if this happens. You can do it, if you try. One more suggestion: don't use a COBOL statement if you are unsure about the syntax or result of its use. Look it up first. Get the syntax right the first time, too. Here are the suggestions again:

1. Plan first.
2. Flowchart.
3. Hand-simulate.
4. Desk-check.
5. Get the syntax right.

TOP-DOWN DESIGN

Top-down design is a method of program design in which the program is designed from the top: starting with a statement of the problem, we keep refining it until we have the program fully laid out. Top-down design is often used instead of flowcharts.

To use top-down design for the payroll program in the previous chapter, first state the problem:

Write a program to read hours and produce paychecks.

The next level of generalization could be:

Initialization.
Reading and processing records.
Termination.

Next, take care of the initialization and termination paragraphs:

Initialization.
    Open files.
    Print headings.
Termination.
    Close files.
    Stop.

Now, move on to the main part of the program:

MAIN (Repeat as needed)
    Read data record.
    Process data record.
    Write data record.

We can expand the process sentence, as follows:

MAIN
    Read data record.
    If overtime hours, perform overtime.
    If regular-time, perform regular-time.
    Do deductions.
    Compute final pay.
    Write data record.

At this point we have the program pretty well laid out. We should hand-simulate the **pseudo-code** with some sample data. If it works, we will start translating it into COBOL code. Pseudo-code is an English-like code that allows us to express the logic of the program in a highly readable manner. Pseudo-code cannot be compiled or executed.

Top-down design is popular because it allows you to take large problems and refine them until a program is designed. Also, like flowcharting, it forces you to organize your program before coding. If you can't write the program in English or pseudo-code, you won't be able to write it in COBOL either. Do it in English first.

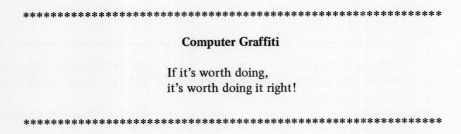

Computer Graffiti

If it's worth doing,
it's worth doing it right!

EFFICIENCY

Program efficiency is often greatly overemphasized. Today's computers are so fast and so large that program efficiency has little meaning. If a program is going to require only a few seconds to execute, it matters little if half a second can be saved. The correctness of the program is much more important than its efficiency. In any case, to improve the efficiency of a program usually requires programmer time, and an hour of programmer time is a bad trade for a small improvement in program performance.

The only time that efficiency is important is in long-running programs which are going to be used continually over a period of time. Even then, the only parts of the program that need to be improved are those which are executed thousands of times inside loops. A **loop** is a part of a program which causes some action or series of actions to be repeated continually until some condition is fulfilled. (A flowchart of a loop would show you how it gets its name.) In COBOL, loops are often created by use of the PERFORM verb. It makes little difference whether or not the initialization and termination paragraphs, which are executed only once, are efficient. All efforts to make the program efficient should be expended on code that is executed many times inside loops. It has been shown that, in a typical program, 3 percent of the code constitutes 50 percent of execution time; we must concentrate on improving this critical 3 percent of the code if the program is to be made efficient. There are programs available, called **profilers**, which accept a program, analyze it, and print a report showing how much time is spent executing each statement in the program. This profiler-generated report can then be used to determine which COBOL statements are worth perfecting.

Computer Graffiti

Every program can be one statement shorter.

Decimal Alignment

In COBOL several things can be done to improve efficiency in programs. One proven technique is to declare variables in a consistent type and size whenever possible, that is, to describe similar fields with identical PICTUREs. For example, when you have the following:

```
77 A   PICTURE  S99V9.
77 B   PICTURE  S99V99.
   MOVE A TO B.
```

the decimal point must be aligned when A is moved to B. If both variables were declared as the same number of decimal positions, that step in execution would be eliminated, and the program would be more efficient.

Unequal Field Lengths

When moving, comparing, or adding fields, it is more efficient to use fields of equal length.

```
77 X   PICTURE  S999.
77 Z   PICTURE  S9999.
```

If the two fields above are compared, the compiler must generate code to pad extra zeros on the lefthand side of variable X so that the fields will be equal in length. If the two fields are already equal in length, this padding code will not be needed, and the program will be more efficient.

Sign

It is important to use a sign on numeric fields being used in computations. When arithmetic is done, a sign is generated for the result field. For example:

```
77 A   TOTAL-A   PICTURE  S9999.
```

If there is no S in the PICTURE clause, the compiler must generate instructions to remove the sign that is automatically generated. For COMPAREs and MOVEs, also, it is more efficient if both fields are signed. Omitting S can be not only inefficient, but wrong: if a result is negative but the resultant field is unsigned, the negative sign will be lost. For both these reasons it is best to use the sign on most computational fields.

Another simple technique for improving efficiency is to be sure to write your program so that no warning messages appear. Even though a program will still execute, efficiency can be seriously impaired by problems flagged by warning messages. Correct any problems indicated by warning messages.

USAGE Clause

The USAGE clause specifies how numeric data are stored. Numeric data can be stored as character data or as numeric data. Data read from cards or printed are always stored as character (alphanumeric) data. Arithmetic can be done using character data, but the character data must first be converted to numeric mode. The code to do this conversion is generated by the compiler.

The general format of the USAGE clause is:

```
USAGE IS  { DISPLAY       }
          { COMPUTATIONAL }
```

DISPLAY mode is used for character data. It is the **default**, that is, if you do not use the USAGE clause, the data is automatically stored in DISPLAY mode. So far in this book we have used DISPLAY mode by default.

The USAGE clause is used in the WORKING-STORAGE SECTION. Card input files and print files are always DISPLAY. Magnetic-tape files, magnetic-disk files, and fields used in internal calculations are often specified as COMPUTATIONAL. Most computers have other options available for the USAGE clause. Consult a manufacturer's COBOL manual to determine what other options are available on the computer you are using.

An example of the USAGE clause is:

```
77 TOTAL   PICTURE S9999V99   USAGE IS COMPUTATIONAL.
```

The IS is not required and is usually omitted. The USAGE clause can be inserted either before or after the PICTURE clause. The USAGE clause can be used at either the group level or the elementary level; when the USAGE clause is on the group level, all elementary items are stored in the stated form. The DISPLAY form is required for all variables which contain alphabetic or special characters. COMPUTA-TIONAL can be used only with variables which have S, V, and 9 in their PICTURE clause.

Here are more examples of the USAGE clause:

```
WORKING-STORAGE SECTION.
77 K   PICTURE S999   VALUE ZERO
          USAGE IS COMPUTATIONAL.
77 L  PICTURE S999   VALUE +1.
77 N  PICTURE S999   VALUE +1.
          USAGE DISPLAY.

01 TOTALS   USAGE COMPUTATIONAL.
   05 TOTAL-HOURS   PICTURE S9999V99.
   05 TOTAL-WAGES   PICTURE S999999V99.
```

In the example above, K is declared COMPUTATIONAL. The variables L and N are DISPLAY. The variable L is DISPLAY by default, and N is explicitly declared DISPLAY. Since the group item TOTALS was declared COMPUTATIONAL, the elementary items TOTAL-HOURS and TOTAL-WAGES are also COMPUTATIONAL.

Considerable computer-time can be saved by employing the USAGE clause to store numeric data as COMPUTATIONAL. Suppose we want to do the following arithmetic, and the variables A and B are DISPLAY:

```
ADD A TO B.
```

The compiler must generate code to do the following:

1. The value in field A must be converted to COMPUTATIONAL mode and stored in a temporary location.

2. The value in field **B** must be converted to **COMPUTATIONAL** mode and stored in a temporary location.

3. The values in the two **COMPUTATIONAL** fields will then be added together.

4. The result must be converted to **DISPLAY** mode and stored in **B**.

As you can see, this causes all numeric calculations to use several times as much machine time as would be required if the variables had been declared **COMPUTATIONAL**. For this reason, most numeric fields (except input/output files) in the **WORKING-STORAGE SECTION** should be declared **COMPUTATIONAL**.

Note:

1. The **USAGE IS COMPUTATIONAL** clause can be used to increase the efficiency of numeric calculations.

2. The **USAGE** clause can be used at any level. If it is used at the group level, it applies to each elementary item within the group.

3. If no **USAGE** is specified, the item is **DISPLAY** by default.

4. If you are performing a sign test, the variable must be declared either implicitly or explicitly as **USAGE DISPLAY**.

Mixed Data Formats

Mixed data formats are different data-types used in operations such as **MOVE, ADD,** or comparisons, for example, comparing a **DISPLAY** variable to a **COMPUTATIONAL** variable. The compiler must generate code to put both variables in the same mode before the operation can be done. Thus, it is most efficient to plan your program so that a minimum number of mixed data formats are used.

REVIEW

1. What is the purpose of the **USAGE** clause? If the **USAGE** is not specified, what **USAGE** is the default?

2. When results are printed, the numbers must be in **DISPLAY** mode. If only one or two calculations were being done, would it be better to declare the numbers in **DISPLAY** mode or in **COMPUTATIONAL** mode?

3. List the clauses which can be used with a **PICTURE** entry. Which can be used at the group level? Which can be used only at the elementary level? Does the order of the clauses matter?

GENERALITY

Generality is the concept of program independence from a particular set of data. It is usually accomplished by using variables instead of constants for parameters. For example, suppose you have a state payroll-tax of 3 percent. Your program could have the following statements:

```
COMPUTE STATE-DEDUCTION = PAY * 0.03.
MOVE 0.03 TO STATE-TAX-OUT.
```

But when the state tax-rate changes, which it surely will, you would have to go through the program and change every occurrence of the state tax-rate. This is a time-consuming and an error-prone process. A better approach is to set up a variable called **STATE-TAX** and initialize it to the tax rate, as follows:

```
77 STATE-TAX    PICTURE S9V99    VALUE 0.03.
      .
      .
      .
    COMPUTE STATE-DEDUCTION = PAY * STATE-TAX.
    MOVE STATE-TAX TO STATE-TAX-OUT.
```

Now, when the state tax changes, you need to change only the **VALUE** clause in order to change **STATE-TAX** throughout the program. Some parameters are read in as data. The disadvantage of this is that the data can too easily be incorrect. It is best to read in parameters as data only when the parameters (for example, a date field) change for every run. There are many places in a program where you can use variables instead of constants, and you should always be on the lookout for them.

PERFORM . . . UNTIL

We have already used two forms of the **PERFORM** verb. They were:

```
PERFORM START-PROCESSING.
PERFORM START-PROCESSING 10 TIMES.
```

Another form of the **PERFORM** verb allows you to **PERFORM** a paragraph until some condition becomes true. The general format of this **PERFORM** statement is:

PERFORM paragraph UNTIL (condition).

The condition can be any legal condition-clause. Condition clauses were discussed in Chapter 8 under **IF** statements. Examples of this type of **PERFORM** are:

```
PERFORM PARA-A UNTIL (TIME > 100).
PERFORM PARA-A UNTIL (AMOUNT < 0).
```

The variables used in the condition clause must be initialized prior to their use in the **PERFORM** statement; in the statement above, the variable **AMOUNT** must have some value in it. You must make sure that the condition will eventually become true, for otherwise the paragraph will be executed until it is shut off by the computer. This is called an **infinite loop**. Infinite loops are expensive—someone must pay for the wasted computer-time. (**Figure 9.1** is a flowchart for the **PERFORM . . . UNTIL** statement.)

Note:

1. In **PERFORM . . . UNTIL**, the paragraph is performed until the condition is true.

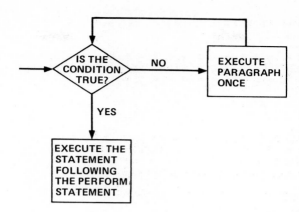

FIGURE 9.1   A Flowchart for PERFORM . . . UNTIL

2. The condition is checked first; if the condition is true at the time the PERFORM is executed, the specified paragraph is not executed.

3. All variables used in the condition clause must already have a value the first time the PERFORM statement is executed.

4. It is important that the condition can eventually be satisfied; if it cannot, your program will go into an infinite loop.

SAMPLE PROGRAM 9A

Ready-Cash Bank needs a program which will read the amount deposited and the interest rate, and then print the yearly interest-rate and new balance, until the original amount has been doubled. These reports are to be given to all new customers as a sales campaign. **Figure 9.2** is Sample Program 9A; **Figure 9.3** is some sample output from this program. For example, if the amount is $1000.00 and the interest rate is 7 percent, then the accumulated interest will be calculated until the new balance is over $2000.00. Let's look at the program:

```
DO-INTEREST.
    COMPUTE CALC-INTEREST = INTEREST * OLD-AMOUNT.
    COMPUTE NEW-AMOUNT = CALC-INTEREST + OLD-AMOUNT.
    MOVE OLD-AMOUNT TO OLD-AMOUNT-LN.
    MOVE CALC-INTEREST TO CALC-INTEREST-LN.
    MOVE NEW-AMOUNT TO NEW-AMOUNT-LN.
    WRITE PRINT-LINE FROM DEPOSIT-LINE AFTER ADVANCING 1 LINES.
    MOVE NEW-AMOUNT TO OLD-AMOUNT.
```

We will go over the statements in this paragraph line by line. First, the calculated interest is calculated by multiplying the interest-rate times the amount deposited. Next, the new amount is calculated by adding the calculated interest to the old amount. The next four sentences in this COBOL paragraph set up the print-line and write out the results. We must move the old amount, the calculated interest, and the new amount to the print-line. Then we write the print-line. In the last line of the paragraph, we move the old amount to the new amount-field, because we must use the new amount (old amount plus interest) to calculate new interest.

```
010010 IDENTIFICATION DIVISION.                                          PROGRM9A
010020 PROGRAM-ID.                                                       PROGRM9A
010030     PROGRM9A.                                                     PROGRM9A
010040* * * * * * * * * * * * * * * * * * * * * * * * * * * * * **PROGRM9A
010050*   CALCULATE BANK BALANCE USING PERFORM ... UNTIL.           *PROGRM9A
010060* * * * * * * * * * * * * * * * * * * * * * * * * * * * * **PROGRM9A
010070                                                                   PROGRM9A
010080 ENVIRONMENT DIVISION.                                             PROGRM9A
010090 INPUT-OUTPUT SECTION.                                             PROGRM9A
010100 FILE-CONTROL.                                                     PROGRM9A
010110     SELECT RECORDS-IN,                                            PROGRM9A
010120         ASSIGN TO UR-2540R-S-SYSIN.                               PROGRM9A
010130     SELECT PRINT-OUT,                                             PROGRM9A
010140         ASSIGN TO UR-1403-S-SYSPRINT.                             PROGRM9A
010150                                                                   PROGRM9A
020010 DATA DIVISION.                                                    PROGRM9A
020020 FILE SECTION.                                                     PROGRM9A
020030 FD  RECORDS-IN                                                    PROGRM9A
020040     LABEL RECORDS ARE OMITTED.                                    PROGRM9A
020050 01  IN-RECORD                    PICTURE X(80).                   PROGRM9A
020060 FD  PRINT-OUT                                                     PROGRM9A
020070     LABEL RECORDS ARE OMITTED.                                    PROGRM9A
020080 01  PRINT-LINE                   PICTURE X(133).                  PROGRM9A
020090                                                                   PROGRM9A
020100 WORKING-STORAGE SECTION.                                          PROGRM9A
020110 77  INTEREST                     PICTURE V9999.                   PROGRM9A
020120 77  TWICE-AMOUNT                 PICTURE S99999V99.               PROGRM9A
020130 77  NEW-AMOUNT                   PICTURE S99999V99.               PROGRM9A
020140 77  OLD-AMOUNT                   PICTURE S99999V99.               PROGRM9A
020150 77  CALC-INTEREST                PICTURE S9999V99.                PROGRM9A
020160                                                                   PROGRM9A
020170 01  HEADING-LINE.                                                 PROGRM9A
020180     05  FILLER       PICTURE X(01).                               PROGRM9A
020190     05  FILLER       PICTURE X(10)    VALUE 'OLD AMOUNT'.         PROGRM9A
020200     05  FILLER       PICTURE X(07)    VALUE SPACES.               PROGRM9A
020210     05  FILLER       PICTURE X(04)    VALUE 'RATE'.               PROGRM9A
020220     05  FILLER       PICTURE X(05)    VALUE SPACES.               PROGRM9A
020230     05  FILLER       PICTURE X(08)    VALUE 'INTEREST'.           PROGRM9A
020240     05  FILLER       PICTURE X(05)    VALUE SPACES.               PROGRM9A
020250     05  FILLER       PICTURE X(10)    VALUE 'NEW AMOUNT'.         PROGRM9A
020255     05  FILLER       PICTURE X(83)    VALUE SPACES.               PROGRM9A
020260                                                                   PROGRM9A
020270 01  DEPOSIT-RECORD.                                               PROGRM9A
020280     05  AMOUNT-RD                PICTURE 9999V99.                 PROGRM9A
020290     05  INTEREST-RD              PICTURE 99V99.                   PROGRM9A
020300     05  FILLER                   PICTURE X(70).                   PROGRM9A
020310                                                                   PROGRM9A
020320 01  DEPOSIT-LINE.                                                 PROGRM9A
020330     05  FILLER                   PICTURE X(01).                   PROGRM9A
020340     05  OLD-AMOUNT-LN            PICTURE $ZZ,ZZZ.99.              PROGRM9A
020350     05  FILLER                   PICTURE X(05).                   PROGRM9A
020360     05  INTEREST-LN              PICTURE ZZ.99.                   PROGRM9A
020370     05  PER-CENT                 PICTURE X.                       PROGRM9A
020380     05  FILLER                   PICTURE X(05).                   PROGRM9A
020390     05  CALC-INTEREST-LN         PICTURE $ZZZZ.99.                PROGRM9A
020400     05  FILLER                   PICTURE X(05).                   PROGRM9A
020410     05  NEW-AMOUNT-LN            PICTURE $ZZ,ZZZ.99.              PROGRM9A
020420     05  FILLER                   PICTURE X(05).                   PROGRM9A
020425     05  FILLER                   PICTURE X(78).                   PROGRM9A
020430                                                                   PROGRM9A


030010 PROCEDURE DIVISION.                                               PROGRM9A
030020     OPEN INPUT RECORDS-IN, OUTPUT PRINT-OUT.                      PROGRM9A
030030     WRITE PRINT-LINE FROM HEADING-LINE AFTER ADVANCING 1 LINES.   PROGRM9A
030040     PERFORM PRINT-BLANK-LINE.                                     PROGRM9A
030050     MOVE SPACES TO DEPOSIT-LINE.                                  PROGRM9A
030060     MOVE '%' TO PER-CENT.                                         PROGRM9A
030070     PERFORM PROCESS-RECORD 10 TIMES.                              PROGRM9A
030080                                                                   PROGRM9A
030090 ALL-DONE.                                                         PROGRM9A
```

```
030100      CLOSE RECORDS-IN, PRINT-OUT.                              PROGRM9A
030110      STOP RUN.                                                 PROGRM9A
030120                                                                PROGRM9A
030130  PRINT-BLANK-LINE.                                             PROGRM9A
030140      MOVE SPACES TO DEPOSIT-LINE.                              PROGRM9A
030150      WRITE PRINT-LINE FROM DEPOSIT-LINE AFTER ADVANCING 1 LINES. PROGRM9A
030160                                                                PROGRM9A
030170  PROCESS-RECORD.                                               PROGRM9A
030180      READ RECORDS-IN INTO DEPOSIT-RECORD                       PROGRM9A
030190          AT END PERFORM ALL-DONE.                              PROGRM9A
030200      MOVE INTEREST-RD TO INTEREST-LN.                          PROGRM9A
030210      COMPUTE INTEREST = INTEREST-RD / 100.                     PROGRM9A
030220      MOVE AMOUNT-RD TO OLD-AMOUNT, NEW-AMOUNT.                 PROGRM9A
030230      COMPUTE TWICE-AMOUNT = 2 * AMOUNT-RD.                     PROGRM9A
030240      PERFORM DO-INTEREST UNTIL (NEW-AMOUNT > TWICE-AMOUNT).    PROGRM9A
030250      PERFORM PRINT-BLANK-LINE 2 TIMES.                         PROGRM9A
030260                                                                PROGRM9A
030270  DO-INTEREST.                                                  PROGRM9A
030280      COMPUTE CALC-INTEREST = INTEREST * OLD-AMOUNT.            PROGRM9A
030290      COMPUTE NEW-AMOUNT = CALC-INTEREST + OLD-AMOUNT.          PROGRM9A
030300      MOVE OLD-AMOUNT TO OLD-AMOUNT-LN.                         PROGRM9A
030310      MOVE CALC-INTEREST TO CALC-INTEREST-LN.                   PROGRM9A
030320      MOVE NEW-AMOUNT TO NEW-AMOUNT-LN.                         PROGRM9A
030330      WRITE PRINT-LINE FROM DEPOSIT-LINE AFTER ADVANCING 1 LINES. PROGRM9A
030340      MOVE NEW-AMOUNT TO OLD-AMOUNT.                            PROGRM9A
```

FIGURE 9.2   Sample Program 9A

OLD AMOUNT	RATE	INTEREST	NEW AMOUNT
$ 1,000.00	7.00%	$ 70.00	$ 1,070.00
$ 1,070.00	7.00%	$ 74.90	$ 1,144.90
$ 1,144.90	7.00%	$ 80.14	$ 1,225.04
$ 1,225.04	7.00%	$ 85.75	$ 1,310.79
$ 1,310.79	7.00%	$ 91.75	$ 1,402.54
$ 1,402.54	7.00%	$ 98.17	$ 1,500.71
$ 1,500.71	7.00%	$ 105.04	$ 1,605.75
$ 1,605.75	7.00%	$ 112.40	$ 1,718.15
$ 1,718.15	7.00%	$ 120.27	$ 1,838.42
$ 1,838.42	7.00%	$ 128.68	$ 1,967.10
$ 1,967.10	7.00%	$ 137.69	$ 2,104.79
$ 1,000.00	7.50	$ 75.00	$ 1,075.00
$ 1,075.00	7.50	$ 80.62	$ 1,155.62
$ 1,155.62	7.50	$ 86.67	$ 1,242.29
$ 1,242.29	7.50	$ 93.17	$ 1,335.46
$ 1,335.46	7.50	$ 100.15	$ 1,435.61
$ 1,435.61	7.50	$ 107.67	$ 1,543.28
$ 1,543.28	7.50	$ 115.74	$ 1,659.02
$ 1,659.02	7.50	$ 124.42	$ 1,783.44
$ 1,783.44	7.50	$ 133.75	$ 1,917.19
$ 1,917.19	7.50	$ 143.78	$ 2,060.97

FIGURE 9.3   Output from Program 9A

Now this paragraph must be executed for each deposit record until the deposit amount has doubled. This is done by the following paragraph:

```
PROCESS-RECORD.
    READ RECORDS-IN INTO DEPOSIT-RECORD
        AT END PERFORM ALL-DONE.
    MOVE INTEREST-RD TO INTEREST-LN.
    COMPUTE INTEREST = INTEREST RD / 100.
    MOVE AMOUNT-RD TO OLD-AMOUNT, NEW-AMOUNT.
    COMPUTE TWICE-AMOUNT = 2 * AMOUNT-RD.
    PERFORM DO-INTEREST UNTIL (NEW-AMOUNT > TWICE-AMOUNT).
```

The first line reads in the data record, which has the deposit amount and interest rate in it. In the next sentence we move the interest rate to the output line. Since interest is read in percent form (e.g., 7%) it must be divided by 100 to get it in decimal form (e.g., 0.07). We do that in the sentence:

```
COMPUTE INTEREST = INTEREST-RD / 100.
```

Next, we want to move the deposit amount from the record to the old-amount and new-amount fields. We must store the deposit amount in OLD-AMOUNT for use in our calculations. We then calculate a variable named TWICE-AMOUNT, which has the value of twice the original amount deposited.

The PERFORM statement then executes the paragraph DO-INTEREST until the new amount is twice the original amount deposited. It is important that all the variables in the condition clause have a value. Notice that the first time the PERFORM statement is executed, the variable NEW-AMOUNT has the value of the original deposit. The previous MOVE statement put that value in NEW-AMOUNT. Each time the paragraph DO-INTEREST is executed, the condition is checked. The paragraph is executed until the condition is true (i.e., NEW-AMOUNT > TWICE-AMOUNT), and each time the paragraph DO-INTEREST is executed the variable NEW-AMOUNT will increase by the calculated interest. Thus, the PERFORM statement will eventually be satisfied.

TESTING

In Chapter 5 we talked a little about testing. We learned how to make sure that the correct columns were being read in the data records. That is very important to check first when testing your program.

Now we have some additional aspects to test—the conditional statements. When we have a conditional statement, such as an IF statement, we usually have at least two possibilities. For example:

```
IF (HOURS > 40) PERFORM OVER-TIME
    ELSE PERFORM REG-TIME.
```

In the example above there are two situations: either there is overtime, or there is not. You must have test data to check both conditions. This is often called a **path test** or a **leg test**, that is, some data must be sent through each path of the program. Good test-data for the hours field would be:

0	Lowest possible.
30	Less than 40.
40	The critical point.
50	Has overtime.
99	One large value.

The set of hours above would give a fairly complete test of the program. Zero is always interesting to use because it ensures that everything is getting reset properly. The 30 is useful because we want to make sure that this employee will not get overtime pay. The **critical point**, that is, the point at which the condition changes, is **40** hours, so we want to test to make sure we have that right. The value **50** allows us to check the overtime calculations, and the value **99** allows us to check what happens with a very large value.

You may have noticed that each number tests a **data class**; for example, the number **30** tests for what happens to the data under 40. If we had several more numbers in this class (e.g., **25, 32, 38**) we would not gain any new knowledge about the correctness of the program. We want to use just enough test-data to ensure that the program works correctly. From now on, be sure that you test each path of your program, and try to use the smallest amount of test data necessary. Don't forget to provide test data to check the other two conditional statements we have had, the **AT END** and **ON SIZE ERROR** clauses. Your test-data should cause each section of code to be executed at least once so that you can see if it works.

Common Testing Errors

1. Not testing all conditions. The test data should test all possible conditions and all combinations of conditions.

2. Using complicated test-data. Simple test-data is easier to hand-check and should be used. For example, for a variable like **HOURS** use 10.0 instead of 17.7. The latter value is much more difficult to hand-calculate.

CHAPTER REVIEW

Vocabulary Review

Paragraphing	Loop	Infinite loop
Alignment	Profiler	Path test (leg test)
Top-down design	Default	Critical point
Pseudo-code	Mixed data format	Data class
Program efficiency	Generality	

Review Questions

1. See how long your present programs take to execute. How much of your time would you be willing to spend to save 10 percent of the execution time? Calculate how much your time is worth and how much the saved computer-time is worth.

2. If you were asked to improve the efficiency of a program and you estimated that it would require four hours of your time, figure out how much computer time would have to be saved to make it worthwhile. Use the current programmer-rate for the calculation.

3. By hand-simulating, determine what the following code segments do:

   a)
```
        COMPUTE A = 1.
        PERFORM PARA-X UNTIL (A = 10).
           .
           .
           .
    PARA-X.
        COMPUTE Y = A ** 2.
        MOVE A TO OUT-A.
        MOVE Y TO OUT-Y.
        WRITE PRINT-LINE FROM OUT-LINE
            AFTER ADVANCING 1 LINES.
        COMPUTE A = A + 2.
```

   b)
```
        COMPUTE INTEREST = 0.050
        PERFORM DO-TABLE UNTIL (INTEREST > 0.100).
    DO-TABLE.
        MOVE 100.00 TO OLD-AMOUNT, NEW-AMOUNT.
        MOVE INTEREST TO INTEREST-LN.
        PERFORM DO-INTEREST UNTIL (NEW-AMOUNT > 200.00).
        COMPUTE INTEREST = INTEREST + 0.005.
    DO-INTEREST.
        COMPUTE CALC-INTEREST = INTEREST * OLD-AMOUNT.
        COMPUTE NEW-AMOUNT = CALC-INTEREST + OLD-AMOUNT.
        MOVE OLD-AMOUNT TO OLD-AMOUNT-LN.
        MOVE CALC-INTEREST TO CALC-INTEREST-LN.
        MOVE NEW-AMOUNT TO NEW-AMOUNT-LN.
        WRITE PRINT-LINE FROM DEPOSIT-LINE AFTER ADVANCING 1 LINES.
        MOVE NEW-AMOUNT TO OLD-AMOUNT.
```

   c)
```
        MOVE ZERO TO T.
        PERFORM DO-IT UNTIL (T > 0).
        CLOSE PRINT-LINE.
        STOP RUN.
    DO-IT.
        COMPUTE T = 0.
        COMPUTE Y = T * 4.0.
        MOVE T TO OUT-T.
        MOVE Y TO OUT-Y.
        WRITE PRINT-LINE FROM OUT-LINE
            AFTER ADVANCING 1 LINES.
        COMPUTE T = T + 1.
```

   d)
```
        MOVE 12 TO T.
        MOVE ZERO TO A.
        PERFORM PARA-A UNTIL (T > 10).
        MOVE A TO OUT-A.
        WRITE PRINT-LINE FROM OUT-LINE AFTER ADVANCING 1 LINES.
        CLOSE PRINT-LINE.
        STOP RUN.
    PARA-A.
        ADD 1 TO A.
```

Program Modifications

1. Try to get a feel for how fast your computer is. Modify a program so that one paragraph does only some arithmetic. Do not print the results within the paragraph. For example:

    ```
    CHECK-IT.
        COMPUTE A = A + 1.
        COMPUTE B = A ** 2.
    ```

    Then do the following:

    a) PERFORM the arithmetic paragraph 100 times.

    b) PERFORM the arithmetic paragraph 1000 times.

    c) PERFORM the arithmetic paragraph 10,000 times.

    Print the results only after the PERFORM statement has finished executing. Compare how long each run takes to execute.

2. Do the above using USAGE IS DISPLAY. Then do the same thing using USAGE IS COMPUTA-TIONAL. How much difference does it make? Does it make any difference if you use the sign on the variables?

3. Do the following:

    ```
    SPEED-TEST.
        COMPUTE PAY = HOURS * RATE.
    ```

    Execute it 100 times. Then execute the program a second time, using an ON SIZE ERROR clause. The PAY field must be small enough that a size error could be generated. Make sure HOURS and RATE are defined. Does the execution time vary significantly?

4. Modify Sample Program 9A so that if the amount or the interest rate in the data record is not positive, the program prints the record and an error message, then goes on to the next data-record.

5. Modify Sample Program 9A so that it prints the year for each printed line. If over 25 years are needed for any input record, stop calculating on that record and go to the next record.

6. Modify Sample Program 9A so that instead of calculating the variable TWICE-AMOUNT in the program, the desired amount is read in as data. Use the variable name NEEDED-AMOUNT. Verify that NEEDED-AMOUNT is greater than the deposit amount; otherwise, print an error message and go on to the next data-record.

7. Modify a previous program so that it prints every third record. Run the program to make sure it works. Then modify the program so it prints every tenth record. Did you design generality into the program?

Programs

1. Write a program to process the following information for Intellect Haven College:

Field	Column	Format
Student name	1-30	X(30)
Student number	31-35	X(05)
Score 1	36-38	999
Score 2	39-41	999
Score 3	42-44	999
Score 4	45-47	999

Calculate the average score for each student. Students are allowed to miss one test without having it count against them. Thus, this must be taken into account when averaging. Missed tests are indicated by a test score of zero. Print a report that gives all pertinent information, including the number of tests used. Label your output.

2. For their credit card, Ready-Cash Bank charges a 1.5 percent service-charge on the first $1,000 of the balance due, and 1 percent on the balance due over $1,000. The service charge is calculated on the new balance due (old balance – payment). Any customer with a balance-due of over $2,000 has exceeded the credit limit and should have the additional message EXCEEDED printed on the righthand side of the detail line. The input record is:

Field	Columns
Customer number	1-5
Customer name	6-25
Balance due	26-31
Payment	32-37

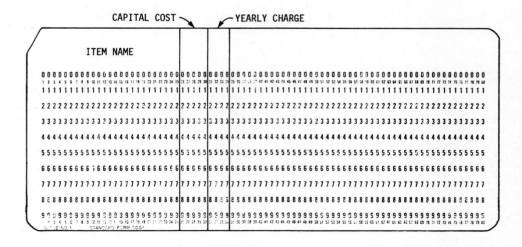

Print and label all fields. Calculate the service charge and new balance due (including the service charge).

3. Write a simple program involving something in which you are interested. Keep the program fairly simple at first, and expand it as you progress in this book.

4. Ready-Cash Bank rents safe-deposit boxes to customers. The bank would like to have a program to see how long it takes the bank to recover its original capital expenses. The input records are:

Field	Columns	
Item name	1–25	
Capital cost	26–30	(dollars)
Yearly charge	31–34	(dollars)

The yearly charge is repeatedly subtracted from capital cost until the capital cost is zero. Since the money used for capital expenses could be used elsewhere, add an 8 percent interest on the present balance at the end of each year. Print all of the information above, including interest, year, and present balance, until the present balance is zero.

Chapter
10

```
*****************************************************
        A young lady robot named Lynch,
        Who longed for an amorous clinch,
           Got wiggly with joy,
           And giggly and coy
        When she felt the economy pinch.

*****************************************************
```

INPUT EDITING

Input data often ends up in large magnetic-tape or disk files. If incorrect input is allowed to get into these files, the files become unreliable and their value decreases drastically. It is very time-consuming and expensive to correct incorrect data-records already in a large data-file. For these reasons, it is important to take measures to avoid incorrect data-records being entered in a large data-file. What must be done is to edit the input before the records are placed in the data-file. This checking of input records is called **input editing** or **input validating**.

In small programs, an additional paragraph or two is used to edit the input records; large systems often use a separate program to edit or validate input-data. Two characteristics are normally checked:

1. Record characteristics.
2. Field characteristics.

RECORD CHARACTERISTICS

Record characteristics are those aspects of the data relating to the structure of each record and the relationships between records. An example is **sequence-checking**: if the records must be in sequence, this can be checked. Another example is that if a single transaction requires two records, the first record must have a 1 in column 80 and the second record must have a 2 in column 80. This can be checked by the program.

FIELD CHARACTERISTICS

Some possible checks of **field characteristics** are:

1. **Missing test**. Normally, each field must have some data: this test checks for empty fields.
2. **Range test**. Most fields can be tested for reasonableness. Some fields have a very restricted choice (e.g., transaction date). Other fields have a wider range (e.g., hours worked). For example, a month field can range from 01–12. Any other value (e.g., 14) would be incorrect.
3. **Code test**. If only certain codes can be used in a field, this test will check for illegal codes.
4. **Character test**. Numeric fields should contain only numbers and a sign. Alphabetic fields should contain only letters. This test checks for incorrect kinds of characters in a field.

****

Computer Graffiti

GIGO—Garbage In, Garbage Out—refers to invalid and mispunched input-data. No matter how good the program is, it can't correct hopelessly incorrect input. When your program abends (*ab*normal *ends*) because of bad input-data, you may find that some computer operator has scribbled GIGO on the report.

****

SAMPLE PROGRAM 10A

Ready-Cash Bank needs a program to edit customer records before the records are put into a master file. Sample Program 10A (**Figure 10.1**) demonstrates how to do input editing. There are several new things going on here. First, the program counts the number of input records. This is done as follows:

```
77 RECORD-COUNT   PICTURE S9(04)   VALUE ZERO.
     .
     .
     .
     READ RECORDS-IN INTO . . .
     ADD 1 TO RECORD-COUNT.
```

The variable **RECORD-COUNT** is declared and initialized to zero. Then each time a record is read, 1 is added to **RECORD-COUNT**. This variable can be used in two ways: (1) when an incorrect record is printed, we can also print the record number so that we know where the incorrect record is in the file; (2) at the end of the job we can print the total number of records read. This is useful information for bookkeeping purposes. The printing of the total number of records is done in the termination paragraph, as follows:

```
ALL-DONE.
     MOVE RECORD-COUNT TO TOTAL-COUNT.
     WRITE PRINT-LINE FROM TOTAL-LINE AFTER ADVANCING 3 LINES.
     CLOSE RECORDS-IN, PRINT-OUT.
     STOP RUN.
```

```
010010 IDENTIFICATION DIVISION.                                          PROGR10A
010020 PROGRAM-ID.                                                       PROGR10A
010030     PROGR10A.                                                     PROGR10A
010040**********************************************************************PROGR10A
010050*     EDIT INPUT RECORDS FOR ERRORS.                              *PROGR10A
010060**********************************************************************PROGR10A
010070                                                                   PROGR10A
010080 ENVIRONMENT DIVISION.                                             PROGR10A
010090 INPUT-OUTPUT SECTION.                                             PROGR10A
010100 FILE-CONTROL.                                                     PROGR10A
010110     SELECT RECORDS-IN,                                            PROGR10A
010120         ASSIGN TO UR-2540R-S-SYSIN.                               PROGR10A
010130     SELECT PRINT-OUT,                                             PROGR10A
010140         ASSIGN TO UR-1403-S-SYSPRINT.                             PROGR10A
010150                                                                   PROGR10A
020010 DATA DIVISION.                                                    PROGR10A
020020 FILE SECTION.                                                     PROGR10A
020030 FD  RECORDS-IN                                                    PROGR10A
020040     LABEL RECORDS ARE OMITTED.                                    PROGR10A
020050 01  IN-RECORD                    PICTURE X(80).                   PROGR10A
020060 FD  PRINT-OUT                                                     PROGR10A
020070     LABEL RECORDS ARE OMITTED.                                    PROGR10A
020080 01  PRINT-LINE                   PICTURE X(133).                  PROGR10A
020090                                                                   PROGR10A
020100 WORKING-STORAGE SECTION.                                          PROGR10A
020110 77  OLD-ACCOUNT                  PICTURE X(05)    VALUE ZERO.     PROGR10A
020120 77  RECORD-COUNT                 PICTURE S9(04)   VALUE ZERO.     PROGR10A
020130                                                                   PROGR10A
020140 01  CUST-REC.                                                     PROGR10A
020150     05  ACCOUNT                  PICTURE X(05).                   PROGR10A
020160     05  NAME                     PICTURE X(20).                   PROGR10A
020170     05  DATES.                                                    PROGR10A
020180         10  MONTHS               PICTURE X(02).                   PROGR10A
020190         10  DAYS                 PICTURE X(02).                   PROGR10A
020200         10  YEARS                PICTURE X(02).                   PROGR10A
020210     05  AMOUNT                   PICTURE X(07).                   PROGR10A
020220     05  FILLER                   PICTURE X(42).                   PROGR10A
020230                                                                   PROGR10A
030010 01  PRINT-CUST-REC.                                               PROGR10A
030020     05  FILLER                   PICTURE X(01).                   PROGR10A
030030     05  RECORD-NUMBER            PICTURE 9(04).                   PROGR10A
030040     05  FILLER                   PICTURE X(05).                   PROGR10A
030050     05  ACCOUNT                  PICTURE X(05).                   PROGR10A
030060     05  FILLER                   PICTURE X(05).                   PROGR10A
030070     05  NAME                     PICTURE X(20).                   PROGR10A
030080     05  FILLER                   PICTURE X(05).                   PROGR10A
030090     05  DATES.                                                    PROGR10A
030100         10  MONTHS               PICTURE X(02).                   PROGR10A
030110         10  FILLER               PICTURE X(01).                   PROGR10A
030120         10  DAYS                 PICTURE X(02).                   PROGR10A
030130         10  FILLER               PICTURE X(01).                   PROGR10A
030140         10  YEARS                PICTURE X(02).                   PROGR10A
030150     05  FILLER                   PICTURE X(05).                   PROGR10A
030160     05  AMOUNT                   PICTURE X(07).                   PROGR10A
030170     05  FILLER                   PICTURE X(05).                   PROGR10A
030180     05  ERROR-MESSAGE            PICTURE X(30).                   PROGR10A
030190     05  FILLER                   PICTURE X(33).                   PROGR10A
030200                                                                   PROGR10A
030210 01  TOTAL-LINE.                                                   PROGR10A
030220     05  FILLER                   PICTURE X(10)    VALUE SPACES.   PROGR10A


030230     05  FILLER                   PICTURE X(12)                    PROGR10A
030240                                  VALUE 'RECORD COUNT'.            PROGR10A
030250     05  TOTAL-COUNT              PICTURE ZZZ9.                    PROGR10A
030260     05  FILLER                   PICTURE X(107)   VALUE SPACES.   PROGR10A
030270                                                                   PROGR10A
040010 PROCEDURE DIVISION.                                               PROGR10A
040020     OPEN INPUT RECORDS-IN, OUTPUT PRINT-OUT.                      PROGR10A
040030     MOVE SPACES TO PRINT-CUST-REC.                                PROGR10A
040040     PERFORM EDIT-FILE 1000 TIMES.                                 PROGR10A
```

```
040050                                                                    PROGR10A
040060  ALL-DONE.                                                         PROGR10A
040070      MOVE RECORD-COUNT TO TOTAL-COUNT.                             PROGR10A
040080      WRITE PRINT-LINE FROM TOTAL-LINE AFTER ADVANCING 3 LINES.     PROGR10A
040090      CLOSE RECORDS-IN, PRINT-OUT.                                  PROGR10A
040100      STOP RUN.                                                     PROGR10A
040110                                                                    PROGR10A
040120  EDIT-FILE.                                                        PROGR10A
040130      READ RECORDS-IN INTO CUST-REC                                 PROGR10A
040140          AT END PERFORM ALL-DONE.                                  PROGR10A
040150      ADD 1 TO RECORD-COUNT.                                        PROGR10A
040160      IF (ACCOUNT OF CUST-REC < OLD-ACCOUNT)                        PROGR10A
040170          MOVE 'RECORDS OUT OF SEQUENCE' TO ERROR-MESSAGE           PROGR10A
040180          PERFORM PRINT-BAD-RECORD.                                 PROGR10A
040190      MOVE ACCOUNT OF CUST-REC TO OLD-ACCOUNT.                      PROGR10A
040200      IF (NAME OF CUST-REC = SPACES)                                PROGR10A
040210          MOVE 'CUSTOMER NAME MISSING' TO ERROR-MESSAGE             PROGR10A
040220          PERFORM PRINT-BAD-RECORD.                                 PROGR10A
040230      IF (MONTHS OF CUST-REC < '01' OR MONTHS OF CUST-REC > '12')   PROGR10A
040240          MOVE 'INVALID MONTH' TO ERROR-MESSAGE                     PROGR10A
040250          PERFORM PRINT-BAD-RECORD.                                 PROGR10A
040260                                                                    PROGR10A
040270  PRINT-BAD-RECORD.                                                 PROGR10A
040280      MOVE RECORD-COUNT TO RECORD-NUMBER.                           PROGR10A
040290      MOVE CORRESPONDING CUST-REC TO PRINT-CUST-REC.                PROGR10A
040300      WRITE PRINT-LINE FROM PRINT-CUST-REC                          PROGR10A
040310          AFTER ADVANCING 1 LINES.                                  PROGR10A
```

FIGURE 10.1   Sample Program 10A

When all records have been read, the **RECORD-COUNT** is moved to a specially set-up print-line for printing the total number of records. Then this total line is printed. The description of the total line is in Program 10A. **Figure 10.2** gives some sample output from this program.

```
0001    00000    00000000000000000000    00 00 00    0000000    INVALID MONTH
0002    07231                            04 23 81    0020000    CUSTOMER NAME MISSING
0003    12547    JERRY LEWIS             00 12 81    0010000    INVALID MONTH
0005    11111    TOM WINGMASTER          13 24 82    0000000    RECORDS OUT OF SEQUENCE
0005    11111    TOM WINGMASTER          13 24 82    0000000    INVALID MONTH
0016    85425    DAN HOLLSWORTH          13 24 82    0005000    INVALID MONTH

        RECORD COUNT    16
```

FIGURE 10.2   **Output from Program 10A**

The next new thing done in Program 10A is sequence-checking of the input records. The records in an input file are ordinarily in a particular order; thus, it is common to have the program verify that the input file is actually in sequence. The input file for this program is supposed to be in customer-account-number sequence. The sequence-checking is done as follows:

```
77 OLD-ACCOUNT   PICTURE X(05)   VALUE ZERO.
      .
      .
      .
    IF (ACCOUNT OF CUST-REC < OLD-ACCOUNT)
        MOVE 'RECORDS OUT OF SEQUENCE' TO ERROR-MESSAGE
        PERFORM PRINT-BAD-RECORD.
    MOVE ACCOUNT OF CUST-REC TO OLD-ACCOUNT.
```

First, a 77-level variable is declared and initialized to zero. (It must be initialized to zero so that the program will have something with which to compare the first record's account number.) The IF statement compares the account number of the record read to the value of the OLD-ACCOUNT. If the records are out of sequence, an error message is printed. Next, the account number of the present record is moved to OLD-ACCOUNT so that the next record can be compared to it.

Two other checks are done in this program. First, the customer name is checked to make sure it is not blank. If there is no customer name, an error message is printed. The second check is done on the month in the date field: months should always be between 01 and 12; anything else would be an error. The month is verified by the program; if it is incorrect, an error message is printed. These checks are done as follows:

```
IF (NAME OF CUST-REC = SPACES)
    MOVE 'CUSTOMER NAME MISSING' TO ERROR-MESSAGE
    PERFORM PRINT-BAD-RECORD.
IF (MONTH OF CUST-REC < '01' OR MONTH OF CUST-REC > '12')
    MOVE 'INVALID MONTH' TO ERROR-MESSAGE
    PERFORM PRINT-BAD-RECORD.
```

Notice that the month field is specified to be alphanumeric (i.e., PICTURE X(02)). Even though any correct month will be numeric, it would be unwise to use a numeric specification because an invalidly typed month could contain alphabetic characters. Since the month field is declared alphanumeric, the comparison must be done by using a character string '01' instead of a number 01.

Note:

1. It is usually best to use alphanumeric fields, not numeric fields (e.g., PICTURE XX, not PICTURE 99), when doing input editing for errors.

2. When testing your program you must have sufficient test-data to test both the error situation and the correct situation. Otherwise, you will never know if the program works in both situations.

REVIEW

1. Find a computer-generated transaction, such as a bill, and indicate how the input record could be checked for errors.

2. Sequence-checking of records is done with the following code:

```
IF (ACCOUNT OF CUST-REC < OLD-ACCOUNT)
    MOVE 'RECORDS OUT OF SEQUENCE' TO ERROR-MESSAGE
    PERFORM PRINT-BAD-RECORD.
MOVE ACCOUNT OF CUST-REC TO OLD-ACCOUNT.
```

The statements above always save the old account-number, even when the file is out of sequence. Moving the account number only when the file was in sequence could be done by dropping the period at the end of the IF statement and using an ELSE MOVE ACCOUNT . . . . Which of the two methods do you think would work better?

Program Modifications

1. Modify Sample Program 10A as follows:

    a) The name field is sometimes punched starting in the wrong column. Check the first column of the customer-name field to make sure it is not blank.

    b) Check for duplicate records. If the account number is the same on two succeeding records, this indicates a duplicate record.

2. Modify Sample Program 10A as follows:

    a) Finish checking the date field, that is, check the day field and year field to make sure they are reasonable.

    b) The minimum customer-transaction is $100.00. Check this.

    c) Any amount over $10,000 may be an error. Print these records so they can be hand-checked.

3. Modify Sample Name-and-Address Program 4B to check for duplicates. If the name field is the same or the street field is the same in two consecutive records, print those records so that they can be checked for possible elimination. Print the total number of records read.

CLASS TEST

If a program is run that has alphabetic data in a numeric field, the program will stop executing each time arithmetic is done with this invalid data. The incorrect data-record must be corrected and the program rerun. If there are ten incorrect data-records in the file, then the program must be run eleven times before a successful run will be completed. This is obviously a very expensive way to get things done. The COBOL language provides an easier way to detect incorrect characters in data fields.

The IF statement can be used to check variables to see whether the value stored in the variable is numeric or alphabetic. Remember, these are the criteria for distinguishing numeric from alphabetic characters:

NUMERIC   The numbers 0 through 9 only, with or without a sign.

ALPHABETIC   The characters A through Z and blank spaces only.

The **alphabetic test** can be performed only on alphabetic variables, that is, variables with PICTURE X or A. The **numeric test** *cannot* be performed on variables with a PICTURE A. Here is a table of valid comparisons:

Type of Field	Valid Tests	
Alphabetic PICTURE A	ALPHABETIC	NOT ALPHABETIC
Alphanumeric PICTURE X	ALPHABETIC NUMERIC	NOT ALPHABETIC NOT NUMERIC
Numeric PICTURE 9	NUMERIC	NOT NUMERIC

The general format for the class test is:

$$\underline{IF}\quad identifier\ IS\ \underline{NOT}\ ]\ \left\{ \begin{array}{l} \underline{NUMERIC} \\ \underline{ALPHABETIC} \end{array} \right\}\ \cdots$$

The identifier being tested with a class test must be declared, implicitly or explicitly, as USAGE DISPLAY. An example of a class test is:

```
IF (ACCOUNT OF CUST-REC IS NOT NUMERIC)
    MOVE 'INVALID ACCOUNT NUMBER' TO ERROR-MESSAGE
    PERFORM PRINT-BAD-RECORD.
```

This checks the account number to verify that it is numeric. If it is not numeric, an error message is printed.

Class tests are often used to check input data for typing errors. If input data is not checked before it is processed, a great deal of computer time is wasted in processing incorrect input-data. The numeric test is more useful than the alphabetic test. An invalid character in a numeric field will usually cause the program to stop executing, while an incorrect alphabetic field usually does not stop the execution of the program. Also, there are few "pure" alphabetic fields. Name fields often contain dashes, apostrophes, and periods, so they cannot be tested as alphabetic. Notice that NOT ALPHABETIC is not the same as NUMERIC and vice versa: for example, the data value X.5Y2 is NOT ALPHABETIC and NOT NUMERIC. Here are some examples:

ZAP *Storage* *Contents*	IF ZAP IS NUMERIC	IF ZAP IS ALPHABETIC
1234	True	False
ABC	False	True
AB23	False	False
2 45	False	False
A-B	False	False

Note:

1. The numeric test can be done only on variables with an alphanumeric or numeric PICTURE (PICTURE A not allowed). For a true condition, *all* characters in the field must be numeric.
2. The alphabetic test can be done only on variables with PICTURE X or A. For a true condition, *all* characters in the field must be alphabetic.
3. If numeric values are signed, the PICTURE clause must have an S.
4. The variable being tested must be declared (implicitly or explicitly) as USAGE DISPLAY.

SAMPLE PROGRAM 10B

The Ready-Cash Bank manager liked the previous editing program, but some of the clerks pointed out that illegal characters (e.g., alphabetic characters in numeric fields) were not discovered by the other editing program. Now we must edit for illegal characters. In this program the account number of the customer record is checked to make sure that it is numeric. The customer name is checked to make

```
*********************************************************
              *** THE FIVE STEP JOB ***

           UH–OH, WOULDN'T YOU KNOW,
             A FIVE STEP JOB IS MY WOE.
           SIT DOWN, CODE, CRUNCH AWAY,
             THE MACHINE IS DOWN HALF THE DAY.
           FLOW CHART, KEYPUNCH, PRINT DESIGN,
             AND HOPE THE SYSTEM'S UP BY NINE.
           NOW THE READER FACES YOU.
             TRY TO GUESS WHAT IT WILL DO.
           READ CHECK, PICK CHECK, STACK CHECK, STOP.
             REREAD THE CARD THAT'S ON TOP.
           YOU CAN SCREAM & KICK & SOB,
             YOU STILL MUST RUN YOUR FIVE STEP JOB.

           ERROR  ERROR  –  JCL
             FROM  I E H  TO  I E L.
           COUNT TO 10; THROW A FIT;
             CORRECT YOUR JOB AND RESUBMIT.

           BY NOW YOUR EYES ARE GETTING RED.
             NOT ONLY THAT—YOU AIN'T BEEN FED.
           WAIT AND WAIT; STAND AROUND,
             UNTIL HASP SAY'S YOUR JOB'S NOT FOUND.
           STATEMENTS WRONG, STATEMENTS IGNORED,
             AT LEAST THE COMPILER WASN'T BORED.
           NOW YOU KNOW YOU CANNOT WIN,
             BUT JUST THE SAME YOU RUN AGAIN.

           THREE-TWENTY-TWO; EIGHT-O-FOUR;
             RAN OUT OF TIME; RAN OUT OF CORE;
           RAN OUT OF PATIENCE; RAN OUT OF STRENGTH;
             RAN OUT OF KNOWLEDGE; RAN OUT OF SENSE;
           RAN OUT OF TEARS; RAN OUT OF HOPE;
           NO TIME TO SPARE; NO TIME TO ROB;
             YOU STILL MUST RUN YOUR FIVE STEP JOB.


*********************************************************
```

sure that it is alphabetic. If either is incorrect, the record is printed along with a error message. Here are those statements:

```
IF (ACCOUNT OF CUST-REC IS NOT NUMERIC)
    MOVE 'INVALID ACCOUNT NUMBER' TO ERROR-MESSAGE
    PERFORM PRINT-BAD-RECORD.
IF (NAME OF CUST-REC NOT ALPHABETIC)
    MOVE 'CHECK CUSTOMER NAME' TO ERROR-MESSAGE
    PERFORM PRINT-BAD-RECORD.
```

It is important that the error message describe exactly what is incorrect so that the clerk correcting the bad records can easily locate and correct the error. (**Figure 10.3** is the sample program. **Figure 10.4** is some sample output.)

```
.010010 IDENTIFICATION DIVISION.                                      PROGR10B
010020 PROGRAM-ID.                                                    PROGR10B
010030     PROGR10B.                                                  PROGR10B
010040************************************************************PROGR10B
010050*    EDIT INPUT RECORDS FOR ERRORS.                         *PROGR10B
010060************************************************************PROGR10B
010070 ENVIRONMENT DIVISION.                                          PROGR10B
010080 INPUT-OUTPUT SECTION.                                          PROGR10B
010090 FILE-CONTROL.                                                  PROGR10B
010100     SELECT RECORDS-IN,                                         PROGR10B
010110        ASSIGN TO UR-2540R-S-SYSIN.                             PROGR10B
010120     SELECT PRINT-OUT,                                          PROGR10B
010130        ASSIGN TO UR-1403-S-SYSPRINT.                           PROGR10B
010140                                                                PROGR10B
020010 DATA DIVISION.                                                 PROGR10B
020020 FILE SECTION.                                                  PROGR10B
020030 FD  RECORDS-IN                                                 PROGR10B
020040     LABEL RECORDS ARE OMITTED.                                 PROGR10B
020050 01  IN-RECORD                PICTURE X(80).                    PROGR10B
020060 FD  PRINT-OUT                                                  PROGR10B
020070     LABEL RECORDS ARE OMITTED.                                 PROGR10B
020080 01  PRINT-LINE               PICTURE X(133).                   PROGR10B
020090                                                                PROGR10B
020100 WORKING-STORAGE SECTION.                                       PROGR10B
020110 77  OLD-ACCOUNT              PICTURE X(05)   VALUE ZERO.       PROGR10B
020120 77  RECORD-COUNT             PICTURE S9(04)  VALUE ZERO.       PROGR10B
020130                                                                PROGR10B
020140 01  CUST-REC.                                                  PROGR10B
020150     05  ACCOUNT              PICTURE X(05).                    PROGR10B
020160     05  NAME                 PICTURE X(20).                    PROGR10B
020170     05  DATES.                                                 PROGR10B
020180         10  MONTHS           PICTURE X(02).                    PROGR10B
020190         10  DAYS             PICTURE X(02).                    PROGR10B
020200         10  YEARS            PICTURE X(02).                    PROGR10B
020210     05  AMOUNT               PICTURE X(07).                    PROGR10B
020220     05  FILLER               PICTURE X(42).                    PROGR10B
020230                                                                PROGR10B
030010 01  PRINT-CUST-REC.                                            PROGR10B
030020     05  FILLER               PICTURE X(01).                    PROGR10B
030030     05  RECORD-NUMBER        PICTURE 9(04).                    PROGR10B
030040     05  FILLER               PICTURE X(05).                    PROGR10B
030050     05  ACCOUNT              PICTURE X(05).                    PROGR10B
030060     05  FILLER               PICTURE X(05).                    PROGR10B
030070     05  NAME                 PICTURE X(20).                    PROGR10B
030080     05  FILLER               PICTURE X(05).                    PROGR10B
030090     05  DATES.                                                 PROGR10B
030100         10  MONTHS           PICTURE X(02).                    PROGR10B
030110         10  FILLER           PICTURE X(01).                    PROGR10B
030120         10  DAYS             PICTURE X(02).                    PROGR10B
030130         10  FILLER           PICTURE X(01).                    PROGR10B
030140         10  YEARS            PICTURE X(02).                    PROGR10B
030150     05  FILLER               PICTURE X(05).                    PROGR10B
030160     05  AMOUNT               PICTURE X(07).                    PROGR10B
030170     05  FILLER               PICTURE X(05).                    PROGR10B
030180     05  ERROR-MESSAGE        PICTURE X(30).                    PROGR10B
030190     05  FILLER               PICTURE X(33).                    PROGR10B
030200                                                                PROGR10B
030210 01  TOTAL-LINE.                                                PROGR10B
030220     05  FILLER               PICTURE X(10)   VALUE SPACES.     PROGR10B
030230     05  FILLER               PICTURE X(12)                     PROGR10B
030240                              VALUE 'RECORD COUNT'.             PROGR10B
030250     05  TOTAL-COUNT          PICTURE ZZZ9.                     PROGR10B
030260     05  FILLER               PICTURE X(107)  VALUE SPACES.     PROGR10B
030270                                                                PROGR10B
040010 PROCEDURE DIVISION.                                            PROGR10B
040020     OPEN INPUT RECORDS-IN, OUTPUT PRINT-OUT.                   PROGR10B
```

```
040030        MOVE SPACES TO PRINT-CUST-REC.                              PROGR10B
040040        PERFORM EDIT-FILE 1000 TIMES.                               PROGR10B
040050                                                                    PROGR10B
040060 ALL-DONE.                                                          PROGR10B
040070        MOVE RECORD-COUNT TO TOTAL-COUNT.                           PROGR10B
040080        WRITE PRINT-LINE FROM TOTAL-LINE AFTER ADVANCING 3 LINES.   PROGR10B
040090        CLOSE RECORDS-IN, PRINT-OUT.                                PROGR10B
040100        STOP RUN.                                                   PROGR10B
040110                                                                    PROGR10B
040120 EDIT-FILE.                                                         PROGR10B
040130        READ RECORDS-IN INTO CUST-REC                              PROGR10B
040140            AT END PERFORM ALL-DONE.                                PROGR10B
040150        ADD 1 TO RECORD-COUNT.                                      PROGR10B
040160        IF (ACCOUNT OF CUST-REC < OLD-ACCOUNT)                      PROGR10B
040170           MOVE 'RECORDS OUT OF SEQUENCE' TO ERROR-MESSAGE          PROGR10B
040180           PERFORM PRINT-BAD-RECORD.                                PROGR10B
040190        MOVE ACCOUNT OF CUST-REC TO OLD-ACCOUNT.                    PROGR10B
040200        IF (ACCOUNT OF CUST-REC IS NOT NUMERIC)                     PROGR10B
040210           MOVE 'INVALID ACCOUNT NUMBER' TO ERROR-MESSAGE           PROGR10B
040220           PERFORM PRINT-BAD-RECORD.                                PROGR10B
040230        IF (NAME OF CUST-REC NOT ALPHABETIC)                        PROGR10B
040240           MOVE 'CHECK CUSTOMER NAME' TO ERROR-MESSAGE              PROGR10B
040250           PERFORM PRINT-BAD-RECORD.                                PROGR10B
040260                                                                    PROGR10B
040270 PRINT-BAD-RECORD.                                                  PROGR10B
040280        MOVE RECORD-COUNT TO RECORD-NUMBER.                         PROGR10B
040290        MOVE CORRESPONDING CUST-REC TO PRINT-CUST-REC.              PROGR10B
040300        WRITE PRINT-LINE FROM PRINT-CUST-REC                        PROGR10B
040310            AFTER ADVANCING 1 LINES.                                PROGR10B
```

FIGURE 10.3   Sample Program 10B

```
0001    00000    00000000000000000000    00 00 00    0000000    CHECK CUSTOMER NAME
0005    11111    TOM WINGMASTER          13 24 82    0000000    RECORDS OUT OF SEQUENCE
0007    42578    TH3MAS ABRAHAMS         12 19 82    0000400    CHECK CUSTOMER NAME
0008    4521M    ARY ANN NELSON          05 24 80    0050000    INVALID ACCOUNT NUMBER
0009    4521M    ARY ANN NELSON          05 24 80    0050000    INVALID ACCOUNT NUMBER
0010    521A2    HARRY WILLOWS           12 02 82    0025000    INVALID ACCOUNT NUMBER

        RECORD COUNT    16
```

FIGURE 10.4   Output from Program 10B

SIGNED FIELDS

Signed fields cause special problems in numeric fields when you are doing a class test. This is because the sign is stored as the rightmost position in a numeric field. Thus, the rightmost digit of a numeric signed field looks like an alphabetic character. To make matters even worse, there is some variance, depending on the machine, on how the class test is done with signed numeric fields. The following rules will work for most computers:

1. A numeric field with a sign (e.g., PICTURE S99) may contain a sign in the data and still be considered numeric.

2. An alphanumeric (e.g., PICTURE XX) field may not have a sign in the data, or it will be evaluated as NOT NUMERIC.

REVIEW

1. Why is it usually necessary to use the alphanumeric (e.g., **PICTURE X**) specification on numeric fields when editing input for errors?

2. Locate a copy of the manufacturer-supplied COBOL language-manual for your compiler. Find out how signed numbers are treated in the class test.

3. The sample programs in this chapter provide a count of the total number of records read. It would be nice if the program could provide a total of the number of invalid records processed. We cannot simply total how many times a bad record is printed to get a total of invalid records, because a single record can have several errors in it and thus be printed several times. See if you can figure out how to print a total of invalid records processed. (In Chapter 12 we will cover switches, and then it will be easy to do.)

4. One way to improve the correctness of input data is to improve the environment in which the data-entry operators work. A good source of information on this subject is *Humanized Input: Techniques for Reliable Input* by Tom Gilb and Gerald M. Weinberg (Cambridge, Mass.: Winthrop, 1977).

5. *Reserved words.* Different COBOL compilers have different reserved words. All COBOL compilers agree on about 97 percent of the reserved words, but each manufacturer adds a few language extensions or drops a few extensions and thus changes the list of reserved words. Sample Program 8B uses the word **DAYS** as a variable name. On a few compilers **DAY** is a reserved word. Check this on your compiler. Have you found any other reserved words that were not in the reserved-word list in this book?

Program Modifications

1. Modify Sample Program 10A as follows:

   a) The account number now has an alphabetic character in the first column and numbers in the rest of the columns. Verify this.

   b) Check the amount field to make sure it is numeric.

2. In Program 10A we had the following statement:

   ```
   IF (MONTH OF CUST-REC < '01' OR MONTH OF CUST-REC > '12')
       MOVE 'INVALID MONTH' TO ERROR-MESSAGE
       PERFORM PRINT-BAD-RECORD.
   ```

   Will this statement completely verify that the month field contains only allowable months? What will happen if the month is typed as '1A'—will the program accept or reject this month? Modify Program 10A so that only numeric months are accepted. (Use a class test.)

3. Edit the payroll records used in Sample Program 7A, using some of the techniques covered in this chapter.

4. Modify a sample program to determine exactly how signed data is handled. Check the following, using the class test **NUMERIC**:

Field Type	Use
PICTURE XX	Unsigned data
PICTURE 99	Unsigned data
PICTURE S99	Signed data

****

A Diversion: What Next?

By now you should have some idea of whether you are interested in computer programming as a career. If you are interested, you may wonder what courses to take next, besides the obvious data-processing or computer-science classes.

If your mathematical background is a little sketchy, you might take a business math class. Some accounting classes would also be useful, since COBOL is heavily used for generating accounting reports. If you are mathematically inclined, you might consider a statistics class, since a lot of statistical processing uses computers.

****

REDEFINES

The **REDEFINES** clause is used when the same storage area is to be referred to by two different variable names, or when it is desirable to describe the same storage area in two different ways. For example, the **REDEFINES** clause can be used to provide a numeric and an alphabetic declaration of the same data-item. The general format is:

> level-number   data-name-1   <u>REDEFINES</u>   data-name-2.

Data-name-1 is the new name for the same storage area. **Data-name-2** is a previously defined storage area which must immediately precede this declaration. The two data-names must have the same level-numbers. The **REDEFINES** simply puts two different names (and sometimes a different format) on the same area of storage. Here is an example:

```
05 RATE-1                   PICTURE 99V99.
05 RATE-2 REDEFINES RATE-1  PICTURE 999V9.
```

If the two lines above were part of the input record, they would count as only four columns of the input record. But notice that the PICTUREs are different in the two fields. Sometimes you have a file which has two different types of input field, depending on some character of the record. This could be handled by describing two distinct record-formats, as follows:

```
01 RATE1-RECORD.
   05 FILLER              PICTURE X(10).
   05 QUANTITY            PICTURE 999.
   05 RATE-1              PICTURE 99V99.
   05 FILLER              PICTURE X(62).
   05 RECORD-TYPE         PICTURE X.
01 RATE2-RECORD.
   05 FILLER              PICTURE X(10).
   05 QUANTITY            PICTURE 999.
   05 RATE-2              PICTURE 999V9.
   05 FILLER              PICTURE X(62).
   05 RECORD TYPE         PICTURE X.
```

Notice that the record descriptions above are the same except that the **PICTURE** of **RATE-1** differs from that of **RATE-2**. The **RECORD-TYPE** field could be used to determine which record-format to use; if this field is a 1, we use the first record-description; if **RECORD-TYPE** is a 2, we use the second record-description. In COBOL, by using the **REDEFINES** clause, we can simplify the example above, as follows:

```
01 RATE-RECORD.
   05 FILLER              PICTURE X(10).
   05 QUANTITY            PICTURE 999.
```

```
   05 RATE-1                         PICTURE 99V99.
   05 RATE-2 REDEFINES RATE-1        PICTURE 999V9.
```

```
   05 FILLER              PICTURE X(62).
   05 RECORD-TYPE         PICTURE X.
      .
      .
      .
   IF RECORD-TYPE = '1' COMPUTE DUE-AMOUNT = RATE-1 * QUANTITY
   ELSE COMPUTE OVER-AMOUNT = RATE-2 * QUANTITY.
```

In the example above, if the **RECORD-TYPE** is 1 we use the format of **RATE-1** for our calculations; otherwise, we use the format of **RATE-2**.

Both group and elementary fields can be redefined. For example:

```
   05 EMPLOYEE-TYPE       PICTURE X.
   05 REGULAR-EMPLOYEE.
      10 SALARY           PICTURE 9999V99.
      10 BONUS            PICTURE 999V99.
   05 TEMP-EMPLOYEE REDEFINES REGULAR-EMPLOYEE.
      10 HOURS            PICTURE 99V9.
      10 RATE             PICTURE 99V99.
      10 FILLER           PICTURE X(04).
```

In the example above a group item is redefined. As you see, the REDEFINES clause can be used to provide an alternate grouping of the same data area. A redefined item must be the same length as the redefining item, which is why the FILLER is needed to fill out the group item TEMP-EMPLOYEE. Pictorially, the storage locations are:

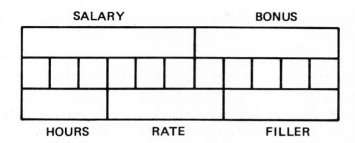

When one field redefines another field, both fields must be at the same level. Also, the redefining field must immediately follow the field being redefined.

The redefining entry cannot contain a VALUE clause, but the field being redefined can contain a VALUE clause. For example:

```
05 FIELD-Z    PICTURE 99    VALUE 16.
05 FIELD-T    PICTURE XX    REDEFINES FIELD-Z.
```

It is acceptable for the first field to contain a VALUE clause, but FIELD-T cannot contain a VALUE clause, which makes sense when you consider that the REDEFINES clause simply puts two data-names on the same area of storage. If each data-name had a VALUE clause, there would be two values stored in the same location. For example:

Incorrect

```
05 ALPHA                    PICTURE XX    VALUE 'T1'.
05 BETA REDEFINES ALPHA     PICTURE XX    VALUE '16'.
```

The example above indicates that two different values, 'T1' and '16', are to be stored in the same location. This is obviously impossible.

Note:

1. The REDEFINES clause can be used at either the group or the elementary level.
2. When a field is redefined, the redefining entry and the field being redefined must be on the same level. The two fields must also be of the same length.
3. The redefining field must immediately follow the field being redefined.
4. The redefining entry must not contain a VALUE clause, but the field being redefined can contain a VALUE clause.

Computer Graffiti

Never trust the data!

EXAMINE

The **EXAMINE** verb is available in the ANSI 1968 COBOL compilers. The ANSI 1974 COBOL compilers replaced the **EXAMINE** verb with the similar but more powerful **INSPECT** verb (which is explained in the next section). Some compilers have both the **EXAMINE** and **INSPECT** verbs. Many computer installations still use the ANSI 1968 COBOL compilers because they were distributed free with the purchase of a computer, while the newer ANSI 1974 COBOL compilers have to be purchased separately.

The **EXAMINE** verb is used for replacing a specified character with a different character. The general format for this statement is:

```
EXAMINE identifier REPLACING
( ALL      )
( LEADING  )
( FIRST    }  literal-1
( UNTIL FIRST )

BY     literal-2.
```

This version of the **EXAMINE** statement is commonly used to replace blank spaces with zeros in numeric fields. An example would be:

    EXAMINE COST REPLACING ALL SPACES BY ZEROS.

After this statement has been executed, any blank spaces will have been changed to zeros. Blank spaces, invalid in numeric fields, are often erroneously left there.

TABLE 10.1   EXAMINE REPLACING EXAMPLES

EXAMINE *Statement*	Z *(before)*	Z *(after)*
EXAMINE Z REPLACING ALL ' ' BY '0'.	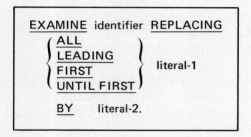	001207
EXAMINE Z REPLACING ALL ' ' BY '-'.	503 99 8765	503-99-8765
EXAMINE Z REPLACING LEADING ZEROS BY '*'.	001204	**1204
EXAMINE Z REPLACING FIRST '0' BY '$'.	DL061208	DL$61208
EXAMINE Z REPLACING UNTIL FIRST '0' BY '*'.	X10160	**0160

The **EXAMINE** statement can be used to insert hyphens in a field. For example:

```
05  SOC-SEC-NO          PICTURE X(09).
05  SOC-SEC-B           PICTURE XXXBXXBXXXX.
    .
    .
    .
    MOVE SOC-SEC-NO TO SOC-SEC-B.
    EXAMINE SOC-SEC-B REPLACING ALL SPACES BY '-'.
```

The **MOVE** statement moves **SOC-SEC-NO** to **SOC-SEC-B** and edits in blank spaces with the **B** edit character. Then the **EXAMINE** statement is used to insert hyphens in the blank spaces.

Any literal used in the **EXAMINE** statement must be of the same class (numeric or alphanumeric) as the field being examined. This means that you cannot replace spaces by zeros in a numeric field. You can get around this restriction by redefining the numeric field as an alphanumeric field. For example:

```
05  PRICE                    PICTURE 9999V99.
05  PRICE-A REDEFINES PRICE  PICTURE X(06).
    .
    .
    .
    EXAMINE PRICE-A REPLACING ALL SPACES BY ZEROS.
```

After the **EXAMINE** statement has been executed, the numeric field **PRICE** will have no blank spaces in it because it was redefined as **PRICE-A**, and all the blank spaces were removed from **PRICE-A** by the **EXAMINE** statement. Now **PRICE** can safely be used as a numeric field.

Note:

1. The identifier being examined must be usage **DISPLAY** (explicitly or implicitly).
2. Any literal used in the statement must be of the same class as the field being examined (numeric or alphanumeric).

INSPECT

The **INSPECT** statement is available on newer COBOL compilers. It is similar to the **EXAMINE** statement. The general format is:

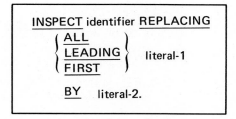

```
INSPECT identifier REPLACING
 ⎧ ALL     ⎫
 ⎨ LEADING ⎬  literal-1
 ⎩ FIRST   ⎭

 BY  literal-2.
```

This form of the **INSPECT** statement works exactly the same as the **EXAMINE** statement discussed above.

Both the EXAMINE and the INSPECT statements have other forms and options not described here. The other forms can count the number of times a specified character occurs in a field, as well as replacing characters. For more information, consult the manufacturer's COBOL manual.

CHAPTER REVIEW

Vocabulary Review

Input editing (input validating)   Missing test   Character test
Record characteristics   Range test   Alphabetic test
Sequence-checking   Code test   Numeric test
Field characteristics

Review Questions

1. Explain:

    a) NUMERIC
    b) ALPHABETIC
    c) NOT NUMERIC
    d) NOT ALPHABETIC

2. Give examples of data which would satisfy each of the class tests in question 1. What type of PICTURE can each of the conditions above test? Give an example of data that is NOT NUMERIC and NOT ALPHABETIC.

3. Give a data value and the necessary PICTURE for each of the following data-classes (for example, 77 A PICTURE 99 VALUE 16.):

    a) NUMERIC.
    b) NOT NUMERIC.
    c) NOT NUMERIC, NOT ALPHABETIC.
    d) ALPHABETIC.

4. When the class test is used, what USAGE must be declared for the variable? What characters may an item being tested as numeric contain?

5. If a numeric item has a sign, and the PICTURE clause does not have an S, what will happen when the class test is done?

6. Given the following declarations, which of the following class tests are valid? Which are invalid? If the test is valid, what will be the result (true or false) of the class test?

```
77 A  PICTURE 999V99      VALUE 16.0.
77 B  PICTURE A(04)       VALUE 'TED'.
77 C  PICTURE X(04)       VALUE '2116'.
77 D  PICTURE X(04)       VALUE 'R2D2'.

IF (A IS NUMERIC)              . . .
IF (A IS NOT NUMERIC)          . . .
IF (A IS ALPHABETIC)           . . .
IF (A IS NOT ALPHABETIC)       . . .
```

(Do the same for variables **B**, **C**, and **D**.)

7. Why is the **REDEFINES** clause used? Where must it be placed? Can a **VALUE** clause be used in a redefined variable or in the variable being redefined? Why is it invalid to have a **VALUE** clause in both the redefined and redefining variables?

```
05  ZEP                   PICTURE X(07).
05  ZAP REDEFINES ZEP.
    10  ZAP-1             PICTURE 999.
    10  ZAP-2             PICTURE X(04).
```

Rewrite the code above so that **ZAP** is defined first and **ZEP** is defined last.

8. Write pseudo-code for a program which reads three numbers in each record. The three numbers can be in any sequence, but the program should print out the three numbers in numeric order.

9. Why is the **EXAMINE** or **INSPECT** statement used? Look up the **EXAMINE** or **INSPECT** verb in the manufacturer's COBOL manual to find out what other forms are available.

Program Modifications

1. Modify Sample Program 8A so that the rate and hours fields are checked to make sure they are numeric. If either one is not numeric, use zero for the value in that field and print the warning message **BAD DATA** on the righthand side of that printed line.

2. Modify one of your older programs as follows:

   a) An input field is declared numeric (**PICTURE 9**s) and the input is not numeric. Use the data in a calculation.

   b) An input field is declared alphabetic (**PICTURE A**) and the input is numeric.

   Do each of the modifications above as a separate run to see what happens when erroneous data is processed.

3. *Errors.* A numeric class test cannot be done on an alphabetic field (e.g., **PICTURE AA**). An alphabetic test cannot be done on a numeric field (e.g., **PICTURE 99**). Try each of these incorrect tests in a separate run to see what happens.

4. Modify Sample Program 10B so that:

   a) If the amount field is numeric, it prints the field, using **PICTURE $99999.99**.

   b) Otherwise, it prints the amount field, using **PICTURE X(09)**.

5. Find out whether your COBOL compiler uses the EXAMINE or the INSPECT verb. One way to find out would be to try using them both in a program. If one is not available, you should get a syntax error message.

6. Modify Program 10B so that any blank spaces in the AMOUNT field are changed to zeros. Use the EXAMINE or INSPECT verb and use some good test-data.

7. Do the previous modification, and also edit the AMOUNT field so that a decimal point and comma print. Do the output editing using standard edit characters. The AMOUNT field will have to be a numeric field.

8. Modify Program 10B so that all blank spaces in the NAME field are changed to dollar signs. Change the first letter A to a #. Print the record before and after it is changed so that you can verify that the modification works.

9. Modify Program 10B so that check protection is provided in the printed AMOUNT field, that is, place a dollar sign on the left and asterisks in the leftmost zero positions. Use the EXAMINE or INSPECT statement to insert these edit characters.

10. Modify Program 10B so that the date field is printed with dashes between the month, day, and year. Use the EXAMINE or INSPECT verb.

Programs

1. The following input records are to be edited:

Field	Columns	
Employee number	1–5	
Employee name	6–25	
Date	26–31	(MMDDYY)
Department code	32–34	
Pay rate	35–38	(two decimal-places)
Hours worked	39–41	(two decimal-places)

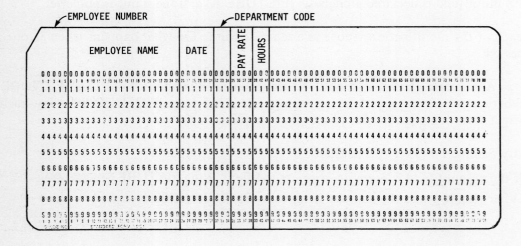

Employee numbers must be in ascending order. Possible department-codes are: 101, 102, 103, 104. Hours are the number of hours worked in one week. Pay rate is hourly pay. Print only the questionable records. Print an error message that indicates what is wrong.

2. The following input record is to be edited:

Field	Columns	
Name	1-20	
Date	21-26	(MMDDYY)
Age	27-29	
Weight	30-32	
Country of birth	33-34	

NAME | DATE | AGE | WEIGHT | COUNTRY

These are high-school seniors' records. The date is the record date. Write a program that will print only the questionable records. Remember, it is better to print a correct record than to miss an incorrect record. Sequence-number records and print the record number of each incorrect record.

3. Process the following data-records:

Field	Input Columns		Output Columns
Production code	1-5		1-5
Description	6-25		11-30
Discount price	26-31	(9999V99)	37-42
Discount rate	26-28	(V999)	—
Retail price	32-37	(9999V99)	49-54
Record type	80		

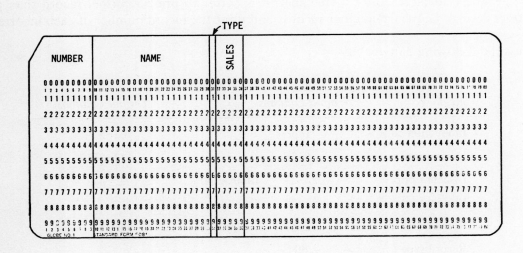

If the record-type field has an **R** in it, the discount price is calculated as follows:

Discount price = Retail price * Discount rate

If the record-type field does not have an **R** in it, use the discount price in the discount-price field in the input record.

4. Write a program to calculate employees' pay, using the following input-records:

Field	Input Columns	
Employee number	1–9	
Employee name	10–30	
Employee type	31	(P or T)
Sales	32–36	

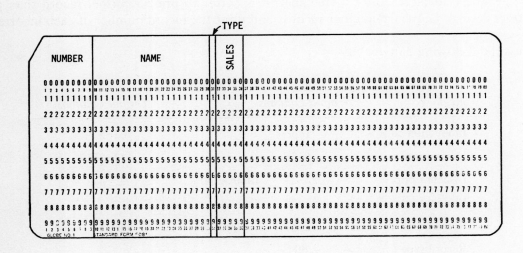

Permanent employees (P in column 31)

Base salary	39–41
Commission rate	42–44 (three decimal-places)

Temporary employees (T in column 31)

Hours	39–41 (one decimal-place)
Rate	42–45 (two decimal-places)

Calculate the pay for permanent employees by adding base salary to (commission rate × sales). For temporary employees, use (hours × rate) to get their pay. Print and label all fields.

****

A robot and man in his prime
Fought often; and at such a time
The man called him "hardware,"
The can called him "software,"
(And this has been hellish to rhyme!).

****

TOTALS AND HEADINGS

When a report is run, it is usually desirable to have a final total printed at the bottom of the report. For example, in Chapter 9 we calculated a payroll; we will need a final total for the pay. In order to accumulate pay we must set up a level-number-77 item to accumulate the total. Here is what we need:

```
77 GROSS-PAY      PICTURE S999V99       VALUE ZERO.
77 TOTAL-PAY      PICTURE S99999V99     VALUE ZERO.
        .
        .
        .
    COMPUTE GROSS-PAY = HOURS * RATE.
    ADD GROSS-PAY TO TOTAL-PAY.
```

We need the variable **TOTAL-PAY** to accumulate the pay for all individuals. This type of variable is usually called an **accumulator**. After the individual's pay has been calculated, the pay is added to **TOTAL-PAY**. Notice that **TOTAL-PAY** must be initialized to zero by a **VALUE** clause; otherwise, **TOTAL-PAY** would be undefined.

GROSS-PAY cannot be an edited variable in a output line, since GROSS-PAY is used in further arithmetic calculations. You will find from now on that most calculations, because they are to be used in several ways, will be put in level-number-77 items. A common mistake for beginners is trying to use edited numeric fields in arithmetic calculations.

PRINTING THE TOTAL

So far, most of our termination paragraphs have only had to close the files and stop the run. Now we wish to print out the totals as well, so we need an output total-line. This is set up in WORKING-STORAGE and is called TOTAL-LINE.

```
01 TOTAL-LINE.
   05 FILLER            PICTURE X(69)            VALUE SPACES.
   05 TOTAL-PAY-LN      PICTURE $ZZ,ZZZ.99.
   05 FILLER            PICTURE X(54)            VALUE SPACES.
```

When all input records have been processed, we must move the TOTAL-PAY to the total-line and print the total-line. This is done in the termination paragraph. In the other programs we only had to close the files and stop the program in the termination paragraph. In this program we must move the totals to a total-line and write the results. Here is the new termination-paragraph:

```
ALL-DONE.
    MOVE TOTAL-PAY TO TOTAL-PAY-LN.
    WRITE PRINT-LINE FROM TOTAL-LINE AFTER ADVANCING 3 LINES.
    CLOSE RECORDS-IN, PRINT-OUT.
    STOP RUN.
```

Common Errors

1. Forgetting to initialize the accumulator to zero.
2. Attempting to add edited values. In the program above, note that GROSS-PAY must be an unedited variable, because the value in GROSS-PAY is added to TOTAL-PAY.

****

Computer Graffiti

Computer programs are 90 percent debugged 50 percent of the time.

****

SAMPLE PROGRAM 11A

The Ready-Cash Bank manager requested that the payroll program be modified so that the pay for each employee will be accumulated and printed as a total at the end of the report. Sample Program 11A (**Figure 11.1**) does this. **Figure 11.2** is some sample output for Program 11A; **Figure 11.3** is a flowchart for it.

```
010010 IDENTIFICATION DIVISION.                                              PROGR11A
010020 PROGRAM-ID.                                                          PROGR11A
010030     PROGRM11A.                                                       PROGR11A
010040* * * * * * * * * * * * * * * * * * * * * * * * * * * * * * * **PROGR11A
010050*    SAMPLE PROGRAM WITH TOTALS.                                       *PROGR11A
010060* * * * * * * * * * * * * * * * * * * * * * * * * * * * * * * **PROGR11A
010070                                                                       PROGR11A
010080 ENVIRONMENT DIVISION.                                                 PROGR11A
010090 INPUT-OUTPUT SECTION.                                                 PROGR11A
010100 FILE-CONTROL.                                                         PROGR11A
010110     SELECT RECORDS-IN                                                 PROGR11A
010120         ASSIGN TO UR-2540R-S-SYSIN.                                   PROGR11A
010130     SELECT PRINT-OUT,                                                 PROGR11A
010140         ASSIGN TO UR-1403-S-SYSPRINT.                                 PROGR11A
010150                                                                       PROGR11A
020010 DATA DIVISION.                                                        PROGR11A
020020 FILE SECTION.                                                         PROGR11A
020030 FD   RECORDS-IN                                                       PROGR11A
020040     LABEL RECORDS ARE OMITTED.                                        PROGR11A
020050 01  IN-RECORD                     PICTURE X(80).                      PROGR11A
020060                                                                       PROGR11A
020070 FD   PRINT-OUT                                                        PROGR11A
020080     LABEL RECORDS ARE OMITTED.                                        PROGR11A
020090 01  PRINT-LINE                    PICTURE X(133).                     PROGR11A
020100                                                                       PROGR11A
020110 WORKING-STORAGE SECTION.                                              PROGR11A
020120 77  GROSS-PAY        PICTURE S999V99        VALUE ZERO.               PROGR11A
020130 77  TOTAL-PAY        PICTURE S99999V99      VALUE ZERO.               PROGR11A
020140                                                                       PROGR11A
020150 01  TOTAL-LINE.                                                       PROGR11A
020160     05  FILLER       PICTURE X(69)          VALUE SPACE.              PROGR11A
020170     05  TOTAL-PAY-LN PICTURE $ZZ,ZZZ.99.                             PROGR11A
020180     05  FILLER       PICTURE X(54)          VALUE SPACE.              PROGR11A
020190                                                                       PROGR11A
030010 01  PAY-CARD.                                                         PROGR11A
030020     05  NAME                      PICTURE X(30).                      PROGR11A
030030     05  EMP-NO                    PICTURE 9(09).                      PROGR11A
030040     05  HOURS                     PICTURE 99V9.                       PROGR11A
030050     05  RATE                      PICTURE 99V99.                      PROGR11A
030060     05  FILLER                    PICTURE X(34).                      PROGR11A
030070                                                                       PROGR11A
030080 01  PAY-LINE.                                                         PROGR11A
030090     05  FILLER                    PICTURE X(01).                      PROGR11A
030100     05  NAME                      PICTURE X(30).                      PROGR11A
030110     05  FILLER                    PICTURE X(05).                      PROGR11A
030120     05  EMP-NO                    PICTURE 999B99B9999.                PROGR11A
030130     05  FILLER                    PICTURE X(05).                      PROGR11A
030140     05  HOURS                     PICTURE Z9.9.                       PROGR11A
030150     05  FILLER                    PICTURE X(05).                      PROGR11A
030160     05  RATE                      PICTURE $ZZ.99.                     PROGR11A
030170     05  FILLER                    PICTURE X(05).                      PROGR11A
030180     05  PAY                       PICTURE $ZZZ.99.                    PROGR11A
030190     05  FILLER                    PICTURE X(54).                      PROGR11A
030200                                                                       PROGR11A
040010 PROCEDURE DIVISION.                                                   PROGR11A
040020     OPEN INPUT RECORDS-IN, OUTPUT PRINT-OUT.                          PROGR11A
040030     MOVE SPACES TO PAY-LINE.                                          PROGR11A
040040     PERFORM CALCULATE-PAY 1000 TIMES.                                 PROGR11A
040050                                                                       PROGR11A
040060 ALL-DONE.                                                             PROGR11A
040070     MOVE TOTAL-PAY TO TOTAL-PAY-LN.                                   PROGR11A



040080     WRITE PRINT-LINE FROM TOTAL-LINE AFTER ADVANCING 3 LINES.        PROGR11A
040090     CLOSE RECORDS-IN, PRINT-OUT.                                      PROGR11A
040100     STOP RUN.                                                         PROGR11A
```

```
040110                                                                        PROGR11A
040120  CALCULATE-PAY.                                                        PROGR11A
040130      READ RECORDS-IN INTO PAY-CARD AT END PERFORM ALL-DONE.            PROGR11A
040140      MOVE CORRESPONDING PAY-CARD TO PAY-LINE.                          PROGR11A
040150      COMPUTE GROSS-PAY = RATE OF PAY-CARD *                            PROGR11A
040160                          HOURS OF PAY-CARD                             PROGR11A
040170      ADD GROSS-PAY TO TOTAL-PAY.                                       PROGR11A
040180      MOVE GROSS-PAY TO PAY.                                            PROGR11A
040190      WRITE PRINT-LINE FROM PAY-LINE AFTER ADVANCING 1 LINES.           PROGR11A
```

FIGURE 11.1   Sample Program 11A

```
BEBBBBBBBBBBBBBBBBBBBBBBBBBBBBBB3      333 33 3333      44.4      $44.44      $973.13
AAAAAAAAAAAAAAAAAAAAAAAAAAAAAAAA       123 45 6789       1.2      $34.56      $ 41.47
JERRY JONES                           123 45 6789      50.0      $ 9.00      $450.00
JUAN GARCIA                           425 74 5865      40.0      $ 8.50      $340.00
MARY ANN WOO                          425 35 2142      30.0      $10.50      $315.00

                                                                           $ 2,119.60
```

FIGURE 11.2   Output from Program 11A

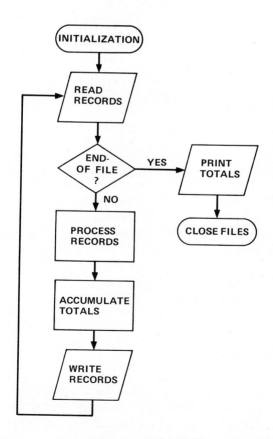

FIGURE 11.3   A Flowchart for Program 11A

REVIEW

1. Why must you place most calculated results in level-number-77 items instead of placing the results directly in the print-line?

2. What is an accumulator used for? Give some examples.

Program Modifications

1. Modify Sample Program 11A so that the hours are accumulated and printed as a total as well. Add the label **FINAL TOTAL** in columns 2–12 on the total-line.

2. Modify Sample Program 9B so that regular pay, overtime pay, and total pay are accumulated and printed as totals at the end of the report.

HEADINGS

In a previous chapter we did a report heading on the first page of the report, but we did not print the headings on the second and following pages of the report. Since reports can be hundreds of pages long, it is not very useful to print headings only on the first page of a report. Now we will set up a program so that it prints a heading on each page of the report.

In order to print headings on each page we must use the **SPECIAL-NAMES** paragraph in the **CONFIGURATION SECTION** of the **ENVIRONMENT DIVISION**. The general format for the **SPECIAL-NAMES** paragraph is

```
CONFIGURATION SECTION.
SPECIAL-NAMES.
      [function-name-1 IS mnemonic-name.]
```

You can have several of the entries above in the **SPECIAL-NAMES** paragraph. The function-name-1 is picked from a set of special names which describe a particular device or function to be performed. These **function names** are called **implementor names** because they are picked by the compiler implementors (the people who wrote the COBOL compiler). As a result, they vary according to the machine you use. These special names are described in your computer-manufacturer COBOL-language manual. The mnemonic-name is a programmer-picked name that is used in the program. Since **SPECIAL-NAMES** is part of the **CONFIGURATION SECTION** we must include this section heading. Here is a sample **SPECIAL-NAMES** paragraph:

```
CONFIGURATION SECTION.
SPECIAL-NAMES.
      C01 IS TOP-OF-PAGE.
```

In the example above, **C01** (use zero, not oh) stands for channel one on a carriage tape. The IBM/370 series uses **C01ˈ** for this function-name, but other computers commonly use other names. Function name **C01** indicates that the printing is to be continued on the first line of the next printed page of output. **TOP-OF-PAGE** is not a reserved word; it is a programmer-picked name that will be used by the program to indicate an advance to a new page. The programmer-picked name is used in the **WRITE** statement as follows:

WRITE PRINT-LINE FROM HEADING-LINE AFTER ADVANCING TOP-OF-PAGE.

This causes a skip to a new page before the heading is printed. The **SPECIAL-NAMES** paragraph provides a means of relating function names to user-specified mnemonic names. We must somehow keep track of when it is time to skip to a new page and print a heading. The usual approach is to keep a count of how many lines have been printed on each page, and when the appropriate number of lines has been reached, to skip to a new page and print a new heading. Here are the code segments for this procedure:

```
WRITE PRINT-LINE FROM PAY-LINE AFTER ADVANCING 1 LINES.
ADD 1 TO LINE-COUNT.
IF (LINE-COUNT > 55) PERFORM HEADING-ROUTINE.
```

The variable **LINE-COUNT** is declared a level-number-77 item which is initialized to **ZERO** (see Sample Program 11B in **Figure 11.4**). Thus, the code above counts the number of lines printed, and when that total is greater than **55** the paragraph **HEADING-ROUTINE** is executed by use of the **PERFORM** verb. (When testing this program you may want to reduce the **55** used in the **IF** statement to **5**, so that you won't need many data-records.) The **HEADING-ROUTINE** could be performed as follows:

```
HEADING-ROUTINE.
    WRITE-PRINT LINE FROM HEADING-LINE AFTER ADVANCING TOP-OF-PAGE.
    MOVE ZERO TO LINE-COUNT.
```

What would happen if we didn't move **ZERO** to **LINE-COUNT**? If you can't figure it out try it and see. Warning: don't use many data-records.

Notice that in Program 11B we **PERFORM** the **HEADING-ROUTINE** from two different places in the program. In order to get the first heading we **PERFORM** the **HEADING-ROUTINE** at the beginning of the program. Then in the main processing paragraph we **PERFORM** the **HEADING-ROUTINE** paragraph conditionally. This example illustrates the power and versatility of the **PERFORM** verb. We can execute the same paragraph from many places in the program by using the **PERFORM** verb, and in this way write shorter programs. This means we will have fewer errors, because there is less code to debug and test. Finally, the **PERFORM** verb allows us to separate the parts of the program, allowing us to have a much neater structure in the main paragraphs of our program.

SAMPLE PROGRAM 11B

The Ready-Cash Bank manager complained that only the first page of all previous reports had a heading line. The manager wants a heading line to be printed on each page of the report. Sample Program 11B provides a heading on each page of the report. **Figure 11.5** is a flowchart for Program 11B.

```
010010 IDENTIFICATION DIVISION.                                          PROGR11B
010020 PROGRAM-ID.                                                        PROGR11B
010030     PROGRM11B.                                                     PROGR11B
010040* * * * * * * * * * * * * * * * * * * * * * * * * * * * * **PROGR11B
010050     SAMPLE PROGRAM WITH HEADINGS ON EACH PAGE OF OUTPUT.           PROGR11B
010060* * * * * * * * * * * * * * * * * * * * * * * * * * * * * **PROGR11B
010070                                                                    PROGR11B
010080 ENVIRONMENT DIVISION.                                              PROGR11B
010090 CONFIGURATION SECTION.                                             PROGR11B
010100 SPECIAL-NAMES.                                                     PROGR11B
010110     C01 IS TOP-OF-PAGE.                                            PROGR11B
010120 INPUT-OUTPUT SECTION.                                              PROGR11B
010130 FILE-CONTROL.                                                      PROGR11B
```

```
010140       SELECT RECORDS-IN                                        PROGR11B
010150           ASSIGN TO UR-2540R-S-SYSIN.                          PROGR11B
010160       SELECT PRINT-OUT,                                        PROGR11B
010170           ASSIGN TO UR-1403-S-SYSPRINT.                        PROGR11B
010180                                                                PROGR11B
020010 DATA DIVISION.                                                 PROGR11B
020020 FILE SECTION.                                                  PROGR11B
020030 FD  RECORDS-IN                                                 PROGR11B
020040     LABEL RECORDS ARE OMITTED.                                 PROGR11B
020050 01  IN-RECORD                    PICTURE X(80).                PROGR11B
020060 FD  PRINT-OUT                                                  PROGR11B
020070     LABEL RECORDS ARE OMITTED.                                 PROGR11B
020080 01  PRINT-LINE                   PICTURE X(133).               PROGR11B
020090                                                                PROGR11B
020100 WORKING-STORAGE SECTION.                                       PROGR11B
020110 77  LINE-COUNT       PICTURE S99          VALUE ZERO.          PROGR11B
020120 77  GROSS-PAY        PICTURE S999V99      VALUE ZERO.          PROGR11B
020130 77  TOTAL-PAY        PICTURE S99999V99    VALUE ZERO.          PROGR11B
020140                                                                PROGR11B
020150 01  TOTAL-LINE.                                                PROGR11B
020160     05  FILLER       PICTURE X(72)        VALUE SPACE.         PROGR11B
020170     05  TOTAL-PAY-LN PICTURE $ZZ,ZZZ.99.                       PROGR11B
020180     05  FILLER       PICTURE X(51)        VALUE SPACE.         PROGR11B
020190                                                                PROGR11B
030010 01  PAY-CARD.                                                  PROGR11B
030020     05  NAME              PICTURE X(30).                       PROGR11B
030030     05  EMP-NO            PICTURE 9(09).                       PROGR11B
030040     05  HOURS             PICTURE 99V9.                        PROGR11B
030050     05  RATE              PICTURE 99V99.                       PROGR11B
030060     05  FILLER            PICTURE X(34).                       PROGR11B
030070                                                                PROGR11B
030080 01  HEADING-LINE.                                              PROGR11B
030090     05  FILLER       PICTURE X(02)        VALUE SPACE.         PROGR11B
030100     05  FILLER       PICTURE X(04)        VALUE 'NAME'.        PROGR11B
030110     05  FILLER       PICTURE X(27)        VALUE SPACE.         PROGR11B
030120     05  FILLER       PICTURE X(17)                            PROGR11B
030130                      VALUE 'EMPLOYEE NUMBER  '.                PROGR11B
030140     05  FILLER       PICTURE X(32)                            PROGR11B
030150          VALUE '  HOURS      RATE      GROSS PAY'.             PROGR11B
030160     05  FILLER       PICTURE X(51)        VALUE SPACE.         PROGR11B
030170                                                                PROGR11B
030180 01  PAY-LINE.                                                  PROGR11B
030190     05  FILLER            PICTURE X(01).                       PROGR11B
030200     05  NAME              PICTURE X(30).                       PROGR11B
030210     05  FILLER            PICTURE X(05).                       PROGR11B
030220     05  EMP-NO            PICTURE 999B99B9999.                 PROGR11B
030230     05  FILLER            PICTURE X(06).                       PROGR11B
030240     05  HOURS             PICTURE Z9.9.                        PROGR11B

030250     05  FILLER            PICTURE X(05).                       PROGR11B
030260     05  RATE              PICTURE $ZZ.99.                      PROGR11B
030270     05  FILLER            PICTURE X(05).                       PROGR11B
030280     05  PAY               PICTURE $Z,ZZZ.99.                   PROGR11B
030290     05  FILLER            PICTURE X(51).                       PROGR11B
030300                                                                PROGR11B
040010 PROCEDURE DIVISION.                                            PROGR11B
040020     OPEN INPUT RECORDS-IN, OUTPUT PRINT-OUT.                   PROGR11B
040030     PERFORM HEADING-ROUTINE.                                   PROGR11B
040040     MOVE SPACES TO PAY-LINE.                                   PROGR11B
040050     PERFORM CALCULATE-PAY 1000 TIMES.                          PROGR11B
040060                                                                PROGR11B
040070 ALL-DONE.                                                      PROGR11B
040080     MOVE TOTAL-PAY TO TOTAL-PAY-LN.                            PROGR11B
040090     WRITE PRINT-LINE FROM TOTAL-LINE AFTER ADVANCING 3 LINES.  PROGR11B
040100     CLOSE RECORDS-IN, PRINT-OUT.                               PROGR11B
040110     STOP RUN.                                                  PROGR11B
040120                                                                PROGR11B
040130 CALCULATE-PAY.                                                 PROGR11B
040140     READ RECORDS-IN INTO PAY-CARD AT END PERFORM ALL-DONE.     PROGR11B
040150     MOVE CORRESPONDING PAY-CARD TO PAY-LINE.                   PROGR11B
040160     COMPUTE GROSS-PAY = RATE OF PAY-CARD *                     PROGR11B
040170                         HOURS OF PAY-CARD.                     PROGR11B
```

```
040180        ADD GROSS-PAY TO TOTAL-PAY.                              PROGR11B
040190        MOVE GROSS-PAY TO PAY.                                   PROGR11B
040200        WRITE PRINT-LINE FROM PAY-LINE AFTER ADVANCING 1 LINES.  PROGR11B
040210        ADD 1 TO LINE-COUNT.                                     PROGR11B
040220        IF (LINE-COUNT > 55) PERFORM HEADING-ROUTINE.            PROGR11B
040230                                                                 PROGR11B
040240 HEADING-ROUTINE.                                                PROGR11B
040250        WRITE PRINT-LINE FROM HEADING-LINE                       PROGR11B
040260                AFTER ADVANCING TOP-OF-PAGE.                     PROGR11B
040270        MOVE ZERO TO LINE-COUNT.                                 PROGR11B
```

FIGURE 11.4   **Sample Program 11B**

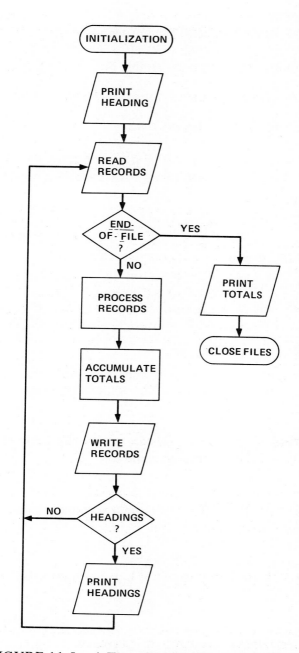

FIGURE 11.5   **A Flowchart for Program 11B**

REVIEW

1. The vertical spacing on your printed output is controlled by something called a carriage tape. Have somebody at your computer center explain to you how a carriage tape is used.

2. If you are not using an IBM/370, find out what function name is used on your compiler for skipping to a new page on output.

3. In Sample Program 11B, if you changed the entry **C01 IS TOP-OF-PAGE** to **C01 IS ZIPPER**, what else would you have to change in the program?

4. In the **HEADING-ROUTINE** paragraph of Program 11B, why is the sentence **MOVE ZERO TO LINE-COUNT** necessary? Exactly what will the program do if that line is left out?

5. Suppose we made the following changes to Sample Program 11B in order to have double-spacing:

    ```
    WRITE PRINT-LINE FROM HEADING-LINE AFTER ADVANCING 2 LINES.
    ADD 2 TO LINE-COUNT
    IF (LINE-COUNT = 55) PERFORM HEADING-ROUTINE.
    ```

    Will this work? If you can't figure out why it won't work correctly, modify Program 11B as above and run the program. Notice that the last line of the code above was changed, too.

Program Modifications

1. Run Sample Program 11B. If you are not using an IBM/370, find out what function name your compiler uses to skip to a new page in output printing.

2. Modify Program 11B so that at the bottom of each page of printout (except the last page) the message **CONTINUED ON NEXT PAGE** is printed in columns 3–24. There should be two blank lines before this message.

3. Modify Program 9B so that proper headings appear on all pages of the printout. Add another heading-line which prints **READY-CASH BANK**. This heading-line should print first and should be centered.

4. Modify Program 11B so that the report pages are numbered. Print on each heading **PAGE nnn** in columns 87–94, where **nnn** is the report page-number.

5. Ready-Cash Bank has international aspirations. Some reports need to be printed to be distributed in another country. The function of the period and comma in numbers is exchanged, as they are in many countries outside North America. That is, in the United States we would print:

    $5,432.97

    but in this foreign country (as well as in much of Europe) they would print:

    #5.432,97

    Notice that a different symbol is used for the currency symbol. Since computers are an international business, there is an option in COBOL to change the function of the period and comma, and an option to change the currency symbol. We need to add some new entries to the SPECIAL-NAMES paragraph, as follows:

```
SPECIAL-NAMES.
     DECIMAL-POINT IS COMMA
     CURRENCY SIGN IS '#'.
```

Notice that there is only one period at the end of all these entries. Then you just switch the characters you use as editing characters when editing output.

Modify Program 11B to include the changes above. (Add the entries above to the SPECIAL-NAMES paragraph, and change the edit characters in the output line).

```
*************************************************************
```

A Diversion: Computer Organizations

There are three major organizations of people working in the computer field. Computer organizations can be classified according to the orientation of their members. In general, computer people are grouped as follows:

a) Business.

b) Academic.

c) Engineering.

Although there is a lot of overlapping of interest (e.g., professors teaching business data-processing or engineering) the categories above serve as general divisions. Here are descriptions of the three major computer organizations.

Association for Computing Machinery, 1133 Avenue of the Americas, New York, New York   10036.

Members of this group are mainly **software**-oriented (that is, they are interested in programming rather than in the machinery itself), and the vast majority of its members are from the academic community. ACM has several publications; all its regular publications tend to be fairly esoteric. ACM also has Special Interest Groups (SIG) who publish newsletters on their areas of interest. The SIG publications are quite timely and readable. Student-discount memberships are available. Some college campuses have student chapters.

Data Processing Management Association, 505 Busse Highway, Park Ridge, Illinois   60068.

DPMA members are usually involved in business data-processing, either in management or programming. There are quite a few local chapters which have monthly meetings. DPMA publishes a monthly magazine, *Data Management*, and it has a student-membership plan.

IEEE Computer Society, 5855 Naples Plaza, Suite 301, Long Beach, California   90803.

Members of this organization are mainly **hardware**-oriented (that is, they are primarily interested in the computers themselves and in various peripheral devices). IEEE members come from both the academic community and the engineering professions. Even though IEEE started out as a hardware-oriented group, they have become interested in software and publish much material in the software areas. They publish several magazines and journals, the most readable of which are *COMPUTER* and *SPECTRUM*; you can probably find these in your library.

All three of the groups above have both regional and national conferences, which are quite interesting to attend. Some areas have regional chapters that sponsor lectures and seminars.

****

DATES

Two types of date are important for printed reports, the report date and the run date. The **report date** is the date which identifies the report. For example, if we were running the January accounts-receivable report, then January would be the report date. This report date should be printed on the report so that anyone reading the report will know what month's processing is being read.

A January report would probably not be run until February, because it takes some time to collect all the January transactions and prepare them for computer processing. So the actual **run date**, when the program is executed by the computer, may be in the middle of February. The run date is useful information to have in a report: sometimes, because of input errors, a report may have to be done twice. Then a run date helps to identify which is the latest, and therefore most likely to be correct, version of the report.

Sample Program 11C

The Ready-Cash Bank manager liked the new headings we provided on the last program, but now the manager has told us that the clerks have difficulty determining what month the reports were run because the reports are not dated. We assured the manager that we can provide a report date on all future reports. Sample Program 11C in **Figure 11.6** does this. **Figure 11.7** is some sample output.

```
010010 IDENTIFICATION DIVISION.                                      PROGR11C
010020 PROGRAM-ID.                                                   PROGR11C
010030    PROGRM11C.                                                 PROGR11C
010040* * * * * * * * * * * * * * * * * * * * * * * * * * * * **PROGR11C
010050*   SAMPLE PROGRAM WITH DATE IN THE HEADING.                  *PROGR11C
010060* * * * * * * * * * * * * * * * * * * * * * * * * * * * **PROGR11C
010070                                                                PROGR11C
010080 ENVIRONMENT DIVISION.                                         PROGR11C
010090 CONFIGURATION SECTION.                                        PROGR11C
010100 SPECIAL-NAMES.                                                PROGR11C
010110    C01 IS TOP-OF-PAGE.                                        PROGR11C
010120 INPUT-OUTPUT SECTION.                                         PROGR11C
010130 FILE-CONTROL.                                                 PROGR11C
010140    SELECT RECORDS-IN                                          PROGR11C
010150       ASSIGN TO UR-2540R-S-SYSIN.                             PROGR11C
010160    SELECT PRINT-OUT,                                          PROGR11C
010170       ASSIGN TO UR-1403-S-SYSPRINT.                           PROGR11C
010180                                                                PROGR11C
020010 DATA DIVISION.                                                PROGR11C
020020 FILE SECTION.                                                 PROGR11C
020030 FD   RECORDS-IN                                               PROGR11C
020040    LABEL RECORDS ARE OMITTED.                                 PROGR11C
020050 01   IN-RECORD              PICTURE X(80).                    PROGR11C
020060 FD   PRINT-OUT                                                PROGR11C
020070    LABEL RECORDS ARE OMITTED.                                 PROGR11C
020080 01   PRINT-LINE             PICTURE X(133).                   PROGR11C
020090                                                                PROGR11C
020100 WORKING-STORAGE SECTION.                                      PROGR11C
020110 77   LINE-COUNT    PICTURE S99        VALUE ZERO.             PROGR11C
020120 77   GROSS-PAY     PICTURE S999V99    VALUE ZERO.             PROGR11C
020130 77   TOTAL-PAY     PICTURE S99999V99  VALUE ZERO.             PROGR11C
020140                                                                PROGR11C
020150 01   TOTAL-LINE.                                              PROGR11C
```

```
020160      05   FILLER        PICTURE X(72)        VALUE SPACE.      PROGR11C
020170      05   TOTAL-PAY-LN  PICTURE $ZZ,ZZZ.99.                    PROGR11C
020180      05   FILLER        PICTURE X(51)        VALUE SPACE.      PROGR11C
020190                                                                PROGR11C
020200 01   DATE-RECORD.                                              PROGR11C
020210      05   FLAG-IN              PICTURE X(01).                  PROGR11C
020220      05   REPORT-DATE-IN       PICTURE X(30).                  PROGR11C
020230      05   FILLER               PICTURE X(59).                  PROGR11C
020240                                                                PROGR11C
030010 01   PAY-CARD.                                                 PROGR11C
030020      05   NAME                 PICTURE X(30).                  PROGR11C
030030      05   EMP-NO               PICTURE 9(09).                  PROGR11C
030040      05   HOURS                PICTURE 99V9.                   PROGR11C
030050      05   RATE                 PICTURE 99V99.                  PROGR11C
030060      05   FILLER               PICTURE X(34).                  PROGR11C
030070                                                                PROGR11C
030080 01   HEADING-LINE.                                             PROGR11C
030090      05   FILLER        PICTURE X(02)        VALUE SPACE.      PROGR11C
030100      05   FILLER        PICTURE X(04)        VALUE 'NAME'.     PROGR11C
030110      05   FILLER        PICTURE X(27)        VALUE SPACE.      PROGR11C
030120      05   FILLER        PICTURE X(17)                         PROGR11C
030130                         VALUE 'EMPLOYEE NUMBER '.              PROGR11C
030140      05   FILLER        PICTURE X(32)                         PROGR11C
030150                 VALUE '  HOURS       RATE       GROSS PAY'.    PROGR11C
030160      05   FILLER        PICTURE X(05)        VALUE SPACE.      PROGR11C
030170      05   RECORD-DATE-HD  PICTURE X(30).                      PROGR11C
030180      05   FILLER        PICTURE X(15)        VALUE SPACE.      PROGR11C
030190                                                                PROGR11C

030200 01   PAY-LINE.                                                 PROGR11C
030210      05   FILLER               PICTURE X(01).                  PROGR11C
030220      05   NAME                 PICTURE X(30).                  PROGR11C
030230      05   FILLER               PICTURE X(05).                  PROGR11C
030240      05   EMP-NO               PICTURE 999B99B9999.            PROGR11C
030250      05   FILLER               PICTURE X(06).                  PROGR11C
030260      05   HOURS                PICTURE Z9.9.                   PROGR11C
030270      05   FILLER               PICTURE X(05).                  PROGR11C
030280      05   RATE                 PICTURE $ZZ.99.                 PROGR11C
030290      05   FILLER               PICTURE X(05).                  PROGR11C
030300      05   PAY                  PICTURE $Z,ZZZ.99.              PROGR11C
030310      05   FILLER               PICTURE X(51).                  PROGR11C
030320                                                                PROGR11C
040010 PROCEDURE DIVISION.                                            PROGR11C
040020      OPEN INPUT RECORDS-IN, OUTPUT PRINT-OUT.                  PROGR11C
040030      READ RECORDS-IN INTO DATE-RECORD AT END PERFORM ALL-DONE. PROGR11C
040040      MOVE REPORT-DATE-IN TO RECORD-DATE-HD.                    PROGR11C
040050      PERFORM HEADING-ROUTINE.                                  PROGR11C
040060      MOVE SPACES TO PAY-LINE.                                  PROGR11C
040070      PERFORM CALCULATE-PAY 1000 TIMES.                         PROGR11C
040080                                                                PROGR11C
040090 ALL-DONE.                                                      PROGR11C
040100      MOVE TOTAL-PAY TO TOTAL-PAY-LN.                           PROGR11C
040110      WRITE PRINT-LINE FROM TOTAL-LINE AFTER ADVANCING 3 LINES. PROGR11C
040120      CLOSE RECORDS-IN, PRINT-OUT.                              PROGR11C
040130      STOP RUN.                                                 PROGR11C
040140                                                                PROGR11C
040150 CALCULATE-PAY.                                                 PROGR11C
040160      READ RECORDS-IN INTO PAY-CARD AT END PERFORM ALL-DONE.    PROGR11C
040170      MOVE CORRESPONDING PAY-CARD TO PAY-LINE.                  PROGR11C
040180      COMPUTE GROSS-PAY = RATE OF PAY-CARD *                    PROGR11C
040190                     HOURS OF PAY-CARD.                         PROGR11C
040200      ADD GROSS-PAY TO TOTAL-PAY.                               PROGR11C
040210      MOVE GROSS-PAY TO PAY.                                    PROGR11C
040220      WRITE PRINT-LINE FROM PAY-LINE AFTER ADVANCING 1 LINES.   PROGR11C
040230      ADD 1 TO LINE-COUNT.                                      PROGR11C
040240      IF (LINE-COUNT > 55) PERFORM HEADING-ROUTINE.             PROGR11C
040250                                                                PROGR11C
040260 HEADING-ROUTINE.                                               PROGR11C
040270      WRITE PRINT-LINE FROM HEADING-LINE                        PROGR11C
040280             AFTER ADVANCING TOP-OF-PAGE.                       PROGR11C
040290      MOVE ZERO TO LINE-COUNT.                                  PROGR11C
```

FIGURE 11.6   Sample Program 11C

```
NAME                    EMPLOYEE NUMBER      HOURS       RATE      GROSS PAY      FEBRUARY 2, 1982
JERRY JONES               123 45 6789        50.0      $ 9.00    $    450.00
JUAN GARCIA               425 74 5865        40.0      $ 8.50    $    340.00
MARY ANN WOO              425 35 2142        30.0      $10.50    $    315.00
FRANK MORRE               742 53 2657        40.0      $11.00    $    440.00
GENE TRACY                425 74 5231        38.0      $10.00    $    380.00

                                                                 $  1,925.00
```

FIGURE 11.7   Output from Program 11C

Report Date

The report date is usually included as the first data-record. We need a complete record-description for this special data-record. It could look like this:

```
01 DATE-RECORD.
   05 FLAG-IN              PICTURE X(01).
   05 REPORT-DATE-IN       PICTURE X(20).
   05 FILLER               PICTURE X(59).
```

Then the first input-record will have, in column 1, identification as a date record (e.g., the letter X) and the date will be placed in columns 2–21. The date can be in any form desired. The date record will be read, and the date will be transferred to the heading-line, as follows:

```
READ RECORDS-IN INTO DATE-RECORD AT END PERFORM ALL-DONE.
MOVE REPORT-DATE-IN TO RECORD-DATE-HD.
```

Thus, we need these two statements in our initialization paragraph in order to get the date into the heading-line before the first heading-line is printed. Sample Program 11C is a program that reads the record date and uses it in the heading-line. **Figure 11.8** is some sample input for this program. Notice that the date record is the *first* data-record.

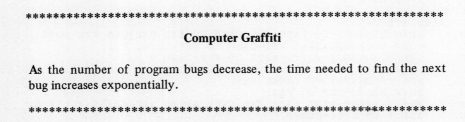

```
XFEBRUARY 2, 1982
JERRY JONES              1234567895000900
JUAN GARCIA              4257458654000850
MARY ANN WOO             4253521423001050
FRANK MORRE              7425326574001100
GENE TRACY               4257452313801000
```

FIGURE 11.8   Sample Input for Program 11C

****

Computer Graffiti

As the number of program bugs decrease, the time needed to find the next bug increases exponentially.

****

END OF JOB

A couple of things are commonly printed at the end of a report. They are:

1. Input-record counts.
2. An END OF JOB message.

These are used to indicate that the program has been successfully completed. As you have probably found out already, it is easy for a computer run to stop before it is completed. One obvious way for this to happen is if the program attempts to divide by zero. On most computers, at that point the program just stops executing. These types of ends are called **abends** (*ab*normal *ends*).

One useful item to put at the end of a report is a count of input records. This is often helpful later on when someone needs to know how many records were processed. Because of various errors, an input record is sometimes omitted from processing. The actual input-record count permits us to verify the record count.

The final item printed should be **END OF JOB**. This indicates that the run has been successfully completed. A separate print-line is usually set up to print this.

REVIEW

1. Find out if there is a local chapter of a computer organization on your campus or in your community. You may enjoy going to one of the meetings.

2. Each computer manufacturer provides a COBOL-language manual which explains the peculiarities of that version of COBOL. Although COBOL is a standard language, you will find that each machine has its own restrictions and extensions. Locate a COBOL-language manual for your computer and read through it.

Program Modifications

1. Sample Program 11C is incomplete because it fails to verify that the first record is the date record. Modify Program 11C so that it checks the first input-record for an **X** in column 1. If the letter **X** is not there, print the warning message **DATE RECORD MISSING** and stop the execution of the program. Also, read a run date from columns 22–29 (MM/DD/YY) of the date record, and print it as a second line of heading, with the label **RUN DATE MM/DD/YY**, in columns 81–97. This run-date is to be printed only on the first page of the report.

2. In any earlier program, at the end of the report print how many records have been read. Print nnn **RECORDS PROCESSED**, where nnn is the number of input records read. Then print **END OF JOB** after the record count.

3. Modify Sample Program 11A or 11B so that at the end of the report the name and pay of the person receiving the largest gross pay is printed.

4. Almost all COBOL compilers have a special reserved word which, when used as a sending field in a MOVE statement, will provide today's date. IBM machines usually use **CURRENT-DATE**. Other machines commonly use **DATE** or something similar. They are used as follows:

MOVE CURRENT-DATE TO DATE-IN-HEADING.

In this **MOVE** statement **CURRENT-DATE** is predefined and it must be moved to a field for use. The date is provided in the form: **January 1, 1982**. Try using the code above to print today's date. If **CURRENT-DATE** or **DATE** does not provide the date, look it up in your manufacturer-supplied COBOL-language manual. Can you find a **TIME** variable there?

DEBUGGING PROGRAMS‡

In Chapter 4 we discussed syntax errors, the errors the compiler finds. These syntax errors are fairly easy for the programmer to locate and correct, since the compiler flags most of the syntax errors.

Another type of error is a **logic error**, which is discovered during execution of the program. Logic errors usually cause one of two things to happen:

1. An abend (abnormal end).
2. Wrong answers.

Abend causes the program to end before processing all the data. Examples of reasons for an abnormal end are:

1. Division by zero.
2. An attempt to READ or WRITE a file which is not OPEN.
3. An attempt to OPEN a file which is already open.
4. Illegal characters in a numeric field which is being used for calculations.

The location of the statements causing these errors can sometimes be very difficult to locate in a program.

The second type of execution error occurs when the program produces the wrong answers. A simple example is when you were supposed to write:

COMPUTE NEW-AMOUNT = OLD-AMOUNT + INTEREST.

and instead you write:

COMPUTE NEW-AMOUNT = OLD-AMOUNT – INTEREST.

Your program will still produce answers, but the answers produced will be incorrect because you subtracted instead of adding.

Debugging Language

A COBOL **debugging language** is available on most IBM versions of COBOL, as well as on some other versions. The debugging language is used to produce output which indicates the content of variables and the flow of execution of the program. The debugging statements must be added to the PROCEDURE DIVISION. These debugging statements are placed in the B area. The debugging output is printed on a separate page from the rest of the output. An extra job control statement is usually needed after the program to direct the debugging output to the printer. Try running the sample program, but, if you get no debugging output, inquire at the computer center for the necessary job control statement.

EXHIBIT

The EXHIBIT statement provides a formatted display of the values of variables. The advantage to using the EXHIBIT statement is that no output line need be defined in the DATA DIVISION. The

‡This section can be skipped by those not using an IBM computer.

primary use of the EXHIBIT statement is to verify that the expected values are actually in the variables.

The general format of the EXHIBIT statement is:

$$\text{EXHIBIT} \left\{ \begin{array}{l} \underline{\text{NAMED}} \\ \underline{\text{CHANGED}} \ \underline{\text{NAMED}} \\ \underline{\text{CHANGED}} \end{array} \right\} \left\{ \begin{array}{l} \text{identifier-1} \\ \text{nonnumeric-literal-1} \end{array} \right\} \left[\begin{array}{l} \text{identifier-2} \\ \text{nonnumeric-literal-2} \end{array} \right] \ \dots$$

EXHIBIT NAMED causes the variable name and its value to be printed each time the statement is executed. For example, suppose we have a variable COST with the value 17 stored in it. Then:

    EXHIBIT NAMED COST.

will cause the following to be printed when the EXHIBIT statement is executed:

    COST = 17

The variable exhibited is labeled with the variable name, and the equals sign is inserted in front of the value.

You can also use nonnumeric literals. For example, if you want to print a paragraph name each time a paragraph is executed you may use this statement:

    EXHIBIT NAMED 'IN START-PROCESSING PARAGRAPH'.

Each time this statement is executed it will print:

    IN START-PROCESSING PARAGRAPH

Several variables and literals can be printed by use of the EXHIBIT statement. For example:

    EXHIBIT NAMED HOURS, 'OLD', RATE.

This version of the EXHIBIT verb prints the values every time the statement is executed.

EXHIBIT CHANGED NAMED causes the values to be printed *only* when the variables have changed in value since the last time the statement was executed. The initial time this statement is executed the values of the variables are printed. If several variables are listed, only the changed variables are printed.

EXHIBIT CHANGED works like the command above, except that the variable name is not printed.

The format of the values printed depends on the PICTURE of the variable. If the value is $123_{\wedge}45$ and the PICTURE is 999.99, the value will be printed as:

    123.45

But if the PICTURE is 999V99, the value will be printed as:

    12345

That is, if the variable being exhibited contains output edit characters, they are used in printing.

TRACE

A **TRACE** statement will indicate each time a paragraph is entered and executed. Depending on the compiler, either the paragraph name or the line number is printed. The paragraph names will be listed in the order in which they are executed. This printout can be used to trace the logical flow within the program. If other debugging statements (such as the **EXHIBIT** statement) are present in the program, the printouts from the various statements will be interspersed.

The general format for the **TRACE** statement is:

$$
\left\{ \begin{array}{l} \underline{READY} \\ \underline{RESET} \end{array} \right\} \quad \underline{TRACE}.
$$

READY TRACE starts the tracing and **RESET TRACE** stops the tracing. If you wish to trace only part of the **PROCEDURE DIVISION**, you can turn the tracing on for some paragraphs of the program and turn it off for later paragrahs of the program. Here is an example:

```
PROCEDURE DIVISION.
INITIALIZATION.
    READY TRACE.
    OPEN INPUT . . .
PROCESS-RECORDS.
    .
    .
    .
PROCESS-ERRORS.
    RESET TRACE.
```

In this code, the **TRACE** is turned on immediately after entering the **INITIALIZATION** paragraph and is turned off after entering the **PROCESS-ERRORS** paragraph. A trace may produce large volumes of output, so the ability to turn a **TRACE** on and off is very valuable.

A **TRACE** is particularly useful when the program ends with an abend. If we insert a **TRACE**, the printed output from the **TRACE** will indicate the last paragraph entered before the abend occurred.

The **TRACE** and **EXHIBIT** statements can also be used with **IF** statements. For example:

```
IF (HOURS > 40) EXHIBIT NAMED HOURS, PAY.
IF (A-B < 0) READY TRACE.
```

ON *Statement*

Most COBOL files are very large, containing thousands of records. If we use the **EXHIBIT** and **TRACE** statements, each record processed may result in several lines of output. We could easily get hundreds of pages of debugging output. COBOL provides the **ON** statement so that we can use the debug commands selectively. The general format is:

```
ON   {integer-1   }  [AND EVERY   {integer-2   }]
     {identifier-1}               {identifier-2}


[UNTIL   {integer-3   }] {imperative-statement}
        {identifier-3}  {NEXT SENTENCE       }

{ELSE     }  {statement . . .}
{OTHERWISE}  {NEXT SENTENCE   }
```

The **ON** statement in a COBOL paragraph is executed when the condition is true. Here is an example:

```
START-PROCESSING.
      ON 301 READY TRACE.
      ON 310 RESET TRACE.
      READ RECORDS-IN . . .
```

The compiler generates an internal counter (called a **count-condition**) for each **ON** statement. This internal counter is incremented each time the **ON** statement is executed. If the count-condition is true, the imperative statement is executed. Thus, the statements above will start the **TRACE** when the paragraph **START-PROCESSING** is executed the 301st time and will stop it on the 310th execution of the paragraph.

Here are some other examples of **ON** statements:

```
ON 15 EXHIBIT NAMED COUNT.
```

The 15th time this statement is executed, the value of **COUNT** will be printed.

```
ON 10 AND EVERY 10 UNTIL 100 EXHIBIT CHANGED NAMED COST, PRICE.
```

This statement will cause the values for **COST** and **PRICE** to be printed every 10th, 20th, 30th, . . . , 90th, and 100th time the paragraph is executed.

```
ON 1 AND EVERY 1 UNTIL 50 EXHIBIT NAMED HOURS, PAY.
```

This **ON** statement will cause the values for **HOURS** and **PAY** to be printed the first 50 times the paragraph is executed.

```
ON 10 AND EVERY 2 UNTIL 80 EXHIBIT NAMED ZAP
   ELSE EXHIBIT NAMED ZIPP.
```

This **ON** statement, starting with the 10th time it was executed up to the 80th time, will cause ZAP to be printed on even-number cycles and ZIPP to be printed on odd-number cycles.

Note:

1. EXHIBIT, TRACE, and ON are used only for debugging. The debugging output is printed separately from the other printed output.
2. Unwise use of debugging statements can produce large volumes of output.
3. The debugging statements should be removed once the program has been debugged, to avoid useless output.

CHAPTER REVIEW

Vocabulary Review

Accumulator	Hardware	Debugging language
Function name (implemen-	Report date	Trace
tor name)	Run date	Count-condition
Currency sign	Abend	
Software	Logic error	

Review Questions

1. List some reasons that a program may provide incorrect results. List some reasons that your program may abend.

2. What does each of the following do?

   a) EXHIBIT NAMED

   b) EXHIBIT CHANGED NAMED

   c) EXHIBIT CHANGED

Program Modifications

1. You may need a new job control statement to use the debugging language. On IBM/370-OS computers you need the statement

   ```
   //GO.SYSOUT DD SYSOUT=A
   ```

   This statement goes after your program, but before the data, if you are using the standard IBM COBOL compiler. Inquire at your computer center for the necessary job control statements.

2. To a program from an earlier chapter add a READY TRACE statement; look at the output. (Use only 3 or 4 data records.) Then add a RESET TRACE in a later paragraph to turn the tracing off, and look at the output.

3. Add an EXHIBIT NAMED statement for some variable to a program from an earlier chapter. Then try EXHIBIT CHANGED NAMED. Finally, try EXHIBIT CHANGED.

4. In a program from an earlier chapter, use the ON statement to print the value of a variable on every 3rd record.

Programs

1. Write a program to process deposit records for Ready-Cash Bank. The input records are:

Field	Columns
Account number	1–9
Date	10–15
Amount	25–32

Print all fields and provide a heading-line. Accumulate a final total for amount.

2. Do the program in question 1, but now process deposit amounts and withdrawals as two separate fields. If the amount field is positive, it is a deposit. If the amount field is negative, it is a withdrawal. Print the deposits in a separate column from the withdrawals. Accumulate a final total for both deposits and withdrawals.

3. Ready-Cash Bank processes the payroll for the We Can Everything Company. The We Can Everything Company hires employees on a piecework rate. Here are the input record and output record:

Field	Columns		Report Field	
Name	1–20		1–20	
Employee number	21–29		26–34	
Item type	30–32		46–48	
Quantity	33–38		60–65	
Item rate	39–41	9V99	75–78	9.99
Earnings	–		85–97	
Department	43		54	

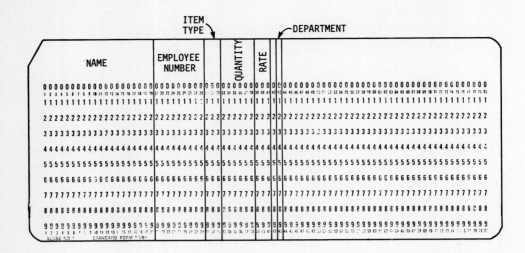

Write a program that reads and prints this information. Calculate earnings. Print headings, and print final totals for quantity and earnings.

4. Ready-Cash Bank has three types of salesperson receiving the following commissions:

Salesperson Code	Employee Type	Commission
1	Supervisor	5%
2	Permanent	30%
3	Trainee	15%

The input and output records are to be as follows:

Field	Input Columns	Report Field
Name	1–20	1–20
Salesperson code	21	–
Office	22–23	26–27
District	24–27	32–35
Sales (in dollars)	28–35	40–50
Commission	–	56–65
Employee type	–	72–81

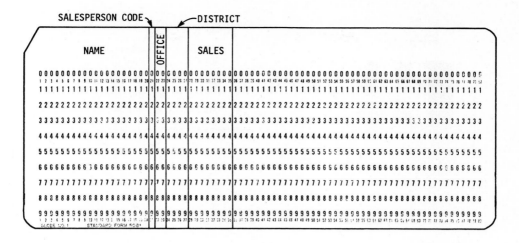

For this report, the program should read the salesperson code (1, 2, or 3) and print the employee type in columns 72–81; for example, if the salesperson code is 1, print SUPERVISOR. Write a program that will print this information. The commission in the output report is calculated by multiplying sales times commission rate. The report should have headings, and final totals for sales and commissions.

****

**All the robots, the engineers say,
Will have man-like muscles someday,
And show off their biceps,
Their quadri- and triceps,
And do sit-ups, and rub with Ben Gay.**

****

MORE ON TOTALS

Ready-Cash Bank would like the payroll program to provide a separate total for each department, in addition to the final total. Here is the new pay record:

```
01 PAY-RECORD.
    05 NAME-RC          PICTURE X(30).
    05 EMP-NO-RC        PICTURE 9(09).
    05 HOURS-RC         PICTURE 99V9.
    05 RATE-RC          PICTURE 99V99.
    05 DIVISION-RC      PICTURE X(02).
    05 DEPT-RC          PICTURE X(02).
    05 SECTION-RC       PICTURE X(03).
    05 FILLER           PICTURE X(27).
```

We have now added a department field in our input record, in columns 49–50. The input file of PAY-RECORDs *must* be in order by department; every time a new department is read we will take a department total. The computer will not automatically order the file by department—you must do this yourself. **Figure 12.1** is some sample printed output from this program.

NAME	EMPLOYEE NO	DIVISION	DEPT	SECTION	HOURS	RATE	GROSS PAY
ZERO TEST	000 00 0000	01	02	000	0.0	$ .00	$ .00
DENNIE VAN TASSEL	456 12 3456	01	02	300	40.0	$12.50	$ 500.00
JERRY CARLSON	147 25 8369	01	02	300	40.0	$ 8.50	$ 340.00
SUE MORRE	753 42 1689	01	02	300	38.0	$10.000	$ 380.00
							$ 1,220.00
ELLOIT WEBSTER	147 25 8635	01	03	010	40.0	$ 9.50	$ 380.00
HUEGA WOO	425 75 8963	01	03	010	40.0	$60.00	$ 400.00
JOHN GARCIA	112 25 8740	01	03	300	35.0	$ 9.00	$ 315.00
							$ 1,095.00
RANDOTH LIEBERSON	754 23 1568	02	05	400	20.0	$ 7.90	$ 158.00
AMAGE BIGFOOT	752 41 3524	02	05	400	40.0	$ 9.00	$ 360.00
							$ 518.00
00000000011111111122222222223	333 33 3333	44	45	555	44.4	$44.44	$ 973.13
							$ 973.13
12345678901234567890123456789 0	123 45 6789	78	90	123	1.2	$34.56	$ 41.47
							$ 41.47
							$ 3,847.60

FIGURE 12.1   Output from Program 12A

Sample Program 12A provides both minor (partial) and final totals. We first need a level-77 item to accumulate our minor totals. The level-77's must now be:

```
WORKING-STORAGE SECTION.
        77 GROSS-PAY              PICTURE S999V99        VALUE ZERO.
        77 DEPARTMENT-TOTAL       PICTURE S9999V99       VALUE ZERO.
        77 FINAL-TOTAL            PICTURE S99999V99      VALUE ZERO.
```

Each time GROSS-PAY is calculated, we must add it to our DEPARTMENT-TOTAL, as follows:

```
COMPUTE GROSS-PAY = RATE-RC * HOURS-RC.
ADD GROSS-PAY TO DEPARTMENT-TOTAL.
MOVE GROSS-PAY TO PAY-LN.
WRITE PRINT-LINE FROM PAY-LINE AFTER ADVANCING 1 LINES.
```

We now need to write code to print the minor totals. There are several ways to do this; we will consider two different ways.

METHOD 1–INITIALIZED VARIABLE

Program 12A (Figure 12.2) shows one method of handling the minor totals. It is not the best method, but it illustrates several programming techniques and demonstrates some common errors. First, we set up a level-77 item for the department, and we initialize it to the first department, which means that we must know what the first department is. For example:

```
77 OLD-DEPT   PICTURE XX   VALUE '02'.
```

Ordinarily, we should know the first department in the input file. In this case the first department is '02'.

```
010010 IDENTIFICATION DIVISION.                                          PROGR12A
010020 PROGRAM-ID.                                                       PROGR12A
010030     PROGR12A.                                                     PROGR12A
010040* * * * * * * * * * * * * * * * * * * * * * * * * * * * * * **PROGR12A
010050*    PROGRAM WITH  MINOR AND FINAL TOTALS.                         *PROGR12A
010060* * * * * * * * * * * * * * * * * * * * * * * * * * * * * * **PROGR12A
010070                                                                   PROGR12A
010080 ENVIRONMENT DIVISION.                                             PROGR12A
010090 CONFIGURATION SECTION.                                            PROGR12A
010100 SPECIAL-NAMES.                                                    PROGR12A
010110     C01 IS TOP-OF-PAGE.                                           PROGR12A
010120 INPUT-OUTPUT SECTION.                                             PROGR12A
010130 FILE-CONTROL.                                                     PROGR12A
010140     SELECT RECORDS-IN,                                            PROGR12A
010150         ASSIGN TO UR-2540R-S-SYSIN.                               PROGR12A
010160     SELECT PRINT-OUT,                                             PROGR12A
010170         ASSIGN TO UR-1403-S-SYSPRINT.                             PROGR12A
010180                                                                   PROGR12A
020010 DATA DIVISION.                                                    PROGR12A
020020 FILE SECTION.                                                     PROGR12A
020030 FD   RECORDS-IN                                                   PROGR12A
020040     LABEL RECORDS ARE OMITTED.                                    PROGR12A
020050 01   IN-RECORD                    PICTURE X(80).                  PROGR12A
020060 FD   PRINT-OUT                                                    PROGR12A
020070     LABEL RECORDS ARE OMITTED.                                    PROGR12A
020080 01   PRINT-LINE                   PICTURE X(133).                 PROGR12A
020090                                                                   PROGR12A
```

```
020100 WORKING-STORAGE SECTION.                                                    PROGR12A
020110 77   LINE-COUNT            PICTURE S99             VALUE ZERO.               PROGR12A
020120 77   GROSS-PAY             PICTURE S999V99         VALUE ZERO.               PROGR12A
020130 77   DEPARTMENT-TOTAL      PICTURE S9999V99        VALUE ZERO.               PROGR12A
020140 77   FINAL-TOTAL           PICTURE S99999V99       VALUE ZERO.               PROGR12A
020150 77   OLD-DEPT              PICTURE XX              VALUE '02'.               PROGR12A
020160                                                                             PROGR12A
020170 01   TOTAL-LINE.                                                            PROGR12A
020180      05   FILLER           PICTURE X(95)           VALUE SPACE.              PROGR12A
020190      05   TOTAL-PAY-LN     PICTURE $ZZ,ZZZ.99.                               PROGR12A
020200      05   FILLER           PICTURE X(28)           VALUE SPACE.              PROGR12A
020210                                                                             PROGR12A
020220 01   PAY-RECORD.                                                            PROGR12A
020230      05   NAME-RC                    PICTURE X(30).                          PROGR12A
020240      05   EMP-NO-RC                  PICTURE 9(09).                          PROGR12A
020250      05   HOURS-RC                   PICTURE 99V9.                           PROGR12A
020260      05   RATE-RC                    PICTURE 99V99.                          PROGR12A
020270      05   DIVISION-RC                PICTURE X(02).                          PROGR12A
020280      05   DEPT-RC                    PICTURE X(02).                          PROGR12A
020290      05   SECTION-RC                 PICTURE X(03).                          PROGR12A
020300      05   FILLER                     PICTURE X(27).                          PROGR12A
020310                                                                             PROGR12A
030010 01   HEADING-LINE.                                                          PROGR12A
030020      05   FILLER           PICTURE X(02)           VALUE SPACE.              PROGR12A
030030      05   FILLER           PICTURE X(04)           VALUE 'NAME'.             PROGR12A
030040      05   FILLER           PICTURE X(27)           VALUE SPACE.              PROGR12A
030050      05   FILLER           PICTURE X(17)                                     PROGR12A
030060                            VALUE '   EMPLOYEE NO  '.                         PROGR12A
030070      05   FILLER           PICTURE X(23)                                     PROGR12A
030080           VALUE 'DIVISION  DEPT   SECTION'.                                  PROGR12A
030090      05   FILLER           PICTURE X(32)                                     PROGR12A
030100           VALUE '   HOURS      RATE      GROSS PAY'.                         PROGR12A
030110      05   FILLER           PICTURE X(28)           VALUE SPACE.              PROGR12A



030120                                                                             PROGR12A
030130 01   PAY-LINE.                                                              PROGR12A
030140      05   FILLER                     PICTURE X(01).                          PROGR12A
030150      05   NAME-LN                    PICTURE X(30).                          PROGR12A
030160      05   FILLER                     PICTURE X(05).                          PROGR12A
030170      05   EMP-NO-LN                  PICTURE 999B99B9999.                    PROGR12A
030180      05   FILLER                     PICTURE X(06).                          PROGR12A
030190      05   DIVISION-LN                PICTURE X(02).                          PROGR12A
030200      05   FILLER                     PICTURE X(06).                          PROGR12A
030210      05   DEPT-LN                    PICTURE X(02).                          PROGR12A
030220      05   FILLER                     PICTURE X(05).                          PROGR12A
030230      05   SECTION-LN                 PICTURE X(03).                          PROGR12A
030240      05   FILLER                     PICTURE X(05).                          PROGR12A
030250      05   HOURS-LN                   PICTURE Z9.9.                           PROGR12A
030260      05   FILLER                     PICTURE X(05).                          PROGR12A
030270      05   RATE-LN                    PICTURE $ZZ.99.                         PROGR12A
030280      05   FILLER                     PICTURE X(05).                          PROGR12A
030290      05   PAY-LN                     PICTURE $Z,ZZZ.99.                      PROGR12A
030300      05   FILLER                     PICTURE X(28).                          PROGR12A
030310                                                                             PROGR12A
040010 PROCEDURE DIVISION.                                                         PROGR12A
040020      OPEN INPUT RECORDS-IN, OUTPUT PRINT-OUT.                               PROGR12A
040030      PERFORM HEADING-ROUTINE.                                               PROGR12A
040040      MOVE SPACES TO PAY-LINE.                                               PROGR12A
040050      PERFORM CALCULATE-PAY 1000 TIMES.                                      PROGR12A
040060                                                                             PROGR12A
040070 ALL-DONE.                                                                   PROGR12A
040080      PERFORM MINOR-TOTAL-ROUTINE.                                           PROGR12A
040090      MOVE FINAL-TOTAL TO TOTAL-PAY-LN.                                      PROGR12A
040100      WRITE PRINT-LINE FROM TOTAL-LINE AFTER ADVANCING 1 LINES.              PROGR12A
040110      CLOSE RECORDS-IN, PRINT-OUT.                                           PROGR12A
040120      STOP RUN.                                                              PROGR12A
040130                                                                             PROGR12A
```

```
040140  CALCULATE-PAY.                                                      PROGR12A
040150      READ RECORDS-IN INTO PAY-RECORD AT END PERFORM ALL-DONE.        PROGR12A
040160      IF (DEPT-RC NOT = OLD-DEPT) PERFORM MINOR-TOTAL-ROUTINE.        PROGR12A
040170      MOVE DEPT-RC TO OLD-DEPT.                                       PROGR12A
040180      MOVE NAME-RC TO NAME-LN.                                        PROGR12A
040190      MOVE EMP-NO-RC TO EMP-NO-LN.                                    PROGR12A
040200      MOVE HOURS-RC TO HOURS-LN.                                      PROGR12A
040210      MOVE RATE-RC TO RATE-LN.                                        PROGR12A
040220      MOVE DEPT-RC TO DEPT-LN.                                        PROGR12A
040230      MOVE SECTION-RC TO SECTION-LN.                                  PROGR12A
040240      MOVE DIVISION-RC TO DIVISION-LN.                                PROGR12A
040250      COMPUTE GROSS-PAY = RATE-RC * HOURS-RC.                         PROGR12A
040260      ADD GROSS-PAY TO DEPARTMENT-TOTAL.                              PROGR12A
040270      MOVE GROSS-PAY TO PAY-LN.                                       PROGR12A
040280      WRITE PRINT-LINE FROM PAY-LINE AFTER ADVANCING 1 LINES.         PROGR12A
040290      ADD 1 TO LINE-COUNT.                                            PROGR12A
040300      IF (LINE-COUNT > 55) PERFORM HEADING-ROUTINE.                   PROGR12A
040310                                                                      PROGR12A
040320  HEADING-ROUTINE.                                                    PROGR12A
040330      WRITE PRINT-LINE FROM HEADING-LINE                              PROGR12A
040340          AFTER ADVANCING TOP-OF-PAGE.                                PROGR12A
040350      MOVE ZERO TO LINE-COUNT.                                        PROGR12A
040360                                                                      PROGR12A
040370  MINOR-TOTAL-ROUTINE.                                                PROGR12A
040380      MOVE DEPARTMENT-TOTAL TO TOTAL-PAY-LN.                          PROGR12A
040390      WRITE PRINT-LINE FROM TOTAL-LINE AFTER ADVANCING 2 LINES.       PROGR12A
040400      ADD DEPARTMENT-TOTAL TO FINAL-TOTAL.                            PROGR12A



040410      MOVE ZERO TO DEPARTMENT-TOTAL.                                  PROGR12A
040420      MOVE SPACES TO PAY-LINE.                                        PROGR12A
040430      WRITE PRINT-LINE FROM PAY-LINE AFTER ADVANCING 2 LINES.         PROGR12A
040440      ADD 4 TO LINE-COUNT.                                            PROGR12A
```

FIGURE 12.2   Sample Program 12A

Then the code used in the main body of the program to execute the minor-total routine may be written as follows:

```
READ RECORDS-IN INTO PAY-RECORD AT END PERFORM ALL-DONE.
IF (DEPT-RC NOT = OLD-DEPT) PERFORM MINOR-TOTAL-ROUTINE.
MOVE DEPT-RC TO OLD-DEPT.
```

The code above reads in a new data-record, and if a new department has been read the code performs the MINOR-TOTAL-ROUTINE. Each time we read a new input record we save the department number in OLD-DEPT so that we can compare the department in the previous record to the department in the new record. The MINOR-TOTAL-ROUTINE might look like this:

```
MINOR-TOTAL-ROUTINE.
    MOVE DEPARTMENT-TOTAL TO TOTAL-PAY-LN.
    WRITE PRINT-LINE FROM TOTAL-LINE AFTER ADVANCING 2 LINES.
    ADD DEPARTMENT-TOTAL TO FINAL-TOTAL.
    MOVE ZERO TO DEPARTMENT-TOTAL.
```

The first two lines of code move the accumulated minor total to the TOTAL-LINE and print the TOTAL-LINE. Next, the DEPARTMENT-TOTAL is accumulated in FINAL-TOTAL so that it can be printed at the end of the report, that is, each time we print a minor total we wish to add the minor-total amount into the final-total accumulator. Finally, we must set DEPARTMENT-TOTAL to zero so that we can accumulate the total for the next department.

The fault or weakness of this program is that the first department may change, that is, the first department may become '01' or '03'. Departments may be added or eliminated, or there could be a reason to run the program with only part of the data. Each time any of these things happens, the program will have to be modified. A program is called **robust** if it still executes correctly when the data changes. This program is not robust. We want a program that will execute even when the first department changes. **Figure 12.3** is some sample input for Program 12A.

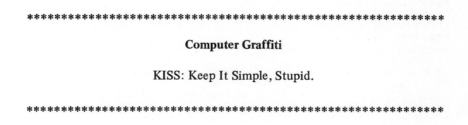

```
ZERO TEST                  000 000 000 00 000 000 10 2000
DENNIE VAN TASSEL          456 1234 5640 012500 102300
JERRY CARLSON              147 2583 6940 008500 102300
SUE MORRE                  753 4216 8938 010000 102300
ELLOIT WEBSTER             147 2586 3540 009500 103010
HUEGA WOO                  425 7589 6340 060000 103010
JOHN GARCIA                112 2587 4035 009000 103300
RANDOTH LIEBERSON          754 2315 682 0007900 205400
AMAGE BIGFOOT              752 4135 2440 009000 205400
000000000 111111111 1222222222 2233333333 334444444444 555555555 556666666666 777777777 8
123456789 012345678 9012345678 9012345678 901234567890 123456789 012345678901 234567890
```

FIGURE 12.3   **Input for Program 12A**

****

Computer Graffiti

KISS: Keep It Simple, Stupid.

****

REVIEW

1. What would happen in Sample Program 12A if the input data records were not in departmental sequence? How could you check for correct input sequence?

Program Modifications

1. Execute Program 12A with some data that starts with department '01' and explain what happens. Then modify the program so that it executes correctly with your new input data.

2. Print record counts for both minor and final totals.

3. Modify Program 12A so that the minor total is printed when the division changes, instead of when the department changes. Accumulate and print the total hours for both levels of totals.

METHOD 2—SWITCHES

Sample Program 12B (Figure 12.4) is a different method of handling the problem. The technique is to set up a variable which will signal us when the first record is being read. A variable used to signal some condition is called a **flag** or a **switch**, so we will use the programmer-picked name SWITCH, which is not a reserved word.

```
010010 IDENTIFICATION DIVISION.                                     PROGR12B
010020 PROGRAM-ID.                                                  PROGR12B
010030    PROGR12B.                                                 PROGR12B
010040* * * * * * * * * * * * * * * * * * * * * * * * * * * **PROGR12B
010050*   PROGRAM WITH  MINOR AND FINAL TOTALS.                    *PROGR12B
010060* * * * * * * * * * * * * * * * * * * * * * * * * * * **PROGR12B
010070                                                              PROGR12B
010080 ENVIRONMENT DIVISION.                                        PROGR12B
010090 CONFIGURATION SECTION.                                       PROGR12B
010100 SPECIAL-NAMES.                                               PROGR12B
010110    C01 IS TOP-OF-PAGE.                                       PROGR12B
010120 INPUT-OUTPUT SECTION.                                        PROGR12B
010130 FILE-CONTROL.                                                PROGR12B
010140    SELECT RECORDS-IN,                                        PROGR12B
010150        ASSIGN TO UR-2540R-S-SYSIN.                           PROGR12B
010160    SELECT PRINT-OUT,                                         PROGR12B
010170        ASSIGN TO UR-1403-S-SYSPRINT.                         PROGR12B
010180                                                              PROGR12B
020010 DATA DIVISION.                                               PROGR12B
020020 FILE SECTION.                                                PROGR12B
020030 FD  RECORDS-IN                                               PROGR12B
020040     LABEL RECORDS ARE OMITTED.                               PROGR12B
020050 01  IN-RECORD                    PICTURE X(80).              PROGR12B
020060 FD  PRINT-OUT                                                PROGR12B
020070     LABEL RECORDS ARE OMITTED.                               PROGR12B
020080 01  PRINT-LINE                   PICTURE X(133).             PROGR12B
020090                                                              PROGR12B
020100 WORKING-STORAGE SECTION.                                     PROGR12B
020110 77  SWITCH              PICTURE 9           VALUE ZERO.      PROGR12B
020120 77  LINE-COUNT          PICTURE S99         VALUE ZERO.      PROGR12B
020130 77  GROSS-PAY           PICTURE S999V99     VALUE ZERO.      PROGR12B
020140 77  DEPARTMENT-TOTAL    PICTURE S9999V99    VALUE ZERO.      PROGR12B
020150 77  FINAL-TOTAL         PICTURE S99999V99   VALUE ZERO.      PROGR12B
020160 77  OLD-DEPT            PICTURE XX          VALUE '02'.      PROGR12B
020170                                                              PROGR12B
020180 01  TOTAL-LINE.                                              PROGR12B
020190     05  FILLER          PICTURE X(95)       VALUE SPACE.     PROGR12B
020200     05  TOTAL-PAY-LN    PICTURE $ZZ,ZZZ.99.                 PROGR12B
020210     05  FILLER          PICTURE X(28)       VALUE SPACE.     PROGR12B
020220                                                              PROGR12B
020230 01  PAY-RECORD.                                              PROGR12B
020240     05  NAME-RC                  PICTURE X(30).              PROGR12B
020250     05  EMP-NO-RC                PICTURE 9(09).              PROGR12B
020260     05  HOURS-RC                 PICTURE 99V9.               PROGR12B
020270     05  RATE-RC                  PICTURE 99V99.              PROGR12B
020280     05  DIVISION-RC              PICTURE X(02).              PROGR12B
020290     05  DEPT-RC                  PICTURE X(02).              PROGR12B
020300     05  SECTION-RC               PICTURE X(03).              PROGR12B
020310     05  FILLER                   PICTURE X(27).              PROGR12B
020320                                                              PROGR12B
030010 01  HEADING-LINE.                                            PROGR12B
030020     05  FILLER          PICTURE X(02)       VALUE SPACE.     PROGR12B
030030     05  FILLER          PICTURE X(04)       VALUE 'NAME'.    PROGR12B
030040     05  FILLER          PICTURE X(27)       VALUE SPACE.     PROGR12B
030050     05  FILLER          PICTURE X(17)                       PROGR12B
030060                         VALUE '  EMPLOYEE NO   '.            PROGR12B
030070     05  FILLER          PICTURE X(23)                       PROGR12B
030080         VALUE 'DIVISION  DEPT  SECTION'.                     PROGR12B
030090     05  FILLER          PICTURE X(32)                       PROGR12B
030100         VALUE '  HOURS      RATE      GROSS PAY'.            PROGR12B

030110     05  FILLER          PICTURE X(28)       VALUE SPACE.     PROGR12B
030120                                                              PROGR12B
```

```
030130 01  PAY-LINE.                                               PROGR12B
030140     05   FILLER            PICTURE X(01).                   PROGR12B
030150     05   NAME-LN           PICTURE X(30).                   PROGR12B
030160     05   FILLER            PICTURE X(05).                   PROGR12B
030170     05   EMP-NO-LN         PICTURE 999B99B9999.             PROGR12B
030180     05   FILLER            PICTURE X(06).                   PROGR12B
030190     05   DIVISION-LN       PICTURE X(02).                   PROGR12B
030200     05   FILLER            PICTURE X(06).                   PROGR12B
030210     05   DEPT-LN           PICTURE X(02).                   PROGR12B
030220     05   FILLER            PICTURE X(05).                   PROGR12B
030230     05   SECTION-LN        PICTURE X(03).                   PROGR12B
030240     05   FILLER            PICTURE X(05).                   PROGR12B
030250     05   HOURS-LN          PICTURE Z9.9.                    PROGR12B
030260     05   FILLER            PICTURE X(05).                   PROGR12B
030270     05   RATE-LN           PICTURE $ZZ.99.                  PROGR12B
030280     05   FILLER            PICTURE X(05).                   PROGR12B
030290     05   PAY-LN            PICTURE $Z,ZZZ.99.               PROGR12B
030300     05   FILLER            PICTURE X(28).                   PROGR12B
030310                                                             PROGR12B
040  0                                                             PROGR12B
040010 PROCEDURE DIVISION.                                         PROGR12B
040020     OPEN INPUT RECORDS-IN, OUTPUT PRINT-OUT.                PROGR12B
040030     PERFORM HEADING-ROUTINE.                                PROGR12B
040040     MOVE SPACES TO PAY-LINE.                                PROGR12B
040050     PERFORM CALCULATE-PAY 1000 TIMES.                       PROGR12B
040060                                                             PROGR12B
040070 ALL-DONE.                                                   PROGR12B
040080     PERFORM MINOR-TOTAL-ROUTINE.                            PROGR12B
040090     MOVE FINAL-TOTAL TO TOTAL-PAY-LN.                       PROGR12B
040100     WRITE PRINT-LINE FROM TOTAL-LINE AFTER ADVANCING 1 LINES.  PROGR12B
040110     CLOSE RECORDS-IN, PRINT-OUT.                            PROGR12B
040120     STOP RUN.                                               PROGR12B
040130                                                             PROGR12B
040140 CALCULATE-PAY.                                              PROGR12B
040150     READ RECORDS-IN INTO PAY-RECORD AT END PERFORM ALL-DONE.  PROGR12B
040160     IF (SWITCH NOT = 0)                                     PROGR12B
040170        IF (DEPT-RC NOT = OLD-DEPT)                          PROGR12B
040180            PERFORM MINOR-TOTAL-ROUTINE.                     PROGR12B
040190     MOVE 1 TO SWITCH.                                       PROGR12B
040200     MOVE DEPT-RC TO OLD-DEPT.                               PROGR12B
040210     MOVE NAME-RC TO NAME-LN.                                PROGR12B
040220     MOVE EMP-NO-RC TO EMP-NO-LN.                            PROGR12B
040230     MOVE HOURS-RC TO HOURS-LN.                              PROGR12B
040240     MOVE RATE-RC TO RATE-LN.                                PROGR12B
040250     MOVE DEPT-RC TO DEPT-LN.                                PROGR12B
040260     MOVE SECTION-RC TO SECTION-LN.                          PROGR12B
040270     MOVE DIVISION-RC TO DIVISION-LN.                        PROGR12B
040280     COMPUTE GROSS-PAY = RATE-RC * HOURS-RC.                 PROGR12B
040290     ADD GROSS-PAY TO DEPARTMENT-TOTAL.                      PROGR12B
040300     MOVE GROSS-PAY TO PAY-LN.                               PROGR12B
040310     WRITE PRINT-LINE FROM PAY-LINE AFTER ADVANCING 1 LINES. PROGR12B
040320     ADD 1 TO LINE-COUNT.                                    PROGR12B
040330     IF (LINE-COUNT > 55) PERFORM HEADING-ROUTINE.           PROGR12B
040340                                                             PROGR12B
040350 HEADING-ROUTINE.                                            PROGR12B
040360     WRITE PRINT-LINE FROM HEADING-LINE                      PROGR12B
040370           AFTER ADVANCING TOP-OF-PAGE.                      PROGR12B
040380     MOVE ZERO TO LINE-COUNT.                                PROGR12B


040390                                                             PROGR12B
040400 MINOR-TOTAL-ROUTINE.                                        PROGR12B
040410     MOVE DEPARTMENT-TOTAL TO TOTAL-PAY-LN.                  PROGR12B
040420     WRITE PRINT-LINE FROM TOTAL-LINE AFTER ADVANCING 2 LINES.  PROGR12B
040430     ADD DEPARTMENT-TOTAL TO FINAL-TOTAL.                    PROGR12B
040440     MOVE ZERO TO DEPARTMENT-TOTAL.                          PROGR12B
040450     MOVE SPACES TO PAY-LINE.                                PROGR12B
040460     WRITE PRINT-LINE FROM PAY-LINE AFTER ADVANCING 2 LINES. PROGR12B
040470     ADD 4 TO LINE-COUNT.                                    PROGR12B
```

FIGURE 12.4   Sample Program 12B

We must set up a level-number-77 item, and initialize it to a value. This is done as follows:

```
77 SWITCH   PICTURE 9   VALUE ZERO.
```

Then this switch will be used as follows:

```
READ RECORDS-IN INTO PAY-RECORD AT END PERFORM ALL-DONE.
IF (SWITCH NOT = 0)
    IF (DEPT-RC NOT = OLD-DEPT)
        PERFORM MINOR-TOTAL-ROUTINE.
MOVE 1 TO SWITCH.
MOVE DEPT-RC TO OLD-DEPT.
```

The code above contains a nested IF statement. The first time this paragraph is exected SWITCH will have the value 0 and the department comparison will not be done. After this paragraph has been executed once, SWITCH will be set to 1 by the MOVE statement and henceforth the department comparison will be done each time the paragraph is executed.

You should study this program until you understand it. The use of switches is a common programming technique. One way to study a program is to hand-simulate it: execute the program three times, keeping track of the status of SWITCH and of when the department comparison is done.

Here is a hand-simulation of this part of the program (notice that the variable SWITCH is set to zero in the initialization):

	SWITCH	*Comparison Done?*
Initialization	0	—
1st record processed	0	No
2nd record processed	1	Yes
3rd record processed	1	Yes

When the first record is read SWITCH is zero, so no comparison is done. Next, SWITCH is set to one, and when the second record is processed the comparison is done, as it is for the third and all following records. Hand-simulation is often used to locate logic errors.

Using a switch is different from simply comparing two quantities. A switch may be set and then not used until later in the program, that is, there is often a time delay before the switch is used. The switch is set, but not used until it is needed.

Using the method in Program 12B means that our program will work no matter which department is processed first. It is important that a program be independent of any particular set of data. The first sample program was dependent upon the first department being 02, while the second, improved program will work correctly independently of what department is first. **Figure** 12.5 is a flowchart for Program 12B.

REVIEW

1. How could you modify Sample Program 12B so that a 1 will be moved to SWITCH *only once* during the execution of the program? Would this matter?

2. Hand-simulate Program 12B for the first three input records, noting the status of the variable SWITCH and whether the department comparison is made.

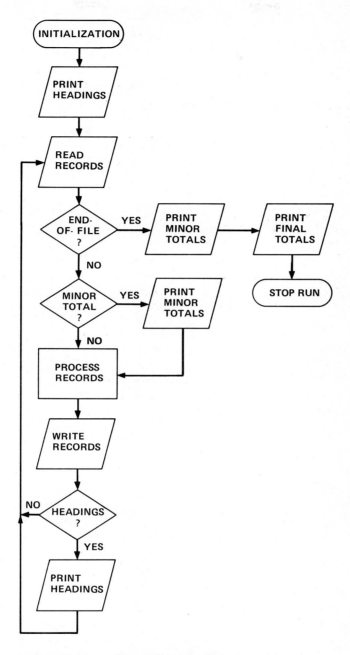

FIGURE 12.5   Flowchart for Program 12B

Program Modifications

1. Sample Program 12B is incomplete because it assumes that the input file is in sequence. Add an IF statement to check for out-of-sequence records. If an input record is out of sequence, perform a paragraph which prints the error message 'INPUT FILE OUT OF SEQUENCE' and stops execution of the program.

2. Modify Program 12B so that on the minor-total line the label MINOR TOTAL is printed in columns 3–14: print one asterisk one space after the total. On the final-total line print FINAL TOTALS, starting in column 3, and print two asterisks after the final total. Accumulate and print the total hours for both levels of totals.

INTERMEDIATE TOTALS

Ready-Cash Bank has divisions as well as departments. The Ready-Cash Bank manager decided that the management would like to have division totals, as well as department totals. Sample Program 12C (**Figure 12.6**) prints an intermediate level of totals as well as a minor total and final total. The intermediate totals are to be taken when the division changes in the input data. Division is a higher level than department, that is, each division can have many departments. The division is given in columns 47–48 of the data record. **Figure 12.7** is some sample output from Program 12C, illustrating the various totals.

```
010010 IDENTIFICATION DIVISION.                                        PROGR12C
010020 PROGRAM-ID.                                                     PROGR12C
010030     PROGR12C.                                                   PROGR12C
010040* * * * * * * * * * * * * * * * * * * * * * * * * * * * * **PROGR12C
010050*     PROGRAM WITH  MINOR, INTERMEDIATE, AND FINAL TOTALS.     *PROGR12C
010060* * * * * * * * * * * * * * * * * * * * * * * * * * * * * **PROGR12C
010070                                                                 PROGR12C
010080 ENVIRONMENT DIVISION.                                           PROGR12C
010090 CONFIGURATION SECTION.                                          PROGR12C
010100 SPECIAL-NAMES.                                                  PROGR12C
010110     C01 IS TOP-OF-PAGE.                                         PROGR12C
010120 INPUT-OUTPUT SECTION.                                           PROGR12C
010130 FILE-CONTROL.                                                   PROGR12C
010140     SELECT RECORDS-IN,                                          PROGR12C
010150         ASSIGN TO UR-2540R-S-SYSIN.                             PROGR12C
010160     SELECT PRINT-OUT,                                           PROGR12C
010170         ASSIGN TO UR-1403-S-SYSPRINT.                           PROGR12C
010180                                                                 PROGR12C
020010 DATA DIVISION.                                                  PROGR12C
020020 FILE SECTION.                                                   PROGR12C
020030 FD   RECORDS-IN                                                 PROGR12C
020040     LABEL RECORDS ARE OMITTED.                                  PROGR12C
020050 01  IN-RECORD                   PICTURE X(80).                  PROGR12C
020060 FD   PRINT-OUT                                                  PROGR12C
020070     LABEL RECORDS ARE OMITTED.                                  PROGR12C
020080 01  PRINT-LINE                  PICTURE X(133).                 PROGR12C
020090                                                                 PROGR12C
020100 WORKING-STORAGE SECTION.                                        PROGR12C
020110 77  SWITCH            PICTURE 9           VALUE ZERO.           PROGR12C
020120 77  LINE-COUNT        PICTURE S99         VALUE ZERO.           PROGR12C
020130 77  GROSS-PAY         PICTURE S999V99     VALUE ZERO.           PROGR12C
020140 77  DEPARTMENT-TOTAL  PICTURE S9999V99    VALUE ZERO.           PROGR12C
020150 77  DIVISION-TOTAL    PICTURE S99999V99   VALUE ZERO.           PROGR12C
020160 77  FINAL-TOTAL       PICTURE S99999V99   VALUE ZERO.           PROGR12C
020170 77  OLD-DEPT          PICTURE XX          VALUE '02'.           PROGR12C
020180 77  OLD-DIVISION      PICTURE XX.                               PROGR12C
020190                                                                 PROGR12C
020200 01  TOTAL-LINE.                                                 PROGR12C
020210     05  FILLER        PICTURE X(95)       VALUE SPACE.          PROGR12C
020220     05  TOTAL-PAY-LN  PICTURE $ZZ,ZZZ.99.                       PROGR12C
020230     05  FILLER        PICTURE X(28)       VALUE SPACE.          PROGR12C
020240                                                                 PROGR12C
020250 01  PAY-RECORD.                                                 PROGR12C
020260     05  NAME-RC               PICTURE X(30).                    PROGR12C
020270     05  EMP-NO-RC             PICTURE 9(09).                    PROGR12C
020280     05  HOURS-RC              PICTURE 99V9.                     PROGR12C
020290     05  RATE-RC               PICTURE 99V99.                    PROGR12C
020300     05  DIVISION-RC           PICTURE X(02).                    PROGR12C
020310     05  DEPT-RC               PICTURE X(02).                    PROGR12C
020320     05  SECTION-RC            PICTURE X(03).                    PROGR12C
020330     05  FILLER                PICTURE X(27).                    PROGR12C
```

```
0 20340                                                                          PROGR12C
030010 01   HEADING-LINE.                                                        PROGR12C
030020      05   FILLER          PICTURE X(02)          VALUE SPACE.             PROGR12C
030030      05   FILLER          PICTURE X(04)          VALUE 'NAME'.            PROGR12C
030040      05   FILLER          PICTURE X(27)          VALUE SPACE.             PROGR12C
030050      05   FILLER          PICTURE X(17)                                   PROGR12C
030060                           VALUE '   EMPLOYEE NO   '.                      PROGR12C
030070      05   FILLER          PICTURE X(23)                                   PROGR12C
030080           VALUE 'DIVISION  DEPT   SECTION'.                               PROGR12C


030090      05   FILLER          PICTURE X(32)                                   PROGR12C
030100           VALUE '   HOURS       RATE      GROSS PAY'.                     PROGR12C
030110      05   FILLER          PICTURE X(28)          VALUE SPACE.             PROGR12C
030120                                                                           PROGR 12C
030130 01   PAY-LINE.                                                            PROGR12C
030140      05   FILLER               PICTURE X(01).                             PROGR12C
030150      05   NAME-LN              PICTURE X(30).                             PROGR12C
030160      05   FILLER               PICTURE X(05).                             PROGR12C
030170      05   EMP-NO-LN            PICTURE 999B99B9999.                       PROGR12C
030180      05   FILLER               PICTURE X(06).                             PROGR12C
030190      05   DIVISION-LN          PICTURE X(02).                             PROGR12C
030200      05   FILLER               PICTURE X(06).                             PROGR12C
030210      05   DEPT-LN              PICTURE X(02).                             PROGR12C
030220      05   FILLER               PICTURE X(05).                             PROGR12C
030230      05   SECTION-LN           PICTURE X(03).                             PROGR12C
030240      05   FILLER               PICTURE X(05).                             PROGR12C
030250      05   HOURS-LN             PICTURE Z9.9.                              PROGR12C
030260      05   FILLER               PICTURE X(05).                             PROGR12C
030270      05   RATE-LN              PICTURE $ZZ.99.                            PROGR12C
030280      05   FILLER               PICTURE X(05).                             PROGR12C
030290      05   PAY-LN               PICTURE $Z,ZZZ.99.                         PROGR12C
030300      05   FILLER               PICTURE X(28).                             PROGR12C
030310                                                                           PROGR12C
040010 PROCEDURE DIVISION.                                                       PROGR12C
040020      OPEN INPUT RECORDS-IN, OUTPUT PRINT-OUT.                             PROGR12C
040030      PERFORM HEADING-ROUTINE.                                            PROGR12C
040040      MOVE SPACES TO PAY-LINE.                                             PROGR12C
040050      PERFORM CALCULATE-PAY 1000 TIMES.                                    PROGR12C
040060                                                                           PROGR12C
040070 ALL-DONE.                                                                 PROGR12C
040080      PERFORM INTERMEDIATE-TOTAL-ROUTINE.                                  PROGR12C
040090      MOVE FINAL-TOTAL TO TOTAL-PAY-LN.                                    PROGR12C
040100      WRITE PRINT-LINE FROM TOTAL-LINE AFTER ADVANCING 1 LINES.            PROGR12C
040110      CLOSE RECORDS-IN, PRINT-OUT.                                         PROGR12C
040120      STOP RUN.                                                            PROGR12C
040130                                                                           PROGR12C
040140 CALCULATE-PAY.                                                            PROGR12C
040150      READ RECORDS-IN INTO PAY-RECORD AT END PERFORM ALL-DONE.             PROGR12C
040160      IF (SWITCH NOT = 0)                                                  PROGR12C
040170         IF (DIVISION-RC NOT = OLD-DIVISION)                               PROGR12C
040180              PERFORM INTERMEDIATE-TOTAL-ROUTINE                           PROGR12C
040190         ELSE IF (DEPT-RC NOT = OLD-DEPT)                                  PROGR12C
040200              PERFORM MINOR-TOTAL-ROUTINE.                                 PROGR12C
040210      MOVE 1 TO SWITCH.                                                    PROGR12C
040220      MOVE DIVISION-RC TO OLD-DIVISION.                                    PROGR12C
040230      MOVE DEPT-RC TO OLD-DEPT.                                            PROGR12C
040240      MOVE NAME-RC TO NAME-LN.                                             PROGR12C
040250      MOVE EMP-NO-RC TO EMP-NO-LN.                                         PROGR12C
040260      MOVE HOURS-RC TO HOURS-LN.                                           PROGR12C
040270      MOVE RATE-RC TO RATE-LN.                                             PROGR12C
040280      MOVE DEPT-RC TO DEPT-LN.                                             PROGR12C
040290      MOVE SECTION-RC TO SECTION-LN.                                       PROGR12C
040300      MOVE DIVISION-RC TO DIVISION-LN.                                     PROGR12C
040310      COMPUTE GROSS-PAY = RATE-RC * HOURS-RC.                              PROGR12C
040320      ADD GROSS-PAY TO DEPARTMENT-TOTAL.                                   PROGR12C
040330      MOVE GROSS-PAY TO PAY-LN.                                            PROGR12C
040340      WRITE PRINT-LINE FROM PAY-LINE AFTER ADVANCING 1 LINES.              PROGR12C
040350      ADD 1 TO LINE-COUNT.                                                 PROGR12C
040360      IF (LINE-COUNT > 55) PERFORM HEADING-ROUTINE.                        PROGR12C
040370                                                                           PROGR12C
```

```
040380  HEADING-ROUTINE.                                                        PROGR 12C
040390      WRITE PRINT-LINE FROM HEADING-LINE                                  PROGR 12C
040400          AFTER ADVANCING TOP-OF-PAGE.                                    PROGR 12C
040410      MOVE ZERO TO LINE-COUNT.                                            PROGR 12C
040420                                                                          PROGR 12C
040430  MINOR-TOTAL-ROUTINE.                                                    PROGR 12C
040440      MOVE DEPARTMENT-TOTAL TO TOTAL-PAY-LN.                              PROGR 12C
040450      WRITE PRINT-LINE FROM TOTAL-LINE AFTER ADVANCING 2 LINES.           PROGR 12C
040460      ADD 2 TO LINE-COUNT.                                                PROGR 12C
040470      ADD DEPARTMENT-TOTAL TO DIVISION-TOTAL.                             PROGR 12C
040480      MOVE ZERO TO DEPARTMENT-TOTAL.                                      PROGR 12C
040490      PERFORM PRINT-BLANK-LINE 2 TIMES.                                   PROGR 12C
040500                                                                          PROGR 12C
040510  INTERMEDIATE-TOTAL-ROUTINE.                                             PROGR 12C
040520      PERFORM MINOR-TOTAL-ROUTINE.                                        PROGR 12C
040530      MOVE DIVISION-TOTAL TO TOTAL-PAY-LN.                                PROGR 12C
040540      WRITE PRINT-LINE FROM TOTAL-LINE AFTER ADVANCING 0 LINES.           PROGR 12C
040550      ADD DIVISION-TOTAL TO FINAL-TOTAL.                                  PROGR 12C
040560      MOVE ZERO TO DIVISION-TOTAL.                                        PROGR 12C
040570      PERFORM PRINT-BLANK-LINE 2 TIMES.                                   PROGR 12C
040580                                                                          PROGR 12C
040590  PRINT-BLANK-LINE.                                                       PROGR 12C
040600      MOVE SPACES TO PAY-LINE.                                            PROGR 12C
040610      WRITE PRINT-LINE FROM PAY-LINE AFTER ADVANCING 1 LINES.             PROGR 12C
040620      ADD 1 TO LINE-COUNT.                                                PROGR 12C
```

FIGURE 12.6   **Sample Program 12C**

We still need to use the switch when we read the first record in the data file. Here is the necessary code to check for both total-levels:

```
READ RECORDS-IN INTO PAY-RECORD AT END PERFORM ALL-DONE.
IF (SWITCH NOT = 0)
    IF (DIVISION-RC NOT = OLD-DIVISION)
        PERFORM INTERMEDIATE-TOTAL-ROUTINE
    ELSE IF (DEPT-RC NOT = OLD-DEPT) PERFORM MINOR-TOTAL-ROUTINE.
MOVE 1 TO SWITCH.
MOVE DIVISION-RC TO OLD-DIVISION.
MOVE DEPT-RC TO OLD-DEPT.
```

Notice that we first check to see if we must do a division total. Always check the highest total-level first: in this case, division is the highest level. Only if there is no need for a division total do we check for a department total. The INTERMEDIATE-TOTAL-ROUTINE could be as follows:

```
INTERMEDIATE-TOTAL-ROUTINE.
    PERFORM MINOR-TOTAL-ROUTINE.
    MOVE DIVISION-TOTAL TO TOTAL-PAY-LN.
    WRITE PRINT-LINE FROM TOTAL-LINE AFTER ADVANCING 0 LINES.
    ADD DIVISION-TOTAL TO FINAL-TOTAL.
    MOVE ZERO TO DIVISION-TOTAL.
```

We will always take a minor total before a division total; when the division changes we must print the department total before we print the division total. The general rule is that we always check the highest level first—in this example, the division is the top level. If the division has not changed, we next check the next lower level, i.e., the department. Then we follow the same pattern as with our previous example for minor total.

The termination paragraph has changed a little. Here are the first two lines:

```
ALL-DONE.
    PERFORM INTERMEDIATE-TOTAL-ROUTINE.
```

NAME	EMPLOYEE NO	DIVISION	DEPT	SECTION	HOURS	RATE	GROSS PAY
ZERO TEST	000 00 0000		02	000	0.0	$ .00	$ .00
DENNIE VAN TASSEL	456 12 3456	01	02	300	40.0	$12.50	$ 500.00
JERRY CARLSON	147 25 8369	01	02	300	40.0	$ 8.50	$ 340.00
SUE MORRE	753 42 1689	01	02	300	38.0	$10.00	$ 380.00
							$ 1,220.00
ELLOIT WEBSTER	147 25 8635	01	03	010	40.0	$ 9.50	$ 380.00
HUEGA WOO	425 75 8963	01	03	010	40.0	$60.00	$ 400.00
JOHN GARCIA	112 25 8740	01	03	300	35.0	$ 9.00	$ 315.00
							$ 1,095.00
							$ 2,315.00
RANDOTH LIEBERSON	754 23 1568	02	05	400	20.0	$ 7.90	$ 158.00
AMAGE BIGFOOT	752 41 3524	02	05	400	40.0	$ 9.00	$ 360.00
							$ 518.00
							$ 518.00
000000000 11111111122222222223	333 33 3333	44	45	555	44.4	$44.44	$ 973.13
							973.13
							$ 973.13
12345678901234567890123456789 0	123 45 6789	78	90	123	1.2	$34.56	$ 41.47
							41.47
							$ 41.47
							$ 3,847.60

FIGURE 12.7   Output from Program 12C

When all input records have been read we wish to force (to print) all totals. The first line of the termination paragraph instructs the computer to perform the intermediate-total routine: the first thing done in the INTERMEDIATE-TOTAL-ROUTINE is to perform the minor-total paragraph. Thus, the minor totals will be printed, then the intermediate totals, and finally the final totals. Reread this code until you thoroughly understand how it works. This is sometimes called **unrolling the totals**.

GROUPING TOTAL FIELDS

Several level-number-77 items may be grouped together under an **01** level instead of using individual level-number-77 items. For example:

```
WORKING-STORAGE SECTION.
77    TOTAL-A    PICTURE S999V99    VALUE ZERO.
77    TOTAL-B    PICTURE S999V99    VALUE ZERO.
```

This could be done as follows:

```
WORKING-STORAGE SECTION.
01 ALL-TOTALS.
   05    TOTAL-A    PICTURE S999V99    VALUE ZERO.
   05    TOTAL-B    PICTURE S999V99    VALUE ZERO.
```

Grouping fields under an **01** description has two main advantages: it allows the programmer to group like fields under one record description, which aids in program documentation, and it permits a single value clause to be used at the group level to zero out all totals or a MOVE statement to be used at either the group or elementary level to zero totals.

REVIEW

1. In Sample Program 12C, why must we always take a minor total first if an intermediate total is to be executed? Why does the program check for intermediate totals before it checks for minor totals? Could this be done in a different order?

Program Modifications

1. Modify Sample Program 12C to accumulate and print the totals for hours for all total levels. Label each total line, as DEPARTMENT TOTAL, DIVISION TOTAL, or FINAL TOTAL. Start these labels in column 3 of the total line. Group the pay-field totals and the hour-field totals separately.

2. Program 12C is incomplete because it fails to check the input file to make sure it is in sequence. Write code to check the input sequence. If the file is out-of-sequence, print the message INPUT FILE OUT OF SEQUENCE and stop execution of the program.

3.   We now need three levels of totals and a final total. Here are the fields:

Level	Field
Major	Division
Intermediate	Department
Minor	Section

The new section code will be in columns 51–53. Modify Program 12C to handle these totals.

4.   On the program-modification sequence above, check the input file. If the input file is out-of-sequence, print the message INPUT FILE OUT OF SEQUENCE and stop execution of the program.

****

Computer Graffiti

They say it's automatic, but you really have to push the button.

****

SUMMARY TOTALS

Often you will have large input files and will not wish to print every input transaction: instead, you will wish to print only the totals, in what is called a **summary report**. Some of the people at Ready-Cash Bank have requested that their version of the report be prepared as a summary report. We will now modify Sample Program 12C to accumulate the totals, but to print only when the department or division changes. We can use the input record of Program 12C, but we will only want to print the division, the department, and the gross pay.

The input-record description does not necessarily change, but since we no longer need the name and employee number, we may as well revise it. Here is the new input record:

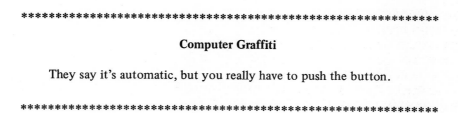

```
01 PAY-RECORD.
    05  FILLER          PICTURE X(39).
    05  HOURS-RC        PICTURE 99V9.
    05  RATE-RC         PICTURE 99V99.
    05  DIVISION-RC     PICTURE X(02).
    05  DEPT-RC         PICTURE X(02).
    05  FILLER          PICTURE X(30).
```

The main processing paragraph is almost the same as that in Program 12C, except that now we do not move any detail information to the print-line, and we do not print a detail line. Here is the main processing paragraph:

```
CALCULATE-PAY.
     READ RECORDS-IN INTO PAY-RECORD AT END PERFORM ALL-DONE.
     IF (SWITCH NOT = 0)
         IF (DIVISION-RC NOT = OLD-DIVISION)
             PERFORM INTERMEDIATE-TOTAL-ROUTINE
         ELSE IF (DEPT-RC NOT = OLD-DEPT)
             PERFORM MINOR-TOTAL-ROUTINE.
     MOVE 1 TO SWITCH.
     MOVE DIVISION-RC TO OLD-DIVISION.
     MOVE DEPT-RC TO OLD-DEPT.
     COMPUTE GROSS-PAY = RATE-RC * HOURS-RC.
     ADD GROSS-PAY TO DEPARTMENT-TOTAL.
```

The paragraph above reads the records, checks for needed totals, and accumulates the pay totals. Notice that no input records are printed.

The MINOR-TOTAL-ROUTINE is also almost the same as in Program 12C. Here is the paragraph:

```
MINOR-TOTAL-ROUTINE.
     MOVE OLD-DEPT TO DEPT-LN.
     MOVE OLD-DIVISION TO DIVISION-LN.
     MOVE DEPARTMENT-TOTAL TO TOTAL-PAY-LN.
     WRITE PRINT-LINE FROM TOTAL-LINE AFTER ADVANCING 1 LINES.
     ADD 1 TO LINE COUNT.
     IF (LINE-COUNT > 55) PERFORM HEADING-ROUTINE.
     ADD DEPARTMENT-TOTAL TO DIVISION-TOTAL.
     MOVE ZERO TO DEPARTMENT-TOTAL.
```

We now move the department and division to the total line; they will print along with the totals.

One last change is to move spaces to the TOTAL-LINE in the INTERMEDIATE-TOTAL-ROUTINE, because we do not wish to print any department or division on the intermediate-total line. Sample Program 12D (Figure 12.8) is the sample program for summary totals. Figure 12.9 is some sample output.

```
010010 IDENTIFICATION DIVISION.                                    PROGR12D
010020 PROGRAM-ID.                                                 PROGR12D
010030      PROGR12D.                                              PROGR12D
010040* * * * * * * * * * * * * * * * * * * * * * * * * * * **PROGR12D
010050*     PROGRAM WITH SUMMARY TOTALS.                           *PROGR12D
010060* * * * * * * * * * * * * * * * * * * * * * * * * * * **PROGR12D
010070                                                             PROGR12D
010080 ENVIRONMENT DIVISION.                                       PROGR12D
010090 CONFIGURATION SECTION.                                      PROGR12D
010100 SPECIAL-NAMES.                                              PROGR12D
010110      C01 IS TOP-OF-PAGE.                                    PROGR12D
010120 INPUT-OUTPUT SECTION.                                       PROGR12D
010130 FILE-CONTROL.                                               PROGR12D
010140      SELECT RECORDS-IN,                                     PROGR12D
010150          ASSIGN TO UR-2540R-S-SYSIN.                        PROGR12D
010160      SELECT PRINT-OUT,                                      PROGR12D
010170          ASSIGN TO UR-1403-S-SYSPRINT.                      PROGR12D
010180                                                             PROGR12D
020010 DATA DIVISION.                                              PROGR12D
020020 FILE SECTION.                                               PROGR12D
020030 FD   RECORDS-IN                                             PROGR12D
020040      LABEL RECORDS ARE OMITTED.                             PROGR12D
020050 01   IN-RECORD                    PICTURE X(80).            PROGR12D
020060 FD   PRINT-OUT                                              PROGR12D
020070      LABEL RECORDS ARE OMITTED.                             PROGR12D
020080 01   PRINT-LINE                   PICTURE X(133).           PROGR12D
```

```
020090                                                                          PROGR12D
020100 WORKING-STORAGE SECTION.                                                 PROGR12D
020110 77  SWITCH              PICTURE 9              VALUE ZERO.                PROGR12D
020120 77  LINE-COUNT          PICTURE S99            VALUE ZERO.                PROGR12D
020130 77  GROSS-PAY           PICTURE S999V99        VALUE ZERO.                PROGR12D
020140 77  DEPARTMENT-TOTAL    PICTURE S9999V99       VALUE ZERO.                PROGR12D
020150 77  DIVISION-TOTAL      PICTURE S99999V99      VALUE ZERO.                PROGR12D
020160 77  FINAL-TOTAL         PICTURE S99999V99      VALUE ZERO.                PROGR12D
020170 77  OLD-DEPT            PICTURE XX             VALUE '02'.                PROGR12D
020180 77  OLD-DIVISION        PICTURE XX.                                       PROGR12D
020190                                                                          PROGR12D
020200 01  PAY-RECORD.                                                          PROGR12D
020210     05  FILLER              PICTURE X(39).                               PROGR12D
020220     05  HOURS-RC            PICTURE 99V9.                                PROGR12D
020230     05  RATE-RC             PICTURE 99V99.                               PROGR12D
020240     05  DIVISION-RC         PICTURE X(02).                               PROGR12D
020250     05  DEPT-RC             PICTURE X(02).                               PROGR12D
020260     05  FILLER              PICTURE X(30).                               PROGR12D
020270                                                                          PROGR12D
030010 01  HEADING-LINE.                                                        PROGR12D
030020     05  FILLER          PICTURE X(03)      VALUE SPACE.                  PROGR12D
030030     05  FILLER          PICTURE X(28)                                    PROGR12D
030040         VALUE 'DIVISION   DEPT      PAY TOTAL'.                          PROGR12D
030050     05  FILLER          PICTURE X(102)     VALUE SPACE.                  PROGR12D
030060                                                                          PROGR12D
030070 01  TOTAL-LINE.                                                          PROGR12D
030080     05  FILLER              PICTURE X(06).                               PROGR12D
030090     05  DIVISION-LN         PICTURE X(02).                               PROGR12D
030100     05  FILLER              PICTURE X(06).                               PROGR12D
030110     05  DEPT-LN             PICTURE X(02).                               PROGR12D
030120     05  FILLER              PICTURE X(06).                               PROGR12D
030130     05  TOTAL-PAY-LN    PICTURE $ZZ,ZZZ.99.                              PROGR12D
030140     05  FILLER          PICTURE X(101)     VALUE SPACE.                  PROGR12D
030150                                                                          PROGR12D


040010 PROCEDURE DIVISION.                                                      PROGR12D
040020     OPEN INPUT RECORDS-IN, OUTPUT PRINT-OUT.                             PROGR12D
040030     PERFORM HEADING-ROUTINE.                                            PROGR12D
040040     MOVE SPACES TO TOTAL-LINE.                                          PROGR12D
040050     PERFORM CALCULATE-PAY 1000 TIMES.                                   PROGR12D
040060                                                                          PROGR12D
040070 ALL-DONE.                                                                PROGR12D
040080     PERFORM INTERMEDIATE-TOTAL-ROUTINE.                                 PROGR12D
040090     MOVE FINAL-TOTAL TO TOTAL-PAY-LN.                                   PROGR12D
040100     WRITE PRINT-LINE FROM TOTAL-LINE AFTER ADVANCING 1 LINES.           PROGR12D
040110     CLOSE RECORDS-IN, PRINT-OUT.                                        PROGR12D
040120     STOP RUN.                                                           PROGR12D
040130                                                                          PROGR12D
040140 CALCULATE-PAY.                                                           PROGR12D
040150     READ RECORDS-IN INTO PAY-RECORD AT END PERFORM ALL-DONE.            PROGR12D
040160     IF (SWITCH NOT = 0)                                                 PROGR12D
040170         IF (DIVISION-RC NOT = OLD-DIVISION)                             PROGR12D
040180             PERFORM INTERMEDIATE-TOTAL-ROUTINE                          PROGR12D
040190         ELSE IF (DEPT-RC NOT = OLD-DEPT)                                PROGR12D
040200             PERFORM MINOR-TOTAL-ROUTINE.                                PROGR12D
040210     MOVE 1 TO SWITCH.                                                   PROGR12D
040220     MOVE DIVISION-RC TO OLD-DIVISION.                                   PROGR12D
040230     MOVE DEPT-RC TO OLD-DEPT.                                           PROGR12D
040240     COMPUTE GROSS-PAY = RATE-RC * HOURS-RC.                             PROGR12D
040250     ADD GROSS-PAY TO DEPARTMENT-TOTAL.                                  PROGR12D
040260                                                                          PROGR12D
040270 HEADING-ROUTINE.                                                         PROGR12D
040280     WRITE PRINT-LINE FROM HEADING-LINE                                  PROGR12D
040290             AFTER ADVANCING TOP-OF-PAGE.                                PROGR12D
040300     MOVE ZERO TO LINE-COUNT.                                            PROGR12D
040310                                                                          PROGR12D
```

```
040320 MINOR-TOTAL-ROUTINE.                                              PROGR12D
040330     MOVE OLD-DEPT TO DEPT-LN.                                      PROGR12D
040340     MOVE OLD-DIVISION TO DIVISION-LN.                             PROGR12D
040350     MOVE DEPARTMENT-TOTAL TO TOTAL-PAY-LN.                        PROGR12D
040360     WRITE PRINT-LINE FROM TOTAL-LINE AFTER ADVANCING 1 LINES.     PROGR12D
040370     ADD 1 TO LINE-COUNT.                                          PROGR12D
040380     IF (LINE-COUNT > 55) PERFORM HEADING-ROUTINE.                 PROGR12D
040390     ADD DEPARTMENT-TOTAL TO DIVISION-TOTAL.                       PROGR12D
040400     MOVE ZERO TO DEPARTMENT-TOTAL.                                PROGR12D
040410                                                                   PROGR12D
040420 INTERMEDIATE-TOTAL-ROUTINE.                                       PROGR12D
040430     PERFORM MINOR-TOTAL-ROUTINE.                                  PROGR12D
040440     MOVE SPACES TO TOTAL-LINE.                                    PROGR12D
040450     MOVE DIVISION-TOTAL TO TOTAL-PAY-LN.                          PROGR12D
040460     WRITE PRINT-LINE FROM TOTAL-LINE AFTER ADVANCING 1 LINES.     PROGR12D
040470     ADD 1 TO LINE-COUNT.                                          PROGR12D
040480     IF (LINE-COUNT > 55) PERFORM HEADING-ROUTINE.                 PROGR12D
040490     ADD DIVISION-TOTAL TO FINAL-TOTAL.                            PROGR12D
040500     MOVE ZERO TO DIVISION-TOTAL.                                  PROGR12D
040510     PERFORM PRINT-BLANK-LINE 2 TIMES.                             PROGR12D
040520                                                                   PROGR12D
040530 PRINT-BLANK-LINE.                                                 PROGR12D
040540     MOVE SPACES TO TOTAL-LINE.                                    PROGR12D
040550     WRITE PRINT-LINE FROM TOTAL-LINE AFTER ADVANCING 1 LINES.     PROGR12D
040560     ADD 1 TO LINE-COUNT.                                          PROGR12D
```

FIGURE 12.8   Sample Program 12D

```
DIVISION   DEPT     PAY TOTAL
   01       02     $ 1,220.00
   01       03     $ 1,095.00
                   $ 2,315.00


   02       05     $   518.00
                   $   518.00


   44       45     $   973.13
                   $   973.13


                   $ 3,806.13
```

FIGURE 12.9   Output from Sample Program 12D

PROGRAM MODIFICATIONS

1. Modify Sample Program 12D so that the total hours are accumulated and printed at each total-level.

2. Modify Program 12D so that DIVISION nn TOTAL (where nn is the division number) is printed on the division total line. This total label should print in columns 35–51.

3. Modify Program 12D so that the minor total is taken by section and the intermediate total is by division.

4. Modify Program 12D so that summary totals are printed at each of the three levels, division, department, and section.

MORE ON SWITCHES

Switches, very useful in programming, are commonly used with the UNTIL clause. Let us modify one of the early programs to use a switch to indicate when there are no more data records. Sample Program 4B could be changed as follows:

```
77 END-SWITCH    PICTURE 9    VALUE ZERO.
        .
        .
        .

    PROCEDURE DIVISION.
        OPEN INPUT RECORDS-IN, OUTPUT PRINT-LINE.
        READ RECORDS-IN INTO ADDRESS-RECORD
            AT END PERFORM WRAP-IT-UP.
        PERFORM PROCESS-RECORDS UNTIL (END-SWITCH = 1).
    WRAP-IT-UP.
        CLOSE RECORDS-IN, PRINT-OUT.
        STOP-RUN.
    PROCESS-RECORDS.
        MOVE NAME-RD TO NAME-LINE.
        MOVE STREET-RD TO STREET-LINE.
        MOVE CITY-RD TO CITY-LINE.
        WRITE PRINT-LINE FROM ADDRESS-LINE
            AFTER ADVANCING 1 LINES.
        READ RECORDS-IN INTO ADDRESS-RECORD
            AT END MOVE 1 TO END-SWITCH.
```

Study the code above to make sure you understand how the switch is used. Notice that we must read the first date-record before we start performing the paragraph PROCESS-RECORDS, because the READ statement must come at the end of the paragraph PROCESS-RECORDS instead of at the beginning of the paragraph. If the READ statement were the first statement in PROCESS-RECORDS, the program would still attempt to move the name, street, and city fields when there were no more data.

****

****

CHAPTER REVIEW

Vocabulary Review

Robust program   Switch   Grouping fields

Flag   Unrolling the totals   Summary report

Review Questions

1. What is a switch? How does it differ from a simple IF statement?

2. In the last COBOL example, why is the READ statement at the end of the paragraph PROCESS-RECORDS instead of the beginning? Would it still work if we moved the READ statement to the beginning?

Program Modifications

1. Modify one of your earlier programs to use a switch to indicate when there are no more data records.

2. Do exercise 1, but use "YES" and "NO" in the switch instead of numbers. Use a more appropriate name than SWITCH, for example, MORE-DATA.

3. In the program you used in exercise 1, move the READ statement from the end of the PROCESS-RECORDS paragraph to the beginning of the paragraph. Run this program and see what happens.

Programs

1. Rewrite the program in question 4 at the end of Chapter 11 so that it takes a minor total on salesperson code, an intermediate total on office, and a major total on district.

2. Write a program to process deposit records for Ready-Cash Bank. The input records are:

Field	Columns
Account number	1–9
Branch	10–13
County	14–16
State	17–18
Amount	19–26

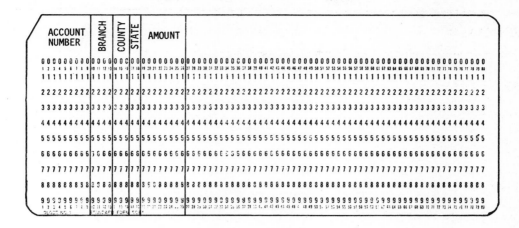

Print all fields and provide a heading line. Take a minor total on branch and an intermediate total on county. Print a final total.

3. Ready-Cash Bank needs a program to process the following data records:

Field	Columns
Account number	1–9
Date	10–15
Branch	16–18
County	19–22
State	23–24
Amount	25–32

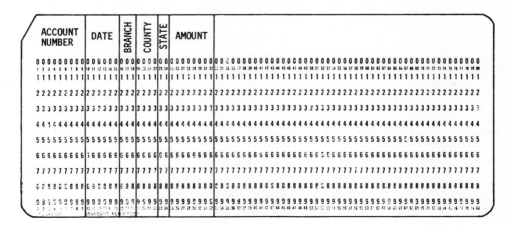

Process these data records, taking an intermediate total on county and a minor total on branch. Print all fields; print a heading line.

4. Rewrite the program above to print only summary information.

****

"Special Forms," The Lady Tells Him.

By the Input/Output Window
Of an I.B.M. 370
Sits an old man—bearded warrior.
Silent. Waiting for his program.

As a young man he submitted
90 cards—a FORTRAN program.
Walked away believing he would
In 2 hours receive his output.

Through the snow and wind returning.
Through the door; up to the window.
Calmly, with a pleasant smile, he
Asks the lady for his output.

"Turnaround," she tells him sharply,
"Turnaround is now 6 hours."
With her hand she indicates the
Blackboard on the wall behind her.

With a shrug he quits the window.
Turns around and climbs the stairwell.
Sits and studies for 6 hours.
Then returns—presents his check stub.

"Special forms," the lady tells him,
"Special forms have now been mounted."
Even planets in their orbits
Halt when special forms are running.

"But," he questions, "I was promised
I'd receive my print out, if I'd
Wait 6 hours for its running."
"Special forms," the lady tells him.

Once again he shrugs his shoulders.
Buys himself a Dr. Pepper.
Buys a couple frozen Twinkees.
Waits until the moon has risen.

Education comes not only
In the classroom; from a teacher.
Mephistopheles grins as they
Tell him that his deck is missing.

Now an odd expression slowly
Spreads across his former calm face.
He sits down next to the window.
Sets his jaw. His eyes become glazed.

By the Input/Output Window
Of an I.B.M. 370
Sits an old man—bearded warrior.
Silent. Waiting for his program.

Dr. D. M. Nessett

****

Chapter
13

****
An old robot versed in geography,
And fond of discussing topography,
Concealed an exotic
Regard for erotic
Postcards and books of pornography.

****

TABLES

You will sometimes need several variables with identical descriptions. For example, suppose you wish to have five pay-rate variables. You could declare them as follows:

```
01 RATE-RECORD.
    05    PAY-RATE-1    PICTURE 99V99.
    05    PAY-RATE-2    PICTURE 99V99.
    05    PAY-RATE-3    PICTURE 99V99.
    05    PAY-RATE-4    PICTURE 99V99.
    05    PAY-RATE-5    PICTURE 99V99.
```

This method works well enough when you need only a few variables, but what if you need 100 or 1,000 pay rates? Then the method above would be much too clumsy.

Fortunately, COBOL provides a simple way to declare a set of identical variables:

```
01 RATE-RECORD.
    05    PAY-RATE    PICTURE 99V99
            OCCURS 5 TIMES.
```

This declares five variables named **PAY-RATE**. This is called a **table** in COBOL. The pay-rate table with values in it could be thought of as looking like this:

PAY-RATE

1	06.00
2	07.00
3	09.50
4	12.00
5	15.00

When a table is declared, space is established for the table but no values are put in the table. Various means for putting values in the table, that is, for **initializing the table**, are discussed in this chapter. The variable used is indicated by the subscript. For example, in:

PAY-RATE (3)

the subscript **3** indicates the *third* pay rate. The subscript is always enclosed in parentheses; it can be either an integer constant or an integer variable.

The complete set of variables, called in mathematics a vector or an array, in COBOL is called a table. Each part of the table is an **element** of the table: the number inside the parentheses which identifies the element is called the **subscript**. In mathematics, tables are subscripted differently. The COBOL subscripts

X(1)   X(2)   X(3)

would be written

X_1 X_2 X_3

in mathematics. Because there is no symbol for the mathematical subscript in COBOL, we put the subscript in parentheses on the same line as the variable.

The **OCCURS** clause is used to indicate how many elements are needed. The general format is

[OCCURS integer TIMES]

Notice that you must use an integer, not a variable, to specify how many elements you want in the table. Use of the reserved word **TIMES** is optional. The **OCCURS** clause may be placed either before or after the **PICTURE** clause. It may be used only with levels 02 through 49, that is, level 01, level 77, and level 88 cannot have an **OCCURS** clause.

SUBSCRIPTS

A subscripted variable may be used in the same ways as other variables, but it must always have its subscript. You must also remember the rules of punctuation regarding parentheses: the left parenthesis must be preceded by a space and the right parenthesis must be followed by a space or period, and the parentheses must be closed up to the subscript. For example:

```
            no space
             ↓ ↓
PAY-RATE (4)
             ↑ ↑
            space
```

(Some of the new COBOL compilers have relaxed the rules; the spacing above may not be mandatory on your compiler.)

The subscript can be an integer constant or an integer variable, but it cannot itself be a subscripted variable. Thus we may have:

```
MOVE PAY-RATE (2) TO PAY-RATE-PR.
```

or

```
MOVE PAY-RATE (L) TO PAY-RATE-PR.
```

L must have been declared and must have a value within the **range of the table**, which is always 1 through the size of the table.

Checking Subscript Range

It is important that the subscript be within the range of the table. For example:

```
05 A   PICTURE 999   OCCURS 3 TIMES.
```

declares three elements in an array. They are:

```
A (1)
A (2)
A (3)
```

If you then wrote the following COBOL statement:

```
MOVE A (6) TO . . .
```

an error would result, because the table has only three elements. Different compilers handle this error differently. Some compilers catch the error, but most compilers will not catch it even if the subscript is a constant. If the subscript is a variable the error can only be caught during execution. Most COBOL compilers do not generate any code to check subscript range.

Whenever the subscript might be outside the permissible range (e.g., when the subscript comes from data), code should be written to make sure that the subscript is within the permissible range. The usual method of checking subscripts for possible incorrect values is with an IF statement. For example:

```
IF (K > 0) AND (K < 4)
    PERFORM PROCESS-RECORD
ELSE PERFORM ERROR-SUBSCRIPT.
```

This code will cause the ERROR-SUBSCRIPT paragraph to be executed whenever the subscript is outside the range of 1 to 3.

Note:

1. The VALUE clause cannot be used with an OCCURS clause.
2. Subscripted variables cannot be level-01, level-77, or level-88 items.
3. Subscripts cannot be subscripted variables.
4. The subscript must be within the range of the table.

****

Computer Graffiti

If the computer were so simple a fool could use it,
only a fool would want to use it.

****

SAMPLE PROGRAM 13A

Ready-Cash Bank has decided to change its payroll records. Instead of typing the hourly rate in each payroll record, a one-digit code will be typed to indicate the pay rate. This will not only save typing time, but will also help to avoid errors in the hourly pay-rate. Sample Program 13A uses subscripted variables to handle some pay-rates. In this program we wish to read in five different pay-rates and store them in a table. Then this table will be used to calculate pay according to the pay code. First, we need an input record, as follows:

```
01 RATE-RECORD.
    05    PAY-RATE          PICTURE 99V99
                  OCCURS 5 TIMES.
    05    FILLER            PICTURE X(60).
```

This describes an 80-column record. The first pay-rate must be in columns 1–4, the second pay-rate in columns 5–8, the third in columns 9–12, etc.

The table is set up in storage somewhat like this:

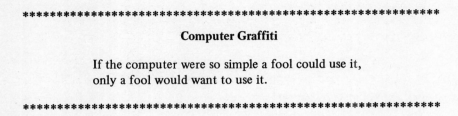

Together, the five pay rates use the first 20 columns of the input record. This RATE-RECORD is the first data-record. It is read as follows:

```
READ RECORDS-IN INTO RATE-RECORD AT END PERFORM ALL-DONE.
```

This READ statement will initialize the pay-rate table. Each detail record must have a code indicating what pay-code is to be used. PAY-CODE is a l-column field in PAY-RECORD. Here is the description of PAY-RECORD:

```
01 PAY-RECORD.
   05 NAME        PICTURE X(30).
   05 EMP-NO      PICTURE 9(09).
   05 HOURS       PICTURE 99V9.
   05 PAY-CODE    PICTURE 9.
   05 FILLER      PICTURE X(37).
```

The PAY-CODE must be a number from 1 to 5. The PAY-RATEs are used as follows:

```
COMPUTE GROSS-PAY = PAY-RATE (PAY-CODE) * HOURS OF PAY-RECORD.
MOVE PAY-RATE (PAY-CODE) TO RATE.
```

These two sentences use PAY-CODE to determine the PAY-RATE to be used for each employee, that is, if the employee's data-record has a 2 in the PAY-CODE field, the second PAY-RATE will be used for the calculation of pay. The use of a code instead of the pay rate saves space in the detail records. It can also simplify changes: all pay-rates can be changed at once by simply altering the pay-rate table. Sample Program 13A (**Figure 13.1**) uses a subscripted array, as described above. **Figure 13.2** is some sample input for this program. Notice that the first record contains the pay rates.

```
010010 IDENTIFICATION DIVISION.                                        PROGR13A
010020 PROGRAM-ID.                                                     PROGR13A
010030     PROGR13A.                                                   PROGR13A
010040* * * * * * * * * * * * * * * * * * * * * * * * * * * * * **PROGR13A
010050*    SAMPLE ONE-DIMENSIONAL TABLES.                            *PROGR13A
010060* * * * * * * * * * * * * * * * * * * * * * * * * * * * * **PROGR13A
010070                                                                 PROGR13A
010080 ENVIRONMENT DIVISION.                                           PROGR13A
010090 INPUT-OUTPUT SECTION.                                           PROGR13A
010100 FILE-CONTROL.                                                   PROGR13A
010110     SELECT RECORDS-IN                                          PROGR13A
010120         ASSIGN TO UR-2540R-S-SYSIN.                            PROGR13A
010130     SELECT PRINT-OUT,                                          PROGR13A
010140         ASSIGN TO UR-1403-S-SYSPRINT.                          PROGR13A
010150                                                                 PROGR13A
020010 DATA DIVISION.                                                  PROGR13A
020020 FILE SECTION.                                                   PROGR13A
020030 FD  RECORDS-IN                                                  PROGR13A
020040     LABEL RECORDS ARE OMITTED.                                 PROGR13A
020050 01  IN-RECORD              PICTURE X(80).                       PROGR13A
020060 FD  PRINT-OUT                                                   PROGR13A
020070     LABEL RECORDS ARE OMITTED.                                 PROGR13A
020080 01  PRINT-LINE             PICTURE X(133).                      PROGR13A
020090                                                                 PROGR13A
020100 WORKING-STORAGE SECTION.                                        PROGR13A
020110 77  TOTAL-PAY         PICTURE S99999V99    VALUE ZERO.          PROGR13A
020120 77  GROSS-PAY         PICTURE S999V99      VALUE ZERO.          PROGR13A
020130                                                                 PROGR13A
020140 01  RATE-RECORD.                                                PROGR13A
020150     05  PAY-RATE           PICTURE 99V99                        PROGR13A
020160              OCCURS 5 TIMES.                                    PROGR13A
020170     05  FILLER             PICTURE X(60).                       PROGR13A
020180                                                                 PROGR13A
020190 01  TOTAL-LINE.                                                 PROGR13A
020200     05  FILLER        PICTURE X(70)        VALUE SPACE.         PROGR13A
020210     05  TOTAL-PAY-LN  PICTURE $ZZ,ZZZ.99.                       PROGR13A
020220     05  FILLER        PICTURE X(53)        VALUE SPACE.         PROGR13A
020230                                                                 PROGR13A
```

```
030010 01  PAY-RECORD.                              PROGR13A
030020     05  NAME          PICTURE X(30).         PROGR13A
030030     05  EMP-NO        PICTURE 9(09).         PROGR13A
030040     05  HOURS         PICTURE 99V9.          PROGR13A
030050     05  PAY-CODE      PICTURE 9.             PROGR13A
030060     05  FILLER        PICTURE X(37).         PROGR13A
030070                                              PROGR13A
030080 01  PAY-LINE.                                PROGR13A
030090     05  FILLER        PICTURE X(01).         PROGR13A
030100     05  NAME          PICTURE X(30).         PROGR13A
030110     05  FILLER        PICTURE X(05).         PROGR13A
030120     05  EMP-NO        PICTURE 999B99B9999.   PROGR13A
030130     05  FILLER        PICTURE X(05).         PROGR13A
030140     05  HOURS         PICTURE Z9.9.          PROGR13A
030150     05  FILLER        PICTURE X(05).         PROGR13A
030160     05  RATE          PICTURE $ZZ.99.        PROGR13A
030170     05  FILLER        PICTURE X(05).         PROGR13A
030180     05  PAY           PICTURE $ZZZZ.99.      PROGR13A
030190     05  FILLER        PICTURE X(53).         PROGR13A
030200                                              PROGR13A
040010 PROCEDURE DIVISION.                          PROGR13A
040020     OPEN INPUT RECORDS-IN, OUTPUT PRINT-OUT. PROGR13A

040030     READ RECORDS-IN INTO RATE-RECORD AT END PERFORM ALL-DONE.  PROGR13A
040040     PERFORM CALCULATE-PAY 1000 TIMES.                          PROGR13A
040050                                                                PROGR13A
040060 ALL-DONE.                                                      PROGR13A
040070     MOVE TOTAL-PAY TO TOTAL-PAY-LN.                            PROGR13A
040080     WRITE PRINT-LINE FROM TOTAL-LINE AFTER ADVANCING 3 LINES.  PROGR13A
040090     CLOSE RECORDS-IN, PRINT-OUT.                               PROGR13A
040100     STOP RUN.                                                  PROGR13A
040110                                                                PROGR13A
040120 CALCULATE-PAY.                                                 PROGR13A
040130     MOVE SPACES TO PAY-LINE.                                   PROGR13A
040140     READ RECORDS-IN INTO PAY-RECORD AT END PERFORM ALL-DONE.   PROGR13A
040150     MOVE CORRESPONDING PAY-RECORD TO PAY-LINE.                 PROGR13A
040160     COMPUTE GROSS-PAY = PAY-RATE (PAY-CODE) *                  PROGR13A
040170                         HOURS OF PAY-RECORD.                   PROGR13A
040180     MOVE PAY-RATE (PAY-CODE) TO RATE.                          PROGR13A
040190     ADD GROSS-PAY TO TOTAL-PAY.                                PROGR13A
040200     MOVE GROSS-PAY TO PAY.                                     PROGR13A
040210     WRITE PRINT-LINE FROM PAY-LINE AFTER ADVANCING 1 LINES.    PROGR13A
```

FIGURE 13.1   Sample Program 13A

```
0800085009000 9751050
HARRY CARLSON        7532453254001
JERRY JONES          1234567895004
JACKIE BERTH         8521453254002
TERRY SMITH          2453256524003
MARY ANN WOO         7542541234205
MICHAEL GARCIA       7453526523005
```

FIGURE 13.2   Input for Program 13A

REVIEW

1. What is the function of the OCCURS clause? What level numbers cannot be used with the OCCURS clause?

2. For what is the subscript used? What type of variable or number must the subscript be? What values cannot be used for a subscript? What is the range of the subscript?

3. On your computer, what happens if the subscript is a constant and the constant is outside the defined range? What happens if the subscript is a variable and its assigned value is outside the defined range?

4. How many positions in storage are reserved for each of the following?

    a) 01 X.
    05 A   PICTURE XX   OCCURS 6 TIMES.

    b) 01 ZZ.
    05 A   PICTURE XX   OCCURS 6 TIMES.
    05 B   PICTURE 9(03).
    05 C   PICTURE 999 OCCURS 4 TIMES.

5. Given the following declaration:

    01 ZAP-REC.
       05 ZZ PICTURE 999
          OCCURS 3 TIMES.

    which of the following MOVE statements are valid? Why are the others invalid?

    a) MOVE ZAP-REC TO OUT-REC.
    b) MOVE ZZ TO AB.
    c) MOVE ZZ (2) TO AC.
    d) MOVE ZZ (0) TO AD.
    e) MOVE ZZ (4) TO AE.
    f) MOVE ZZ (ZZ (2)) TO AF.

    (Assume that the receiving variable has been correctly defined for each of these MOVEs.)

Program Modifications

1. Sample Program 13A is incomplete because it fails to check the PAY-CODE field to see if it falls within the defined range of 1 to 5. Run the program using some data with an incorrect PAY-CODE (try 0 or 9) and see what happens. Then modify the program so that if an incorrect PAY-CODE is read the program does the following:

    a) Uses a pay rate of zero.
    b) Prints the error message BAD PAY-CODE three columns to the right of the last output field.

    Provide a heading line for the output.

2. Program 13A is incomplete because it fails to verify that the first data-record contains the pay rates. Modify the program so that it does the following:

   a) Requires that the pay-rate record has an X in column 80.

   b) If the pay-rate record is missing, prints the error message RATE RECORD MISSING and stops the program.

   Provide a heading line for the output.

3. Modify Program 13A so that the tax rate is also read in as data. The tax rates are:

tax rate 1	0.0%
tax rate 2	4.0%
tax rate 3	7.5%
tax rate 4	9.0%

   The tax rates above can be placed on the same input records as the pay rates.

   The detail records now have a field for tax rate, in column 65. This column should always contain a 1, 2, 3, or 4. Use the tax rate to calculate withholding tax and deduct it from the pay. Print and label all pertinent data.

4. Modify Program 13A so that it reads in twenty pay rates. Then do the following:

   a) Print the average pay-rate.

   b) Print the smallest pay-rate.

   c) Print the largest pay-rate.

5. Each pay-rate is now on a separate record. The pay-rate is in the first 4 columns of each pay-record. The last pay-rate is zero. There are never more than ten pay-rates, and the pay-rate records are read in first. Modify Program 13A to use these pay-rate records.

SAMPLE PROGRAM 13B

Last week the pay-rate record was typed incorrectly—all fields were off by one column. All the Ready-Cash Bank paychecks were wrong; the job had to be rerun. The Ready-Cash Bank manager wants the payroll program modified to prevent this from happening again. In Sample Program 13A the pay rates were read in as data. This is undesirable because someone must make sure that the first data-record is the pay rates. This pay-rate record could easily be left off or be typed incorrectly, and then the printed report would be incorrect. Since the pay rates seldom change, it would be better to have them as part of the program instead of the data. This is an example of a basic rule in programming: whenever possible, make variables which are constants part of the program instead of part of the data. Once the variables have been set correctly in the program, they remain correct, and one more source of possible error has been eliminated.

Remember, a VALUE clause cannot be used in an entry with an OCCURS clause. This makes sense, since a VALUE clause initializes one variable and an OCCURS clause declares several variables. There are ways around this, however. One method is to move the pay rates into the table. For example:

```
MOVE  8.00 TO PAY-RATE (1).
MOVE  8.50 TO PAY-RATE (2).
MOVE  9.00 TO PAY-RATE (3).
MOVE  9.75 TO PAY-RATE (4).
MOVE 10.50 TO PAY-RATE (5).
```

This code initializes the five pay-rates in the tables, but this method would involve a great deal of code if there were many pay-rates.

A better way to initialize the table is as follows:

```
01 RATE-VALUES.
    05    RATE-1      PICTURE 99V99      VALUE 8.00.
    05    RATE-2      PICTURE 99V99      VALUE 8.50.
    05    RATE-3      PICTURE 99V99      VALUE 9.00.
    05    RATE-4      PICTURE 99V99      VALUE 9.75.
    05    RATE-5      PICTURE 99V99      VALUE 10.50.
01 RATE-RECORD REDEFINES RATE-VALUES.
    05    PAY-RATE   OCCURS 5 TIMES  PICTURE 99V99.
```

Notice that RATE-VALUES has five elementary items, each of which is 4 positions long. Each of these elements must be the same size and must have the same description. The VALUE clause is used to initialize each of the five rates. The REDEFINES clause declares that RATE-RECORD is another name for RATE-VALUES. RATE-RECORD is composed of a table named PAY-RATE, and PAY-RATE has five elements, each of which is 4 positions in length.

There are some strict rules about use of the OCCURS clause and use of the REDEFINES clause. The VALUE clause cannot be used in the same entry with a REDEFINES clause: you must first code the values of a table, and then redefine the storage area. In the code above, RATE-VALUES and RATE-RECORD are simply two different names for the same storage area, but RATE-VALUES must initialize the storage areas first. All fields in RATE-VALUES must be the same length.

In this example we have used a REDEFINES clause to initialize an array. The PAY-RATE array will have the following values:

```
PAY-RATE (1) _ _ _ _ 8.00
PAY-RATE (2) _ _ _ _ 8.50
PAY-RATE (3) _ _ _ _ 9.00
PAY-RATE (4) _ _ _ _ 9.75
PAY-RATE (5) _ _ _ 10.50
```

Notice that RATE-VALUES is five 4-column numeric fields and RATE-RECORD—which is redefined as RATE-VALUES—is also five 4-column numeric fields. Thus

```
MOVE PAY-RATE (3) TO . . . .
```

will cause the third rate (i.e., 9.00) to be moved. You can see that the initialization table in Sample Program 13B (**Figure 13.3**) is the same as that in Program 13A, except that we no longer have to read in the pay rates as data.

****

Computer Graffiti

Computer (com-pew-ter): an incredibly fast moron.

****

```
010010 IDENTIFICATION DIVISION.                                                          PROGR13B
010020 PROGRAM-ID.                                                                       PROGR13B
010030      PROGRM13B.                                                                   PROGR13B
010040* * * * * * * * * * * * * * * * * * * * * * * * * * * * * * * * **PROGR13B
010050*    RATE TABLE INITIALIZED IN PROGRAM.                                   *PROGR13B
010060* * * * * * * * * * * * * * * * * * * * * * * * * * * * * * * * **PROGR13B
010070                                                                                   PROGR13B
010080 ENVIRONMENT DIVISION.                                                             PROGR13B
010090 INPUT-OUTPUT SECTION.                                                             PROGR13B
010100 FILE-CONTROL.                                                                     PROGR13B
010110     SELECT RECORDS-IN                                                             PROGR13B
010120         ASSIGN TO UR-2540R-S-SYSIN.                                               PROGR13B
010130     SELECT PRINT-OUT,                                                             PROGR13B
010140         ASSIGN TO UR-1403-S-SYSPRINT.                                             PROGR13B
010150                                                                                   PROGR13B
020010 DATA DIVISION.                                                                    PROGR13B
020020 FILE SECTION.                                                                     PROGR13B
020030 FD RECORDS-IN                                                                     PROGR13B
020040     LABEL RECORDS ARE OMITTED.                                                    PROGR13B
020050 01  IN-RECORD                     PICTURE X(80).                                  PROGR13B
020060 FD PRINT-OUT                                                                      PROGR13B
020070     LABEL RECORDS ARE OMITTED.                                                    PROGR13B
020080 01  PRINT-LINE                    PICTURE X(133).                                 PROGR13B
020090                                                                                   PROGR13B
020100 WORKING-STORAGE SECTION.                                                          PROGR13B
020110 77  GROSS-PAY           PICTURE S999V99        VALUE ZERO.                        PROGR13B
020120 77  TOTAL-PAY           PICTURE S99999V99      VALUE ZERO.                        PROGR13B
020130                                                                                   PROGR13B
020140 01  RATES-VALUE.                                                                  PROGR13B
020150     05  RATE-1    PICTURE 99V99    VALUE 8.00.                                    PROGR13B
020160     05  RATE-2    PICTURE 99V99    VALUE 8.50.                                    PROGR13B
020170     05  RATE-3    PICTURE 99V99    VALUE 9.00.                                    PROGR13B
020180     05  RATE-4    PICTURE 99V99    VALUE 9.75.                                    PROGR13B
020190     05  RATE-5    PICTURE 99V99    VALUE 10.50.                                   PROGR13B
020200 01  RATE-RECORD  REDEFINES RATES-VALUE.                                           PROGR13B
020210     05  PAY-RATE    OCCURS 5 TIMES  PICTURE 99V99.                                PROGR13B
020220                                                                                   PROGR13B
030010 01  TOTAL-LINE.                                                                   PROGR13B
030020     05  FILLER           PICTURE X(70)           VALUE SPACE.                     PROGR13B
030030     05  TOTAL-PAY-LN     PICTURE $ZZ,ZZZ.99.                                      PROGR13B
030040     05  FILLER           PICTURE X(53)           VALUE SPACE.                     PROGR13B
030050                                                                                   PROGR13B
030060 01  PAY-RECORD.                                                                   PROGR13B
030070     05  NAME                      PICTURE X(30).                                  PROGR13B
030080     05  EMP-NO                    PICTURE 9(09).                                  PROGR13B
030090     05  HOURS                     PICTURE 99V9.                                   PROGR13B
030100     05  PAY-CODE                  PICTURE 9.                                      PROGR13B
030110     05  FILLER                    PICTURE X(37).                                  PROGR13B
030120                                                                                   PROGR13B
030130 01  PAY-LINE.                                                                     PROGR13B
030140     05  FILLER                    PICTURE X(01).                                  PROGR13B
030150     05  NAME                      PICTURE X(30).                                  PROGR13B
030160     05  FILLER                    PICTURE X(05).                                  PROGR13B
030170     05  EMP-NO                    PICTURE 999B99B9999.                            PROGR13B
030180     05  FILLER                    PICTURE X(05).                                  PROGR13B
030190     05  HOURS                     PICTURE Z9.9.                                   PROGR13B
030200     05  FILLER                    PICTURE X(05).                                  PROGR13B
030210     05  RATE                      PICTURE $ZZ.99.                                 PROGR13B
030220     05  FILLER                    PICTURE X(05).                                  PROGR13B
030230     05  PAY                       PICTURE $ZZZZ.99.                               PROGR13B
030240     05  FILLER                    PICTURE X(53).                                  PROGR13B



030250                                                                                   PROGR13B
040010 PROCEDURE DIVISION.                                                               PROGR13B
040020     OPEN INPUT RECORDS-IN, OUTPUT PRINT-OUT.                                      PROGR13B
040030     MOVE SPACES TO PAY-LINE.                                                      PROGR13B
040040     PERFORM CALCULATE-PAY 1000 TIMES.                                             PROGR13B
```

```
040050                                                                    PROGR13B
040060 ALL-DONE.                                                          PROGR13B
040070     MOVE TOTAL-PAY TO TOTAL-PAY-LN.                                PROGR13B
040080     WRITE PRINT-LINE FROM TOTAL-LINE AFTER ADVANCING 3 LINES.      PROGR13B
040090     CLOSE RECORDS-IN, PRINT-OUT.                                   PROGR13B
040100     STOP RUN.                                                      PROGR13B
040110                                                                    PROGR13B
040120 CALCULATE-PAY.                                                     PROGR13B
040130     READ RECORDS-IN INTO PAY-RECORD AT END PERFORM ALL-DONE.       PROGR13B
040140     MOVE CORRESPONDING PAY-RECORD TO PAY-LINE.                     PROGR13B
040150     COMPUTE GROSS-PAY = PAY-RATE (PAY-CODE) *                      PROGR13B
040160                          HOURS OF PAY-RECORD.                      PROGR13B
040170     MOVE PAY-RATE (PAY-CODE) TO RATE.                             PROGR13B
040180     ADD GROSS-PAY TO TOTAL-PAY.                                    PROGR13B
040190     MOVE GROSS-PAY TO PAY.                                         PROGR13B
040200     WRITE PRINT-LINE FROM PAY-LINE AFTER ADVANCING 1 LINES.        PROGR13B
```

FIGURE 13.3   Sample Program 13B

REVIEW

1. What restrictions are there on including an OCCURS clause, REDEFINES clause, and VALUE clause in the same data-description entry? How may these restrictions be overcome?

2. Write code to set up a table called TAX-TABLE. Initialize the table as follows:

   Tax Rate

   0.0%

   4.0%

   7.5%

   9.0%

3. When should a programmer read values into a program, and when should the programmer make the values constants in the program?

Program Modifications

1. Modify Sample Program 13B so that there are the following 6 pay rates:

Number	Rate
1	7.50
2	8.70
3	9.50
4	12.00
5	14.00
6	16.50

2. Modify Program 13B so that the following tax-rates are part of the program instead of being read in as data:

    Tax Rates
    0.0%
    4.0%
    7.5%
    9.0%

    The detail records now have a code field for tax rate, in column 65; it should always be a 1, 2, 3, or 4. Use the tax-rate code to calculate withholding tax and deduct it from the pay. Print and label all the pertinent data.

3. Modify Program 13B so that it counts the number of employees at each pay-rate. Print this total at the end of the report.

SUBSCRIPTED GROUP ITEMS

We have used the **OCCURS** clause only for elementary items, but it is often convenient to use **subscripted group items**. Here is an example:

```
01 BOOKS.
    05 BOOK-INFO OCCURS 100 TIMES.
        10 TITLE          PICTURE X(25).
        10 AUTHORS        PICTURE X(25).
        10 YEARS          PICTURE X(04).
        10 CALL-NUMBER    PICTURE X(16).
        10 ORDER-DEPT     PICTURE X(10).
```

A single group-item, **BOOK-INFO**, is 80 characters long. The complete table is 8000 characters long (**80 ∗ 100**). We can now subscript at two different levels.

BOOK-INFO (3)	refers to 80 characters.
TITLE (14)	refers to 25 characters.
AUTHORS (7)	refers to 25 characters.
YEARS (3)	refers to 4 characters.
CALL-NUMBER (85)	refers to 16 characters.
ORDER-DEPT (16)	refers to 10 characters.

RECORD STORAGE IN TABLES

The **OCCURS** clause cannot be used at the 01 level. This could be a major disadvantage if we wish to have a table of records, but there is an easy way to get around this restriction. For example:

```
01 IN-RECORD.
    05 BOOK-STUFF        PICTURE X(80).
01 BOOKS.
    05 BOOK-INFO OCCURS 100 TIMES.
        10 TITLE          PICTURE X(25).
        10 AUTHORS        PICTURE X(25).
        10 YEARS          PICTURE X(04).
        10 CALL-NUMBER    PICTURE X(16).
        10 ORDER-DEPT     PICTURE X(10).
            .
            .
            .

    READ DATA-IN INTO IN-RECORD AT END PERFORM PROCESS-BOOKS.
    ADD 1 TO K.
    MOVE BOOK-STUFF TO BOOK-INFO (K).
```

The code above allows us to keep a table of all the records in storage. This is useful for internal sorting and comparing. These two techniques will be discussed in later chapters.

REVIEW

1. How many positions of storage does each of the following require?

    a) 01 QUARTER-DAY-RECORD.
    ```
        05 QTR-NAME      PICTURE X(06)   OCCURS 4 TIMES.
        05 DAY-COUNT     PICTURE 9(02)   OCCURS 4 TIMES.
    ```
    b) 01 QUARTER-DAY-RECORD.
    ```
        03 PERIOD-DAY      OCCURS 4 TIMES.
            05 QTR-NAME    PICTURE  X(06).
            05 DAY-COUNT   PICTURE  9(02).
    ```

    How, if at all, do the two declarations differ? Draw a picture of how each will be laid out in storage.

Program Modifications

1. Modify Sample Program 13A so that it uses two tables, as follows:

Pay Rate	Tax Rate
6.00	0.0%
7.00	4.0%
9.50	7.5%
12.00	9.0%
15.00	10.0%

    Use an OCCURS clause at a group level. (The tax-rate code is in column 65 of the data records.)

TWO-DIMENSIONAL TABLES

COBOL also allows two-dimensional and three-dimensional tables. A two-dimensional table is defined like this:

```
01 A.
   05 B OCCURS 4 TIMES.
      10 C OCCURS 3 TIMES   PICTURE XX.
```

A occupies 24 storage locations altogether (i.e., 4 X 3 X 2 = 24). A is divided into 4 elements: B (1), B (2), B (3), and B (4). Each element of B is composed of three elements: B (1) is composed of C (1,1), C (1,2), and C (1,3); B (3) is composed of C (3,1), C (3,2), and C (3,3). Each C element is two positions long.

Subscripting

In two-dimensional tables the first subscript is the row and the second subscript is the column. You can picture the table above, with the element C (3,2), like this:

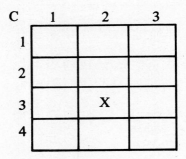

C has 4 rows and 3 columns: 12 elements in all. C (3,2) (where the "X" is in the diagram above) indicates the element in the third row and second column. When using tables, remember the rules of spacing punctuation: the left parenthesis must be preceded by a space; the right parenthesis must be followed by a space; a comma must be followed by a space. Here is an example:

```
    no spaces
    ↓   ↓
C (3, 2)
  ↑  ↑
  space
```

If you space incorrectly, however, most compilers will process your program correctly anyway, but they will generate a warning message.

SAMPLE PROGRAM 13C

Ready-Cash Bank's salespeople sell banking services. They need a summary report giving the total sales for each quarter and each sales region. In Sample Program 13C (**Figure 13.4**) we accumulate the sales totals into a two-dimensional table by quarter and region. Our table will look like this:

SALES-TABLE Region

Quarter

The table above will be declared as follows:

```
01 SALES-TABLE.
    05 SALES-QUARTER OCCURS 4 TIMES.
        10 SALES-REGION-TABLE OCCURS 3 TIMES   PICTURE 99999V99.
```

There are 4 quarters and 3 regions: the whole table is composed of 12 elements. Our input record defines the quarters, region, and sales as follows:

```
01 SALES-RECORD.
    05 FILLER          PICTURE X(10).
    05 QUARTER-RC      PICTURE 9(01).
    05 REGION-RC       PICTURE 9(01).
    05 SALES-RC        PICTURE 99999V99.
    05 FILLER          PICTURE X(61).
```

Now we can use the SALES-TABLE to accumulate totals by quarter and region. We need to set the whole SALES-TABLE to zero, like this:

```
MOVE ZERO TO SALES-TABLE.
```

This single sentence moves zeros into all 12 elements of the table. We accumulate the sales from each record as follows:

```
PROCESS-DATA.
    READ RECORDS-IN INTO SALES-RECORD AT END PERFORM ALL-DONE.
    ADD SALES-RC TO SALES-REGION-TABLE (QUARTER-RC, REGION-RC).
```

The paragraph above reads the input records and accumulates the sales totals by quarter and region. Each input record contains the quarter and region; the quarter and region are used as subscripts to accumulate the sales in the correct element in the table.

Next, we wish to print the accumulated table. This will be done after all the records have been read, in the termination paragraph. **Figure 13.5** shows printed output from Program 13C. We label the rows by quarter by using a table and REDEFINES:

```
01 QUARTERS-VALUE.
    05 QUARTER-1    PICTURE X(08)    VALUE 'FIRST'.
    05 QUARTER-2    PICTURE X(08)    VALUE 'SECOND'.
    05 QUARTER-3    PICTURE X(08)    VALUE 'THIRD'.
    05 QUARTER-4    PICTURE X(08)    VALUE 'FOURTH'.
01 QUARTERS-RECORD REDEFINES QUARTERS-VALUE.
    05 QUARTER      PICTURE X(08)  OCCURS 4 TIMES.
```

```
010010 IDENTIFICATION DIVISION.                                              PROGR13C
010020 PROGRAM-ID.                                                           PROGR13C
010030    PROGR13C.                                                          PROGR13C
010040* * * * * * * * * * * * * * * * * * * * * * * * * * * * * * * * * **PROGR13C
010050*    TWO DIMENSIONAL TABLES.                                          PROGR13C
010060*    SAMPLE PROGRAM USING TABLES.                                     PROGR13C
010070* * * * * * * * * * * * * * * * * * * * * * * * * * * * * * * * * **PROGR13C
010080                                                                       PROGR13C
010090 ENVIRONMENT DIVISION.                                                 PROGR13C
010100 INPUT-OUTPUT SECTION.                                                 PROGR13C
010110 FILE-CONTROL.                                                         PROGR13C
010120    SELECT RECORDS-IN                                                  PROGR13C
010130       ASSIGN TO UR-2540R-S-SYSIN.                                     PROGR13C
010140    SELECT PRINT-OUT,                                                  PROGR13C
010150       ASSIGN TO UR-1403-S-SYSPRINT.                                   PROGR13C
010160                                                                       PROGR13C
020010 DATA DIVISION.                                                        PROGR13C
020020 FILE SECTION.                                                         PROGR13C
020030 FD  RECORDS-IN                                                        PROGR13C
020040    LABEL RECORDS ARE OMITTED.                                         PROGR13C
020050 01  IN-RECORD                   PICTURE X(80).                        PROGR13C
020060 FD  PRINT-OUT                                                         PROGR13C
020070    LABEL RECORDS ARE OMITTED.                                         PROGR13C
020080 01  PRINT-LINE                  PICTURE X(133).                       PROGR13C
020090                                                                       PROGR13C
020100 WORKING-STORAGE SECTION.                                              PROGR13C
020110 77  K           PICTURE S9     VALUE +1  USAGE IS COMPUTATIONAL.      PROGR13C
020120                                                                       PROGR13C
020130 01  QUARTERS-VALUE.                                                   PROGR13C
020140    05  QUARTER-1   PICTURE X(08)   VALUE 'FIRST'.                     PROGR13C
020150    05  QUARTER-2   PICTURE X(08)   VALUE 'SECOND'.                    PROGR13C
020160    05  QUARTER-3   PICTURE X(08)   VALUE 'THIRD'.                     PROGR13C
020170    05  QUARTER-4   PICTURE X(08)   VALUE 'FOURTH'.                    PROGR13C
020180 01  QUARTERS-RECORD REDEFINES QUARTERS-VALUE.                         PROGR13C
020190    05  QUARTER     PICTURE X(08) OCCURS 4 TIMES.                      PROGR13C
020200                                                                       PROGR13C
020210 01  SALES-TABLE.                                                      PROGR13C
020220    05  SALES-QUARTER OCCURS 4 TIMES.                                  PROGR13C
020230       10 SALES-REGION-TABLE  OCCURS 3 TIMES  PICTURE 99999V99.        PROGR13C
020240                                                                       PROGR13C
030010 01  SALES-RECORD.                                                     PROGR13C
030020    05  FILLER        PICTURE X(10).                                   PROGR13C
030030    05  QUARTER-RC    PICTURE 9(01).                                   PROGR13C
030040    05  REGION-RC     PICTURE 9(01).                                   PROGR13C
030050    05  SALES-RC      PICTURE 99999V99.                                PROGR13C
030060    05  FILLER        PICTURE X(61).                                   PROGR13C
030070                                                                       PROGR13C
030080 01  SALES-LINE.                                                       PROGR13C
030090    05  FILLER              PICTURE X(01).                             PROGR13C
030100    05  QUARTER-LN          PICTURE X(08).                             PROGR13C
030110    05  FILLER              PICTURE X(08).                             PROGR13C
030120    05  SALES-PRINT OCCURS 3 TIMES.                                    PROGR13C
030130       10  REGION-LN        PICTURE $ZZ,ZZZ.99.                        PROGR13C
030140       10  FILLER           PICTURE X(10).                             PROGR13C
030150    05  FILLER              PICTURE X(56).                             PROGR13C
030160                                                                       PROGR13C
040010 PROCEDURE DIVISION.                                                   PROGR13C
040020    OPEN INPUT RECORDS-IN, OUTPUT PRINT-OUT.                           PROGR13C
040030    MOVE ZERO TO SALES-TABLE.                                          PROGR13C
040040    MOVE SPACES TO SALES-LINE.                                         PROGR13C


040050    PERFORM PROCESS-DATA 1000 TIMES.                                   PROGR13C
040060                                                                       PROGR13C
040070 ALL-DONE.                                                             PROGR13C
040080    PERFORM DO-TOTALS 4 TIMES.                                         PROGR13C
040090    CLOSE RECORDS-IN, PRINT-OUT.                                       PROGR13C
040100    STOP RUN.                                                          PROGR13C
040110                                                                       PROGR13C
```

```
040120 DO-TOTALS.                                                          PROGR13C
040130     MOVE QUARTER (K) TO QUARTER-LN.                                  PROGR13C
040140     MOVE  SALES-REGION-TABLE (K, 1) TO  REGION-LN (1).               PROGR13C
040150     MOVE  SALES-REGION-TABLE (K, 2) TO  REGION-LN (2).               PROGR13C
040160     MOVE  SALES-REGION-TABLE (K, 3) TO  REGION-LN (3).               PROGR13C
040170     WRITE PRINT-LINE FROM SALES-LINE AFTER ADVANCING 1 LINES.        PROGR13C
040180     ADD 1 TO K.                                                      PROGR13C
040190                                                                      PROGR13C
040200 PROCESS-DATA.                                                        PROGR13C
040210     READ RECORDS-IN INTO SALES-RECORD AT END PERFORM ALL-DONE.       PROGR13C
040220     ADD SALES-RC TO SALES-REGION-TABLE (QUARTER-RC, REGION-RC).      PROGR13C
```

FIGURE 13.4   Sample Program 13C

```
FIRST       $ 5,040.00      $ 3,422.44      $ 1,200.45
SECOND      $ 4,230.00      $ 5,203.55      $ 2,055.66
THIRD       $ 8,203.00      $12,033.00      $20,300.00
FOURTH      $15,230.00      $ 2,830.00      $ 1,850.00
```

FIGURE 13.5   Output from Program 13C

These four row-labels must be moved to the print-line. The print-line is declared as follows:

```
01 SALES-LINE.
    05 FILLER            PICTURE X(01).
    05 QUARTER-LN        PICTURE X(08).
    05 FILLER            PICTURE X(08).
    05 SALES-PRINT OCCURS 3 TIMES.
        10 REGION-LN     PICTURE $ZZ,ZZZ.99.
        10 FILLER        PICTURE X(10).
    05 FILLER            PICTURE X(86).
```

This allows space for the quarter label and for the three sales-totals for each line.
Finally, we move the information into the print-line and print it.

```
ALL-DONE.
    PERFORM DO-TOTALS 4 TIMES.
        .
        .
        .
DO-TOTALS.
    MOVE QUARTER (K) TO QUARTER-LN.
    MOVE SALES-REGION-TABLE (K, 1) TO REGION-LN (1).
    MOVE SALES-REGION-TABLE (K, 2) TO REGION-LN (2).
    MOVE SALES-REGION-TABLE (K, 3) TO REGION-LN (3).
    WRITE PRINT-LINE FROM SALES-LINE AFTER ADVANCING 1 LINES.
    ADD 1 TO K.
```

Paragraph DO-TOTALS is executed four times because we want to print the four lines of our table. The variable K is initialized to 1 by a level-number-77 item. The first time this paragraph is executed K has the value 1 and it processes row 1. Then K is incremented by the ADD sentence, and the second row is processed and printed. This is done four times to print all four rows of the table. This use of K is called **indexing**. In the next chapter we will see how this can be done more conveniently by a PERFORM sentence.

This program is a little different from the earlier programs: there may be thousands of input records, but only four lines of output will be printed.

Level-number-77 variables used for subscript calculations should be declared USAGE COMPUTATIONAL. For example:

```
77 K PICTURE S99    VALUE 1    USAGE COMPUTATIONAL.
```

Subscript variables declared any other way may cause a substantial loss of efficiency.

CHAPTER REVIEW

Vocabulary Review

COBOL table
Initializing the table
Element of a table

Subscript
Range of the table

Subscripted group items

Indexing

Review Questions

1. Discuss the OCCURS clause. What are its uses? What rules govern its use?

2. Write code to define a three-dimensional table named ZAP with the size of (4,3,5). Draw a picture of how the storage is laid out.

3. List all the clauses which may be used in the WORKING-STORAGE SECTION. Which clauses may be used only at the elementary level? Which clauses may be used only at the group level? Which may appear at the 01 level?

4. Are any of the clauses discussed in question 3 required to be in a particular order? Which clauses cannot be used in the same entry?

5. What are the rules for spacing when using subscripts?

6. Given the following code:

```
05 A OCCURS 2 TIMES.
  10 B OCCURS 3 TIMES.
    15 C OCCURS 3 TIMES    PICTURE XX.
```

how many positions of storage are required? Given the above declaration, how many characters are moved in each of the following statements?

a) MOVE C(1,1,1) TO . . .

b) MOVE A(2) TO . . .

c) MOVE B(1,2) TO . . .

Draw a picture for each, showing exactly what elements are being moved.

7. Using the table in question 6, which of the following would be correct? If invalid, state why.

a) MOVE A(3) TO . . .

b) MOVE B(4) TO . . .

c) MOVE A(K) TO . . .

d) MOVE C(1,1,1) TO . . .

e) MOVE B(3,3) TO . . .

f) MOVE B(L,1) TO . . .

g) MOVE B(L-6,I) TO . . .

h) MOVE B(0,K) TO . . .

8. What is the largest array you can declare on your computer? For example, could you have

05 A PICTURE XX OCCURS 1000 TIMES.

in a COBOL program? Could you write OCCURS 1000000 TIMES? You can probably find out how big the OCCURS clause may be by trying different table sizes.

Program Modifications

1. Sample Program 13C is incomplete because it fails to check both quarter and region for correct codes. Run the program with an incorrect region (try 0 or 6) and see what happens. Then modify the program so that any input records with incorrect regions or codes are not accumulated. Print the incorrect records on a separate page. After the printed table, print two lines of output giving the number of incorrect records read and the number of correct records read.

2. Modify Sample Program 13B so that it deducts insurance payments from the paycheck. Insurance fees are calculated according to the following two-dimensional table:

	Class	
Category	1	2
1	0.00	5.00
2	4.00	7.00
3	8.00	10.00

Read in the insurance fees as data. The class code is in column 66 of the detail record. The category code is in column 67 of the detail record.

3. In the program in question 2, do not read in the insurance fees as data. Initialize the insurance table in the WORKING-STORAGE SECTION.

4. Modify Program 13C so that instead of using 4 quarters it uses 12 months. On the output, label the 12 months JANUARY, FEBRUARY, etc. Type some new input records to test the program.

5. Modify Program 13B so that the program handles the following alphabetic pay-codes:

Pay Code	Pay Rate
A	7.00
N	9.00
M	10.00

The pay codes are now alphabetic, that is, the detail records have alphabetic codes in the pay-code field. Your program will have to translate the alphabetic code into a numeric code for the subscript.

6. When alphanumeric variables are initialized with a VALUE clause, the character string is left-justified in the field. We can right-justify the character string if we add the clause JUSTIFIED RIGHT, as follows:

    05 MONTH1   PICTURE X(06)   VALUE 'JAN'   JUSTIFIED RIGHT.

Now the field MONTH1 will be right-justified, with any needed blanks added on the left side. This clause can only be used for elementary items. When the receiving field of a MOVE statement has a JUSTIFIED RIGHT clause, truncation will occur on the left side if the receiving field is too short. Modify Program 13C so that the fields QUARTER-1, QUARTER-2, etc., are right-justified.

Programs

1. Intellect Haven College has the following student records:

Field	Input Columns	Output Columns
Student number	1–6	1–6
Student name	7–32	13–38
Division code	34	46
Division name	–	52–72

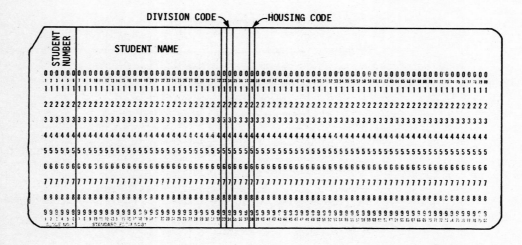

The division codes are as follows:

Code	Division
1	Natural sciences
2	Social sciences
3	Humanities
4	Medicine
5	Business

Write a program to read the input records above; have the program print the output record described. You must read the division codes and then print the division name from a table of division names stored in the program. If the division code is incorrect, print the error message INCORRECT CODE instead of the division name.

2. After writing the program in question 1, we have the following new fields to process:

Field	Input Columns	Output Columns
Housing code	38	69
Housing name	–	75–86

The housing codes are:

Code	Name
1	On-campus
2	Campus group
3	Off-campus
4	Unknown

Your program should now also print the housing information above. If the housing code is incorrect, print it as Unknown.

3. The new manager of the Ready-Cash Bank has a theory that more employees tend to report in sick on Monday or Friday than on any other day. She has decided to ask you to write a program to accumulate statistics on this. The input record is as follows:

Field	Columns
Employee name	1–30
Day absent	42
Employee type	48

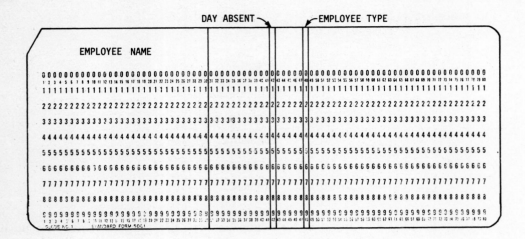

The codes for days absent are:

Code	Day
1	Monday
2	Tuesday
3	Wednesday
4	Thursday
5	Friday

The codes for employee type are:

Code	Employee Type
1	Manager
2	Standard
3	Temporary

You are to read the input record above and print a two-dimensional table. Label the rows—days—and columns—employee type—of the table using the information above.

4. Write a program to process the following input records for Intellect Haven College:

Field	Columns	
Telephone number	1–7	
Unit code	9	
Number of message units	10–13	
Starting time	14–17	(HHMM)
Department	20–40	

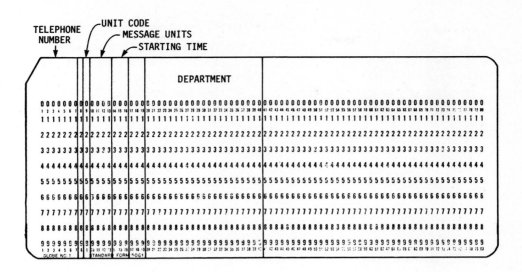

The rates for the unit codes are:

Unit Code	Rate/Message Unit
1	$0.20
2	$0.28
3	$0.37
4	$0.43
5	$0.51

These rates are charged for each message unit, that is, with a unit code of 3 and 12 message units, the charge will be 0.37 × 12. In addition, calls not started within the time period 0800 to 1700 receive a 20 percent discount. Set up a carefully laid-out report.

****
**Employed for diagnostic impression,
A robot disgraced that profession
By treating a dame
For testicular shame,
And a man for post-natal depression.**

****

MORE ON PERFORM AND TABLES

We have already used the PERFORM verb when we wished to execute a single paragraph once. For example:

    PERFORM HEADING-ROUTINE.

With this code, the paragraph HEADING-ROUTINE will be executed only once. We have also used PERFORM to execute a single paragraph several times. For example:

    PERFORM PRINT-BLANK-LINE 3 TIMES.

In this case the single paragraph PRINT-BLANK-LINE will be executed three times. In this chapter we will discuss the other forms of the PERFORM verb.

PERFORM WITH THE THRU OPTION

Another form of the PERFORM verb allows you to execute several consecutive paragraphs. For example:

PERFORM PARA-A THRU PARA-X.

This code executes all the paragraphs from **PARA-A** to **PARA-X**. This can include as few as two paragraphs and as many as are needed, that is, there may be several paragraphs between **PARA-A** and **PARA-X**. This form of **PERFORM** can be combined with the **TIMES** clause, as follows:

PERFORM PARA-A THRU PARA-X 4 TIMES.

The general formats for these **PERFORM** statements are:

```
PERFORM paragraph-1.

PERFORM paragraph-1 [THRU paragraph-n].

PERFORM paragraph-1 [THRU paragraph-n]
  { identifier }
  {            }  TIMES.
  { integer    }
```

SECTION NAMES

Instead of using paragraph names, programmer-picked **section names** may be used. In the PROCE-DURE DIVISION, SECTION names are chosen by the programmer. SECTION names are used to group consecutive paragraphs. For example:

PERFORM PARA-A THRU PARA-T.
.
.
.
PARA-A.
.
.
.
PARA-T.

SECTION names may be substituted for the PERFORM THRU option. We could do the following:

PERFORM ZAPPER.
.
.
.
ZAPPER SECTION.
PARA-A.
.
.
.
PARA-T.
.
.
.
NEW-X SECTION.

PERFORM ZAPPER will execute all the paragraphs in the ZAPPER SECTION. A SECTION is ended only by a new SECTION; therefore we need the new name NEW-X SECTION.

PERFORM WITH THE VARYING OPTION

Another form of the PERFORM allows us to increment an index. For example:

    PERFORM DO-TOTALS VARYING K FROM 1 BY 1 UNTIL (K > 4).

This code executes the paragraph DO-TOTALS four times, starting K at 1 and incrementing by 1 until K is greater than 4. The general form of this PERFORM sentence is:

```
PERFORM paragraph [THRU paragraph-n]
VARYING identifier-1 FROM {literal-2    }
                         {identifier-2  }
BY {literal-3    }   UNTIL  condition-1.
   {identifier-3 }
```

We can now modify Sample Program 13C to use this VARYING clause. Program 13C had the following segments of code:

    PERFORM DO-TOTALS 4 TIMES.
        .
        .
        .
    DO-TOTALS.
        MOVE QUARTER (K) TO QUARTER-LN.
        MOVE SALES-REGION-TABLE (K, 1) TO REGION-LN (1).
        MOVE SALES-REGION-TABLE (K, 2) TO REGION-LN (2).
        MOVE SALES-REGION-TABLE (K, 3) TO REGION-LN (3).
        WRITE PRINT-LINE FROM SALES-LINE AFTER ADVANCING 1 LINES.
        ADD 1 TO K.

This segment of code can be changed to the following:

    PERFORM DO-TOTALS VARYING K FROM 1 BY 1 UNTIL (K > 4).
        .
        .
        .
    DO-TOTALS.
        MOVE QUARTER (K) TO QUARTER-LN.
        MOVE SALES-REGION-TABLE (K, 1) TO REGION-LN (1).
        MOVE SALES-REGION-TABLE (K, 2) TO REGION-LN (2).
        MOVE SALES-REGION-TABLE (K, 3) TO REGION-LN (3).
        WRITE PRINT-LINE FROM SALES-LINE AFTER ADVANCING 1 LINES.

Notice that we no longer need the sentence ADD 1 TO K in the DO-TOTALS paragraph, since the PERFORM sentence does the incrementing of K. Sample Program 14A (**Figure 14.1**) includes the modifications above. **Figure 14.2** is a flowchart of the PERFORM ... VARYING statement.

```
010010 IDENTIFICATION DIVISION.                                          PROGR14A
010020 PROGRAM-ID.                                                       PROGR14A
010030     PROGR14A.                                                     PROGR14A
010040* * * * * * * * * * * * * * * * * * * * * * * * * * * * * * * **PROGR14A
010050*    SAMPLE PROGRAM USING TABLES AND PERFORM UNTIL.               *PROGR14A
010060* * * * * * * * * * * * * * * * * * * * * * * * * * * * * * * **PROGR14A
```

```
010070                                                                    PROGR14A
010080 ENVIRONMENT DIVISION.                                              PROGR14A
010090 INPUT-OUTPUT SECTION.                                              PROGR14A
010100 FILE-CONTROL.                                                      PROGR14A
010110     SELECT RECORDS-IN                                             PROGR14A
010120         ASSIGN TO UR-2540R-S-SYSIN.                               PROGR14A
010130     SELECT PRINT-OUT,                                             PROGR14A
010140         ASSIGN TO UR-1403-S-SYSPRINT.                             PROGR14A
010150                                                                    PROGR14A
020010 DATA DIVISION.                                                     PROGR14A
020020 FILE SECTION.                                                      PROGR14A
020030 FD   RECORDS-IN                                                    PROGR14A
020040     LABEL RECORDS ARE OMITTED.                                    PROGR14A
020050 01  IN-RECORD                 PICTURE X(80).                      PROGR14A
020060 FD   PRINT-OUT                                                     PROGR14A
020070     LABEL RECORDS ARE OMITTED.                                    PROGR14A
020080 01  PRINT-LINE                PICTURE X(133).                     PROGR14A
020090                                                                    PROGR14A
020100 WORKING-STORAGE SECTION.                                           PROGR14A
020110 77  K          PICTURE 9      VALUE 1.                            PROGR14A
020120                                                                    PROGR14A
020130 01  QUARTERS-VALUE.                                                PROGR14A
020140     05  QUARTER-1  PICTURE X(08)    VALUE 'FIRST'.               PROGR14A
020150     05  QUARTER-2  PICTURE X(08)    VALUE 'SECOND'.              PROGR14A
020160     05  QUARTER-3  PICTURE X(08)    VALUE 'THIRD'.               PROGR14A
020170     05  QUARTER-4  PICTURE X(08)    VALUE 'FOURTH'.              PROGR14A
020180 01  QUARTERS-RECORD REDEFINES QUARTERS-VALUE.                      PROGR14A
020190     05  QUARTER    PICTURE X(08) OCCURS 4 TIMES.                  PROGR14A
020200                                                                    PROGR14A
020210 01  SALES-TABLE.                                                   PROGR14A
020220     05  SALES-QUARTER OCCURS 4 TIMES.                             PROGR14A
020230         10 SALES-REGION-TABLE  OCCURS 3 TIMES  PICTURE 99999V99. PROGR14A
020240                                                                    PROGR14A
030010 01  SALES-RECORD.                                                  PROGR14A
030020     05  FILLER          PICTURE X(10).                           PROGR14A
030030     05  QUARTER-RC      PICTURE 9(01).                           PROGR14A
030040     05  REGION-RC       PICTURE 9(01).                           PROGR14A
030050     05  SALES-RC        PICTURE 99999V99.                        PROGR14A
030060     05  FILLER          PICTURE X(61).                           PROGR14A
030070                                                                    PROGR14A
030080 01  SALES-LINE.                                                    PROGR14A
030090     05  FILLER              PICTURE X(01).                       PROGR14A
030100     05  QUARTER-LN          PICTURE X(08).                       PROGR14A
030110     05  FILLER              PICTURE X(08).                       PROGR14A
030120     05  SALES-PRINT OCCURS 3 TIMES.                               PROGR14A
030130         10  REGION-LN       PICTURE $ZZ,ZZZ.99.                  PROGR14A
030140         10  FILLER          PICTURE X(10).                       PROGR14A
030150     05  FILLER              PICTURE X(56).                       PROGR14A
030160                                                                    PROGR14A
040010 PROCEDURE DIVISION.                                                PROGR14A
040020     OPEN INPUT RECORDS-IN, OUTPUT PRINT-OUT.                      PROGR14A
040030     MOVE ZERO TO SALES-TABLE.                                    PROGR14A
040040     MOVE SPACES TO SALES-LINE.                                   PROGR14A
040050     PERFORM PROCESS-DATA 1000 TIMES.                             PROGR14A

040060                                                                    PROGR14A
040070 ALL-DONE.                                                          PROGR14A
040080     PERFORM DO-TOTALS VARYING K FROM 1 BY 1 UNTIL (K > 4).       PROGR14A
040090     CLOSE RECORDS-IN, PRINT-OUT.                                 PROGR14A
040100     STOP RUN.                                                    PROGR14A
040110                                                                    PROGR14A
040120 DO-TOTALS.                                                         PROGR14A
040130     MOVE QUARTER (K) TO QUARTER-LN.                              PROGR14A
040140     MOVE  SALES-REGION-TABLE (K, 1) TO  REGION-LN (1).           PROGR14A
040150     MOVE  SALES-REGION-TABLE (K, 2) TO  REGION-LN (2).           PROGR14A
040160     MOVE  SALES-REGION-TABLE (K, 3) TO  REGION-LN (3).           PROGR14A
040170     WRITE PRINT-LINE FROM SALES-LINE AFTER ADVANCING 1 LINES.    PROGR14A
040180                                                                    PROGR14A
040190 PROCESS-DATA.                                                      PROGR14A
040200     READ RECORDS-IN INTO SALES-RECORD AT END PERFORM ALL-DONE.   PROGR14A
040210     ADD SALES-RC TO SALES-REGION-TABLE (QUARTER-RC, REGION-RC).  PROGR14A
```

FIGURE 14.1   Sample Program 14A

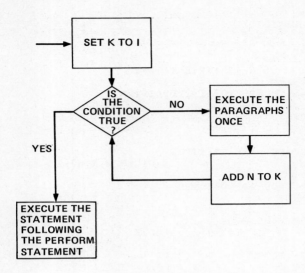

FIGURE 14.2   A Flowchart of PERFORM . . . VARYING

**PERFORM PARA VARYING K FROM I
BY N UNTIL (I > L).**

Note:

1. The **identifier-1** is set to the initial value specified in the **FROM** clause.
2. The condition in the **UNTIL** clause is tested. If the condition is true the statement after the **PERFORM** statement is executed next.
3. If the condition is false the paragraph(s) is (are) executed again.
4. The operand in the **BY** clause is used to increment the controlling variable, then the steps starting with that given in number 2 above are executed.

COUNTING THE LOOPS

There is often some confusion about how many times a paragraph will be executed by the **PERFORM** verb. If the code is:

    PERFORM PARA.

the paragraph **PARA** is executed only once. If the code is:

    PERFORM PARA 3 TIMES.

PARA is executed three times, unless, that is, you have made the following error:

        PERFORM PARA 3 TIMES.
        .
        .
        .
    PARA.
        MOVE A TO B.

If there is no code to prevent **PARA** from being executed the fourth time, **PARA** will be executed three times by the **PERFORM** sentence and once because the paragraph **PARA** follows the **PERFORM** statement.

The usual way to prevent this error is to put all paragraphs which are to be **PERFORM**ed at the end of the program after the **STOP RUN**. For example:

```
    PERFORM PARA 3 TIMES.
      .
      .
      .
    STOP RUN.
PARA.
    MOVE A TO B.
```

The code above will execute paragraph **PARA** only three times.

The following code:

```
PERFORM PARA VARYING K FROM 1 BY 1 UNTIL (K = 11).
```

will execute the paragraph **PARA** ten times, because the **UNTIL** is checked immediately after K is incremented. The code above could also be written as:

```
PERFORM PARA VARYING K FROM 1 BY 1 UNTIL (K > 10).
```

It is usually better to use "greater than," rather than the equality test, for the condition.

NESTED LOOPS

Loops may occur within loops. This is called a **nested loop** or double loop. For example:

```
    PERFORM PARA 10 TIMES.
    STOP RUN.
PARA.
    PERFORM PARX 12 TIMES.
PARX.
      .
      .
      .
```

Paragraph **PARA** will be executed 10 times; paragraph **PARX** will be executed 120 (10 * 12) times because of the double loop.

REVIEW

1. Write **PERFORM** statements to do the following:

   a) Execute paragraph **PARA** while K takes the values 3, 4, 5, 6, . . . , 11.

   b) Execute paragraphs **PARA** through **PARX** while L takes the values 2, 4, 6, 8, . . . , 20.

   c) Execute paragraph **PARZ** while T takes all odd values from 4 to 18.

2. How many times is PARA performed with the following code?

```
        PERFORM PARX 10 TIMES.
        .
        .
        .
        STOP RUN.
    PARX.
        PERFORM PARA 15 TIMES.
    PARA.
        MOVE ZAP TO ZIP.
```

INFINITE LOOPS

It is important that the UNTIL clause eventually be satisfied; otherwise, we will have an **infinite loop**. For example:

```
    PERFORM PARA-A VARYING K FROM 1 BY 2 UNTIL (K = 10).
```

What will happen in the situation above? Did you notice that K will never equal 10? K will equal 1, 3, 5, 7, 9, 11, etc., but never 10. The statement above will cause an infinite loop; it will continue to execute until the program is shut off by the computer. There are two lessons to be learned from this PERFORM statement:

1. Make sure your UNTIL clause will be satisfied.

2. Equality is a very poor conditional statement.

The UNTIL clause should be changed to:

```
    UNTIL (K > 9).
```

Many program errors are caused through use of an equality test. It is usually better to use a "greater than" test or a "less than" test.

SAMPLE PROGRAM 14B

Sample Program 14A does not total the sales by region. The Ready-Cash Bank manager has requested that the total sales be summed for each region so that the clerks will not have to do this by hand. This can easily be done with the PERFORM ... VARYING statement, but first we must set up some variables to accumulate the regional totals. The easiest way to do this is simply to add another row on the bottom of our table:

```
    05 SALES-QUARTER      OCCURS 5 TIMES.
```

The SALES-QUARTER had occurred four times. We will use the fifth SALES-QUARTER to accumulate the regional table. The necessary code to sum the totals by region is:

```
ALL-DONE.
    PERFORM SUM-REGION-COLUMN VARYING K FROM 1 BY 1 UNTIL (K > 3).
    .
    .
    .

SUM-REGION-COLUMN.
    PERFORM SUM-COLUMN VARYING L FROM 1 BY 1 UNTIL (L > 4).
SUM-COLUMN.
    ADD SALES-REGION-TABLE (L, K) TO SALES-REGION-TABLE (5, K).
```

This code collects the regional totals in the fifth row of the table. Then we must print all five rows, labeling the fifth row as a total row. Sample Program 14B (**Figure 14.3**) does this. **Figure 14.4** is some sample output from this program.

```
010010 IDENTIFICATION DIVISION.                                          PROGR14B
010020 PROGRAM-ID.                                                       PROGR14B
010030     PROGR14B.                                                     PROGR14B
010040* * * * * * * * * * * * * * * * * * * * * * * * * * * * **PROGR14B
010050*    SAMPLE PROGRAM  WITH TABLES AND TOTALS.                *PROGR14B
010060* * * * * * * * * * * * * * * * * * * * * * * * * * * * **PROGR14B
010070                                                                   PROGR14B
010080 ENVIRONMENT DIVISION.                                             PROGR14B
010090 INPUT-OUTPUT SECTION.                                             PROGR14B
010100 FILE-CONTROL.                                                     PROGR14B
010110     SELECT RECORDS-IN                                             PROGR14B
010120         ASSIGN TO UR-2540R-S-SYSIN.                               PROGR14B
010130     SELECT PRINT-OUT,                                             PROGR14B
010140         ASSIGN TO UR-1403-S-SYSPRINT.                             PROGR14B
010150                                                                   PROGR14B
020010 DATA DIVISION.                                                    PROGR14B
020020 FILE SECTION.                                                     PROGR14B
020030 FD  RECORDS-IN                                                    PROGR14B
020040     LABEL RECORDS ARE OMITTED.                                    PROGR14B
020050 01  IN-RECORD                     PICTURE X(80).                  PROGR14B
020060 FD  PRINT-OUT                                                     PROGR14B
020070     LABEL RECORDS ARE OMITTED.                                    PROGR14B
020080 01  PRINT-LINE                    PICTURE X(133).                 PROGR14B
020090                                                                   PROGR14B
020100 WORKING-STORAGE SECTION.                                          PROGR14B
020110 77  K            PICTURE 9.                                       PROGR14B
020120 77  L            PICTURE 9.                                       PROGR14B
020130                                                                   PROGR14B
020140 01  QUARTERS-VALUE.                                               PROGR14B
020150     05  QUARTER-1  PICTURE X(08)    VALUE 'FIRST'.                PROGR14B
020160     05  QUARTER-2  PICTURE X(08)    VALUE 'SECOND'.               PROGR14B
020170     05  QUARTER-3  PICTURE X(08)    VALUE 'THIRD'.                PROGR14B
020180     05  QUARTER-4  PICTURE X(08)    VALUE 'FOURTH'.               PROGR14B
020190     05  QUARTER-5  PICTURE X(08)    VALUE 'TOTAL'.                PROGR14B
020200 01  QUARTERS-RECORD REDEFINES QUARTERS-VALUE.                     PROGR14B
020210     05  QUARTER    PICTURE X(08) OCCURS 5 TIMES.                  PROGR14B
020220                                                                   PROGR14B
030010 01  SALES-TABLE.                                                  PROGR14B
030020     05  SALES-QUARTER OCCURS 5 TIMES.                             PROGR14B
030030         10 SALES-REGION-TABLE  OCCURS 3 TIMES  PICTURE 99999V99.  PROGR14B
030040                                                                   PROGR14B
030050 01  SALES-RECORD.                                                 PROGR14B
030060     05  FILLER       PICTURE X(10).                               PROGR14B
030070     05  QUARTER-RC   PICTURE 9(01).                               PROGR14B
030080     05  REGION-RC    PICTURE 9(01).                               PROGR14B
030090     05  SALES-RC     PICTURE 99999V99.                            PROGR14B
030100     05  FILLER       PICTURE X(61).                               PROGR14B
030110                                                                   PROGR14B
030120 01  SALES-LINE.                                                   PROGR14B
030130     05  FILLER                   PICTURE X(01).                   PROGR14B
030140     05  QUARTER-LN               PICTURE X(08).                   PROGR14B
```

```
030150      05    FILLER                    PICTURE X(08).          PROGR14B
030160      05    SALES-PRINT OCCURS 3 TIMES.                       PROGR14B
030170            10   REGION-LN            PICTURE $ZZ,ZZZ.99.     PROGR14B
030180            10   FILLER               PICTURE X(10).          PROGR14B
030190      05    FILLER                    PICTURE X(56).          PROGR14B
030200                                                              PROGR14B
040010 PROCEDURE DIVISION.                                          PROGR14B
040020      OPEN INPUT RECORDS-IN, OUTPUT PRINT-OUT.                PROGR14B
040030      MOVE ZERO TO SALES-TABLE.                               PROGR14B


040040      MOVE SPACES TO SALES-LINE.                              PROGR14B
040050      PERFORM PROCESS-DATA 1000 TIMES.                        PROGR14B
040060                                                              PROGR14B
040070 ALL-DONE.                                                    PROGR14B
040080      PERFORM SUM-REGION-COLUMN VARYING K FROM 1 BY 1         PROGR14B
040085                          UNTIL (K > 3).                      PROGR14B
040090      PERFORM DO-TOTALS VARYING K FROM 1 BY 1 UNTIL (K > 5).  PROGR14B
040100      CLOSE RECORDS-IN, PRINT-OUT.                            PROGR14B
040110      STOP RUN.                                               PROGR14B
040120                                                              PROGR14B
040130 PROCESS-DATA.                                                PROGR14B
040140      READ RECORDS-IN INTO SALES-RECORD AT END PERFORM ALL-DONE.  PROGR14B
040150      ADD SALES-RC TO SALES-REGION-TABLE (QUARTER-RC, REGION-RC).  PROGR14B
040160                                                              PROGR14B
040170 SUM-REGION-COLUMN.                                           PROGR14B
040180      PERFORM SUM-COLUMN VARYING L FROM 1 BY 1 UNTIL (L > 4).  PROGR14B
040190                                                              PROGR14B
040200 SUM-COLUMN.                                                  PROGR14B
040210      ADD SALES-REGION-TABLE (L, K) TO SALES-REGION-TABLE (5, K).  PROGR14B
040220                                                              PROGR14B
040230 DO-TOTALS.                                                   PROGR14B
040240      MOVE QUARTER (K) TO QUARTER-LN.                         PROGR14B
040250      MOVE  SALES-REGION-TABLE (K, 1) TO  REGION-LN (1).      PROGR14B
040260      MOVE  SALES-REGION-TABLE (K, 2) TO  REGION-LN (2).      PROGR14B
040270      MOVE  SALES-REGION-TABLE (K, 3) TO  REGION-LN (3).      PROGR14B
040280      WRITE PRINT-LINE FROM SALES-LINE AFTER ADVANCING 1 LINES.  PROGR14B
```

FIGURE 14.3   Sample Program 14B

FIRST	$ 5,040.00	$ 3,422.44	$ 1,200.45
SECOND	$ 4,230.00	$ 5,203.55	$ 2,055.66
THIRD	$ 8,203.00	$12,033.00	$20,300.00
FOURTH	$15,230.00	$ 2,830.00	$ 1,850.00
TOTAL	$32,703.00	$23,488.99	$25,406.11

FIGURE 14.4   Output from Program 14B

PERFORM . . . UNTIL

There is one other form of the PERFORM statement. Here is an example:

PERFORM DO-TOTALS UNTIL (K > 4).

In this example DO-TOTALS will be executed until the condition (K > 4) is satisfied. The general format for this type of PERFORM statement is:

PERFORM paragraph-1 [THRU paragraph-n] UNTIL (condition).

In this way one or more paragraphs can be executed continuously until some condition becomes true. You must make sure that the condition *will* become true, of course, or you will have an infinite loop.

Note:

1. The paragraphs are performed until the condition becomes true.
2. The condition is checked first: thus, if the condition is already true at the time the PERFORM statement is executed, the specified paragraphs are never executed.

SAMPLE PROGRAM 14C

In Sample Program 14C (**Figure 14.5**) the PERFORM . . . UNTIL is used to calculate new balances for savings accounts at a bank. The program reads a deposit amount and interest rate, and calculates the new balance each year for a period of years. The input record is:

```
01 DEPOSIT-RECORD.
    05 AMOUNT-RC         PICTURE 999999V99.
    05 INTEREST-RC       PICTURE V999.
    05 START-YEAR-RC     PICTURE 9999.
    05 END-YEAR-RC       PICTURE 9999.
    05 FILLER            PICTURE X(61).
```

Then the yearly interest must be calculated and added to the amount from the starting year to the ending year. This is done as follows:

```
    READ RECORDS-IN INTO DEPOSIT-RECORD AT END PERFORM ALL-DONE.
    MOVE AMOUNT-RC TO NEW-AMOUNT.
    MOVE START-YEAR-RC TO PRESENT-YEAR.
    PERFORM CALCULATE-NEW-PRINCIPAL
        UNTIL (PRESENT-YEAR > END-YEAR-RC).
    .
    .
    .
CALCULATE-NEW-PRINCIPAL.
    MOVE NEW-AMOUNT TO AMOUNT-LN.
    MOVE PRESENT-YEAR TO YEAR-LN.
    WRITE PRINT-LINE FROM AMOUNT-LINE AFTER ADVANCING 1 LINES.
    COMPUTE NEW-AMOUNT = NEW-AMOUNT + NEW-AMOUNT * INTEREST-RC.
    ADD 1 TO PRESENT-YEAR.
```

The variables NEW-AMOUNT and PRESENT-YEAR are level-number-77 items.
    Let's look at the UNTIL clause:

```
    PERFORM CALCULATE-NEW-PRINCIPAL
        UNTIL (PRESENT-YEAR > END-YEAR-RC).
```

Notice that PRESENT-YEAR is the deposit starting-year. Then, inside the paragraph CALCULATE-NEW-PRINCIPAL, we add 1 to PRESENT-YEAR each time the paragraph is executed. Therefore PRESENT-YEAR will eventually become larger then END-YEAR so that the UNTIL condition will be satisfied. Remember, it is very important to check that your condition will eventually be satisfied, or your program will run forever.

```
010010 IDENTIFICATION DIVISION.
010020 PROGRAM-ID.                                                         PROGR14C
010030     PROGR14C.                                                       PROGR14C
010040* * * * * * * * * * * * * * * * * * * * * * * * * * * * * **PROGR14C
010050*    SAMPLE PROGRAM USING PERFORM ... UNTIL.                  *PROGR14C
010060* * * * * * * * * * * * * * * * * * * * * * * * * * * * * **PROGR14C
010070                                                                     PROGR14C
010080 ENVIRONMENT DIVISION.                                               PROGR14C
010090 INPUT-OUTPUT SECTION.                                               PROGR14C
010100 FILE-CONTROL.                                                       PROGR14C
010110     SELECT RECORDS-IN                                               PROGR14C
010120         ASSIGN TO UR-2540R-S-SYSIN.                                 PROGR14C
010130     SELECT PRINT-OUT,                                               PROGR14C
010140         ASSIGN TO UR-1403-S-SYSPRINT.                               PROGR14C
010150                                                                     PROGR14C
020010 DATA DIVISION.                                                      PROGR14C
020020 FILE SECTION.                                                       PROGR14C
020030 FD  RECORDS-IN                                                      PROGR14C
020040     LABEL RECORDS ARE OMITTED.                                      PROGR14C
020050 01  IN-RECORD                   PICTURE X(80).                      PROGR14C
020060 FD  PRINT-OUT                                                       PROGR14C
020070     LABEL RECORDS ARE OMITTED.                                      PROGR14C
020080 01  PRINT-LINE                  PICTURE X(133).                     PROGR14C
020090                                                                     PROGR14C
020100 WORKING-STORAGE SECTION.                                            PROGR14C
020110 77  NEW-AMOUNT                  PICTURE 999999V99.                  PROGR14C
020120 77  PRESENT-YEAR                PICTURE 9999.                       PROGR14C
020130                                                                     PROGR14C
020140 01  DEPOSIT-RECORD.                                                 PROGR14C
020150     05  AMOUNT-RC               PICTURE 999999V99.                  PROGR14C
020160     05  INTEREST-RC             PICTURE V999.                       PROGR14C
020170     05  START-YEAR-RC           PICTURE 9999.                       PROGR14C
020180     05  END-YEAR-RC             PICTURE 9999.                       PROGR14C
020190     05  FILLER                  PICTURE X(61).                      PROGR14C
020200                                                                     PROGR14C
020210 01  AMOUNT-LINE.                                                    PROGR14C
020220     05  FILLER                  PICTURE X(01).                      PROGR14C
020230     05  YEAR-LN                 PICTURE 9999.                       PROGR14C
020240     05  FILLER                  PICTURE X(10).                      PROGR14C
020250     05  AMOUNT-LN               PICTURE $ZZZ,ZZZ.99.                PROGR14C
020260     05  FILLER                  PICTURE X(107).                     PROGR14C
020270                                                                     PROGR14C
030010 PROCEDURE DIVISION.                                                 PROGR14C
030020     OPEN INPUT RECORDS-IN, OUTPUT PRINT-OUT.                        PROGR14C
030030     MOVE SPACES TO AMOUNT-LINE.                                     PROGR14C
030040     READ RECORDS-IN INTO DEPOSIT-RECORD AT END PERFORM ALL-DONE. PROGR14C
030050     MOVE AMOUNT-RC TO NEW-AMOUNT.                                   PROGR14C
030060     MOVE START-YEAR-RC TO PRESENT-YEAR.                             PROGR14C
030070     PERFORM CALCULATE-NEW-PRINCIPAL                                 PROGR14C
030080         UNTIL (PRESENT-YEAR > END-YEAR-RC).                         PROGR14C
030090                                                                     PROGR14C
030100 ALL-DONE.                                                           PROGR14C
030110     CLOSE RECORDS-IN, PRINT-OUT.                                    PROGR14C
030120     STOP RUN.                                                       PROGR14C
030130                                                                     PROGR14C
030140 CALCULATE-NEW-PRINCIPAL.                                            PROGR14C
030150     MOVE NEW-AMOUNT TO AMOUNT-LN.                                   PROGR14C
030160     MOVE PRESENT-YEAR TO YEAR-LN.                                   PROGR14C
030170     WRITE PRINT-LINE FROM AMOUNT-LINE AFTER ADVANCING 1 LINES.    PROGR14C
030180     COMPUTE NEW-AMOUNT = NEW-AMOUNT + NEW-AMOUNT * INTEREST-RC.   PROGR14C




030190     ADD 1 TO PRESENT-YEAR.                                          PROGR14C
```

FIGURE 14.5   Sample Program 14C

****

RAVIN'

Laverne Ruby

Once upon a midday dreary, while I pondered, weak and weary,
Over many a quaint and curious volume of computer lore,
As I nodded, nearly snoring, suddenly there came a roaring,
As of someone gently boring, boring through tape number four.
" 'Tis the octal load," I muttered, "reading cards into the core—
Only this and nothing more."

Ah, distinctly I'm recalling all about the sound appalling
And my skin began a-crawling as I heard that sound once more.
Eagerly I wished the morrow, vainly I had sought to borrow
From my booze surcease of sorrow—sorrow that I had this chore—
Working on this vile computer which the coders all deplore,
Nameless here forevermore.

Then the flutter, sad, unsteady, of the light that flashed, "Not Ready"
Thrilled me—filled me—with fantastic terrors never felt before;
And to still my heart's quick pounding, fiercely I began expounding
" 'Tis the octal load resounding as it reads cards into core,
Just the octal load resounding as it reads cards into core,
This it is, and nothing more."

Presently my soul grew sicker, for the lights began to flicker,
And I thought I heard a snicker from behind the tape drive door.
Hereupon discarding vanity, hoping but to save my sanity,
Uttered I some choice profanity of the rugged days of yore,
For the grim machine was looping! I, to display console, tore—
Darkness there, and nothing more!

Deep into that blank scope staring, long I stood there, cursing, swearing,
Sobbing, screaming screams no mortal ever dared to scream before;
But the looping was unbroken, and the darkness gave no token,
And the only word there spoken was the whispered word (CENSORED),
This I whispered, and an echo murmured back the word (CENSORED),
Merely this, and nothing more,

Back then toward the printer speeding, all my soul within me bleeding,
Soon again I heard a roaring, somewhat louder than before.
"Surely," said I, "as sure as heck, something's wrong with my octal deck,
Let me see then, let me check, and this mystery explore—
Let my heart be still a moment, and this mystery explore—
'Tis the cards, and nothing more!"

Open here I flung a listing, with the noisy roar persisting,
Out there fluttered two control cards, cards I had forgot before;
Not the least deferment made I, not a moment stopped or stayed I,
Launching on a foul tirade, I started up the beast once more.
But, the monster, after reading both the cards into the core,
Blinked, and sat, and nothing more.

Then this foul machine beguiling my sad fancy to reviling.
Turned I back toward the printer, answer then I did implore:
"Though my nerves are all a-splinter, thou," I said, "art sure no stinter,
Ghastly, grim and ancient printer, printer of computer lore.
Tell me what the trouble here is, for I surely need no more!"
                                                                      Quoth the printer, "Nevermore!"

Much I marveled this contraption should give birth to such a caption,
Though its answer little meaning—little relevancy bore:
For it's sure that vile invective would deter the best detective,
Render such a one defective, stupid as a sophomore.
Why should such a steel invention as the printer on the floor,
                                                                      Say such a word as "Nevermore?"

But the printer, sitting lonely on the concrete floor, spoke only
That one word as if by saying that one word it jinxed a score;
Nothing further then was written, and it purred on like a kitten,
'Till I stood there, conscience-smitten, "Other woes were fixed before—
On the morrow 'twill be ended, as my woes have flown before."
                                                                      Quoth the printer, "Nevermore!"

Then methought the air grew smoggy, presently my head grew groggy,
Gripped by madness, then I spoke, my voice containing thirst for gore:
"Beast!" I cried, "Let Satan take thee! Let the devil roast and bake thee!
After, get the fiends who make thee! Let them sizzle four by four!
Let them sizzle, boil, and sputter! Let them fry forevermore!"
                                                                      Quoth the printer, "Nevermore!"

"Monster!" said I, "Thing of evil! Black invention of the devil!
By the Hell that fries below us, by the Fiend we both abhor!
Tell this soul with sorrow shackled, the meaning of the word you cackled.
What's this job that I have tackled, never mind the metaphor!
Tell me just wherein I've failed, by signal, sign, or semaphore!"
                                                                      Quoth the printer, "Nevermore!"

"Stop repeating words inanely, ghastly fiend," I shrieked insanely.
"May the gods come and destroy thee, and my shattered nerves restore."
While I stood my curse invoking, suddenly I started choking,
For the printer started smoking, and I started for the door.
"I'll win yet, machine infernal!" This I said and this I swore.
                                                                      Quoth the printer, "Nevermore!"

And the monster, always whooping, still is looping, still is looping,
In the self-same program looping, that elusive part of core.
And its lights have all the seeming of a demon that is scheming,
And the coders all blaspheming throw their programs on the floor—
And my soul from out those programs that lie scattered on the floor,
                                                                      Shall be lifted—nevermore!

Reprinted with the permission of System Development Corporation.

****

CHAPTER REVIEW

Vocabulary Review

Section name   Nested loop (double loop)   Infinite loop

Review Questions

1. What is an infinite loop? How does this happen? How can you prevent it?

2. Which of the following are valid **PERFORM** statements?
   a) PERFORM A.
   b) PERFORM A TO I.
   c) PERFORM A VARYING I FROM 10 BY – 1 UNTIL (I < 1).
   d) PERFORM ZAP VARYING K FROM 1 BY 3 UNTIL (K = 9).
   e) PERFORM ZAP VARYING L BY 1 UNTIL (L = 10).

3. How many times will the paragraph **ZAP** be executed if the following code is executed?

   a)   PERFORM ZAP 3 TIMES.
           ADD 1 TO COUNT.
        ZAP.
           MOVE OUTTER TO INNER.

   b)   PERFORM ZAP VARYING L FROM 1 BY 1 UNTIL (L = 5).
           STOP RUN.
        ZAP.
           MOVE OUTTER TO INNER.

   c)   PERFORM ZAP VARYING L FROM 1 BY 1 UNTIL (L > 4).
           STOP RUN.
        ZAP.
           MOVE OUTTER TO INNER.

Program Modifications

1. Modify Sample Program 14B so that it prints the row totals. Be sure to sum the fifth row to give a grand total. Label the columns. Print the total sales on a line by itself after the table. Label this total-line **TOTAL SALES**.

2. Modify Sample Program 14C as follows:
   a) The program won't work correctly unless the starting year is less than the ending year. Check for this; if it isn't true, print an error message and stop the program.
   b) Change the program so that it prints the old balance, yearly interest, and new balance. Provide a total for the interest.
   c) Print headings.

3. Do the modifications listed in question 2. Calculate the interest twice a year instead of annually. (The program should still read in the annual interest rate as data.)

4. Generalize the modification in question 3, that is, read in a variable which indicates how many times a year interest is paid.

Programs

1. Write a program to read in a deposit amount and annual interest rate. Calculate the new principal after 10 years for:

    a) Annual interest.

    b) Semiannual interest.

    c) Quarterly interest.

    d) Monthly interest.

    e) Daily interest.

2. Compound interest can be calculated either by performing a paragraph repeatedly or by use of an interest formula. If you calculated the interest in question 3 by using a PERFORM loop, look up the compound-interest formula and try it that way; if you used the formula, calculate it now using PERFORM. Do you get exactly the same answer both ways?

3. The Indians sold Manhattan Island for $24.00 in 1626. Write a program to calculate the amount of money they would now have if they had instead deposited their $24.00 in the Bank of England at 6 percent annual interest.

4. Write a program to calculate loan amortization. The input record is as follows:

Field	Input Columns	
Loan number	1–6	
Customer name	7–25	
Loan date	26–31	
Principal	32–39	(two decimal-places)
Annual interest	40–43	(two decimal-places)
Monthly payment	44–49	(two decimal-places)

****

Computer Graffiti

Show me a program that works perfectly,
and I will show you a program that does not do much.

****

The program should print all the information above, and then print the total payment, interest payment, principal payment, and new balance for each month until the loan has been paid back.

5. *Sum-of-the-year depreciation.* Depreciation for any year can be calculated by the following formula:

Depreciation = COST × Y/SY

where

COST = original cost.
Y = the year in reverse order.
SY = the sum of the years.

For example, if you have some machinery worth $15,000 which is to be depreciated over 5 years, then

$SY = 5 + 4 + 3 + 2 + 1 = 15$

and the calculated depreciation for each year will be:

Year 1 depreciation = $15,000 x 5/15 = $5,000
Year 2 depreciation = $15,000 x 4/15 = $4,000
Year 3 depreciation = $15,000 x 3/15 = $3,000
Year 4 depreciation = $15,000 x 2/15 = $2,000
Year 5 depreciation = $15,000 x 1/15 = $1,000

Notice that the sum of the yearly depreciations equals the original cost. Write a program to read in original cost and number of years and calculate depreciation. There is a simple formula for SY:

$$SY = \frac{n * (n + 1)}{2}$$

where n = the number of years. Your program should print the machinery's value and its depreciation for each year. The input record is:

Field	Input Columns
Item number	1–5
Item name	6–25
Item value	26–30
Years	31–32

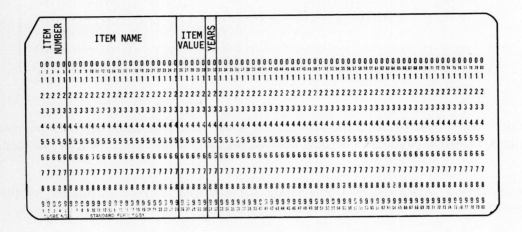

6. *Declining-balance depreciation.* Write a program to compute depreciation using the declining-balance method. Input records are as follows:

Field	Input Columns	
Item number	1–5	
Item name	6–25	
Item value	26–30	
Years	31–32	
Rate	33–35	(two decimal-places)

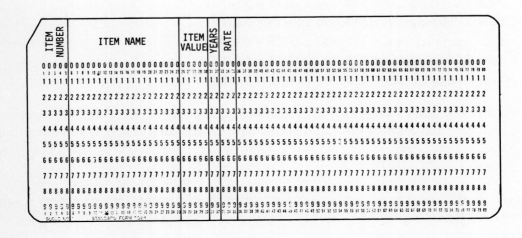

Rate = the rate of depreciation; years = the number of years the item is to be depreciated. Thus, if the original value was $1,000, the depreciation rate = 0.20, and years = 5.

Years	Present Value	Present Depreciation	Accumulated Depreciation
0	$1,000.00	$ 00.00	$ 00.00
1	800.00	200.00	200.00
2	640.00	160.00	360.00
3	512.00	128.00	488.00
4	409.60	102.40	590.40
5	327.68	81.92	672.32

The depreciation rate is multiplied by the present value each year in order to get the new yearly depreciation.

Chapter

15

****

A surgical robot named Clyde,
As med students probed his inside,
_And dismantled a part
Of his fiberglass heart,
Sat up and announced, "I just died!"

****

SEARCHING

Our previous programs containing tables were able to use a subscript to locate an item in a table directly. Often, however, this is not possible. For example, suppose we had the following two-dimensional table:

Discipline Code	Discipline Name
401	Mathematics
107	Chemistry
204	Biology
195	Computer science
310	Psychology
185	English
158	Physics
155	Religious studies
188	Philosophy
999	Unknown

Here the first column is the discipline code and the second column is the discipline name. Each detail record will have a discipline code in it. In order to print the discipline name, the program would have to search through the discipline codes to find the matching code. This table searching is called a **table lookup**.

While it would be convenient, from the point of view of programming, to have a discipline code used as a subscript, this would often require too many other changes in the bureaucracy requiring the program. This is a common situation! Seldom can you request an organization to change their habits just to make your program easier to write.

****

Computer Graffiti

It is easier to change a program
than to change a bureaucracy.

****

Table searching is very common in programming, for example, to match job codes or part numbers to a desired list, or in calculating taxes, where the income is compared to a tax table to determine the tax rate.

SAMPLE PROGRAM 15A

Intellect Haven College needs a program to process some student records. Sample Program 15A (**Figure 15.1**) reads student detail-records which have a discipline code and then does a table lookup to find the discipline name. The first task is to read in the records for the discipline table. The format of the discipline records is as follows:

Field	Columns
Discipline code	1-3
Discipline name	4-30

The final discipline record will have a discipline code of **999**. The COBOL statements necessary to read and initialize the discipline table are as follows:

```
WORKING-STORAGE SECTION.
77 K                    PICTURE S99   VALUE +1
                        USAGE COMPUTATIONAL.
77 TABLE-SIZE           PICTURE S99.
01 DISCIPLINE-TABLE.
   05 DISCIPLINES       OCCURS 10 TIMES.
      10 DISC-CODE      PICTURE XXX.
      10 DISC-NAME      PICTURE X(27).

01 DISCIPLINE-RECORD.
   05 DISCIPLINE-IN.
      10 DISC-CODE-IN   PICTURE X(03).
      10 DISC-NAME-IN   PICTURE X(27).
   05 FILLER            PICTURE X(50).
```

First, K and TABLE-SIZE are defined. The variable K will be a subscript in the table, and TABLE-SIZE will keep track of the table size. If the table size is variable, we can declare the table larger than we need and use the variable TABLE-SIZE to keep track of the actual size of the table. Next, DISCIPLINE-TABLE is declared to hold the discipline codes and the discipline names. Finally, DISCIPLINE-RECORD is defined so we can read in the discipline records. These declare the variables necessary for reading in and setting up the discipline table. In order to read in and store the discipline records, we need to execute a paragraph over and over until all the discipline-table records have been read. The final table-record contains the discipline code 999. A PERFORM UNTIL statement will initialize the table. Here are the necessary statements to initialize the DISCIPLINE-TABLE:

```
        PERFORM READ-IN-TABLE UNTIL (DISC-CODE-IN = '999').
        COMPUTE TABLE-SIZE = K - 1.
        .
        .
        .
    READ-IN-TABLE.
        READ RECORDS-IN INTO DISCIPLINE-RECORD
            AT END PERFORM ALL-DONE.
        MOVE DISC-CODE-IN TO DISC-CODE (K).
        MOVE DISC-NAME-IN TO DISC-NAME (K).
        ADD 1 TO K.
```

The paragraph READ-IN-TABLE will read in discipline records and move the discipline code and discipline name to the discipline table. If the table items are numerous and subject to frequent change, they should be read in as data. If the table items are few and unchanging, they should be made part of the WORKING-STORAGE SECTION.

The student detail-records are as follows:

Field	Columns
Student number	1–9
Student name	10–30
Student discipline	31–33

The student-discipline field in the detail record, a three-column alphanumeric field, is used to print the discipline name. Since there is no subscript-like relationship between the discipline code and the discipline name, the program must search the table for a match in discipline code in order to print the discipline name. The COBOL code to do this is as follows:

```
    PROCESS-RECORDS.
        READ RECORDS-IN INTO STUDENT-RECORD
            AT END PERFORM ALL-DONE.
        MOVE CORRESPONDING STUDENT-RECORD TO STUDENT-LINE.
        MOVE 1 TO L.
        PERFORM SEARCH-DISCIPLINE TABLE-SIZE TIMES.
        WRITE PRINT-LINE FROM STUDENT-LINE AFTER ADVANCING 1 LINES.
    SEARCH-DISCIPLINE.
        IF (STUDENT-DISCIPLINE OF STUDENT-RECORD = DISC-CODE (L))
            MOVE DISC-NAME (L) TO DISCIPLINE-NAME.
        ADD 1 TO L.
```

The COBOL statements above are executed for each detail record. The READ statement reads in the detail records; the MOVE CORRESPONDING statement moves all fields, except the discipline name, to the print area. The variable L is set to 1; then the table is searched for the matching discipline code. When the discipline code has been found, the discipline name is moved to the print-line. Finally, the output line is printed. **Figure 15.2** is some sample output from Program 15A.

```
010010 IDENTIFICATION DIVISION.                                      PROGR15A
010020 PROGRAM-ID.                                                   PROGR15A
010030      PROG15A.                                                 PROGR15A
010040* * * * * * * * * * * * * * * * * * * * * * * * * * * * * **PROGR15A
010050*     SIMPLE TABLE SEARCH USING A PERFORM.                    *PROGR15A
010060* * * * * * * * * * * * * * * * * * * * * * * * * * * * * **PROGR15A
010070                                                               PROGR15A
010080 ENVIRONMENT DIVISION.                                         PROGR15A
010090 INPUT-OUTPUT SECTION.                                         PROGR15A
010100 FILE-CONTROL.                                                 PROGR15A
010110      SELECT RECORDS-IN,                                       PROGR15A
010120          ASSIGN TO UR-2540R-S-SYSIN.                          PROGR15A
010130      SELECT PRINT-OUT,                                        PROGR15A
010140          ASSIGN TO UR-1403-S-SYSPRINT.                        PROGR15A
010150                                                               PROGR15A
020010 DATA DIVISION.                                                PROGR15A
020020 FILE SECTION.                                                 PROGR15A
020030 FD  RECORDS-IN                                                PROGR15A
020040      LABEL RECORDS ARE OMITTED.                               PROGR15A
020050 01  IN-RECORD                      PICTURE X(80).             PROGR15A
020060 FD  PRINT-OUT                                                 PROGR15A
020070      LABEL RECORDS ARE OMITTED.                               PROGR15A
020080 01  PRINT-LINE                     PICTURE X(133).            PROGR15A
020090                                                               PROGR15A
020100 WORKING-STORAGE SECTION.                                      PROGR15A
020110 77  K                    PICTURE S99      VALUE +1            PROGR15A
020120                          USAGE COMPUTATIONAL.                 PROGR15A
020130 77  L                    PICTURE S99      VALUE +1            PROGR15A
020140                          USAGE COMPUTATIONAL.                 PROGR15A
020150 77  TABLE-SIZE           PICTURE S99.                         PROGR15A
020160                                                               PROGR15A
020170 01  DISCIPLINE-TABLE.                                         PROGR15A
020180      05  DISCIPLINES       OCCURS 10 TIMES.                   PROGR15A
020190          10  DISC-CODE     PICTURE XXX.                       PROGR15A
020200          10  DISC-NAME     PICTURE X(27).                     PROGR15A
020210                                                               PROGR15A
030010 01  DISCIPLINE-RECORD.                                        PROGR15A
030020      05  DISCIPLINE-IN.                                       PROGR15A
030030          10  DISC-CODE-IN    PICTURE XXX.                     PROGR15A
030040          10  DISC-NAME-IN    PICTURE X(27).                   PROGR15A
030050      05  FILLER              PICTURE X(50).                   PROGR15A
030060                                                               PROGR15A
030070 01  STUDENT-RECORD.                                           PROGR15A
030080      05  STUDENT-NUMBER           PICTURE X(09).              PROGR15A
030090      05  STUDENT-NAME             PICTURE X(25).              PROGR15A
030100      05  STUDENT-DISCIPLINE       PICTURE X(03).              PROGR15A
030110      05  FILLER                   PICTURE X(43).              PROGR15A
030120                                                               PROGR15A
030130 01  STUDENT-LINE.                                             PROGR15A
030140      05  FILLER                   PICTURE X(01).              PROGR15A
030150      05  STUDENT-NUMBER           PICTURE X(09).              PROGR15A
030160      05  FILLER                   PICTURE X(06).              PROGR15A
030170      05  STUDENT-NAME             PICTURE X(25).              PROGR15A
030180      05  FILLER                   PICTURE X(06).              PROGR15A
030190      05  STUDENT-DISCIPLINE       PICTURE X(03).              PROGR15A
030200      05  FILLER                   PICTURE X(06).              PROGR15A
030210      05  DISCIPLINE-NAME          PICTURE X(27).              PROGR15A
030220      05  FILLER                   PICTURE X(50).              PROGR15A
030230                                                               PROGR15A
040010 PROCEDURE DIVISION.                                           PROGR15A
040020      OPEN INPUT RECORDS-IN, OUTPUT PRINT-OUT.                 PROGR15A
```

```
040030       MOVE SPACES TO STUDENT-LINE.                              PROGR15A
040040       MOVE ZERO TO DISC-CODE-IN.                                PROGR15A
040050       PERFORM READ-IN-TABLE UNTIL (DISC-CODE-IN = '999').       PROGR15A
040060       COMPUTE TABLE-SIZE = K - 1.                               PROGR15A
040070       PERFORM PROCESS-RECORDS 1000 TIMES.                       PROGR15A
040080                                                                 PROGR15A
040090 ALL-DONE.                                                       PROGR15A
040100       CLOSE RECORDS-IN, PRINT-OUT.                              PROGR15A
040110       STOP RUN.                                                 PROGR15A
040120                                                                 PROGR15A
040130 READ-IN-TABLE.                                                  PROGR15A
040140     READ RECORDS-IN INTO DISCIPLINE-RECORD                      PROGR15A
040150         AT END PERFORM ALL-DONE.                                PROGR15A
040160     MOVE DISC-CODE-IN TO DISC-CODE (K).                         PROGR15A
040170     MOVE DISC-NAME-IN TO DISC-NAME (K).                         PROGR15A
040180     ADD 1 TO K.                                                 PROGR15A
040190                                                                 PROGR15A
040200 PROCESS-RECORDS.                                                PROGR15A
040210     READ RECORDS-IN INTO STUDENT-RECORD                         PROGR15A
040220         AT END PERFORM ALL-DONE.                                PROGR15A
040230     MOVE CORRESPONDING STUDENT-RECORD TO STUDENT-LINE.          PROGR15A
040240     MOVE 1 TO L.                                                PROGR15A
040250     PERFORM SEARCH-DISCIPLINE TABLE-SIZE TIMES.                 PROGR15A
040260     WRITE PRINT-LINE FROM STUDENT-LINE AFTER ADVANCING 1 LINES. PROGR15A
040270                                                                 PROGR15A
040280 SEARCH-DISCIPLINE.                                              PROGR15A
040290     IF (STUDENT-DISCIPLINE OF STUDENT-RECORD = DISC-CODE (L))   PROGR15A
040300         MOVE DISC-NAME (L) TO DISCIPLINE-NAME.                  PROGR15A
040310     ADD 1 TO L.                                                 PROGR15A
```

FIGURE 15.1   Sample Program 15A

```
245387564       HOSE GARCIA            401       MATHEMATICS
425786356       OMI WANG               195       COMPUTER SCIENCE
142536898       MARY JONES             107       CHEMISTRY
754215352       MICHAEL RAMIZES        188       PHILOSOPHY
852412356       ALAN GREENSPUR         158       PHYSICS
752415968       HOSE SMITH             195       COMPUTER SCIENCE
```

FIGURE 15.2   Output from Program 15A

REVIEW

1. If the table search were stopped as soon as a match was found, how much table-searching time would be saved, on the average?

2. In Sample Program 15A, what would happen if there were fewer than 10 discipline-table records? Would the program still work correctly? If you cannot determine the answer, try using only 5 discipline-table records.

3. In Program 15A, what would happen if the number of discipline-table records exceeded the amount of space declared for them in the OCCURS clause? What would happen if the discipline-table record with a discipline code of 999 were missing?

4. What would happen if no match were found for the discipline code?

Program Modifications

1. Sample Program 15A is incomplete because it assumes that the number of discipline records will not exceed the limits for the table. Add statements to check, and, if there are too many discipline records, to print an error message and stop the program.

2. Modify Program 15A so that the first input-record indicates the number of table entries. Use this number to control the PERFORM statement (do not use the UNTIL clause).

3. Modify Program 15A so that the table is initialized in the WORKING-STORAGE SECTION instead of being read in as data.

4. Program 15A is incomplete because it assumes that a matching discipline code will always be found. Provide a detail record with an unmatched discipline-code and rerun the program. What happens in this case? Modify the program so that it prints the major name UNKNOWN whenever the discipline code is unmatched.

5. Program 15A is inefficient because it always searches the whole table even if a match occurs on the first or second discipline. Modify the program so that it stops searching as soon as a match is found.

6. Modify Program 15A so that it prints the lowest and the highest discipline-code. Print the subscript values of the lowest and the highest discipline-code.

The SEARCH Statement

Table searching is so common that there is a special COBOL verb, the SEARCH verb, that will do table searching. The programmer should use the SEARCH verb for the following reasons:

1. The SEARCH verb is much more efficient than programmer-written code.
2. The use of the SEARCH verb will eliminate many programming errors.

The second reason brings us to another basic rule of programming: let the computer and the programming language do as much work as possible. This will allow you, the programmer, to avoid much work and many errors.

INDEXES

To use the SEARCH verb, we must declare an **index**—a special variable used to identify a particular element in a table—when we declare the array. Here is an example:

```
01 DISCIPLINE-TABLE.
   05 DISCIPLINES        OCCURS 10 TIMES
                         INDEXED BY DISC-INDEX.
      10 DISC-CODE       PICTURE X(03).
      10 DISC-NAME       PICTURE X(27).
```

The general form of the INDEXED BY clause is:

```
INDEXED BY index-name-1 [index-name-2 . . . ]
```

Notice that the INDEXED BY clause is part of the entry containing the OCCURS clause. The index name is associated with a particular table; it is not declared anywhere else in the program. An index name must be initialized in a SET or PERFORM statement before it can be used. An index name is different from a subscript: the index refers to the position in a table. For example:

```
05 ZAP OCCURS 10 TIMES
    INDEXED BY ZAP-INDEX.
    10 Z     PICTURE 99.
    10 T     PICTURE XXXX.
```

ZAP Table									
ZAP(1)		ZAP(2)					ZAP(10)		
Z	T	Z	T				Z	T	

The valid subscripts are 1, 2, 3, 4, . . . ,10, but ZAP-INDEX refers to the position of displacement from the beginning. Valid displacements are 0, 6, 12, 18, . . . , 54. Thus, subscript-value 1 corresponds to index-value 0; subscript-value 2 corresponds to index-value 6; subscript-value 3 corresponds to index-value 12. When the index is set, the index-value is calculated automatically by the COBOL statements. The **occurrence number** minus 1 is multiplied by the length of the indexed entry. For the table above, the value of the third index would be:

$$\text{ZAP-INDEX} = (3 - 1) * 6 = 12.$$

The index can be set by the SET statement.

The SET Statement

The SET statement will initialize an index name to a value associated with the table elements. An index name *cannot* be initialized by a MOVE or COMPUTE statement, because the displacement must be calculated at the time that the index is set. The general format of the SET statement is:

```
SET index-name-1 TO  { index-name-2 }
                     { identifier    } .
                     { literal       }
```

Both identifiers and literals must be integer variables, and their values must be positive. When an identifier or literal is used, its position is calculated for the index, that is, the literal or variable should have the desired subscript-value. For example:

    SET ZAP-INDEX TO 3.

This code will set ZAP-INDEX to point at the third element in the table. The index name must have been initialized by a SET statement if a SEARCH is to be executed.

PERFORM with Indexes

The PERFORM verb with the VARYING clause can be used with indexes. The PERFORM . . . VARYING with indexes works like other PERFORMs except that we must use indexes instead of variables. The general format is:

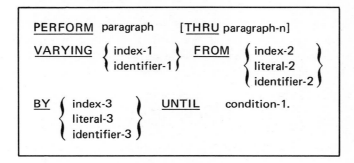

An example of a PERFORM with an index (if ZAP-INDEX is an index) is:

    PERFORM PARA-X VARYING ZAP-INDEX
        FROM 1 BY 1 UNTIL (ZAP-INDEX > 10).

A substantial amount of execution machine-time can be saved by using indexes when you are manipulating large tables.

Note:

1. The INDEXED BY clause defines the index for use with a specific table. The index is not defined anywhere else in the program.
2. The SET clause uses the occurrence number and calculates the corresponding position.
3. The SET statement must be executed in order to initialize the index before the SEARCH statement can be used.

The SEARCH Verb

The SEARCH statement is used to search a table. If the element desired is found, the index variable is set to the occurrence number. The WHEN clause of the SEARCH will be executed if the element is found; the AT END clause will be executed if the element is not found. Here is the general form of the SEARCH statement:

```
SEARCH identifier-1
    AT END imperative-statement-1
    WHEN    condition    imperative-statement-2.
```

The variable used as identifier-1 *must* be the variable described in the DATA DIVISION, which must contain both an OCCURS clause and the INDEXED BY option. Identifier-1 must refer to the whole table, and must not be subscripted or indexed. The NEXT SENTENCE clause can be used in place of the imperative-statements.

The AT END clause will be executed if the condition is not satisfied within the permitted range of the index. If the condition is satisfied, the imperative statement in the WHEN clause will be executed. The condition is evaluated in this way: If the condition is not satisfied, the index name for identifier-1 is incremented to reference the next element in the table, then the condition is evaluated again. This process continues until the end of the table is reached or until the condition is satisfied. The search terminates as soon as the condition has been satisfied. The index name is automatically set to point to the index value satisfying the condition. The statements used to search in Sample Program 15A were the following:

```
PERFORM SEARCH-DISCIPLINE TABLE-SIZE TIMES.
    .
    .
    .
SEARCH-DISCIPLINE.
    IF (STUDENT-DISCIPLINE OF STUDENT-RECORD = DISC-CODE (L))
        MOVE DISC-NAME (L) TO DISCIPLINE-NAME.
    ADD 1 TO L.
```

The code above fails to check to see if no match can be made, but this is relatively easy to fix: when the search has been done, check to see if L is larger than the size of the table.

The equivalent statements using SEARCH are the following:

```
SET DISC-INDEX TO 1.
SEARCH DISCIPLINES
    AT END MOVE 'UNKNOWN' TO DISCIPLINE-NAME
    WHEN (DISC-CODE (DISC-INDEX) = STUDENT-DISCIPLINE OF STUDENT-RECORD)
        MOVE DISC-NAME (DISC-INDEX) TO DISCIPLINE-NAME.
```

The code above sets DISC-INDEX to point at the first element in the table by using the SET statement. The SEARCH command then automatically searches through the table, entry by entry, until the condition has been satisfied or until the end of the table has been reached. If the condition in the WHEN clause is satisfied, the MOVE statement in the code above will be executed. If the condition is never satisfied, the AT END clause will be executed.

The SEARCH statement eliminates the necessity for the programmer to write code to step through the table, and it also solves the problem of going beyond the limits of the table. When you are using the SEARCH verb, you must make sure that the table is no larger than you need, because the SEARCH command searches through the whole table. If the table is declared larger than necessary, errors may occur which will cause mismatching or program abends. Sample Program 15B (**Figure 15.3**) uses the SEARCH verb.

```
010010 IDENTIFICATION DIVISION.                                          PROGR15B
010020 PROGRAM-ID.                                                       PROGR15B
010030    PROG15B.                                                       PROGR15B
010040* * * * * * * * * * * * * * * * * * * * * * * * * * * * * * **PROGR15B
010050*    SIMPLE TABLE SEARCH USING A SEARCH VERB.                   *PROGR15B
010060* * * * * * * * * * * * * * * * * * * * * * * * * * * * * * **PROGR15B
010070                                                                   PROGR15B
010080 ENVIRONMENT DIVISION.                                             PROGR15B
010090 INPUT-OUTPUT SECTION.                                             PROGR15B
010100 FILE-CONTROL.                                                     PROGR15B
010110    SELECT RECORDS-IN,                                             PROGR15B
010120       ASSIGN TO UR-2540R-S-SYSIN.                                 PROGR15B
010130    SELECT PRINT-OUT,                                              PROGR15B
010140       ASSIGN TO UR-1403-S-SYSPRINT.                               PROGR15B
010150                                                                   PROGR15B
020010 DATA DIVISION.                                                    PROGR15B
020020 FILE SECTION.                                                     PROGR15B
020030 FD   RECORDS-IN                                                   PROGR15B
020040    LABEL RECORDS ARE OMITTED.                                     PROGR15B
020050 01   IN-RECORD                    PICTURE X(80).                  PROGR15B
020060 FD   PRINT-OUT                                                    PROGR15B
020070    LABEL RECORDS ARE OMITTED.                                     PROGR15B
020080 01   PRINT-LINE                   PICTURE X(133).                 PROGR15B
020090                                                                   PROGR15B
020100 WORKING-STORAGE SECTION.                                          PROGR15B
020110 77   K                    PICTURE S99      VALUE +1               PROGR15B
020120                           USAGE COMPUTATIONAL.                    PROGR15B
020130                                                                   PROGR15B
020140 01   DISCIPLINE-TABLE.                                            PROGR15B
020150    05   DISCIPLINES       OCCURS 10 TIMES                         PROGR15B
020160                           INDEXED BY DISC-INDEX.                  PROGR15B
020170       10   DISC-CODE      PICTURE X(03).                          PROGR15B
020180       10   DISC-NAME      PICTURE X(27).                          PROGR15B
020190                                                                   PROGR15B
030010 01   DISCIPLINE-RECORD.                                           PROGR15B
030020    05   DISCIPLINE-IN.                                            PROGR15B
030030       10   DISC-CODE-IN      PICTURE X(03).                       PROGR15B
030040       10   DISC-NAME-IN      PICTURE X(27).                       PROGR15B
030050    05   FILLER              PICTURE X(50).                        PROGR15B
030060                                                                   PROGR15B
030070 01   STUDENT-RECORD.                                              PROGR15B
030080    05   STUDENT-NUMBER          PICTURE X(09).                    PROGR15B
030090    05   STUDENT-NAME            PICTURE X(25).                    PROGR15B
030100    05   STUDENT-DISCIPLINE      PICTURE X(03).                    PROGR15B
030110    05   FILLER                  PICTURE X(43).                    PROGR15B
030120                                                                   PROGR15B
030130 01   STUDENT-LINE.                                                PROGR15B
030140    05   FILLER                  PICTURE X(01).                    PROGR15B
030150    05   STUDENT-NUMBER          PICTURE X(09).                    PROGR15B
030160    05   FILLER                  PICTURE X(06).                    PROGR15B
030170    05   STUDENT-NAME            PICTURE X(25).                    PROGR15B
030180    05   FILLER                  PICTURE X(06).                    PROGR15B
030190    05   STUDENT-DISCIPLINE      PICTURE X(03).                    PROGR15B
030200    05   FILLER                  PICTURE X(06).                    PROGR15B
030210    05   DISCIPLINE-NAME         PICTURE X(27).                    PROGR15B
030220    05   FILLER                  PICTURE X(50).                    PROGR15B
030230                                                                   PROGR15B
040010 PROCEDURE DIVISION.                                               PROGR15B
040020    OPEN INPUT RECORDS-IN, OUTPUT PRINT-OUT.                       PROGR15B
040030    MOVE SPACES TO STUDENT-LINE.                                   PROGR15B
040040    MOVE ZERO TO DISC-CODE-IN.                                     PROGR15B


040050    PERFORM READ-IN-TABLE UNTIL (DISC-CODE-IN = '999').           PROGR15B
040060    PERFORM PROCESS-RECORDS 1000 TIMES.                           PROGR15B
040070                                                                   PROGR15B
040080 ALL-DONE.                                                         PROGR15B
040090    CLOSE RECORDS-IN, PRINT-OUT.                                   PROGR15B
040100    STOP RUN.                                                      PROGR15B
040110                                                                   PROGR15B
040120 READ-IN-TABLE.                                                    PROGR15B
```

```
040130        READ RECORDS-IN INTO DISCIPLINE-RECORD                    PROGR15B
040140            AT END PERFORM ALL-DONE.                              PROGR15B
040150        MOVE DISC-CODE-IN TO DISC-CODE (K).                       PROGR15B
040160        MOVE DISC-NAME-IN TO DISC-NAME (K).                       PROGR15B
040170        ADD 1 TO K.                                               PROGR15B
040180                                                                  PROGR15B
040190 PROCESS-RECORDS.                                                 PROGR15B
040200        READ RECORDS-IN INTO STUDENT-RECORD                       PROGR15B
040210            AT END PERFORM ALL-DONE.                              PROGR15B
040220        MOVE CORRESPONDING STUDENT-RECORD TO STUDENT-LINE.        PROGR15B
040230        SET DISC-INDEX TO 1.                                      PROGR15B
040240        SEARCH DISCIPLINES                                        PROGR15B
040250            AT END MOVE 'UNKNOWN' TO DISCIPLINE-NAME              PROGR15B
040260            WHEN (DISC-CODE (DISC-INDEX) = STUDENT-DISCIPLINE OF  PROGR15B
040270                                      STUDENT-RECORD)             PROGR15B
040280                MOVE DISC-NAME (DISC-INDEX) TO DISCIPLINE-NAME.   PROGR15B
040290        WRITE PRINT-LINE FROM STUDENT-LINE AFTER ADVANCING 1 LINES. PROGR15B
```

FIGURE 15.3   Sample Program 15B

REVIEW

1. How does an index differ from a subscript? How is each declared? What are the advantages of using indexes rather than subscripts? What are the disadvantages?

2. What is the purpose of the SET statement? How does a SET statement differ from a COMPUTE statement? For example, explain how

    COMPUTE K = 1

differs from

    SET K-INDEX TO 1.

What value does this SET statement place in K-INDEX?

3. What three statements can modify an index?

4. Notice that the search starts at the first entry of the table and proceeds toward the last, stopping either when a match is found or at the end of the table. How could you arrange entries in the table to speed up the search?

5. When using the SEARCH statement, is it permissible to declare the table larger than necessary? If not, why not?

Program Modifications

1. The SEARCH verb used with indexes searches a table much more quickly than a PERFORM with subscripts. Increase the table size in Sample Program 15A to at least 50 elements and run the program. Then increase the size of the table in Program 15B and run it. Determine how much time is saved by using SEARCH.

2. The **SEARCH** can be made more efficient by placing the most commonly needed entries at the beginning of the table. Run Program 15B, placing the most common elements at the end of the table. Then place the most common elements at the beginning of the table, and rerun the program to see how much faster it executes.

3. Modify Program 15A to use indexes instead of subscripts to do the search. Indexes can be increased or decreased by the following:

$$\underline{SET} \text{ index-name } \left\{ \begin{array}{c} \underline{UP} \\ \underline{DOWN} \end{array} \right\} \underline{BY} \text{ integer.}$$

For example (L-INDEX is defined as in index):

    SET L-INDEX UP BY 1.

4. Do the same as in modification 3, but use **PERFORM** with indexes instead of the **SET** . . . **UP** statement.

INTERNAL SORTING

The discipline table was not in any particular order, but often table items must be in order. As you have seen, **ordering the table** permits a much more efficient SEARCH.

You have already done some exercises in ordering small groups of data. How may the variables X, Y, Z be checked for the smallest value? Assuming that the variables X, Y, Z, and SMALL are defined and that X, Y, and Z have values, COBOL code to solve this problem may be written as follows:

```
MOVE X TO SMALL.
IF (Y < SMALL) MOVE Y TO SMALL.
IF (Z < SMALL) MOVE Z TO SMALL.
```

Hand-simulate the code above to determine how it works. These three lines of code will place the smallest value in the variable SMALL. It is important that you thoroughly understand this example before you go on.

Now let's modify the problem a little: the goal is to put the smallest value in X and leave the other two values in Y and Z. In Sample Program 15C (**Figure 15.6**) we need a temporary storage location called TEMP. Here is the code for placing the smallest value in X and leaving the other two values in Y and Z:

```
IF (Y < X)
    MOVE X TO TEMP
    MOVE Y TO X
    MOVE TEMP TO Y.
IF (Z < X)
    MOVE X TO TEMP
    MOVE Z TO X
    MOVE TEMP TO Z.
```

The first IF statement compares Y and X and interchanges them if Y is less than X. The second IF statement compares Z and X and interchanges them if Z is less than X. When these statements have been executed, the smallest value is in the variable X. A similar technique would be used to order Y and Z. This code does work, but you can imagine how cumbersome it would get if you were working with 100 or even 10 variables.

Notice that the two IF statements are very similar. Whenever statements are similar there is a good chance that a loop or a PERFORM may be used to shorten the coding.

Let's go back to Sample Program 15B and look at the discipline table. The table was declared as follows:

```
01 DISCIPLINE-TABLE.
      05 DISCIPLINES       OCCURS 10 TIMES
                           INDEXED BY DISC-INDEX.
          10 DISC-CODE     PICTURE X(03).
          10 DISC-NAME     PICTURE X(27).
```

After the table has been filled, we may write code to order the table by discipline code. The method used is similar to the method used for placing X, Y, and Z in sequence. The first step is to put the smallest value in the first entry in the table. This is done by comparing the first discipline-code to the second discipline-code; if they are out of order, they are interchanged. Then the first discipline-code is compared to the third discipline-code; if they are out of order, they are interchanged. This process is continued until the first discipline-code has been compared to all the other discipline-codes. The smallest value will now be in the first entry of the table. **Figure 15.4** is a picture of this comparison. The necessary COBOL code to accomplish this is as follows:

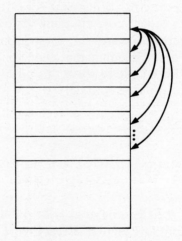

FIGURE 15.4   Ordering by Discipline Code: 1st Record Comparison

```
OUTER-SORT.
      PERFORM INNER-SORT VARYING L FROM K BY 1 UNTIL (L > 10).
INNER-SORT.
      IF (DISC-CODE (L) < DISC-CODE (K))
          MOVE DISCIPLINES (K) TO TEMP
          MOVE DISCIPLINES (L) TO DISCIPLINES (K)
          MOVE TEMP TO DISCIPLINES (L).
```

Assuming that K has the value of 1, the first entry of the table is the smallest. The next step is to get the second smallest entry in the second entry of the table, that is, we compare the second entry to the third entry and interchange them if they are out of sequence, then we compare the second entry to the fourth entry, and so on. **Figure 15.5** is a pictorial representation of this process.

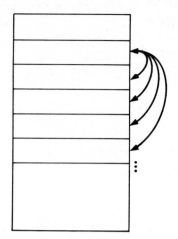

FIGURE 15.5   Ordering by Discipline Code: 2nd Record Comparison

After the second entry is in order, we must repeat the process for the third, the fourth, and all succeeding entries. In this way the table will eventually be placed in sequence. Here is the code to finish the sort:

```
SORT-TABLE.
    PERFORM OUTER-SORT VARYING K FROM 1 BY 1 UNTIL (K > 10).
```

This type of sort is called a **linear sort with exchange** because the sort is done in a linear order. Another type of sort is a **bubble sort**. Suppose you had a table of 10 items. To do a bubble sort, compare item 9 with item 10; if they are out of order, interchange them. Then compare item 8 and item 9, and interchange them if they are out of sequence. Then compare item 7 and item 8, and interchange them if they are out of sequence. Continue this process until you reach the top of the table. When this is done once the smallest item will be in the top element in the table, that is, the smallest value has *bubbled* to the top. Now repeat this process with items 10 through 2. Then do the same with items 10 through 3, etc. When you are done, the entire table will be in order.

REVIEW

1. Write code to place the values of X, Y, and Z in order: X should contain the smallest value, Y the second smallest, and Z the largest value.

2. Write code to order four variables, A, B, C, and D, using linear sort with exchange. Is there a better method for sorting four variables?

3. The linear sort is inefficient: the first time INNER-SORT is executed L and K are equals. This comparison is not necessary. How could you correct this?

4. In a linear sort with exchange, how many comparisons are needed for a table of 10 items? How many comparisons for a table of 20 items? Of 100 items? Of 1,000 items?

5. How many comparisons will be needed for a bubble sort with a table of 10 elements? With 100 elements? With 1,000 elements?

```
010010 IDENTIFICATION DIVISION.                                           PROGR15C
010020 PROGRAM-ID.                                                        PROGR15C
010030    PROG15C.                                                        PROGR15C
010040* * * * * * * * * * * * * * * * * * * * * * * * * * * * **PROGR15C
010050*    TABLE SORT AND SEARCH.                                      *PROGR15C
010060* * * * * * * * * * * * * * * * * * * * * * * * * * * * * **PROGR15C
010070                                                                    PROGR15C
010080 ENVIRONMENT DIVISION.                                              PROGR15C
010090 INPUT-OUTPUT SECTION.                                              PROGR15C
010100 FILE-CONTROL.                                                      PROGR15C
010110    SELECT RECORDS-IN,                                              PROGR15C
010120       ASSIGN TO UR-2540R-S-SYSIN.                                  PROGR15C
010130    SELECT PRINT-OUT,                                               PROGR15C
010140       ASSIGN TO UR-1403-S-SYSPRINT.                                PROGR15C
010150                                                                    PROGR15C
020010 DATA DIVISION.                                                     PROGR15C
020020 FILE SECTION.                                                      PROGR15C
020030 FD  RECORDS-IN                                                     PROGR15C
020040    LABEL RECORDS ARE OMITTED.                                      PROGR15C
020050 01  IN-RECORD                    PICTURE X(80).                    PROGR15C
020060 FD  PRINT-OUT                                                      PROGR15C
020070    LABEL RECORDS ARE OMITTED.                                      PROGR15C
020080 01  PRINT-LINE                   PICTURE X(133).                   PROGR15C
020090                                                                    PROGR15C
020100 WORKING-STORAGE SECTION.                                           PROGR15C
020110 77  L                 PICTURE S99.                                 PROGR15C
020120 77  K                 PICTURE S99      VALUE +1                    PROGR15C
020130                        USAGE COMPUTATIONAL.                        PROGR15C
020140 77  TEMP              PICTURE X(30).                               PROGR15C
020150                                                                    PROGR15C
020160 01  DISCIPLINE-TABLE.                                              PROGR15C
020170    05  DISCIPLINES        OCCURS 10 TIMES                          PROGR15C
020180                           INDEXED BY DISC-INDEX.                   PROGR15C
020190       10  DISC-CODE    PICTURE X(03).                             PROGR15C
020200       10  DISC-NAME    PICTURE X(27).                             PROGR15C
020210                                                                    PROGR15C
030010 01  DISCIPLINE-RECORD.                                             PROGR15C
030020    05  DISCIPLINE-IN.                                              PROGR15C
030030       10  DISC-CODE-IN    PICTURE X(03).                          PROGR15C
030040       10  DISC-NAME-IN    PICTURE X(27).                          PROGR15C
030050    05  FILLER              PICTURE X(50).                         PROGR15C
030060                                                                    PROGR15C
030070 01  STUDENT-RECORD.                                                PROGR15C
030080    05  STUDENT-NUMBER            PICTURE X(09).                    PROGR15C
030090    05  STUDENT-NAME              PICTURE X(25).                    PROGR15C
030100    05  STUDENT-DISCIPLINE        PICTURE X(03).                    PROGR15C
030110    05  FILLER                    PICTURE X(43).                    PROGR15C
030120                                                                    PROGR15C
030130 01  STUDENT-LINE.                                                  PROGR15C
030140    05  FILLER                    PICTURE X(01).                    PROGR15C
030150    05  STUDENT-NUMBER            PICTURE X(09).                    PROGR15C
030160    05  FILLER                    PICTURE X(06).                    PROGR15C
030170    05  STUDENT-NAME              PICTURE X(25).                    PROGR15C
030180    05  FILLER                    PICTURE X(06).                    PROGR15C
030190    05  STUDENT-DISCIPLINE        PICTURE X(03).                    PROGR15C
030200    05  FILLER                    PICTURE X(06).                    PROGR15C
030210    05  DISCIPLINE-NAME           PICTURE X(27).                    PROGR15C
030220    05  FILLER                    PICTURE X(50).                    PROGR15C
030230                                                                    PROGR15C
040010 PROCEDURE DIVISION.                                                PROGR15C
040020    OPEN INPUT RECORDS-IN, OUTPUT PRINT-OUT.                        PROGR15C


040030    MOVE SPACES TO STUDENT-LINE.                                    PROGR15C
040040    MOVE ZERO TO DISC-CODE-IN.                                      PROGR15C
040050    PERFORM READ-IN-TABLE UNTIL (DISC-CODE-IN = '999').            PROGR15C
040060    PERFORM SORT-TABLE.                                             PROGR15C
040070    PERFORM PROCESS-RECORDS 1000 TIMES.                             PROGR15C
040080                                                                    PROGR15C
040090 ALL-DONE.                                                          PROGR15C
040100    CLOSE RECORDS-IN, PRINT-OUT.                                    PROGR15C
040110    STOP RUN.                                                       PROGR15C
```

```
040120                                                             PROGR15C
040130 READ-IN-TABLE.                                              PROGR15C
040140     READ RECORDS-IN INTO DISCIPLINE-RECORD                  PROGR15C
040150         AT END PERFORM ALL-DONE.                            PROGR15C
040160     MOVE DISC-CODE-IN TO DISC-CODE (K).                     PROGR15C
040170     MOVE DISC-NAME-IN TO DISC-NAME (K).                     PROGR15C
040180     ADD 1 TO K.                                             PROGR15C
040190                                                             PROGR15C
040200                                                             PROGR15C
040210 SORT-TABLE.                                                 PROGR15C
040220     PERFORM OUTER-SORT VARYING K FROM 1 BY 1 UNTIL (K > 10).PROGR15C
040230                                                             PROGR15C
040240 OUTER-SORT.                                                 PROGR15C
040250     PERFORM INNER-SORT VARYING L FROM K BY 1 UNTIL (L > 10).PROGR15C
040260                                                             PROGR15C
040270 INNER-SORT.                                                 PROGR15C
040280     IF (DISC-CODE (L) < DISC-CODE (K))                      PROGR15C
040290         MOVE DISCIPLINES (K) TO TEMP                        PROGR15C
040300         MOVE DISCIPLINES (L) TO DISCIPLINES (K)             PROGR15C
040310         MOVE TEMP TO DISCIPLINES (L).                       PROGR15C
040320 PROCESS-RECORDS.                                            PROGR15C
040330     READ RECORDS-IN INTO STUDENT-RECORD                     PROGR15C
040340         AT END PERFORM ALL-DONE.                            PROGR15C
040350     MOVE CORRESPONDING STUDENT-RECORD TO STUDENT-LINE.      PROGR15C
040360     SET DISC-INDEX TO 1.                                    PROGR15C
040370     SEARCH DISCIPLINES                                      PROGR15C
040380         AT END MOVE 'UNKNOWN' TO DISCIPLINE-NAME            PROGR15C
040390         WHEN (DISC-CODE (DISC-INDEX) = STUDENT-DISCIPLINE OF PROGR15C
040400                               STUDENT-RECORD)               PROGR15C
040410             MOVE DISC-NAME (DISC-INDEX) TO DISCIPLINE-NAME. PROGR15C
040420     WRITE PRINT-LINE FROM STUDENT-LINE AFTER ADVANCING 1 LINES. PROGR15C
```

FIGURE 15.6   **Sample Program 15C**

6. The bubble sort described can be greatly improved. Notice that if the bubble sort goes through the table without interchanging two items, it means that the table is in sequence. How could this information be used to improve the sort?

7. There are many other methods available for sorting tables. Two good sources on sorting are:

   a) *The Art of Computer Programming. Volume 3: Sorting and Searching,* by Donald E. Knuth (Reading, Mass.: Addison-Wesley, 1973).

   b) *Software Tools,* by Brian W. Kernighan and P. J. Plauger (Reading, Mass.: Addison-Wesley, 1976).

Program Modifications

1. Add the necessary statements for sorting the table in Sample Program 15B. Then add statements to print the table both before and after it has been sorted so that you can see whether the sort works.

2. Modify Program 15C so that the table is in descending sequence instead of ascending sequence, that is, the largest value should be at the top of the table. Print the table both before and after it has been sorted.

3. Modify Program 15C so that the discipline *names* are put in sequence instead of the discipline *codes*. Print the table both before and after it has been sorted.

4. Instead of subscripts, indexes may be used for sorting. Modify Program 15C so that an index is used in the PERFORM statement instead of a subscript variable. You will need two indexes (several indexes can be defined in the same INDEXED BY clause).

5. Program a bubble sort.

6. *Merge*. Modify Program 15C to include two tables of discipline, both of which must be in order. Write COBOL code to merge the two tables into a single third table. The final table must also be in order.

7. Figure out another type of sort and program it.

SEARCH ALL

Our use of the SEARCH verb has been somewhat inefficient because the search starts at the beginning of the table and continues to search through the table. This is called a **linear search**. On large tables this type of search can be very time-consuming. Another method that is more efficient is the SEARCH statement with the ALL option. The general form is like that of SEARCH, but the word ALL must follow the word SEARCH. For example:

    SEARCH ALL identifier . . .

instead of

    SEARCH identifier . . .

When a table is in order, a **binary search** can eliminate half the table on each comparison. The first comparison is done with the middle element of the table. In a table in ascending order, if the value being sought is less than the middle element, the lower half of the table will be eliminated from the search. The second comparison will then be done with the middle element in the first half of the table. This comparison will eliminate one-fourth of the table. This process of "comparison to the middle element" in the table is continued until a match is found. Suppose we have a table containing the integers 1 to 1,000 and we wish to find the matching element in the table for ZAP, where ZAP contains 488. Then we do a binary search as follows:

    ZAP < 500: search between 1 and 499
    ZAP > 250: search between 251 and 499
    ZAP > 375: search between 376 and 499
    ZAP > 438: search between 439 and 499
    ZAP > 469: search between 470 and 499
    ZAP > 485: search between 486 and 499
    ZAP < 492: search between 486 and 491
    ZAP < 489: search between 486 and 488
    ZAP > 487: search between 488 and 488
    ZAP = 488: search is complete.

The number 488 causes the largest possible number of comparisons to be made, yet the search only took ten comparisons. This type of search is very fast even for a large table. It is called a *binary* search because each comparison eliminates *half* the table.

ASCENDING KEY CLAUSE

If a SEARCH ALL is to be used, the KEY option must be used with the INDEXED BY clause. The KEY clause indicates by what variable the table is ordered. For example, here is our discipline-table with the KEY option:

```
01 DISCIPLINE-TABLES.
    05 DISCIPLINES      OCCURS 10 TIMES
                        INDEXED BY DISC-INDEX
                        ASCENDING KEY IS DISC-CODE.
        10 DISC-CODE    PICTURE X(03).
        10 DISC-NAME    PICTURE X(27).
```

The ASCENDING KEY clause indicates which field in the table is used for ordering the table: in this example, the table is in order by DISC-CODE. The general form of the KEY option is:

The table can be in either ASCENDING or DESCENDING sequence. A binary search (SEARCH ALL) requires that the table be in sequence and that the sequence key be indicated by the KEY clause.

Note:

1. The KEY option is used in conjunction with the INDEXED BY option in the execution of a SEARCH ALL statement.
2. The data name in the KEY clause must be either the name of the entry containing an OCCURS clause or an entry subordinate to the entry containing the OCCURS clause.
3. The table must be in order by the key variable.

CHAPTER REVIEW

Vocabulary Review

Table lookup	Ordering the table	Linear search
Index	Linear sort with exchange	Binary search
Occurrence number	Bubble sort	

Review Questions

1. Explain:

   a) **INDEXED BY** clause.
   b) **SET** statement.
   c) **ASCENDING KEY** clause.

2. What is the difference between a **SEARCH** and a **SEARCH ALL**? When can either be used?

Program Modification

1. Modify Sample Program 15C so that it uses the **SEARCH ALL** statement instead of the **SEARCH** statement. Rerun the program.

Programs

1. Write a program to process the following pay-records for Ready-Cash Bank:

Field	Columns
Name	1–25
Employee number	26–34
Pay code	35–37
Hours worked	38–40 (xx.x)

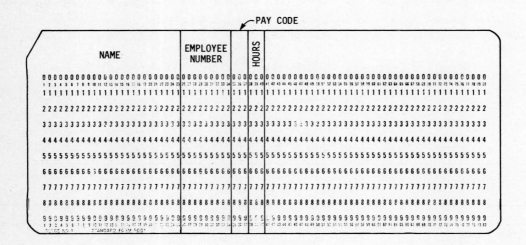

The pay code is a three-digit number that must be used to find the pay rate. The pay-rate table is as follows:

Pay Code	Pay Rate
101	8.00
204	9.00
209	9.50
411	9.50
312	9.75
128	10.25

Use the SEARCH verb to find the pay rate and then calculate the total pay (pay rate × hours worked). Print and label all pertinent values.

2. Write a program to read and process the following input-records:

Field	Columns
Student number	1–9
Student name	10–35
Score	36–38

The score ranges from 0 to 100. The input file is not in sequence. Write COBOL code to do one or more of the following:

a) Print the input record for all students with a score of 90 or above.

b) Print the input records in student-name sequence.

c) Print the input record if the student number has a nine in column 1.

3. Write a program to read the following records for Intellect Haven College:

Field	Columns
Name	1-30
Major	32-45
Grade	46-48

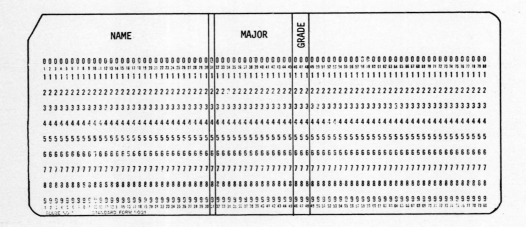

The input file is not in sequence. Print the file once in name sequence and once in grade sequence. There are no more than 30 names.

4. The input records for a pricing table are:

Field	Columns
Code	1-4
Cost	5-8 (xx.xx)

The detail records are:

Field	Columns
Account	1-10
Code	11-14
Length	15-18
Width	19-22

Find the price by searching the table for the cost, then multiply the cost times the square units (length times width). Print and label all fields.

****

An athletic robot is flogging
Himself into fitness by logging
Up miles and miles
And miles and miles
Each morning in memory-jogging.

****

MAGNETIC TAPE

Punched cards have been in use since the 1890s. They were an obvious material to use for computer input. After computers began to develop, it became clear that a better and faster process of transferring information into the computer was needed. To fill this need, magnetic tape was developed.

Magnetic tape continues to be popular in medium- to large-scale computer installations. It has several advantages: high-density packing of data: high-speed processing: low-cost compact storage; and it is reusable—a tape can be rerun with the same data, or it can be erased and new data can be written on it. Magnetic tape thus qualifies as one of the most economical and versatile forms of storage. **Figure 16.1** is a picture of a magnetic tape.

CHARACTERISTICS OF PUNCHED CARDS

In order better to understand the advantages of magnetic tape, let us consider some familiar characteristics of punched cards. Punched cards contain 80 columns, and therefore can contain 80

FIGURE 16.1   **A Magnetic Tape**
Photo Courtesy of IBM.

characters. If you have information that requires more than 80 columns, you must use multiple cards. This can become both space- and time-consuming, since each card must have a sequence number and card number. If, on the other hand, your information requires fewer than 80 columns, some of the space on each card is wasted. Cards are classified as **unit-record storage**, that is, each card is read or punched as one unit. Each set of information is called a record, and only one transaction or record is recorded in a card.

Advantages of Cards

Even though magnetic tape has obvious advantages, in many situations punched cards are most useful. The major advantage of cards is that users readily learn how to keypunch cards and how to make corrections. Also, as long as card decks are small, it is easy to make changes to them, and cards are readable by the human eye. Computer soothsayers have long been predicting that cards will be replaced, but they remain the most convenient form of storing small amounts of data.

Disadvantages of Cards

One major disadvantage of card files is that they are bulky. If you wish to save a card file of 100,000 cards for two or three years, the storage costs can be expensive. Also, to locate one or two cards in a file this size can cost a good deal of time. Cards stored for a long period may warp so that they are no longer machine-readable.

CHARACTERISTICS OF MAGNETIC TAPE

Magnetic tape is similar to the tape used for audio tape-machines, but computer tape is wider and is more carefully made. Information may be written on the tape and then read at a later date. A tape may be read over and over without destroying the information on it. Whenever it is desirable to do so, the old information may be erased as the new data is recorded. The same magnetic-tape drive will either read or write on a magnetic tape.

On audio tape, sound is recorded in a continuous mode, but on computer magnetic-tape, information is recorded in small magnetic spots called **bits**. Any legal character can be written on a magnetic tape. One way to visualize magnetic tape is to think of it as a continuous string of punched cards on which data is represented by magnetic spots instead of holes. The small magnetized spots on the tape are not visible to the eye, but if fine iron particles are sprinkled on a tape, they will cling to the magnetized areas, which can then be seen through a magnifying glass. If the magnetic spots were visible, they would look like **Figure 16.2**. The presence or absence of magnetic spots is used to record data. If the bit is on (that is, magnetized) it is a **1**; if the bit is off, it is a **0**.

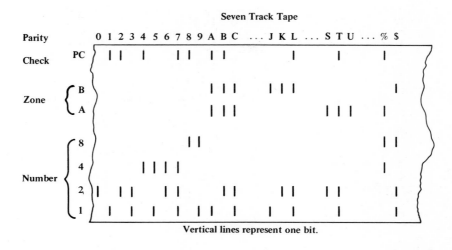

FIGURE 16.2   **A Magnetized Tape**

The information is recorded in **frames** perpendicular to the tape. A frame can accommodate a character or part of a binary word. A **word** is four bytes of data. On the IBM/370 one computer character, a **byte**, can be recorded as one frame on a 9-track tape, and one computer word (32 bits) will occupy four frames.

Thus, a frame is roughly equivalent to a card column. If a line were drawn across the width of the tape, the information represented on the tape would constitute one frame.

The **density** of a tape is the number of frames recorded per inch. Since one character can be recorded in a frame, the density is also commonly referred to as characters per inch or **bpi** (bits per inch): for example, a density of 1600 bpi equals 1600 characters per linear inch of tape. An 80-column card would occupy 1/20 of an inch at this density. Early tape-drives used to write at 200 bpi. Other common densities are:

bits per inch

556
800
1600
6250

The technology in this area is advancing so rapidly that even greater densities may already be available at your installation.

The term **track** (also called **channel**) refers to a horizontal row of bits. If a frame is approximately equivalent to a card column, a track is equivalent to a horizontal punching-row on a card. Some computer manufacturers use a 9-track tape-drive and other manufacturers use a 7-track tape drive. The same magnetic-tape can be used on either system, but a tape drive will write and read 9-track tape or 7-track tape but not both, that is, a tape written on a 7-track tape drive cannot be read by a 9-track drive, and vice versa. **Figure 16.3** illustrates the coding for a 9-track tape.

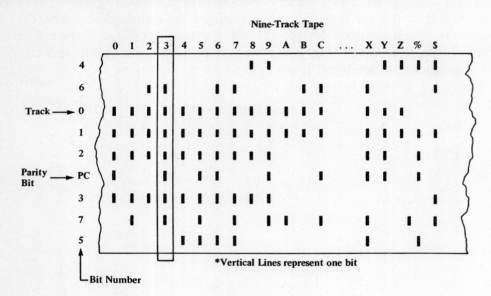

FIGURE 16.3   **Coding for a 9-Track Tape**

Advantages of Magnetic Tape

Magnetic tape eliminates most of the disadvantages of card files. Here are some of the advantages of magnetic tape:

Low-Cost Storage

A large amount of data can be stored on a magnetic tape inexpensively. *Theoretically*, one standard tape could hold 560,000 cards. Magnetic tapes offer the lowest cost per character storage—they are even cheaper than cards. Tapes are also easy to store and are compact. Thus tapes are an inexpensive form for long-term storage of data, especially if the data is seldom used. Some data, such as tax records, must be stored for many years. If magnetic tapes were not available, the cost of storing large amounts of data would be very high.

Faster Processing

Data can be read much faster from magnetic tape than from cards. Millions of characters per minute can be read from magnetic tape, while only thousands of characters per minute can be read from punched cards.

Repeated Use

The same tape can be read many times without destroying the data on it. Then, when the data is no longer needed, the old data can be erased as new data is recorded on the tape. Once a card has been punched, it cannot be used for another purpose, and long-term storage may destroy its readability.

Any Record-Size

A substantial advantage is that records can be any size: they are not restricted to a maximum of 80 columns, as card records are. Records as small as 18 characters can be handled efficiently with no wasted space. The size of the record can be determined by the size needed, instead of by the physical length of the card.

Greater Durability

Magnetic tapes are much more durable than cards: after repeated use, cards tend to become dog-eared and to jam in the machine.

Off-Line Usage

Peripheral equipment can be used to transfer information from cards or paper tape to magnetic tape. Thus, the computer is needed only for transferring information from the compact input-medium of magnetic tape, instead of the less dense (and slower) medium of cards. Information can be stored on magnetic tape by the computer and an off-line peripheral printer can be used for printing results, so that valuable computer-time is saved and the computer is free for actual calculations rather than slow reading and printing.

Disadvantages of Magnetic Tape

Even though magnetic tape has many advantages compared to punched cards, there are also a few disadvantages:

Invisible to the Eye

A disadvantage of magnetic tape is that a magnetic tape cannot be read by human beings, that is, it must be processed by a machine in order for it to be readable. Sometimes it is desirable to be able to read the data; in that case, data-processing cards must be used instead of tape.

Still Too Slow

Even though tape reading is fast, it is slow in comparison to the computer. The reason for this is that the tape is read mechanically, while the computer calculates electronically.

Cards Still Needed

Often, the data must still be punched on cards before it can be placed on tape. Then the cards are read and the information is written onto a tape. Once the data has been put on tape it can be used speedily many times from the tape. Machines are available to key the data directly onto the tape, but card input is still common.

No Inserting of Records

You cannot make changes on a tape already created. There is no way to insert a record between the fifth and sixth records without rewriting the whole tape. Similarly, you cannot change part of a record without rewriting the complete tape. Any change needed in the tape requires that you read the tape and then rewrite the whole tape onto a new tape. Records cannot be updated in place on magnetic tape.

Physical and Environmental Problems

Heat and humidity must be carefully controlled to prevent tape damage. In addition, dust should be filtered out of the air. Dust on a tape prevents correct contact of the read/write head of the tape drive. Dust, heat, and humidity can all be controlled by a good air-conditioning unit.

Sequential Organization

Data on a tape must be ordered sequentially. If you wish to read the fifth record on a tape, you must read the first four records first. If you wish to read the last record on the tape you must read the whole tape first. Magnetic-disk files can be read directly, that is, on disk files a record can be read without first reading the preceding records.

Large File, Little Activity

The entire magnetic tape file must be processed at the same time, due to its sequential organization. If the file is large (say, over 100,000 records) and the number of records to be updated is small (say, under 100 records), magnetic tape is very inefficient. The complete file must be copied for each update, no matter how small the proportion of records changing. This type of file could be processed much more efficiently using magnetic disk.

****

Computer Graffiti

Sign on computer-center wall:
Mistakes made while you wait.

****

INTERBLOCK GAPS (IBG)

Tape drives can move tape at speeds from 12.5 inches per second to 200.0 inches per second. One of the most commonly used tape-drives moves tape at 200 inches per second—over eleven miles per hour. This tape drive cannot get to full speed immediately nor can it stop immediately. For a 9-track tape, it requires 3/10 of an inch to go from a stationary position to full speed, and it requires 3/10 of an inch to stop the tape. Information on a tape can only be read or written when the tape is moving at full speed, so a 9-track tape requires 3/10 of an inch of blank tape for starting and 3/10 of an inch of blank tape for stopping. Since records follow one another, 6/10 of an inch of blank tape must be left between each block of information. These are called **interblock gaps (IBG)**. The tape drive makes these gaps automatically. (Seven-track tapes use an interblock gap of 3/4 of an inch.)

On a tape with a recording density of 1600 bpi, 80 characters, or one punched card, would need 0.05 inch. Since the interblock gap takes 0.6 inch, the tape would look like **Figure 16.4** The unblocked tape shows that the ratio of IBG to data is 12 to 1; thus, a great deal of tim~ ~nt in reading the IBG. The tape contains 12 times as much space as data. The tape drive al~ ~rts reading at each interblock gap.

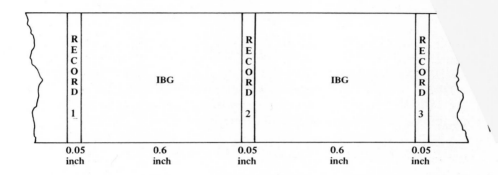

FIGURE 16.4   **A Tape with Interblock Gaps**

Several conclusions can be reached from the illustration above. First, the fewer the number of IBG, the greater the amount of information that can be placed on the tape. Second, starting and stopping after a small block of information takes a large proportion of the reading time. Information on tape would be processed much more quickly if the tape drive were moving continuously. The obvious way to improve tape performance is to increase the amount of information between each IBG. This is called blocking information.

BLOCKING

Blocking is a method of grouping records in a file for more efficient tape-processing. The amount of information processed by one read or write command in the program is called a **logical record**. A set of logical records grouped into a block is called a **physical record**. The number of logical records in each physical record is called the **blocking factor**. If 6 logical records are included in each physical record, the blocking factor is 6. If the blocking factor is 1, the records are **unblocked**.

If we block information into groups of 20 card-images, we need space for 1600 (80 × 20) characters. With a density of 1600 bpi, this requires 1 inch of tape for data and a 0.6 inch IBG on a 9-track tape. The ratio of IBG to data is about 6 to 10. If we increase the block size to 120 card-images, we need space for 9600 (80 × 120) characters. This requires 6 inches of tape at 1600 bpi and a 0.6 inch IBG. Now the ratio of IBG to data is 1 to 10. **Figure 16.5** shows some data with a blocking factor of 6.

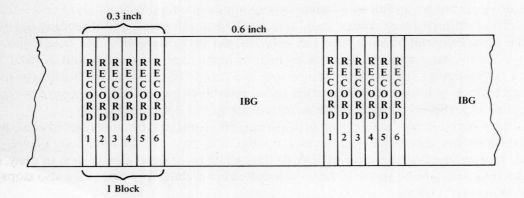

FIGURE 16.5   **Data with a Blocking Factor of 6**

As you can see, the larger the block size the more efficient the tape processing, since less tape will be required for interblock gaps. Using large blocks of data does not require the programmers to change the way their program processes data; instead, either the job control language (JCL) of the program or the FD entry of the COBOL program indicates the size of the logical record and the size of the block. All the blocking and unblocking will be done in a buffer.

BUFFERS

If records are unblocked, then each time a record is read, it is read from the tape. This is inefficient, since the time needed to read a record from a tape is usually considerably more than the amount of time needed to process the record.

If records are blocked, the complete block of records is read into a special storage area called a **buffer.** The operating system automatically reads a block of records into a buffer: the programmer simply specifies the record size and block size. The block size is used as the buffer size.

An example of what happens is the following: you are processing card images of 80 columns, and you want a blocking factor of 10. Your record size is then 80, and your block size is 800 (10 × 80). The computer will automatically read in a block of 800 characters from the tape. Every time a read command is executed in your program, 80 columns will be read from the buffer area. The first read command will cause the first 80 columns to be read from the buffer, the second will cause the second 80 columns to be read, and so on, until all 800 characters have been read from the buffer. Then a new block of 800 characters is read from the tape. The reading of a new block and the determination of which 80 characters to read in a block are handled automatically by the operating system.

In addition, input/output is usually double-buffered, which means that two blocks are available for processing: a second block of records can be transferred automatically to the second buffer while the first is being processed. There should always be a buffer of data available for reading to eliminate waiting for input/output.

Computer centers usually charge for input/output requests. By blocking records in groups of 10, nine I/O requests are eliminated, since the charge is for the reading or writing of physical records, not logical records.

INFINITE BLOCKS

All this may lead you to assume that it is best to use the largest possible blocks. The perfect block-size for the tape would be one that would hold all the data for the tape, so that we wouldn't waste any blank space on IBG between blocks of data. This isn't possible, however.

The first problem concerns the computer: on the IBM/370, blocks cannot be larger than 32,760 bytes. The second problem concerns input/output errors: if you have an input/output error on a tape, you often lose a whole block. If this is one record then the loss is less serious than if the block were 400 records. If tape I/O errors are common at your computer center, you should use small blocks. Most I/O errors are caused by dirty tape-drives, so this problem can easily be remedied by having the tape drives kept clean.

The third problem concerns storage requirements. In this case, execution efficiency costs storage: a larger block size means less time, but more storage, will be needed. Each buffer requires storage. If there are two buffers and your block size is 32,760 bytes, then the buffers use 65,520 bytes of storage. If your program is large or your computer size is small, then this block size will not even be possible. Therefore, smaller blocks are usually used.

DATA-TRANSMISSION SPEED

Cards are usually read at a speed of 1,000 cards per minute. Each card has 80 columns, so 80,000 characters can be read per minute. By dividing this number by 60, we obtain a figure of 1,333 characters per second as the maximum **data-transmission speed** for reading cards.

Two factors determine the data-transmission speed for tape—density, and tape-drive speed. The greater the density and the faster the tape drive, the greater the input/output transmission speed. Data transmission can be expressed by the following formula:

Density × Inches per second = Characters per second

Tape density varies from 200 to 6250 characters per inch. Tape-drive speeds vary from 12.5 to 200 inches per second. A common density is 1600, and a common tape-drive speed is 200 inches per second. By using these two figures in our formula, we obtain the following:

1600 × 200 = 320,000 characters per second

As you see, magnetic tape allows for very high data-transmission rates. This is over 100 times faster than reading punched cards.

THE VALUE OF BLOCKING RECORDS

Here are some calculations which demonstrate the savings in time and space due to blocking of records.

Tape Read-Time

The time necessary for reading a tape is directly dependent on the blocking factor used with the records. If you have 100,000 *unblocked* records to be processed, each record contains 120 characters, and the reading speed is 320,000 characters per second, with a start/stop time of 0.003 second per IBG, then:

$$\text{Read time} = \frac{100,000 \text{ records} \times 120 \text{ characters per record}}{320,000 \text{ characters per second}} = 37.5 \text{ seconds}$$

and

$$\text{Start/stop time} = 99,999 \text{ IBG's} \times 0.003 \text{ second per IBG} \cong 300 \text{ seconds}$$

so the total time is 337.5 seconds.

If you have the same situation, but the records are in *blocks* of 100:

$$\text{Read time} = \frac{100,000 \text{ records} \times 120 \text{ characters per record}}{320,000 \text{ characters per second}} = 37.5 \text{ seconds}$$

but now

$$\text{Start/stop time} = 999 \text{ IBG} \times 0.003 \text{ second per IBG} \cong 3.0 \text{ seconds}$$

so the total time is 40.5 seconds.

Tape Storage-Length

The length of tape used is also directly dependent on the blocking factor used with the records. If you have 100,000 *unblocked* records to be processed, each record contains 120 characters, the tape density is 1600 bpi, and the IBG is 6/10 inch, then:

$$\text{Tape for records} = \frac{100,000 \text{ records} \times 120 \text{ characters per inch}}{1600 \text{ characters per inch}} = 7500 \text{ inches}$$

and

$$\text{Tape for IBG} = 99,999 \text{ IBG} \times 0.6 \text{ inch} = 59999.4 \text{ inches}$$

so the total tape-length is 67499.4 inches, or almost 5625 feet.

If you use the same figures, except that the records are in *blocks* of 100, then:

$$\text{Tape for records} = \frac{100,000 \text{ records} \times 120 \text{ characters per second}}{1600 \text{ characters per inch}} = 7500 \text{ inches}$$

as before, but

$$\text{Tape for IBG} = 999 \text{ IBG} \times 0.6 \text{ inch} = 599.4 \text{ inches}$$

so the total tape-length is only 8099.4 inches or about 675 feet.

FILE PROTECTION

The operator must insert a write-enable, or **file-protection, ring** in the tape reel before writing can occur. This prevents accidental writing on a tape. The easy way to remember this is:

No Ring—No Write

Whenever you are reading a tape, you should request that the file-protection ring be removed. When the ring is removed, only reading can take place. **Figure 16.6** shows a file-protection ring.

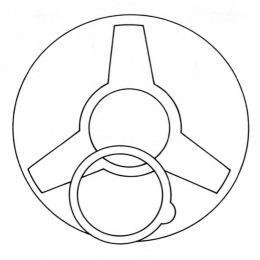

FIGURE 16.6   **A File-Protection Ring**

TAPE LABELS

One magnetic tape looks just like another magnetic tape, unless some identification is added to it. Magnetic tapes are identified in two ways: first, an external adhesive label is placed on each tape. This label usually has a file name, the date the tape was written, and a few other pieces of information concerning the computer center. **Figure 16.7** is a sample external table-of-contents label.

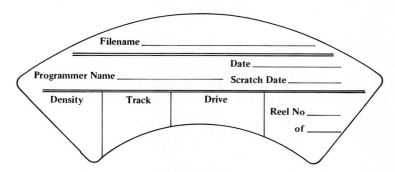

FIGURE 16.7   **A External Magnetic-Tape Label**

Second, an internal tape-label is written. Some 80 column-records are written by the operating system on the beginning and end of each data set. These label records usually include a volume identification, data-set name, date written, record type, record length, and block length, as well as other miscellaneous information. This information can be used when a tape is read to help ensure that the correct magnetic-tape is being used. **Figure 16.8** is a picture of how data is organized on a magnetic tape.

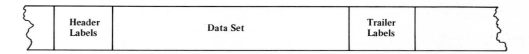

FIGURE 16.8   **Data Organization on a Magnetic Tape**

****

A Diversion: How Much Data Can We Put on One Magnetic Tape?

Assuming a 2400-foot 9-track tape writing data at 1600 bpi with a block size of 32,760 bytes, we could write 560,000 80-character records. A box of cards contains 2,000 cards, so we could store 280 boxes of computer cards. A magnetic tape would surely be lighter than 280 boxes of cards.

That doesn't really give us a good picture, though. Instead, let's look at it this way. If we realize that 560,000 records are equivalent to about 14,000 pages of the average book, we see that we could store 13 copies of *Gone with the Wind* on one reel of computer tape—or 110 copies of *The Old Man and the Sea,* or 29 copies of *For Whom the Bell Tolls.* People do put books on magnetic tape: in fact, some books now are typeset using magnetic tape. Magnetic tapes are now available with the Bible, Shakespeare's plays, and Eugene O'Neill's plays.

****

Photo Courtesy of IBM.

REVIEW

1. List some advantages and some disadvantages of magnetic tape.

2. What is the cost of a magnetic tape at your computer installation? What density is used on the magnetic tape-drive at your installation? Does your installation use a 7-track or a 9-track tape drive?

3. A reel of magnetic tape is usually 2400 feet long. Using the proper density, calculate the number of characters which could theoretically be written continuously on a magnetic tape.

4. Using a density of 1600 bpi (or your tape-drive density) how many columns of data can be written using card images? Remember the interblock gaps. What percentage of the tape is data, and what percentage is interblock gap?

5. Do the same calculations as in question 4, but use a blocking factor of 10 card-images. Next, use a blocking factor of 400 card-images.

6. Obtain a magnetic tape and look at the write-enable ring. Watch a magnetic tape being processed at your computer installation.

7. At a density of 1600 bpi and a speed of 200 inches per second, how many characters per second can a tape drive process?

8. If you wanted to obtain a magnetic tape of information from another computer installation, what would you have to tell the other computer installation to make sure you could read the tape at your installation?

THE ENVIRONMENT DIVISION

The **SELECT** entry indicates the type of device used for input or output. In Chapter 4 we covered the **SELECT** entry in some detail.

You may remember that the **SELECT** entry is very machine- and installation-dependent, so this is only a general description. You will have to check with your own computer center to see how it is coded at your installation. The most commonly used **SELECT** clause is:

```
SELECT TAPE-FILE ASSIGN TO UT-2400-S-SYSTAPE.
```

The user-picked file-name is **TAPE-FILE**. Remember, there must be a matching **FD** entry for this file. The device class is **UT**, which stands for utility. The most commonly used device-name for a tape drive is **2400**. The S stands for sequential, since, as we saw, magnetic-tape files are sequential. The programmer-picked external name is **SYSTAPE**. You will need a job-control card with an external name on it, but you must find out the exact form of the job-control statements at your computer center.

THE FILE SECTION

Each **SELECT** entry must have a matching file-description entry. We have previously used a very abbreviated form of the file-description entry; we will now cover it in more detail. The general format is:

```
FD filename
    LABEL RECORDS clause
    [RECORDING MODE clause]
    [RECORD CONTAINS integer CHARACTERS]
    [BLOCK CONTAINS integer RECORDS].
```

The first item needed is the file name. This must be the file name used in the **SELECT** entry. The other clauses may be in any order within the **FD**.

The **LABEL RECORDS** clause indicates whether there are standard label-records on the tape. The choices are:

```
LABEL RECORDS ARE   { OMITTED  }
                    { STANDARD }
```

On card and print files, label records are always omitted. On tape files, the label records are usually standard. If standard tape-labels are used, the operating system writes 80-column header-records at the beginning and end of the data-set on the tape. The operating system does this automatically to identify the magnetic-tape volume and to identify the data-set on the tape. These internal tape-labels are very useful for identifying the tape volume. A **volume** is a external-storage unit. For magnetic-tape drives, it is a reel of tape. A computer installation can easily have several thousand magnetic-tape volumes and the internal labels are used to verify that the correct magnetic tape is mounted on the tape drive.

RECORDING MODE CLAUSE

The **RECORDING MODE** clause indicates the type of record used. Some non-IBM computers do not use this clause. The general form of this clause is:

```
                     { F }
RECORDING MODE IS    { U }
                     { V }
```

This clause refers to the length of the record. **F** stands for fixed, **U** stands for undefined, and **V** stands for variable. If the records are of fixed length, we use **F** for the recording mode. On some types of record the record length is not fixed: for example, a bank may have a 100-column master record containing account information, followed by 20 columns for each transaction completed during the month. Some customers will have no transactions, while others will have hundreds of transactions. Undefined is similar to variable, except that on variable-length records the record length must be variable according to some predetermined pattern. In the bank record example above, there is always a 100-column master record followed by some 20-column detail records. Undefined records do not have to fit any pattern. Undefined length is not much used.

RECORD CONTAINS CLAUSE

The RECORD CONTAINS clause indicates the number of characters in the logical record. The clause is optional and is often omitted. We have been restricted to the record length of the printer or card reader; now, with magnetic tape, we can use any size of record we wish. The minimum length for a record is usually 18 characters. If we were using card images, this clause could be as follows:

    RECORD CONTAINS 80 CHARACTERS

If more or fewer characters are needed, simply change the number of characters in the clause.

BLOCK CONTAINS CLAUSE

This clause is required when records are to be blocked. Only a rank amateur would fail to block tape files, so we will always use this clause. The general format is:

```
BLOCK CONTAINS integer RECORDS
```

This indicates the number of records to be written in each block. Here is a sample clause:

    BLOCK CONTAINS 10 RECORDS

Remember, the operating system takes care of blocking and unblocking the records. If there is a partial block at the end of the data set, that is also automatically handled correctly.

SUMMARY

Here are some sample statements necessary for using magnetic tape:

```
    SELECT TAPE-FILE
        ASSIGN TO UT-2400-S-SYSTAPE.
    .
    .
    .
FD TAPE-FILE
    LABEL RECORDS ARE STANDARD
    RECORDING MODE IS F
    RECORD CONTAINS 80 CHARACTERS
    BLOCK CONTAINS 10 RECORDS.
```

Hint: Each time you submit a job using a magnetic tape, an operator has to mount the magnetic tape. If your program has syntax errors, then the magnetic tape will not be used. In order to help the computer operator, many programmers use the printer to test their program instead of having the magnetic tape mounted each time; that is, when writing on a magnetic tape, you should use the printer for output until the program has been debugged. To do this, you will have to change the program so that the SELECT entry and the FD entry point at the printer instead of the magnetic tape. Using the printer as the output device while debugging also makes it easier to check for errors in the output file.

SAMPLE PROGRAM 16A

Sample Program 16A (**Figure 16.9**) is a sample card-to-tape program. This program reads card images and writes the card images onto the magnetic tape. Notice that the magnetic-tape file must be opened and closed just as files have been in earlier sample programs. You may have to change the ASSIGN clause to make it work at your installation. Remember, you will need job-control statements to identify the tape.

```
010010 IDENTIFICATION DIVISION.                                          PROGR16A
010020 PROGRAM-ID.                                                       PROGR16A
010030    PROGR16A.                                                      PROGR16A
010040************************************************************************PROGR16A
010050*      SAMPLE CARD TO TAPE PROGRAM.                                *PROGR16A
010060************************************************************************PROGR16A
010070                                                                   PROGR16A
010080 ENVIRONMENT DIVISION.                                             PROGR16A
010090 INPUT-OUTPUT SECTION.                                             PROGR16A
010100 FILE-CONTROL.                                                     PROGR16A
010110    SELECT RECORDS-IN                                             PROGR16A
010120       ASSIGN TO UR-2540R-S-SYSIN.                                PROGR16A
010130    SELECT TAPE-OUT                                               PROGR16A
010140       ASSIGN TO UT-2400-S-SYSTAPE.                               PROGR16A
010150                                                                   PROGR16A
020010 DATA DIVISION.                                                    PROGR16A
020020 FILE SECTION.                                                     PROGR16A
020030 FD  RECORDS-IN                                                    PROGR16A
020040    LABEL RECORDS ARE OMITTED.                                    PROGR16A
020050 01  IN-RECORD                   PICTURE X(80).                    PROGR16A
020060                                                                   PROGR16A
020070 FD  TAPE-OUT                                                      PROGR16A
020080    LABEL RECORDS ARE STANDARD                                    PROGR16A
020090    RECORDING MODE IS F                                           PROGR16A
020100    RECORD CONTAINS 80 CHARACTERS                                 PROGR16A
020110    BLOCK CONTAINS 10 RECORDS.                                    PROGR16A
020120 01  TAPE-RECORD                 PICTURE X(80).                    PROGR16A
020130                                                                   PROGR16A
030010 PROCEDURE DIVISION.                                               PROGR16A
030020    OPEN INPUT RECORDS-IN, OUTPUT TAPE-OUT.                        PROGR16A
030030    PERFORM START-PROCESSING 1000 TIMES.                          PROGR16A
030040                                                                   PROGR16A
030050 WRAP-IT-UP.                                                       PROGR16A
030060    CLOSE RECORDS-IN, TAPE-OUT.                                   PROGR16A
030070    STOP RUN.                                                     PROGR16A
030080                                                                   PROGR16A
030090 START-PROCESSING.                                                 PROGR16A
030100    READ RECORDS-IN                                               PROGR16A
030110       AT END PERFORM WRAP-IT-UP.                                 PROGR16A
030120    MOVE IN-RECORD TO TAPE-RECORD.                                PROGR16A
030130    WRITE TAPE-RECORD.                                            PROGR16A
```

FIGURE 16.9   **Sample Program 16A**

Note:

1. Have someone at your installation check the ASSIGN clause to make sure it is correct.
2. You will need job-control statements to identify your magnetic tape. Since these are installation-dependent, you will have to find out the necessary format for your installation.

REVIEW

1. Find out exactly how the SELECT clause must be written at your installation to use magnetic tape. At the same time, find out what job-control statements are needed. How do you indicate when you are writing a tape and when you are only reading a tape?

2. To find out more about magnetic tape labels, read *OS/VS Tape Labels* (IBM Corp. Publication C26-3795).

Program Modifications

1. Type Sample Program 16A and run it at your installation. (Check the SELECT clause and the job control language before trying to execute the program.)

2. Modify Program 16A so that it can read the magnetic tape you created in exercise 1. Print the records from the magnetic tape.

3. Modify Program 16A to use a blocking factor of 15 records. You may have to change both the program and the job control statements.

4. Modify Program 16A so that record lengths of 60 characters, instead of 80 characters, are written on the magnetic tape.

5. Use Program 16A to write card images on a magnetic tape, then modify one of your earlier programs so that it uses the magnetic tape as its input device.

6. *Merge.* Use Program 16A to write card images on a magnetic tape. (The card file should have a sequence number in columns 1-9, and the card file should be in sequential order.) Then write a program to read the magnetic-tape file and another card file (in sequence) and print the file (in sequence) on the printer. The program will have to read the card file and tape file, and print the merged file on the printer.

Programs

1. The bookstore at Intellect Haven College has decided to automate its book inventory. Write a program to create the original master file using the following input records:

Field	Columns	
Book number	1-5	
Title	6-25	
Author	26-50	
Cost	51-54	(99.99)
Minimum stock	55-57	
Present stock	58-60	
Publisher	61-80	

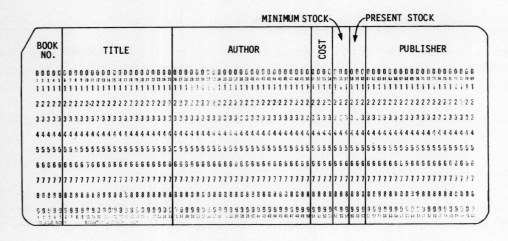

FIGURE 16.10

Books which the bookstore wants to keep in stock permanently have a non-zero number in the minimum-stock field. A minimum number of zero means that there is no minimum number of copies to be kept in stock.

2. Write a program to read the magnetic-tape file for the book inventory and to print the numbers and titles of all books that should be reordered. A book should be reordered if the present stock is less than the minimum stock.

ORGANIZATION ON A TAPE

Records on a tape are always written in sequential order according to some sequential identification field. The sequence number can be, e.g., a part number (for an inventory file), an employee number (for a payroll file), or a subscript number (for a large table). There must be some means of identifying which record you are reading. The telephone directory is an example of a sequential file in which the names are in ascending alphabetic sequence according to the last name of the customer.

Since tape files are organized sequentially, changes must be organized sequentially. If records on tape are to be modified, the whole tape must be read and rewritten: therefore, it is not economical to make only one change. Changes are usually accumulated until there are enough of them to process the tape economically. Collecting changes is called **batching** transactions. Finally, the master file and the change file must be in the same sequence to facilitate speedy processing.

The sequence in which the individual records are stored on the tape is an important factor in processing. Sometimes it is not immediately clear which field should be used for the sequence number. This is apt to be true when one file serves a number of different purposes. A good deal of thought should be given to the arrangement of information within the files.

An example of a file for which two different identification sequences would be desirable is a file of customer transactions. It is desirable to have the file in customer sequence in order to process all transactions for payment, but it is also desirable to process the transactions by inventory number in order to adjust the inventory levels after sales.

It is not practical to keep two files—one in customer-number sequence and one in inventory-number sequence—because then *both* files would have to be maintained and updated. If you did decide to update two files, you would soon find that errors would creep in and the two files would soon differ. The best procedure always is to update one file and to sort the file if another sequence is needed.

TAPE-PROCESSING CHARACTERISTICS

Most files change. In an inventory file, items are sold and new items are received. To change records on a tape file, the changes are sorted in the same sequence as the tape file. Then the master tape-file and the changes file are merged to create a new master-tape. **Figure 16.11** shows a sample tape-update procedure.

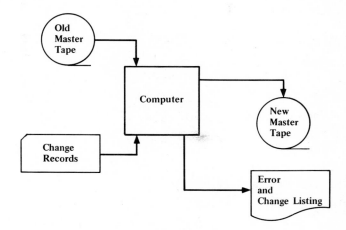

FIGURE 16.11   **A Sample Tape-Update Procedure**

A new computer-tape must be written each time changes to the original tape are made. It is not possible to make a change on the original tape, for several reasons. The first is that the record you wish to change has already been read, so the tape unit would have to back up in order to write the changed record in the same place. This would be very inefficient.

Another reason for not attempting to make a change in the original tape is that the original tape would then no longer be available. If, after a tape was updated, you noticed that the update had been done incorrectly, the usual procedure would be to take the original tape and update it again. If, however, the update was done on the original tape, this would no longer be possible, since the original tape would no longer exist. Another obvious problem is that you may wish to add a new record. Since the original tape has each record written in sequence, there would be no room to insert a new record.

The major reason why you can't make changes on the original tape, however, is that there is no guarantee that the record will be written in the same place. The hardware does not permit exact back-up procedures: the tape could easily be backed up a little too much or not quite enough.

Finally, tape-write errors could occur. Each time a tape drive encounters a spot on a tape that does not record a bit of information, it stops, backs up, and attempts to rewrite the information. If it fails after ten such retries, the tape drive moves the tape ahead about 3-1/2 inches to a new area of the tape. You can imagine the data loss that might occur in this way if you were to attempt to change a single record in a recorded tape.

UPDATING A FILE

Files must be **updated** in order to keep the files current and correct. New employees are hired and old ones quit, so the payroll file must be updated. People move, so a name-and-address file must be updated. New information is collected, so a statistical file must be updated to include the new information.

When updating a file, you must have both a master file and a change file, and the two files must be in the same sequence. Here is a very general description of an update algorithm.

First, read your input tape and the changes. If there is no change for the current input-record, simply copy the record onto the new tape. If the change is an addition, insert the new record in its proper place on the new tape. If it is a deletion, do not copy the old record onto the new tape. If it is truly a change, make the change and add the modified record to the output file.

To accomplish a change, the transactions for the update must include the following:

1. Sequence identification.
2. Change code.
3. New information.

The changes are sorted in identification sequence, then the master tape and change tape are merged to produce a new tape.

Note, to perform an update:

1. Read a record from the transaction file.
2. Read a record from the master file.
3. If the master sequence-number is less than the transaction sequence-number, write the *unchanged* master record onto the new master-tape file. Go back to step 2.
4. If the master sequence-number is equal to the transaction sequence-number, either a deletion or a change is to occur on the master record. If it is a change, write the *changed* master record onto the master file. Go back to step 1. If it is a deletion, write *nothing* onto the master file. Go back to step 1.
5. If the transaction sequence-number is less than the master sequence-number, the transaction is an addition. Write the new master-record onto the new master-file. Go back to step 1.

This is a very general description of an update. The following checks should be added:

1. Sequence-check both the master file and the transaction file.
2. The transaction fields should be edited for correctness.
3. The description of the update does not consider the case of two changes to the master record occurring in sequence.
4. A change or deletion can be requested on a record not in the master file.
5. An addition can be requested when there is a record with the same sequence-number.
6. The description of the update procedure is an endless loop.

CHAPTER REVIEW

Vocabulary Review

Unit-record storage	Track (channel)	Buffer
Bit	Interblock gap (IBG)	Data-transmission speed
Frame	Blocking	File-protection ring

Byte	Logical record	Volume
Word	Physical record	Batching
Density	Blocking factor	Updating
Bpi	Unblocked records	

Review Questions

1. Find out approximately how many magnetic tapes are in your installation's magnetic-tape library. How is a particular tape identified? That is, what numbering scheme does your installation use?

2. Explain how blocking of records saves space and speeds up processing on magnetic tape.

3. If you have a file in account-number sequence and you must change an account number, how would you do this? Can you simply change the account number? Would the file still be in sequence?

Programs

1. Write a program to read the block size, then calculate how many characters of data can be written on a magnetic tape. (A magnetic tape is 2400 feet long.) Find out what density is used at your installation, or use 1600 bpi for density. Use 0.6 inch IBG for 9-track tapes and 0.75 IBG for 7-track tapes. Calculate how long it would take to read the magnetic tape.

2. Use Sample Program 16A to write the following card-images on a magnetic tape:

Field	Columns
Account number	1-9
Name	10-30
Street	31-50
City	51-78

The input file should be ordered by account number or be sorted before being written on the magnetic tape. Now a simple update-program is needed.

Update records have the following format:

Field	Columns
Account number	1–9
Update code	10–11
Update field	12–41

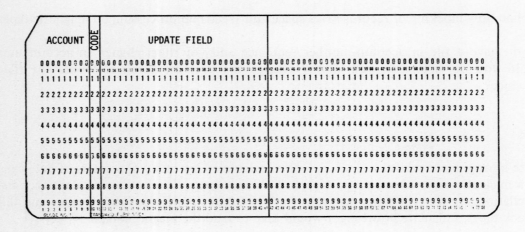

The update field is the new information for the file. The update codes are:

Update Code	Meaning
11	Name
14	Street
17	City

For example, an update code of 17 would indicate a change in the city field. The update file must also be in account-number sequence.

To check the program, print the input record, the change record, and the output record. Now, add the following update-codes to the program:

Update Code	Meaning
01	New record
99	Delete record

When the code is **01**, the whole new record will be on the update record. When there is a deletion, the update record contains only the account number and the deletion code.

3. Intellect Haven College needs an inventory program for its stockroom. The magnetic-tape file contains the following records:

Field	Columns	
Item number	1–6	
Item name	7–20	
Price	21–26	(9999.99)
Quantity available	27–30	
Reorder point	31–34	

First, create a magnetic-tape file using the record formats above. The magnetic-tape file must be in item-number sequence. Next, the magnetic-tape file must be updated. The following records are used to indicate what has been ordered:

Field	Columns
Item number	1–6
Quantity ordered	7–10
Department code	11–14
Department address	15–30

These records must be in item-number sequence. The quantity ordered must be subtracted from the quantity available on the master record. A new master inventory-file must be written. To test your program, print the new master inventory-file.

Some possible problems: item numbers could be incorrect; departments might order more stock than is available.

4. Using the information above, write a program to print the billing information for each department. The department code and department address should be printed, and the bill should be calculated (quantity × price) and printed.

Chapter
17

****
A tall, handsome robot named Dorf,
Was proud of the way he could dwarf
The robotical ranks
Resembling tanks,
Since he was an Anthropomorph.

****

MAGNETIC DISK

If you wish to read the 250th record in a magnetic-tape file, you must read the previous 249 records first, since data on a magnetic tape must be processed sequentially. This can be very time-consuming when you have large files with little activity. To solve this problem, storage devices were developed to permit **direct access** to the desired record. With magnetic-disk storage, stored data can be recorded and retrieved either sequentially or directly, or both in combination. A magnetic disk looks somewhat like a phonograph record.

HISTORY

The first commercially available magnetic disk appeared in 1956, but it was not until 1961 that people realized the importance of magnetic-disk use. Today, even small systems usually have disk storage. Before use of disks became widespread, most installations used magnetic tape to store necessary programs or data. In 1964 IBM announced the 360 system, which relied on the use of disk storage for its new operating system. **Table 17.1** shows the advance of disk technology during the 1960s:

TABLE 17.1

Date	IBM Disk Number	Bits per Inch	Capacity (Million Bytes)	Tracks per Inch
1956	305	100	?	20
1961	1311	500	2.0	50
1965	2311	1100	7.25	65
1966	2314	2200	29.0	65
1970	3330	4040	100.00	70

As you can see, disk capacity grew in a period of ten years from 2 million to 100 million bytes (characters). This suggests that the maximum capacity has not yet been reached: someone must have a lot of information to store. The number of tracks per inch has not increased very rapidly, however, which suggests the likelihood of technological or cost restrictions involved in increasing the density. Since 1970 disk technology has improved rapidly. Disks now on the market can hold over 300 million bytes on one disk pack. Because of their large storage capacity, magnetic disks are commonly called **mass storage devices. Figure 17.1** shows a magnetic disk.

FIGURE 17.1   **A Magnetic Disk**
Photo Courtesy of IBM.

MAGNETIC-DISK APPLICATIONS

A familiar example of use of direct access is the seat-reservation system of a major airline: requests for seat reservations must be processed immediately. Direct access is also desirable for a large inventory file. Inquiries about inventory status are to be answered immediately, so a method must be available to access the desired information directly and efficiently. Here, since we wish to access only one piece of information, speed is not very important.

The reading of magnetic tape is usually faster—you can read tens of thousands of characters per second—but most of the time will usually be spent in reading inactive items. Since sequential processing requires that all files be handled in the same sequence, a great deal of time must be spent in sorting the files.

Magnetic disks can be used in the same way that magnetic tape is used, that is, files or programs can be stored on a disk in a sequential order. In addition, however, files can be organized for direct access, and they can also be set up as combinations of direct and sequential access.

Another use of direct access is to extend memory. Some users want a nearly infinite amount of memory, but core storage is expensive, so there is usually a shortage. Either the program or the data can be temporarily stored on a disk. The older way to do this is to overlay the program, that is, divide it into segments and then call the segments into memory as they are needed. The programmer must plan for this when writing the program. This method is commonly used on small or older computers. **Virtual memory**, which is available nowadays, does this for you so that you can write the program as though the computer had a very large memory.

CHARACTERISTICS OF MAGNETIC DISK

A **magnetic-disk pack** can be visualized as a stack of phonograph records permanently attached to a single vertical shaft which revolves at high speed. There can be as few as one metal disk on a shaft for some small computers, to as many as 25 metal disks on a shaft for some very large disk systems. Each disk plate is a thin round piece of metal coated on both sides with magnetic oxide.

The metal disks are similar to phonograph records, except that concentric *circles*, called **tracks**, cover both sides of the disk. Some units have 500 tracks; others have 200 tracks. The tracks are accessed for reading or writing by positioning a read/write head over the correct track. Information is processed while the disk is spinning. On any track a user can write a set number of characters (bytes). On one common type of disk 13,030 characters can be written on one track. The disk is designed so that the same number of bytes is written on each track, that is, you cannot write more information on an outer track than on an inner track. **Figure 17.2** illustrates the track system.

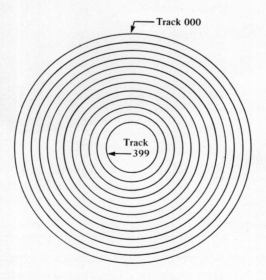

FIGURE 17.2   **Track Arrangement on a Magnetic Disk**

The cost of these disks is high, so data files used only a few times a year would be stored on magnetic tape, not on a magnetic disk. In a disk/tape installation one normally stores currently used data on a disk pack and historical (out-of-date) data on a tape.

Each physical record has a discrete location and a unique address, that is, records are stored in such a way that the location of any record can be determined without extensive searching.

Advantages of Magnetic Disk

Direct Access

The major advantage of magnetic disk storage is ability to address a single record in a file without first sequentially processing the complete file in order to reach the desired record.

Insertion and Modification of Records

If the file is not ordered sequentially, individual records can be added, deleted, or modified without reprocessing the whole file.

Similarity to Tape

Anything that can be done with magnetic tape can be done on a magnetic disk. Thus we may have records of any size, we may use the disk over and over, and we can process data very quickly.

Disadvantages of Magnetic Disk

Cost

The major disadvantage is cost. Not only is the individual disk expensive, but the disk drive that reads/writes on the disk is also very costly. A disk pack which holds as much as a magnetic tape costs about 100 times as much as the magnetic tape, and the disk drive costs several times what a magnetic-tape drive costs. **Figure 17.3** shows a magnetic disk drive.

FIGURE 17.3   **A Magnetic Disk Drive**
Photo Courtesy of IBM.

Speed

For sequential files, tape processing is usually faster, and memory-storage access is much faster than disk-storage access.

Invisible to Eye

An obvious disadvantage is that data stored on a disk cannot be read without the aid of a computer. This brings up the corollary fact that programs using disks are usually not trivial and require knowledgeable programming techniques and interaction with the operating system.

DISK DRIVE

The disk drive can be placed anywhere in the computer room, connected by cable to the computer. The disk drive is usually near the rest of the computer so that the operator can change disk packs easily. Most installations have both public and private disk-packs. The public disk-packs are always on the system. In addition, some users prefer to use private disk-packs, either because they have very large files or because they are dealing with confidential material. Private disk-files are only mounted on the system when the user's program requests them. Some disk drives use permanently mounted disk-packs; other disk drives allow users to dismount one disk-pack and mount another one. A movable disk-pack has the advantage of being transportable to another computer installation.

When the disk pack is mounted on the spindle of the disk drive, the disk pack spins very rapidly. Enough space is left between adjacent disks to permit a comb-like **access arm** to move horizontally in and out freely, reading any track of either the upper or lower side of any of the disks in the pack. The access mechanism contains a separate read/write head for each usable disk surface. **Figure 17.4** is a picture of the comb-type access mechanism.

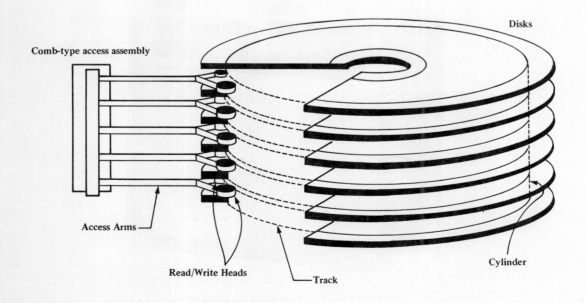

FIGURE 17.4   **Comb-Type Access Mechanism**

The Cylinder Concept

Each recording side has an access arm. All the arms are connected; when the arm is in position on a particular track on the first surface, the other arms are on the same track on the other surfaces. A **cylinder** of data is the amount accessible in one positioning of the access mechanism. Any movement of the access arm represents a significant portion of the time needed to access and transfer data. The top and bottom surfaces are not usually used for storing data. **Figure 17.5** illustrates the cylinder concept.

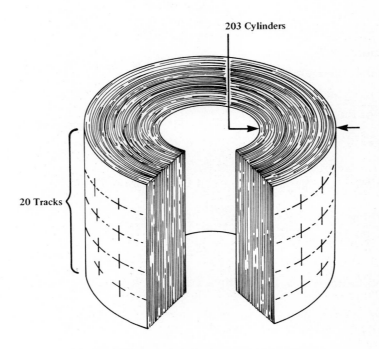

203 Cylinders

20 Tracks

FIGURE 17.5 Cylinder Concept

STATISTICS CONCERNING DISK

The following table shows characteristics of some of the common magnetic disks:

TABLE 17.2

IBM Disk Number	Tracks per Cylinder	Cylinders per Pack	Bytes per Track	Million Bytes per Pack
2311	10	200	3,625	7.25
2314	20	200	7,294	29.17
3330	19	404	13,030	100.00
3340	12	348	8,368	34.90
3350	30	555	19,069	317.50

Many other disks, both smaller and larger, are also available. Even within each type listed above, different models can be obtained which have half or double the listed capacity.

REVIEW

1. Go look at a magnetic-disk pack. Count the number of disk plates on the pack. Then watch the disk in operation.

2. Find out the following information about your installation:

    a) The disk manufacturer.
    b) How many disks there are on your system.
    c) The number of cylinders per disk.
    d) The number of tracks per cylinder.
    e) The number of characters per track.

    Now calculate the number of characters (bytes) that can be stored on one magnetic disk. Next, calculate the number of characters that can be stored on all the on-line disks at your installation.

3. Compare the storage capacity of magnetic tape and disks: using a reasonably large blocking factor for magnetic tape (e.g., 10,000 characters), how many magnetic tapes are equivalent to one magnetic disk?

4. Find out the approximate cost of buying a private disk-pack at your installation.

5. To gain a better understanding of magnetic disk, read *Introduction to IBM Direct-Access Storage Devices and Organization Methods* (IBM Corp. Publication C20-1649).

6. Since magnetic disks are expensive, most computer installations charge the user for each track used on a magnetic disk. Find out the track charge at your installation. Calculate the cost of renting a whole disk, track by track.

7. Name some applications where it would be desirable to use magnetic tape instead of magnetic disk, and vice versa. See if you can develop some general guidelines concerning when to use magnetic tape and when to use magnetic disk.

Program Modifications

1. Modify Sample Program 16A so that it writes card images on magnetic disk. You will have to change the **SELECT** entry and provide new job control statements to identify the disk. No other changes should be necessary.

2. After you have done question 1, modify the program so that it reads and prints the disk file.

3. If you wrote one of the programs suggested at the end of Chapter 16, modify the program so that magnetic disk is used instead of magnetic tape.

****

A Diversion: What Next

Having come this far, you may want to continue your study of COBOL. First, if you have not already done so, obtain the COBOL manual supplied by your computer manufacturer. This manual will provide you with a wealth of information on COBOL. Some textbooks on advanced COBOL are:

High Level COBOL, by Gerald M. Weinberg (Cambridge, Mass.: Winthrop Publishers, 1977).

Advanced ANSI COBOL with Structured Programming, by Gary D. Brown (New York: John Wiley and Sons, 1977).

Effective Use of ANS COBOL Computer Programming Language, by Laurence S. Cohn (New York: John Wiley and Sons, 1975).

****

FILE CHARACTERISTICS

The file characteristics will influence the method of file organization. Some characteristics are:

1. Size
2. Activity
3. Volatility
4. Growth

Size

The size of the file will greatly influence the type of file organization. If the file is very small, a simple sequential card-file is usually sufficient. At the other extreme is a file so large that it cannot be kept on-line on one magnetic disk. Large files must be more carefully organized if they are going to be processed efficiently.

Activity

Activity refers to the percentage of records referred to in the file. A file each record of which is referred to each time it is processed would have 100 percent activity and be a very high-activity file, while a file that has fewer than 50 records referred to out of 1000 would have 5 percent activity, a low-activity file.

An activity estimate is used to help decide how to organize a file for most efficient processing. A file with high activity should probably be organized sequentially; a file with low activity should be organized so that individual records can be located without having to process the complete file.

Another consideration is the distribution of activity. Some methods of organization permit certain records to be located more easily than others. If some records will be needed often, they should be located so that they can be found quickly. Records frequently referred to are often placed at the beginning of the file.

The amount of activity will influence the importance of file organization. If a file is very inactive, it may be immaterial how the file is organized. At the other extreme, a frequently referred-to file must be organized very carefully to provide efficient processing.

Volatility

A **volatile file** is one that has a high rate of additions and deletions. A **static file** is one that has a low rate of additions and deletions. Some methods of file organization allow for more efficient handling of additions and deletions than others.

Growth

The potential growth of a file is often overlooked in the original planning. If the file grows, it should still be processed efficiently without changing the method of file organization.

FILE ORGANIZATION

Magnetic-disk storage devices provide the computer with the ability to record and retrieve stored data in four ways:

1. Sequential.
2. By partition.
3. Indexed sequential.
4. Directly (random).

Sequential Organization

Records are organized according to the physical location of the file. The records are usually in sequence according to their keys (the sequence field). This is the way tape and card files are organized. If the program must be able to read a file from both tape and disk, the file must be a sequential file.

Partitioned Organization

A **partitioned data-set** is a collection of sequential data-sets called **members**. Each member has a unique name and belongs to a **library** or family. The library or data-set name is the name stored in the Volume Table of Contents (**VTOC**). The VTOC points to the beginning of the data set. At the beginning of the data set is a directory which points to the individual members. Members can be individually called, deleted, or replaced. New members can be added to the partitioned data-set. The records within each member are stored sequentially. An obvious use for a partitioned file is to store subprograms. It allows for sequential storing of the subprograms and easy deleting or adding of any one subprogram without disturbing the rest of the subprograms. Tables that can be partitioned are also stored as partitioned files.

Indexed Sequential Organization

Indexed sequential files have some characteristics of both sequential and direct organization. An indexed sequential file is organized sequentially with indexes established so that any record can be located rapidly for random processing. A separate area is established for additions so that a rewrite of the entire file is not necessary.

These added records will not be in correct physical location for sequential organization, but the indexes are used to keep track of added records. Records in this type of file can be used randomly and can also rapidly be processed sequentially. In this type of file structure, the programming system locates individual records; very little I/O programming is necessary.

An example of use of this type of file organization is an inventory system to process order requests in a random order as they are received during the day. Then at the close of each work day sequential summary reports to indicate file status can be generated.

Direct (Random) Organization

Random files are characterized by a predictable relationship between the key of a record and the physical address of that record on the disk. This organization is used when the time spent locating an individual record must be kept to a minimum. Files with this organization are rarely processed sequentially. The programmer must derive an efficient algorithm for locating each of the records, which may prove difficult to do. An example of use of this kind of organization is in an airline reservation-system, where individuals call in to request seat reservations, cancel reservations, and request information. It is not possible to batch-process this type of request and use sequential files.

DISK EFFICIENCY

Since there are so many different types of magnetic disks, it is a little risky to make general statements on how to use magnetic disks, but here are a few guidelines. These rules apply best to sequential files. The block size should be as close as possible to (but *not* more than) the track size, so that a written block of data will take one track. It is important not to write blocks larger than one track, because severe inefficiencies in speed and use of storage will result. For example, if the track size is 13,030 characters and a block size of 14,000 characters is used, each block will require 2 tracks but the second track will be almost empty. Also, the track overflow requires extra calculations to locate the second track for each block.

Short blocks on sequential files also cause inefficiencies in speed and use of storage. Short blocks mean that data must be written often. Each block requires a little overhead (like the interblock gaps on magnetic tape). On the IBM 3330 disk, on one track you can write either one block of 13,030 characters or two blocks of 6447 characters. We can calculate how many characters are lost by using the smaller blocks:

    13,030 - (2 × 6447) =
    13,030 - 12,894 = 136

In each track, 136 characters are lost. As the size of the block decreases we lose more space; for example, only 10 blocks of 1181 characters each can be written on one track.

TIMING

The time required to transfer data to a magnetic disk is affected by three factors: access motion, rotational delay, and data transfer.

Access-Motion Time

This is the time necessary to position the access mechanism at the correct cylinder. If the mechanism is already at the correct cylinder, access time is zero.

Rotational Delay

This is the time necessary for the disk to rotate so that the read/write head can start to read or write.

Data Transfer

This is the time necessary to transfer data between core storage and the device.

The only factor the programmer has much control over is the access-motion time. Requesting disk storage by cylinders can eliminate most of the access-motion time. This request can usually be made in the job control statements specifying the amount of disk space needed.

EXTERNAL SORTING

Business files must be sorted in many ways. A file of customer accounts must be sorted into customer-number sequence for some reports and into customer-name sequence for others. Most files are too large to sort in an internal table within the COBOL program, so COBOL provides a means to sort files on external-storage devices such as magnetic tape or magnetic disk.

Remember, files can be in ascending or descending sequence. The collating sequence is the arrangement of all valid characters in the order of their precedence. The collating sequence of the alphabet is A, B, C, D, ... The collating sequence for all characters is listed in Chapter 8.

When records are sorted, one or more fields are used to order the records. The fields used for ordering the records in the file are the **key fields**. For example, suppose we had the following records:

Field	Columns
Account number	1–9
Name	10–30
Date	31–36
Amount	41–46

If the account-number field is to be used to sequence the file, then account number is the key field for the sort. It is usual to have several keys to determine the order. If you have two key fields, one is the major key-field and one is the minor key-field, that is, the minor key-field is to be placed in sequence within the major key-field.

In order to sort we need a file to be used as work space to do the sorting. The sort is done on magnetic disks or magnetic tapes. Magnetic disk is usually used whenever there is enough disk space available. We need a **SELECT** clause to indicate the devices to be used for the temporary space for sorting. For example:

```
SELECT SORT-FILE
     ASSIGN TO UT-2314-S-SORTWK.
```

The programmer-picked file name is **SORT-FILE**. (Any file name could be used here.) The class of device is utility (i.e., **UT**). The device name is **2314**. The organization is sequential (**S**). The external name is **SORTWK**.

FILE SECTION

For each **SELECT** clause we need an entry in the **FILE SECTION**. For example:

```
SD SORT-FILE.
01 SORT-RECORD.
   05 SEQ-FIELD      PICTURE X(09).
   05 FILLER         PICTURE X(71).
```

For sort files we must use an **SD** instead of an **FD** in the **FILE SECTION**. The SD stands for **sort description**. The other entries ordinarily in a File Description (**FD**) are not needed; most are not even allowed. The record description must indicate the key field used for the sort. In this file the field **SEQ-FIELD** will be the key field.

SORT Verb

The general form of the sort statement is as follows:

```
┌─────────────────────────────────────────────────────────────┐
│  SORT file-name-1 ON  ⎧ ASCENDING      KEY data-name-1 ... ⎫ │
│                       ⎩ DESCENDING                         ⎭ │
│                                                               │
│      ⎡ ON ⎧ ASCENDING  ⎫ KEY data-name-2 ... ⎤               │
│      ⎣    ⎩ DESCENDING ⎭                      ⎦               │
│                                                               │
│  USING file-name-2.                                           │
│  GIVING file-name-3.                                          │
└─────────────────────────────────────────────────────────────┘
```

The first data-name is the major key-field, the second data-name is the intermediate key-field, and the third data-name is the minor key-field. **File-name-1** is the file described in the sort description **SD**. Each data-name in the key field is used for the sequence of the file. **File-name-2** is the input file to be sorted. **File-name-3** is the place for the sorted output. A sample **SORT** statement is:

```
SORT SORT-FILE ON ASCENDING KEY SEQ-FIELD
     USING RECORDS-IN
     GIVING PRINT-OUT.
```

There are several interesting features of the SORT verb. Notice that we did not have to OPEN or CLOSE any files. In fact, it would be an error to OPEN any of the files mentioned in the SORT. The SORT does the following:

1. Opens all files mentioned.
2. Reads in the input file.
3. Sorts the input file.
4. Writes the output file.
5. Closes all the files.

Thus, the files used in the sort must not be opened when the sort is executed. The input file can be used before the sort and the output file can be used after the sort, but then they have to be opened and closed.

SAMPLE PROGRAM 17A

Sample Program 17A (**Figure 17.6**) accepts the input file RECORDS-IN, sorts it, and prints it in the output file PRINT-OUT. This is the simplest possible way to use a sort. You should try to run this program. You may have to change the SELECT entry, and you will need some job control statements to define the work space for sorting.

```
010010 IDENTIFICATION DIVISION.                                    PROGR17A
010020 PROGRAM-ID.                                                 PROGR17A
010030     PROGR17A.                                               PROGR17A
010040 ****************************************************************PROGR17A
010050*     SAMPLE EXTERNAL SORT PROGRAM.                          *PROGR17A
010060 ****************************************************************PROGR17A
010070                                                             PROGR17A
010080 ENVIRONMENT DIVISION.                                       PROGR17A
010090 INPUT-OUTPUT SECTION.                                       PROGR17A
010100 FILE-CONTROL.                                               PROGR17A
010110     SELECT RECORDS-IN                                       PROGR17A
010120        ASSIGN TO UR-2540R-S-SYSIN.                          PROGR17A
010130     SELECT PRINT-OUT                                        PROGR17A
010140        ASSIGN TO UR-1403-S-SYSPRINT.                        PROGR17A
010150     SELECT SORT-FILE                                        PROGR17A
010160        ASSIGN TO UT-2314-S-SORTWK.                          PROGR17A
010170                                                             PROGR17A
020010 DATA DIVISION.                                              PROGR17A
020020 FILE SECTION.                                               PROGR17A
020030 FD  RECORDS-IN                                              PROGR17A
020040     LABEL RECORDS ARE OMITTED.                              PROGR17A
020050 01  IN-RECORD                    PICTURE X(80).             PROGR17A
020060 FD  PRINT-OUT                                               PROGR17A
020070     LABEL RECORDS ARE OMITTED.                              PROGR17A
020080 01  PRINT-IT                     PICTURE X(133).            PROGR17A
020090                                                             PROGR17A
020100 SD  SORT-FILE.                                              PROGR17A
020110 01  SORT-RECORD.                                            PROGR17A
020120     05  SEQ-FIELD                PICTURE X(09).             PROGR17A
020130     05  FILLER                   PICTURE X(71).             PROGR17A
020140                                                             PROGR17A
030010 PROCEDURE DIVISION.                                         PROGR17A
030020     SORT SORT-FILE ASCENDING SEQ-FIELD                      PROGR17A
030030        USING RECORDS-IN                                     PROGR17A
030040        GIVING PRINT-OUT.                                    PROGR17A
030050     STOP RUN.                                               PROGR17A
```

FIGURE 17.6   **Sample Program 17A**

CHAPTER REVIEW

Vocabulary Review

Direct access	Cylinder	Library
Mass storage device	File activity	VTOC
Virtual memory	Volatile file	Indexed sequential file
Magnetic-disk pack	Static file	Random file
Magnetic-disk track	Partitioned data-set	Key field
Access arm	Member	Sort description

Review Questions

1. Explain:

   a) ASCENDING and DESCENDING.

   b) SD.

2. How many files are needed for a sort? What is the purpose of each file?

3. Given the following sort statement:

   ```
   SORT SORT-FILE ON ASCENDING KEY MAJOR
              DESCENDING KEY DATE
          USING MAST-FILE
          GIVING TEST-FILE.
   ```

   answer the following questions:

   a) Which file is the input file?

   b) Which file is the output file?

   c) How will the file be ordered after the sort?

   d) Which file is the work file?

   e) What file must be described in an SD?

4. Given the following sort statement:

   ```
   SORT SORT-IN ON ASCENDING ZAP ZIP TIP
       USING . . .
   ```

   answer the following questions:

   a) What is the major key?

   b) What is the minor key?

   c) What is the intermediate key?

5. There are many options and rules for the SORT verb, many of which are hardware-dependent, so consult a *COBOL Programmers' Guide* to learn more about SORT.

Program Modifications

1. Type Sample Program 17A and run it. Be sure to check the proper form for the **SELECT** entry and the necessary job control statements at your installation.

2. Modify Program 17A so that the file is sorted in descending sequence.

3. Add a field called **DATE** in columns 10–15 of Program 17A. Then do the sort using **DATE** as the minor sequence-field.

4. After you have done the modification in question 3, use **SEQ-FIELD** as the major field in ascending sequence, and date as the minor field in descending sequence.

5. Modify Sample Program 4B to sort the records by city field.

6. Type all the characters on the keypunch, one character per record in column 1 of each record. Then read these records and sort them so you can see what the collating sequence is. After they have been sorted, print the records.

AMERICAN NATIONAL STANDARD COBOL GLOSSARY

ACCESS. The manner in which files are referenced by the computer. Access can be sequential (records are referred to one after another in the order in which they appear on the file), or it can be random (the individual records can be referred to in a nonsequential manner).

Actual Decimal Point. The physical representation, using either of the decimal point characters (. or ,), of the decimal point position in a data item. When specified, it will appear in a printed report, and it requires an actual space in storage.

ACTUAL KEY. A key which can be directly used by the system to locate a logical record on a mass storage device. An ACTUAL KEY must be a data item of 5 to 259 bytes in length.

Alphabetic Character. A character which is one of the 26 characters of the alphabet, or a space. In COBOL, the term does *not* include any other characters.

Alphanumeric Character. Any character in the computer's character set.

Alphanumeric Edited Character. A character within an alphanumeric character string which contains at least one B or 0.

Arithmetic Expression.   A statement containing any combination of data-names, numeric literals, and figurative constants, joined together by one or more arithmetic operators in such a way that the statement as a whole can be reduced to a single numeric value.

Arithmetic Operator.   A symbol (single character or 2-character set) or COBOL verb which directs the system to perform an arithmetic operation. The following list shows arithmetic operators:

Meaning	*Symbol*
Addition	+
Subtraction	–
Multiplication	*
Division	/
Exponentiation	**

Assumed Decimal Point.   A decimal point position which does not involve the existence of an actual character in a data item. It does not occupy an actual space in storage, but is used by the compiler to align a value properly for calculation.

BLOCK.   In COBOL, a group of characters or records which is treated as an entity when moved into or out of the computer. The term is synonymous with the term Physical Record.

Buffer.   A portion of main storage into which data is read or from which it is written.

Byte.   A sequence of eight adjacent binary bits. When properly aligned, two bytes form a halfword, four bytes a fullword, and eight bytes a doubleword.

Channel.   A device that directs the flow of information between the computer main storage and the input/output devices.

Character.   One of a set of indivisible symbols that can be arranged in sequences to express information. These symbols include the letters A through Z, the decimal digits 0 through 9, punctuation symbols, and any other symbols which will be accepted by the data-processing system.

Character Set.   All the valid COBOL characters. The complete set of 51 characters is listed in Chapter 2.

Character String.   A connected sequence of characters. All COBOL characters are valid.

Class Condition.   A statement that the content of an item is wholly alphabetic or wholly numeric. It may be true or false.

Clause.   A set of consecutive COBOL words whose purpose is to specify an attribute of an entry. There are three types of clauses: data, environment, and file.

COBOL Character.   Any of the 51 valid characters (see CHARACTER) in the COBOL character set. The complete set is listed in Chapter 2.

Collating Sequence.   The arrangement of all valid characters in the order of their relative precedence. The collating sequence of a computer is part of the computer design—each acceptable character has a predetermined place in the sequence. A collating sequence is used primarily in comparison operations.

Comment.   An annotation in the Identification Division or Procedure Division of a COBOL source program. A comment is ignored by the compiler. As an IBM extension, comments may be included at any point in a COBOL source program.

Compile Time.   The time during which a COBOL source program is translated by the COBOL compiler into a machine language object program.

Compiler. A program which translates a program written in a higher level language into a machine language object program.

- PROCEDURE DIVISION, which consists of statements directing the processing of data in a specified manner at execution time.

Division Header. The COBOL words that indicate the beginning of a particular division of a COBOL program. The four division headers are:

- IDENTIFICATION DIVISION.

- ENVIRONMENT DIVISION.

- DATA DIVISION.

- PROCEDURE DIVISION.

Division-name. The name of one of the four divisions of a COBOL program.

EBCDIC Character. Any one of the symbols included in the eight-bit EBCDIC (Extended Binary-Coded-Decimal Interchange Code) set. All 51 COBOL characters are included.

Editing Character. A single character or a fixed two-character combination used to create proper formats for output reports.

Elementary Item. A data item that cannot logically be subdivided.

Entry. Any consecutive set of descriptive clauses terminated by a period, written in the Identification, Environment, or Procedure Divisions of a COBOL program.

ENVIRONMENT DIVISION. One of the four main component parts of a COBOL program. The Environment Division describes the computers upon which the source program is compiled and those on which the object program is executed, and provides a linkage between the logical concept of files and their records, and the physical aspects of the devices on which files are stored (see "Environment Division" for full details).

Execution Time. The time at which an object program actually performs the instructions coded in the Procedure Division, using the actual data provided.

Exponent. A number, indicating how many times another number (the base) is to be repeated as a factor. Positive exponents denote multiplication, negative exponents denote division, fractional exponents denote a root of a quantity. In COBOL, exponentiation is indicated with the symbol ** followed by the exponent.

F-mode Records. Records of a fixed length. Blocks may contain more than one record.

Figurative Constant. A reserved word that represents a numeric value, a character, or a string of repeated values or characters. The word can be written in a COBOL program to represent the values or characters without being defined in the Data Division.

FILE-CONTROL. The name and header of an Environment Division paragraph in which the data files for a given source program are named and assigned to specific input/output devices.

File Description. An entry in the File Section of the Data Division that provides information about the identification and physical structure of a file.

File-name. A name assigned to a set of input data or output data. A file-name must include at least one alphabetic character.

FILE SECTION. A section of the Data Division that contains descriptions of all externally stored data (or files) used in a program. Such information is given in one or more file description entries.

Function-name. A name, specified by IBM, that identifies system logical units, printer and card punch control characters, and report codes. When a function-name is associated with a mnemonic name in the Environment Division, the mnemonic-name may then be substituted in any format in which such substitution is valid.

Group Item. A data item made up of a series of logically related elementary items. It can be part of a record or a complete record.

Header Label. A record that identifies the beginning of a physical file or a volume.

High-Order. The leftmost position in a string of characters.

IDENTIFICATION DIVISION. One of the four main component parts of a COBOL program. The Identification Division identifies the source program and the object program and, in addition, may include such documentation as the author's name, the installation where written, date written, etc., (see "Identification Division" for full details).

Identifier. A data-name, unique in itself, or made unique by the syntactically correct combination of qualifiers, subscripts, and/or indexes.

Imperative-Statement. A statement consisting of an imperative verb and its operands, which specifies that an action be taken, unconditionally. An imperative-statement may consist of a series of imperative-statements.

Index. A computer storage position or register, the contents of which identify a particular element in a table.

Index-name. A name, given by the programmer, for an index of a specific table. An index-name must contain at least one alphabetic character. It is one word (4 bytes) in length.

INPUT-OUTPUT SECTION. In the Environment Division, the section that names the files and external media needed by an object program. It also provides information required for the transmission and handling of data during the execution of an object program.

Integer. A numeric data item or literal that does not include any character positions to the right of the decimal point, actual or assumed. Where the term "integer" appears in formats, "integer" must not be a numeric data item.

I-O-CONTROL. The name, and the header, for an Environment Division paragraph in which object program requirements for specific input/output techniques are specified. These techniques include rerun checkpoints, sharing of same areas by several data files, and multiple file storage on a single tape device.

KEY. One or more data items, the contents of which identify the type or the location of a record, or the ordering of data.

Key Word. A reserved word whose employment is essential to the meaning and structure of a COBOL statement. In this manual, key words are indicated in the formats of statements by *underscoring*. Key words are included in the reserved word list.

Level Indicator. Two alphabetic characters that identify a specific type of file, or the highest position in a hierarchy. The level indicators are: FD, RD, SD.

Level Number. A numeric character or 2-character set that identifies the properties of a data description entry. Level numbers 01 through 49 define group items, the highest level being identified as 01, and the subordinate data items within the hierarchy being identified with level numbers 02 through 49. Level numbers 66, 77, and 88 identify special properties of a data description entry in the Data Division.

Literal. A character string whose value is implicit in the characters themselves. The numeric literal 7 expresses the value 7, and the nonnumeric literal 'CHARACTERS' expresses the value CHARACTERS.

Logical Operator. A COBOL word that defines the logical connections between relational operators. The three logical operators and their meanings are:

OR (logical inclusive—either or both)

AND (logical connective—both)

NOT (logical negation)

(See "Procedure Division" for a more detailed explanation.)

Logical Record. The most inclusive data item, identified by a level-01 entry. It consists of one or more related data items.

Low-Order. The rightmost position in a string of characters.

Mass Storage. A storage medium—disk, drum, or data cell—in which data can be collected and maintained in a sequential, direct, indexed or relative organization.

Mass Storage File. A collection of records assigned to a mass storage device.

Mnemonic-name. A programmer-supplied word associated with a specific function-name in the Environment Division. It then may be written in place of the function-name in any format where such a substitution is valid.

MODE. The manner in which records of a file are accessed or processed.

Name. A word composed of not more than 30 characters, which defines a COBOL operand.

Noncontiguous Item. A data item in the Working-Storage Section of the Data Division which bears no relationship to other data items.

Nonnumeric Literal. A character string bounded by quotation marks, which means literally itself. For example, 'CHARACTER' is the literal for, and means, CHARACTER. The string of characters may include any characters in the computer's set, with the exception of the quotation mark. Characters that are not COBOL characters may be included.

Numeric Character. A character that belongs to one of the set of digits 0 through 9.

Numeric Edited Character. A numeric character which is in such a form that it may be used in a printed output. It may consist of external decimal digits 0 through 9, the decimal point, commas, the dollar sign, etc., as the programmer wishes (see "Data Division" for a fuller explanation).

Numeric Item. An item whose description restricts its contents to a value represented by characters chosen from the digits 0 through 9; if signed, the item may also contain a + or −, or other representation of an operational sign.

Numeric Literal. A numeric character or string of characters whose value is implicit in the characters themselves. Thus, 777 is the literal as well as the value of the number 777.

OBJECT-COMPUTER. The name of an Environment Division paragraph in which the computer upon which the object program will be run is described.

Object Program. The set of machine language instructions that is the output from the compilation of a COBOL source program. The actual processing of data is done by the object program.

Object Time. The time during which an object program is executed.

Operand. The "object" of a verb or an operator. That is, the data or equipment governed or directed by a verb or operator.

Operational Sign.   An algebraic sign associated with a numeric data item, which indicates whether the item is positive or negative.

Optional Word.   A reserved word included in a specific format only to improve the readability of a COBOL statement. If the programmer wishes, optional words may be omitted.

Paragraph.   A set of one or more COBOL sentences, making up a logical processing entity, and preceded by a paragraph-name or a paragraph header.

Paragraph Header.   A word followed by a period that identifies and precedes all paragraphs in the Identification Division and Environment Division.

Paragraph-name.   A programmer-defined word that identifies and precedes a paragraph.

Physical Record.   A physical unit of data, synonymous with a block. It can be composed of a portion of one logical record, of one complete logical record, or of a group of logical records.

Procedure.   One or more logically connected paragraphs or sections within the Procedure Division, which direct the computer to perform some action or series of related actions.

PROCEDURE DIVISION.   One of the four main component parts of a COBOL program. The Procedure Division contains instructions for solving a problem. The Procedure Division may contain imperative-statements, conditional statements, paragraphs, procedures, and sections (see "Procedure Division" for full details).

Procedure-name.   A word that precedes and identifies a procedure, used by the programmer to transfer control from one point of the program to another.

Process.   Any operation or combination of operations on data.

Program-name.   A word in the Identification Division that identifies a COBOL source program.

Punctuation Character.   A comma, semicolon, period, quotation mark, left or right parenthesis, or a space.

Qualifier.   A group data-name that is used to reference a non-unique data-name at a lower level in the same hierarchy, or a section-name that is used to reference a non-unique paragraph. In this way, the data-name or the paragraph-name can be made unique.

Random Access.   An access mode in which specific logical records are obtained from or placed into a mass storage file in a nonsequential manner.

RECORD.   A set of one or more related data items grouped for handling either internally or by the input/output systems (see "Logical Record").

Record Description.   The total set of data description entries associated with a particular logical record.

Record-name.   A data-name that identifies a logical record.

REEL.   A module of external storage associated with a tape device.

Relation Character.   A character that expresses a relationship between two operands. The following are COBOL relation characters:

Character	Meaning
>	Greater than
<	Less than
=	Equal to

Relation Condition. A statement that the value of an arithmetic expression or data item has a specific relationship to another arithmetic expression or data item. The statement may be true or false.

Relational Operator. A reserved word, or a group of reserved words, or a group of reserved words and relation characters. A relational operator plus programmer-defined operands make up a relational expression. A complete listing is given in "Procedure Division."

Reserved Word. A word used in a COBOL source program for syntactical purposes. It must not appear in a program as a user-defined operand.

Routine. A set of statements in a program that causes the computer to perform an operation or series of related operations.

SECTION. A logically related sequence of one or more paragraphs. A section must always be named.

Section Header. A combination of words that precedes and identifies each section in the Environment, Data, and Procedure Divisions.

Section-name. A word specified by the programmer that precedes and identifies a section in the Procedure Division.

Sentence. A sequence of one or more statements, the last ending with a period followed by a space.

Separator. An optional word or character that improves readability.

Sequential Access. An access mode in which logical records are obtained from or placed into a file in such a way that each successive access to the file refers to the next subsequent logical record in the file. The order of the records is established by the programmer when creating the file.

Sequential Processing. The processing of logical records in the order in which records are accessed.

Sign Condition. A statement that the algebraic value of a data item is less than, equal to, or greater than zero. It may be true or false.

Simple Condition. An expression that can have two values, and causes the object program to select between alternate paths of control, depending on the value found. The expression can be true or false.

Sort File. A collection of records that is sorted by a SORT statement. The sort file is created and used only while the sort function is operative.

Sort-File-Description Entry. An entry in the File Section of the Data Division that names and describes a collection of records that is used in a SORT statement.

Sort-file-name. A data-name that identifies a Sort File.

Sort-key. The field within a record on which a file is sorted.

Sort-work-file. A collection of records involved in the sorting operation as this collection exists on intermediate device(s).

SOURCE-COMPUTER. The name of an Environment Division paragraph. In it, the computer upon which the source program will be compiled is described.

Source Program. A problem-solving program written in COBOL.

Special Character. A character that is neither numeric nor alphabetic. Special characters in COBOL include the space ( ), the period (.), as well as the following: + - * / = $, ; ") (

SPECIAL-NAMES. The name of an Environment Division paragraph, and the paragraph itself, in which names supplied by IBM are related to mnemonic-names specified by the programmer. In addition, this paragraph can be used to exchange the functions of the comma and the period, or to specify a substitution character for the currency sign, in the PICTURE string.

Special Register. Compiler-generated storage areas primarily used to store information produced with the use of specific COBOL features. The special registers are: TALLY, LINE-COUNTER, PAGE-COUNTER, CURRENT-DATE, TIME-OF-DAY, LABEL-RETURN, RETURN-CODE, SORT-RETURN, SORT-FILE-SIZE, SORT-CORE-SIZE, and SORT-MODE-SIZE.

Statement. A syntactically valid combination of words and symbols written in the Procedure Division. A statement combines COBOL reserved words and programmer-defined operands.

Subject of entry. A data-name or reserved word that appears immediately after a level indicator or level number in a Data Division entry. It serves to reference the entry.

Subscript. An integer or a variable whose value references a particular element in a table.

SYSIN. The system logical input device.

SYSOUT. The system logical output device.

SYSPUNCH. The system logical punch device.

System-name. A name that identifies any particular external device used with the computer, and characteristics of files contained within it.

Table. A collection and arrangement of data in a fixed form for ready reference. Such a collection follows some logical order, expressing particular values (functions) corresponding to other values (arguments) by which they are referenced.

Table Element. A data item that belongs to the set of repeated items comprising a table.

Test Condition. A statement that, taken as a whole, may be either true or false, depending on the circumstances existing at the time the expression is evaluated.

Trailer Label. A record that identifies the ending of a physical file or of a volume.

U-mode Records. Records of unspecified length. They may be fixed or variable in length; there is only one record per block.

Unary Operator. An arithmetic operator (+ or –) that can precede a single variable, a literal, or a left parenthesis in an arithmetic expression. The plus sign multiplies the value by +1; the minus sign multiplies the value by – 1.

UNIT. A module of external storage. Its dimensions are determined by IBM.

V-mode Records. Records of variable length. Blocks may contain more than one record. Each record contains a record length field, and each block contains a block length field.

Variable. A data item whose value may be changed during execution of the object program.

Verb. A COBOL reserved word that expresses an action to be taken by a COBOL compiler or an object program.

Volume. A module of external storage. For tape devices it is a reel; for mass storage devices it is a unit.

WORD:

1. In COBOL: A string of not more than 30 characters, chosen from the following: the letters A through Z, the digits 0 through 9, and the hyphen (-). The hyphen may not appear as either the first or last character.

2. In System/360: A fullword is four bytes of storage; a doubleword is eight bytes of storage; a halfword is two bytes of storage.

Word Boundary. Any particular storage position at which data must be aligned for certain processing operations in System/360. The halfword boundary must be divisible by 2, the fullword boundary must be divisible by 4, the doubleword boundary must be divisible by 8.

WORKING-STORAGE SECTION. A section-name (and the section itself) in the Data Division. The section describes records and noncontiguous data items that are not part of external files, but are developed and processed internally. It also defines data items whose values are assigned in the source program.

AMERICAN NATIONAL STANDARD COBOL FORMAT SUMMARY

The general format of a COBOL program is illustrated in these format summaries. Included within the general format is the specific format for each valid COBOL statement. All clauses are shown as though they were required by the COBOL source program, although within a given context many are optional.

IDENTIFICATION DIVISION — BASIC FORMATS

<u>IDENTIFICATION</u> <u>DIVISION</u>.
<u>PROGRAM-ID</u>. *program name*.
<u>AUTHOR</u>. [*comment-entry*] . . .
<u>INSTALLATION</u>. [*comment entry*] . . .
<u>DATE-WRITTEN</u>. [*comment-entry*] . . .
<u>DATE-COMPILED</u>. [*comment-entry*] . . .
<u>SECURITY</u>. [*comment-entry*] . . .
<u>REMARKS</u>. [*comment-entry*] . . .

ENVIRONMENT DIVISION — BASIC FORMATS

ENVIRONMENT DIVISION.
CONFIGURATION SECTION.
SOURCE-COMPUTER. *computer-name.*
OBJECT COMPUTER. *computer-name.*
SPECIAL-NAMES.
    [*function-name* IS *mnemonic-name*] . . .
   [CURRENCY SIGN IS literal] .
   [DECIMAL-POINT IS COMMA] .
INPUT-OUTPUT SECTION.
FILE-CONTROL.
   {SELECT [OPTIONAL] *file name.*
   ASSIGN TO [*integer-1*] *system-name-1*
   [*system-name-2*] . . .

DATA DIVISION — BASIC FORMATS

DATA DIVISION.
FILE SECTION.
FD *file-name.*
    BLOCK CONTAINS [*integer-1* TO] *integer-2* $\begin{Bmatrix} \text{CHARACTERS} \\ \text{RECORDS} \end{Bmatrix}$

    RECORD CONTAINS [*integer-1* TO] *integer-2* CHARACTERS

    LABEL $\begin{Bmatrix} \text{RECORD IS} \\ \text{RECORDS ARE} \end{Bmatrix} \begin{Bmatrix} \text{OMITTED} \\ \text{STANDARD} \end{Bmatrix}$

    DATA $\begin{Bmatrix} \text{RECORD IS} \\ \text{RECORDS ARE} \end{Bmatrix}$ *data-name-1* [*data-name-2*] . . .

01-49 $\begin{Bmatrix} \textit{data-name-1} \\ \text{FILLER} \end{Bmatrix}$

    REDEFINES *data-name-2*
    BLANK WHEN ZERO
    $\begin{Bmatrix} \text{JUSTIFIED} \\ \text{JUST} \end{Bmatrix}$ RIGHT
    $\begin{Bmatrix} \text{PICTURE} \\ \text{PIC} \end{Bmatrix}$ IS *character string*

[USAGE IS] $\left\{ \begin{array}{l} \text{INDEX} \\ \text{DISPLAY} \\ \begin{Bmatrix} \text{COMPUTATIONAL} \\ \text{COMP} \end{Bmatrix} \\ \begin{Bmatrix} \text{COMPUTATIONAL-1} \\ \text{COMP-1} \end{Bmatrix} \\ \begin{Bmatrix} \text{COMPUTATIONAL-2} \\ \text{COMP-2} \end{Bmatrix} \\ \begin{Bmatrix} \text{COMPUTATIONAL-3} \\ \text{COMP-3} \end{Bmatrix} \\ \text{DISPLAY-ST} \end{array} \right\}$

88 *condition-name* $\begin{Bmatrix} \text{VALUE IS} \\ \text{VALUE ARE} \end{Bmatrix}$ *literal-1* [THRU *literal-2*]

    [*literal-3* [THRU *literal-4*]] . . . .

66 *data-name-1* RENAMES *data-name-2* [THRU *data-name-3*] .

NOTE: Formats for the OCCURS Clause are included with
             Formats for the TABLE HANDLING feature.

WORKING-STORAGE SECTION.

77 *data-name-1*

01 49 $\begin{Bmatrix} \text{\textit{data-name-1}} \\ \underline{\text{FILLER}} \end{Bmatrix}$

$\qquad$ <u>REDEFINES</u> *data-name-2*

$\qquad$ <u>BLANK</u> WHEN <u>ZERO</u>

$\qquad$ $\begin{Bmatrix} \underline{\text{JUSTIFIED}} \\ \underline{\text{JUST}} \end{Bmatrix}$ RIGHT

$\qquad$ $\begin{Bmatrix} \underline{\text{PICTURE}} \\ \underline{\text{PIC}} \end{Bmatrix}$ IS *character string*

$\qquad$ $\begin{Bmatrix} \underline{\text{SYNCHRONIZED}} \\ \underline{\text{SYNC}} \end{Bmatrix} \begin{bmatrix} \underline{\text{LEFT}} \\ \underline{\text{RIGHT}} \end{bmatrix}$

$\qquad$ [USAGE IS] $\left\{\begin{array}{l} \underline{\text{INDEX}} \\ \underline{\text{DISPLAY}} \\ \begin{Bmatrix} \underline{\text{COMPUTATIONAL -1}} \\ \underline{\text{COMP-1}} \end{Bmatrix} \\ \begin{Bmatrix} \underline{\text{COMPUTATIONAL-2}} \\ \underline{\text{COMP-2}} \end{Bmatrix} \\ \begin{Bmatrix} \underline{\text{COMPUTATIONAL-3}} \\ \underline{\text{COMP-3}} \end{Bmatrix} \\ \underline{\text{DISPLAY ST}} \end{array}\right\}$

$\qquad$ <u>VALUE</u> IS *literal*.

88 *condition name* $\dfrac{\underline{\text{VALUE}} \text{ IS}}{\underline{\text{VALUES}} \text{ ARE}}$ *literal-1* [<u>THRU</u> *literal-2*]

$\qquad$ [*literal-3* [<u>THRU</u> *literal-4*]] . . . .

66 *data-name-1* <u>RENAMES</u> *data-name-2* [<u>THRU</u> *data-name-3*] .

NOTE: Formats for the OCCURS Clause are included with
$\qquad$ Formats for the TABLE HANDLING feature.

PROCEDURE DIVISION — BASIC FORMATS

<u>PROCEDURE</u> <u>DIVISION</u>

ADD statement

Format 1

$\qquad$ <u>ADD</u> $\begin{Bmatrix} \text{\textit{identifier-1}} \\ \text{\textit{literal-1}} \end{Bmatrix} \begin{bmatrix} \text{\textit{identifier-2}} \\ \text{\textit{literal-2}} \end{bmatrix}$ . . . <u>TO</u> *identifier-m* [<u>ROUNDED</u>]

$\qquad\qquad$ [*identifier-n* [<u>ROUNDED</u>]] . . . [ON <u>SIZE</u> <u>ERROR</u> *imperative-statement*]

Format 2

$\qquad$ <u>ADD</u> $\begin{Bmatrix} \text{\textit{identifier-1}} \\ \text{\textit{literal-1}} \end{Bmatrix} \begin{Bmatrix} \text{\textit{identifier-2}} \\ \text{\textit{literal-2}} \end{Bmatrix} \begin{bmatrix} \text{\textit{identifier-3}} \\ \text{\textit{literal-3}} \end{bmatrix}$ . . . <u>GIVING</u>

$\qquad\qquad$ *identifier-m* [<u>ROUNDED</u>] [ON <u>SIZE</u> <u>ERROR</u> *imperative-statement*]

Format 3

$\qquad$ <u>ADD</u> $\begin{Bmatrix} \underline{\text{CORRESPONDING}} \\ \underline{\text{CORR}} \end{Bmatrix}$ *identifier-1* TO *identifier-2* [<u>ROUNDED</u>]

$\qquad\qquad$ [ON <u>SIZE</u> <u>ERROR</u> *imperative-statement*]

CLOSE statement.

Format 1

CLOSE *file-name-1* $\left[\begin{matrix} \underline{REEL} \\ \underline{UNIT} \end{matrix}\right]$ [WITH $\left\{\begin{matrix} \underline{NO} \ \underline{REWIND} \\ \underline{LOCK} \end{matrix}\right\}$]

COMPUTE Statement

COMPUTE *identifier-1* [ROUNDED] = $\left\{\begin{matrix} \textit{arithmetic-expression} \\ \textit{identifier-2} \\ \textit{literal-1} \end{matrix}\right\}$

[ON SIZE ERROR *imperative-statement*]

DECLARATIVE Section

PROCEDURE DIVISION.

DECLARATIVES.

{*section-name* SECTION. USE *sentence.*

{*paragraph-name.* (*sentence*) ... }...}...

END DECLARATIVES.

DIVIDE Statement

Format 1

DIVIDE $\left\{\begin{matrix} \textit{identifier-1} \\ \textit{literal-1} \end{matrix}\right\}$ INTO *identifier-2* [ROUNDED)

[ON SIZE ERROR *imperative-statement*]

Format 2

DIVIDE $\left\{\begin{matrix} \textit{identifier-1} \\ \textit{literal-1} \end{matrix}\right\}\left\{\begin{matrix} \underline{INTO} \\ \underline{BY} \end{matrix}\right\}\left\{\begin{matrix} \textit{identifier-2} \\ \textit{literal-2} \end{matrix}\right\}$ GIVING *identifier-3*

[ROUNDED] [REMAINDER *identifier-4*] [ON SIZE ERROR *imperative-statement*]

EXAMINE Statement

Format 1

EXAMINE *identifier* TALLYING $\left\{\begin{matrix} \underline{UNTIL} \ \underline{FIRST} \\ \underline{ALL} \\ \underline{LEADING} \end{matrix}\right\}$ *literal-1*

[REPLACING BY *literal-2*]

Format 2

EXAMINE *identifier* REPLACING $\left\{\begin{matrix} \underline{ALL} \\ \underline{LEADING} \\ \underline{FIRST} \\ \underline{UNTIL} \ \underline{FIRST} \end{matrix}\right\}$ *literal-1* BY *literal-2*

GO TO *Statement*

Format 1

GO TO *procedure-name-1*

Format 2

GO TO *procedure-name-1* [*procedure-name-2*] ... DEPENDING ON *identifier*

Format 3

GO TO.

IF Statement

IF condition THEN { NEXT SENTENCE / statement-1 } { OTHERWISE / ELSE } { NEXT SENTENCE / statement-2 }

MOVE Statement

Format 1

MOVE { identifier-1 / literal-1 } TO identifier-2 [identifier-3] ...

Format 2

MOVE { CORRESPONDING / CORR } identifier-1 TO identifier-2

MULTIPLY Statement

Format 1

MULTIPLY { identifier-1 / literal-1 } BY identifier-2 [ROUNDED]

[ON SIZE ERROR imperative-statement]

Format 2

MULTIPLY { identifier-1 / literal-1 } BY { identifier-2 / literal-2 } GIVING identifier-3

[ROUNDED] [ON SIZE ERROR imperative-statement]

OPEN Statement

Format 1

OPEN [INPUT { file-name [REVERSED / WITH NO REWIND] } ...]

[OUTPUT { file-name [WITH NO REWIND] } ...]

PERFORM Statement

Format 1

PERFORM procedure-name-1 [THRU procedure-name-2]

Format 2

PERFORM procedure-name-1 [THRU procedure-name-2] { identifier-1 / integer-1 } TIMES

Format 3

PERFORM procedure-name-1 [THRU procedure-name-2] UNTIL condition-1

Format 4

PERFORM procedure-name-1 [THRU procedure-name-2]

VARYING { index-name-1 / identifier-1 } FROM { index-name-2 / literal-2 / identifier-2 } BY { literal-3 / identifier-3 } UNTIL condition 1

[AFTER { index-name-4 / identifier-4 } FROM { index-name-5 / literal-5 / identifier-5 } BY { literal-6 / identifier-6 } UNTIL condition 2

[AFTER { index-name-7 / identifier-7 } FROM { index-name-8 / literal-8 / identifier-8 } BY { literal-9 / identifier-9 } UNTIL condition 3]]

READ Statement

   READ *file-name* RECORD [INTO *identifier*]

$$\left\{ \begin{matrix} \text{AT END} \\ \text{INVALID KEY} \end{matrix} \right\} \textit{imperative-statement}$$

STOP Statement

   STOP $\left\{ \begin{matrix} \text{RUN} \\ \textit{literal} \end{matrix} \right\}$

SUBTRACT Statement

Format 1

   SUBTRACT $\left\{ \begin{matrix} \textit{identifier-1} \\ \textit{literal-1} \end{matrix} \right\}$ $\left[\begin{matrix} \textit{identifier-2} \\ \textit{literal-2} \end{matrix} \right]$ ... FROM *identifier-m* [ROUNDED]

      [*identifier-n* [ROUNDED]] ... [ON SIZE ERROR *imperative-statement*]

Format 2

   SUBTRACT $\left\{ \begin{matrix} \textit{identifier-1} \\ \textit{literal-1} \end{matrix} \right\}$ $\left[\begin{matrix} \textit{identifier-2} \\ \textit{literal-2} \end{matrix} \right]$ ... FROM $\left\{ \begin{matrix} \textit{identifier-m} \\ \textit{literal-m} \end{matrix} \right\}$ GIVING *identifier-n*

      [ROUNDED] [ON SIZE ERROR *imperative-statement*]

Format 3

   SUBTRACT $\left\{ \begin{matrix} \text{CORRESPONDING} \\ \text{CORR} \end{matrix} \right\}$ *identifier-1* FROM *identifier-2* [ROUNDED]

      [ON SIZE ERROR *imperative-statement*]

WRITE Statement

Format 1

   WRITE *record-name* [FROM *identifier-1*] [$\left\{ \begin{matrix} \text{BEFORE} \\ \text{AFTER} \end{matrix} \right\}$ ADVANCING

      $\left\{ \begin{matrix} \textit{identifier-2} \text{ LINES} \\ \textit{integer} \text{ LINES} \\ \textit{mnemonic-name} \end{matrix} \right\}$] [AT $\left\{ \begin{matrix} \text{END-OF-PAGE} \\ \text{EOP} \end{matrix} \right\}$ *imperative-stament*]

SORT — BASIC FORMATS

Environment Division Sort Formats

FILE-CONTROL PARAGRAPH — SELECT SENTENCE

SELECT Sentence (for GIVING option only)

   SELECT *file-name*

      ASSIGN TO [*integer-1*] *system-name-1* [*system-name-2*] ...

         OR *system-name-3* [FOR MULTIPLE $\left\{ \begin{matrix} \text{REEL} \\ \text{UNIT} \end{matrix} \right\}$]

            [RESERVE $\left\{ \begin{matrix} \textit{integer-2} \\ \text{NO} \end{matrix} \right\}$ ALTERNATE $\left[\begin{matrix} \text{AREA} \\ \text{AREAS} \end{matrix} \right]$].

SELECT Sentence (for Sort Work Files)

   SELECT *sort-file-name*

      ASSIGN TO [*integer*] *system-name-1* [*system-name-2*] ...

Data Division Sort Formats

SORT-FILE DESCRIPTION

$\underline{SD}$ *sort-file-name*

$\underline{RECORDING}$ MODE IS *mode*

DATA $\left\{ \begin{array}{l} \underline{RECORD} \text{ IS} \\ \underline{RECORDS} \text{ ARE} \end{array} \right\}$ *data-name-1* [*data-name-2*] ...

$\underline{RECORD}$ CONTAINS [*integer-1* $\underline{TO}$] *integer-2* CHARACTERS

Procedure Division Sort Formats

SORT Statement

$\underline{SORT}$ *file-name-1* ON $\left\{ \begin{array}{l} \underline{DESCENDING} \\ \underline{ASCENDING} \end{array} \right\}$ KEY *data-name-1* ...

ON $\left\{ \begin{array}{l} \underline{DESCENDING} \\ \underline{ASCENDING} \end{array} \right\}$ KEY *data-name-2* ...] ...

$\left\{ \begin{array}{l} [\underline{INPUT} \ \underline{PROCEDURE} \text{ IS } \textit{section-name-1} \ [\underline{THRU} \ \textit{section-name-2}] \\ [\underline{USING} \ \textit{file-name-2} \end{array} \right.$

$\left\{ \begin{array}{l} [\underline{OUTPUT} \ \underline{PROCEDURE} \text{ IS } \textit{section-name-3} \ [\underline{THRU} \ \textit{section-name-4}] \\ [\underline{GIVING} \ \textit{file-name-3} \end{array} \right.$

TABLE HANDLING — BASIC FORMATS

Data Division Table Handling Formats

OCCURS Clause

Format 1

$\underline{OCCURS}$ *integer-2* TIMES

[$\left\{ \begin{array}{l} \underline{ASCENDING} \\ \underline{DESCENDING} \end{array} \right\}$ KEY IS *data-name-3* ...] ...

[$\underline{INDEXED}$ BY *index-name-1* [*index-name-2*] ...]

Format 2

$\underline{OCCURS}$ *integer-1* $\underline{TO}$ *integer-2* TIMES [$\underline{DEPENDING}$ ON *data-name-1*]

[$\left\{ \begin{array}{l} \underline{ASCENDING} \\ \underline{DESCENDING} \end{array} \right\}$ KEY IS *data-name-2* [*data-name-3*] ...] ...

[$\underline{INDEXED}$ BY *index-name-1* [*index-name-2*] ...]

USAGE Clause

[$\underline{USAGE}$ IS] $\underline{INDEX}$

Procedure Division Table Handling Formats

SEARCH Statement

Format 1

$\underline{SEARCH}$ *identifier-1* [$\underline{VARYING}$ $\left\{ \begin{array}{l} \textit{index-name-1} \\ \textit{identifier-2} \end{array} \right\}$]

[AT $\underline{END}$ *imperative-statement-1*]

$\underline{WHEN}$ *condition -1* $\left\{ \begin{array}{l} \textit{imperative-statement-2} \\ \underline{NEXT} \ \underline{SENTENCE} \end{array} \right\}$

[$\underline{WHEN}$ *condition-2* $\left\{ \begin{array}{l} \textit{imperative-statement-3} \\ \underline{NEXT} \ \underline{SENTENCE} \end{array} \right\}$] ...

Format 2

> SEARCH ALL *identifier-1* [AT END *imperative-statement-1*]
>
> WHEN *condition-1* $\begin{Bmatrix} imperative\text{-}statement\text{-}2 \\ \underline{NEXT\ SENTENCE} \end{Bmatrix}$

SET Statement

Format 1

> $\underline{SET}$ $\begin{Bmatrix} index\text{-}name\text{-}1\ [index\text{-}name\text{-}2]\ldots \\ identifier\text{-}1\ \ \ \ [identifier\text{-}2\ \ ]\ldots \end{Bmatrix}$ $\underline{TO}$ $\begin{Bmatrix} index\text{-}name\text{-}3 \\ identifier\text{-}3 \\ literal\text{-}1 \end{Bmatrix}$

Format 2

> $\underline{SET}$ *index-name-4* [*index-name-5*] ... $\begin{Bmatrix} \underline{UP}\ \underline{BY} \\ \underline{DOWN}\ \underline{BY} \end{Bmatrix}$ $\begin{Bmatrix} identifier\text{-}4 \\ literal\text{-}2 \end{Bmatrix}$

DEBUGGING LANGUAGE — BASIC FORMATS

Procedure Division Debugging Formats

EXHIBIT Statement

> $\underline{EXHIBIT}$ $\begin{Bmatrix} \underline{NAMED} \\ \underline{CHANGED}\ \underline{NAMED} \\ \underline{CHANGED} \end{Bmatrix}$ $\begin{Bmatrix} identifier\text{-}1 \\ nonnumeric\text{-}literal\text{-}1 \end{Bmatrix}$ $\begin{bmatrix} identifier\text{-}2 \\ nonnumeric\text{-}literal\ 2 \end{bmatrix}$ ...

ON (Count-Conditional) Statement

> $\underline{ON}$ *integer-1* [$\underline{AND}$ $\underline{EVERY}$ *integer-2*] [$\underline{UNTIL}$ *integer-3*]
>
> $\begin{Bmatrix} imperative\text{-}statement\ldots \\ \underline{NEXT}\ \underline{SENTENCE} \end{Bmatrix}$ $\begin{Bmatrix} \underline{ELSE} \\ \underline{OTHERWISE} \end{Bmatrix}$ $\begin{Bmatrix} statement\ldots \\ \underline{NEXT}\ \underline{SENTENCE} \end{Bmatrix}$

TRACE Statement

> $\begin{Bmatrix} \underline{READY} \\ \underline{RESET} \end{Bmatrix}$ $\underline{TRACE}$

Compile-Time Debugging Packet

DEBUG Card

$\underline{DEBUG}$ *location*

Structure of <u>system-name</u>

class [-device] -organization-name

    class — a two-character field representing device class.
        Allowable combinations are:
      DA mass storage
      UT utility
      UR unit record

    device — a four- or five-digit field that represents device
        number.
          Allowable numbers for each device class
          are:
          DA 2311, 2321, 2314
          UT 2400, 2311, 2314, 2321, 1442R, 1442P,
              1403, 1404 (continuous forms only),
              1443, 2501, 2520R, 2520P, 2540R,
              2540P

organization — a one-character field that specifies file
organization.
Allowable characters are:

S for standard sequential files
D for direct files

name — a one- to eight-character field that specifies the
external-name by which the file is known to the
system

Symbols Allowed in the PICTURE Clause

Symbol	Meaning
A	Alphabetic character or space
B	Space insertion character
P	Decimal scaling position (not counted in size of data item)
S	Operational sign (not counted in size of data item)
V	Assumed decimal point (not counted in size of data item)
X	Alphanumeric character (any from the EBCDIC set)
Z	Zero suppression character
9	Numeric character
0	Zero insertion character
,	Decimal point or period editing control character
.	Decimal point or period editing control character
+	Plus sign insertion editing control character
−	Minus sign editing control character
CR	Credit editing control characters
DB	Debit editing control characters
*	Check protect insertion character
$	Currency sign insertion character

Appendix C

ACKNOWLEDGMENTS

The following information is reprinted from *COBOL Edition 1965,* published by the Conference on Data Systems Languages (CODASYL), and printed by the U.S. Government Printing Office.

"Any organization interested in reproducing the COBOL report and specifications in whole or in part, using ideas taken from this report as the basis for an instruction manual or for any other purpose is free to do so. However, all such organizations are requested to reproduce this section as part of the introduction to the document. Those using a short passage, as in a book review, are requested to mention "COBOL" in acknowledgment of the source, but need not quote this entire section.

"COBOL is an industry language and is not the property of any company or group of companies, or of any organization or group of organizations.

"No warranty, expressed or implied, is made by any contributor or by the COBOL Committee as to the accuracy and functioning of the programming system and language. Moreover, no responsibility is assumed by any contributor, or by the committee, in connection therewith.

"Procedures have been established for the maintenance of COBOL. Inquiries concerning the procedures for proposing changes should be directed to the Executive Committee of the Conference on Data Systems Languages.

"The authors and copyright hc'ders of the copyrighted material used herein

FLOW-MATIC (Trademark of Sperry Rand Corporation), Programming for the Univac (R) I and II, Data Automation Systems copyrighted 1958, 1959, by Sperry Rand Corporation; IBM Commercial Translator Form No. F28-8013, copyrighted 1959 by IBM; FACT, DSI 27A52602760, copyrighted 1960 by Minneapolis-Honeywell

have specifically authorized the use of this material in whole or in part, in the COBOL specifications. Such authorization extends to the reproduction and use of COBOL specifications in programming manuals of similar publications."

Appendix D

FORMS

MULTIPLE-CARD LAYOUT FORM

```
9999999999999999999999999999999999999999999999999999999999999999999999999999999
1 2 3 4 5 6 7 8 9 10 11 12 13 14 15 16 17 18 19 20 21 22 23 24 25 26 27 28 29 30 31 32 33 34 35 36 37 38 39 40 41 42 43 44 45 46 47 48 49 50 51 52 53 54 55 56 57 58 59 60 61 62 63 64 65 66 67 68 69 70 71 72 73 74 75 76 77 78 79 80

9999999999999999999999999999999999999999999999999999999999999999999999999999999
1 2 3 4 5 6 7 8 9 10 11 12 13 14 15 16 17 18 19 20 21 22 23 24 25 26 27 28 29 30 31 32 33 34 35 36 37 38 39 40 41 42 43 44 45 46 47 48 49 50 51 52 53 54 55 56 57 58 59 60 61 62 63 64 65 66 67 68 69 70 71 72 73 74 75 76 77 78 79 80

9999999999999999999999999999999999999999999999999999999999999999999999999999999
1 2 3 4 5 6 7 8 9 10 11 12 13 14 15 16 17 18 19 20 21 22 23 24 25 26 27 28 29 30 31 32 33 34 35 36 37 38 39 40 41 42 43 44 45 46 47 48 49 50 51 52 53 54 55 56 57 58 59 60 61 62 63 64 65 66 67 68 69 70 71 72 73 74 75 76 77 78 79 80

9999999999999999999999999999999999999999999999999999999999999999999999999999999
1 2 3 4 5 6 7 8 9 10 11 12 13 14 15 16 17 18 19 20 21 22 23 24 25 26 27 28 29 30 31 32 33 34 35 36 37 38 39 40 41 42 43 44 45 46 47 48 49 50 51 52 53 54 55 56 57 58 59 60 61 62 63 64 65 66 67 68 69 70 71 72 73 74 75 76 77 78 79 80

9999999999999999999999999999999999999999999999999999999999999999999999999999999
1 2 3 4 5 6 7 8 9 10 11 12 13 14 15 16 17 18 19 20 21 22 23 24 25 26 27 28 29 30 31 32 33 34 35 36 37 38 39 40 41 42 43 44 45 46 47 48 49 50 51 52 53 54 55 56 57 58 59 60 61 62 63 64 65 66 67 68 69 70 71 72 73 74 75 76 77 78 79 80

9999999999999999999999999999999999999999999999999999999999999999999999999999999
1 2 3 4 5 6 7 8 9 10 11 12 13 14 15 16 17 18 19 20 21 22 23 24 25 26 27 28 29 30 31 32 33 34 35 36 37 38 39 40 41 42 43 44 45 46 47 48 49 50 51 52 53 54 55 56 57 58 59 60 61 62 63 64 65 66 67 68 69 70 71 72 73 74 75 76 77 78 79 80
```

MULTIPLE-CARD LAYOUT FORM

Company _____

Application _____

by _____   Date _____   Job No. _____   Sheet No. _____

MULTIPLE-CARD LAYOUT FORM

```
9 9 9 9 9 9 9 9 9 9 9 9 9 9 9 9 9 9 9 9 9 9 9 9 9 9 9 9 9 9 9 9 9 9 9 9 9 9 9 9 9 9 9 9 9 9 9 9 9 9 9 9 9 9 9 9 9 9 9 9 9 9 9 9 9 9 9 9 9 9 9 9 9 9 9 9 9 9 9 9
1 2 3 4 5 6 7 8 9 10 11 12 13 14 15 16 17 18 19 20 21 22 23 24 25 26 27 28 29 30 31 32 33 34 35 36 37 38 39 40 41 42 43 44 45 46 47 48 49 50 51 52 53 54 55 56 57 58 59 60 61 62 63 64 65 66 67 68 69 70 71 72 73 74 75 76 77 78 79 80
```

```
9 9 9 9 9 9 9 9 9 9 9 9 9 9 9 9 9 9 9 9 9 9 9 9 9 9 9 9 9 9 9 9 9 9 9 9 9 9 9 9 9 9 9 9 9 9 9 9 9 9 9 9 9 9 9 9 9 9 9 9 9 9 9 9 9 9 9 9 9 9 9 9 9 9 9 9 9 9 9 9
1 2 3 4 5 6 7 8 9 10 11 12 13 14 15 16 17 18 19 20 21 22 23 24 25 26 27 28 29 30 31 32 33 34 35 36 37 38 39 40 41 42 43 44 45 46 47 48 49 50 51 52 53 54 55 56 57 58 59 60 61 62 63 64 65 66 67 68 69 70 71 72 73 74 75 76 77 78 79 80
```

```
9 9 9 9 9 9 9 9 9 9 9 9 9 9 9 9 9 9 9 9 9 9 9 9 9 9 9 9 9 9 9 9 9 9 9 9 9 9 9 9 9 9 9 9 9 9 9 9 9 9 9 9 9 9 9 9 9 9 9 9 9 9 9 9 9 9 9 9 9 9 9 9 9 9 9 9 9 9 9 9
1 2 3 4 5 6 7 8 9 10 11 12 13 14 15 16 17 18 19 20 21 22 23 24 25 26 27 28 29 30 31 32 33 34 35 36 37 38 39 40 41 42 43 44 45 46 47 48 49 50 51 52 53 54 55 56 57 58 59 60 61 62 63 64 65 66 67 68 69 70 71 72 73 74 75 76 77 78 79 80
```

```
9 9 9 9 9 9 9 9 9 9 9 9 9 9 9 9 9 9 9 9 9 9 9 9 9 9 9 9 9 9 9 9 9 9 9 9 9 9 9 9 9 9 9 9 9 9 9 9 9 9 9 9 9 9 9 9 9 9 9 9 9 9 9 9 9 9 9 9 9 9 9 9 9 9 9 9 9 9 9 9
1 2 3 4 5 6 7 8 9 10 11 12 13 14 15 16 17 18 19 20 21 22 23 24 25 26 27 28 29 30 31 32 33 34 35 36 37 38 39 40 41 42 43 44 45 46 47 48 49 50 51 52 53 54 55 56 57 58 59 60 61 62 63 64 65 66 67 68 69 70 71 72 73 74 75 76 77 78 79 80
```

```
9 9 9 9 9 9 9 9 9 9 9 9 9 9 9 9 9 9 9 9 9 9 9 9 9 9 9 9 9 9 9 9 9 9 9 9 9 9 9 9 9 9 9 9 9 9 9 9 9 9 9 9 9 9 9 9 9 9 9 9 9 9 9 9 9 9 9 9 9 9 9 9 9 9 9 9 9 9 9 9
1 2 3 4 5 6 7 8 9 10 11 12 13 14 15 16 17 18 19 20 21 22 23 24 25 26 27 28 29 30 31 32 33 34 35 36 37 38 39 40 41 42 43 44 45 46 47 48 49 50 51 52 53 54 55 56 57 58 59 60 61 62 63 64 65 66 67 68 69 70 71 72 73 74 75 76 77 78 79 80
```

```
9 9 9 9 9 9 9 9 9 9 9 9 9 9 9 9 9 9 9 9 9 9 9 9 9 9 9 9 9 9 9 9 9 9 9 9 9 9 9 9 9 9 9 9 9 9 9 9 9 9 9 9 9 9 9 9 9 9 9 9 9 9 9 9 9 9 9 9 9 9 9 9 9 9 9 9 9 9 9 9
1 2 3 4 5 6 7 8 9 10 11 12 13 14 15 16 17 18 19 20 21 22 23 24 25 26 27 28 29 30 31 32 33 34 35 36 37 38 39 40 41 42 43 44 45 46 47 48 49 50 51 52 53 54 55 56 57 58 59 60 61 62 63 64 65 66 67 68 69 70 71 72 73 74 75 76 77 78 79 80
```

MULTIPLE-CARD LAYOUT FORM

Company _____

Application _____

by _____

Date _____

Job No. _____

Sheet No. _____

```
9 9 9 9 9 9 9 9 9 9 9 9 9 9 9 9 9 9 9 9 9 9 9 9 9 9 9 9 9 9 9 9 9 9 9 9 9 9 9 9
1 2 3 4 5 6 7 8 9 10 11 12 13 14 15 16 17 18 19 20 21 22 23 24 25 26 27 28 29 30 31 32 33 34 35 36 37 38 39 40 41 42 43 44 45 46 47 48 49 50 51 52 53 54 55 56 57 58 59 60 61 62 63 64 65 66 67 68 69 70 71 72 73 74 75 76 77 78 79 80
```

```
9 9 9 9 9 9 9 9 9 9 9 9 9 9 9 9 9 9 9 9 9 9 9 9 9 9 9 9 9 9 9 9 9 9 9 9 9 9 9 9
1 2 3 4 5 6 7 8 9 10 11 12 13 14 15 16 17 18 19 20 21 22 23 24 25 26 27 28 29 30 31 32 33 34 35 36 37 38 39 40 41 42 43 44 45 46 47 48 49 50 51 52 53 54 55 56 57 58 59 60 61 62 63 64 65 66 67 68 69 70 71 72 73 74 75 76 77 78 79 80
```

```
9 9 9 9 9 9 9 9 9 9 9 9 9 9 9 9 9 9 9 9 9 9 9 9 9 9 9 9 9 9 9 9 9 9 9 9 9 9 9 9
1 2 3 4 5 6 7 8 9 10 11 12 13 14 15 16 17 18 19 20 21 22 23 24 25 26 27 28 29 30 31 32 33 34 35 36 37 38 39 40 41 42 43 44 45 46 47 48 49 50 51 52 53 54 55 56 57 58 59 60 61 62 63 64 65 66 67 68 69 70 71 72 73 74 75 76 77 78 79 80
```

```
9 9 9 9 9 9 9 9 9 9 9 9 9 9 9 9 9 9 9 9 9 9 9 9 9 9 9 9 9 9 9 9 9 9 9 9 9 9 9 9
1 2 3 4 5 6 7 8 9 10 11 12 13 14 15 16 17 18 19 20 21 22 23 24 25 26 27 28 29 30 31 32 33 34 35 36 37 38 39 40 41 42 43 44 45 46 47 48 49 50 51 52 53 54 55 56 57 58 59 60 61 62 63 64 65 66 67 68 69 70 71 72 73 74 75 76 77 78 79 80
```

```
9 9 9 9 9 9 9 9 9 9 9 9 9 9 9 9 9 9 9 9 9 9 9 9 9 9 9 9 9 9 9 9 9 9 9 9 9 9 9 9
1 2 3 4 5 6 7 8 9 10 11 12 13 14 15 16 17 18 19 20 21 22 23 24 25 26 27 28 29 30 31 32 33 34 35 36 37 38 39 40 41 42 43 44 45 46 47 48 49 50 51 52 53 54 55 56 57 58 59 60 61 62 63 64 65 66 67 68 69 70 71 72 73 74 75 76 77 78 79 80
```

```
9 9 9 9 9 9 9 9 9 9 9 9 9 9 9 9 9 9 9 9 9 9 9 9 9 9 9 9 9 9 9 9 9 9 9 9 9 9 9 9
1 2 3 4 5 6 7 8 9 10 11 12 13 14 15 16 17 18 19 20 21 22 23 24 25 26 27 28 29 30 31 32 33 34 35 36 37 38 39 40 41 42 43 44 45 46 47 48 49 50 51 52 53 54 55 56 57 58 59 60 61 62 63 64 65 66 67 68 69 70 71 72 73 74 75 76 77 78 79 80
```

PRINTCHART FORM

PROG. ID _____

PAGE _____

(SPACING: 150 POSITION SPAN, AT 10 CHARACTERS PER INCH, 6 LINES PER VERTICAL INCH)

DATE _____

PROGRAM TITLE _____

PROGRAMMER OR DOCUMENTALIST: _____

CHART TITLE _____

PRINTCHART FORM PROG. ID _____ PAGE _____

(SPACING: 150 POSITION SPAN, AT 10 CHARACTERS PER INCH, 6 LINES PER VERTICAL INCH)   DATE _____

PROGRAM TITLE _____

PROGRAMMER OR DOCUMENTALIST: _____

CHART TITLE _____

CARRIAGE CONTROL
TAPE   CHAN.

PRINTCHART FORM   PROG. ID

(SPACING: 150 POSITION SPAN, AT 10 CHARACTERS PER INCH, 6 LINES PER VERTICAL INCH)

PAGE

DATE

PROGRAM TITLE

PROGRAMMER OR DOCUMENTALIST:

CHART TITLE

PRINTCHART FORM   PROG. ID _____   PAGE _____

(SPACING: 150 POSITION SPAN, AT 10 CHARACTERS PER INCH, 6 LINES PER VERTICAL INCH)   DATE _____

PROGRAM TITLE _____

PROGRAMMER OR DOCUMENTALIST: _____

CHART TITLE _____

CARRIAGE CONTROL
TAPE   CHAN.

COBOL CODING FORM

PAGE NO	PROGRAM		PAGE	OF
1 3	PROGRAMMER	DATE	IDENT. 73	80

LINE NO

4 | 6 7 | 8 | 12 | 16 | 40 | 72

01
02
03
04
05
06
07
08
09
10
11
12
13
14
15
16
17
18
19
20
21
22
23
24
25

COBOL CODING FORM

PAGE NO	PROGRAM		PAGE	OF
1 3	PROGRAMMER	DATE	IDENT.	80
			73	

LINE NO								
4 6 7 8	12	16		40			72	
01								
02								
03								
04								
05								
06								
07								
08								
09								
10								
11								
12								
13								
14								
15								
16								
17								
18								
19								
20								
21								
22								
23								
24								
25								

COBOL CODING FORM

PAGE NO	PROGRAM		PAGE	OF
1 3	PROGRAMMER	DATE	IDENT.	73 80

LINE NO

4 6 7 8 12 16 40 72

01
02
03
04
05
06
07
08
09
10
11
12
13
14
15
16
17
18
19
20
21
22
23
24
25

COBOL CODING FORM

PAGE NO	PROGRAM				PAGE	OF
1 3	PROGRAMMER		DATE		IDENT.	73 80

LINE NO							72
4 6	7	8	12	16	40		
01							
02							
03							
04	*						
05							
06							
07							
08							
09							
10							
11							
12							
13							
14							
15							
16							
17							
18							
19							
20							
21							
22							
23							
24							
25							

COBOL CODING FORM

PAGE NO 1 3	PROGRAM			PAGE	OF
	PROGRAMMER		DATE	IDENT. 73	80

LINE NO

4 6 7 8	12	16	40	72
01				
02				
03				
04				
05				
06				
07				
08				
09				
10				
11				
12				
13				
14				
15				
16				
17				
18				
19				
20				
21				
22				
23				
24				
25				

COBOL CODING FORM

PAGE NO 1 3	PROGRAM		PAGE	OF
	PROGRAMMER	DATE	IDENT. 73	80

LINE NO									
4 6 7 8	12	16		40				72	
01									
02									
03									
04									
05									
06									
07									
08									
09									
10									
11									
12									
13									
14									
15									
16									
17									
18									
19									
20									
21									
22									
23									
24									
25									

COBOL CODING FORM

PAGE NO 1 3	PROGRAM			PAGE	OF
	PROGRAMMER		DATE	IDENT. 73	80

LINE NO 4 6 7 8	12	16		40	72
01					
02					
03					
04					
05					
06					
07					
08					
09					
10					
11					
12					
13					
14					
15					
16					
17					
18					
19					
20					
21					
22					
23					
24					
25					

COBOL CODING FORM

PAGE NO	PROGRAM		PAGE	OF
1 3	PROGRAMMER	DATE	IDENT.	
			73	80

LINE NO							
4 6 7 8	12	16		40		72	
01							
02							
03							
04							
05							
06							
07							
08							
09							
10							
11							
12							
13							
14							
15							
16							
17							
18							
19							
20							
21							
22							
23							
24							
25							

INDEX